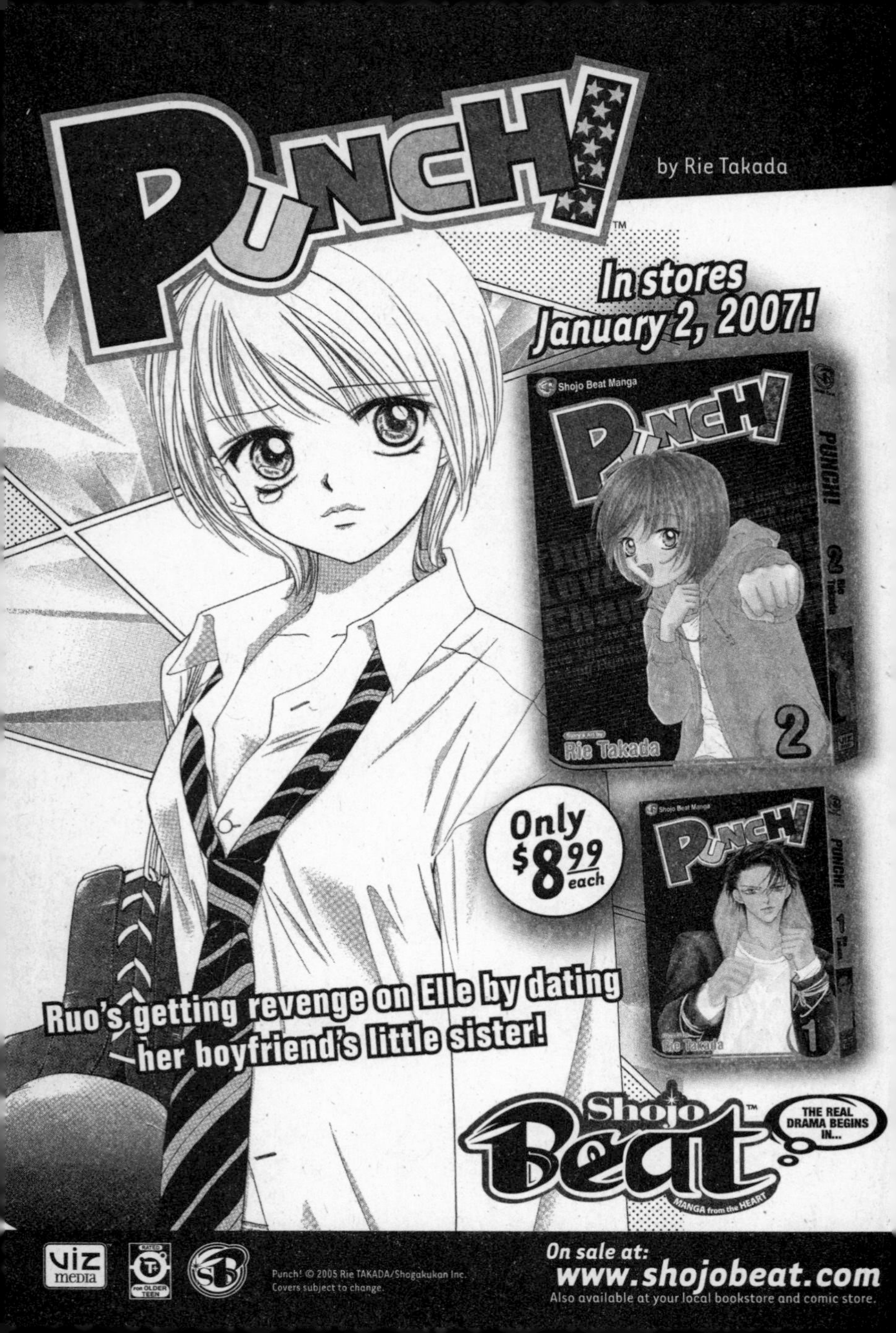

PUNCH!™
by Rie Takada
In stores January 2, 2007!
Shojo Beat Manga
PUNCH!
Rie Takada
2
Only $8.99 each
Shojo Beat Manga
PUNCH!
Rie Takada
1
Ruo's getting revenge on Elle by dating her boyfriend's little sister!
Shojo Beat™
THE REAL DRAMA BEGINS IN...
MANGA from the HEART
viz media
RATED T+ FOR OLDER TEEN
Punch! © 2005 Rie TAKADA/Shogakukan Inc.
Covers subject to change.
On sale at:
www.shojobeat.com
Also available at your local bookstore and comic store.

Ouran High School Host Club™

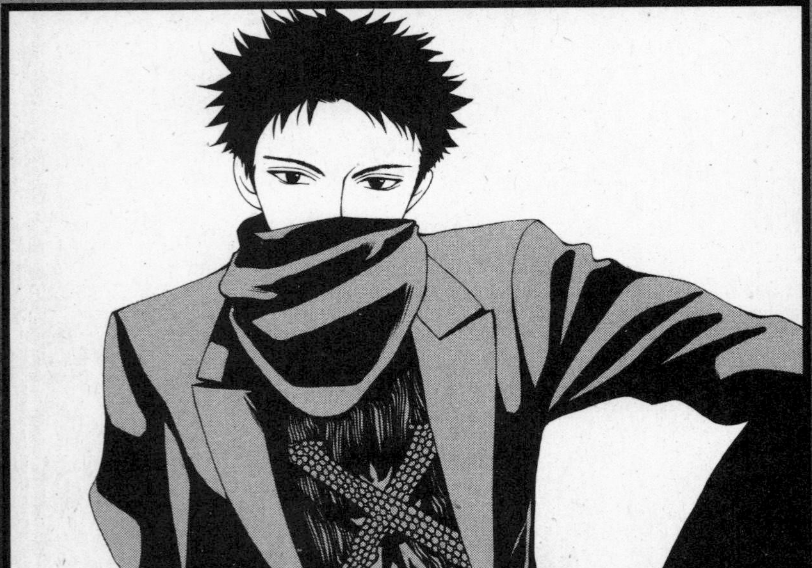

BRAC

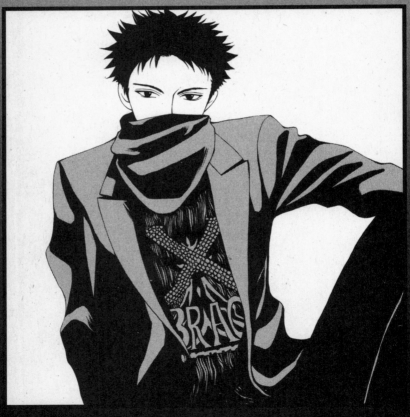

Vol. 8

Bisco Hatori

Ouran High School

Host Club™

Vol. 8

CONTENTS

CAST

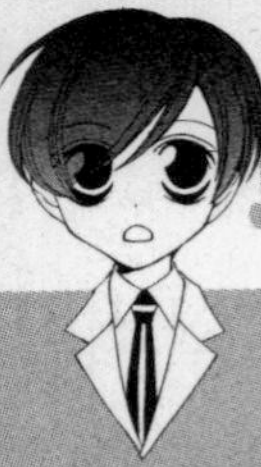

HARUHI FUJIOKA <1-A>
A SCHOLARSHIP STUDENT WITH A BLUNT PERSONALITY. THE CLUB'S CUSTOMERS ARE UNAWARE THAT SHE IS A GIRL. ♥

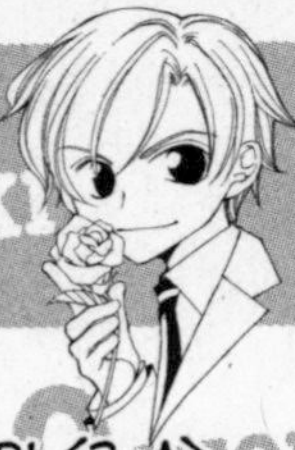

TAMAKI SUOH <2-A>
HOST CLUB PRESIDENT AND SUPPOSEDLY THE MOST REQUESTED HOST. SOMEWHAT NARCISSISTIC AND SLIGHTLY DENSE.

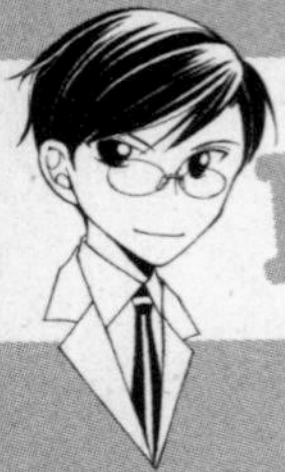

KYOYA OHTORI <2-A>
HOST CLUB VICE PRESIDENT. A COOL STRATEGIST. WHAT IS HE THINKING BEHIND THAT SMILE?

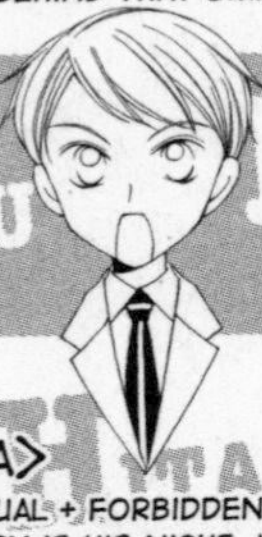

HIKARU HITACHIIN <1-A>
EASYGOING AND LIVES BY THE PHILOSOPHY OF "OTHERS = TOYS." THE OLDEST OF THE TWINS. VIRGO.

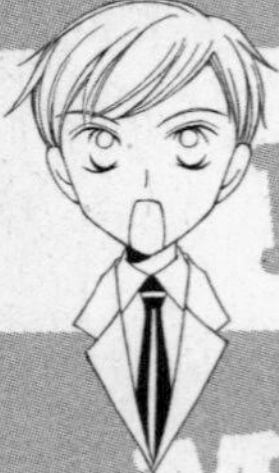

KAORU HITACHIIN <1-A>
HANDSOME HOMOSEXUAL + FORBIDDEN LOVE BETWEEN RELATIVES + SYMMETRY IS HIS NICHE. VIRGO.

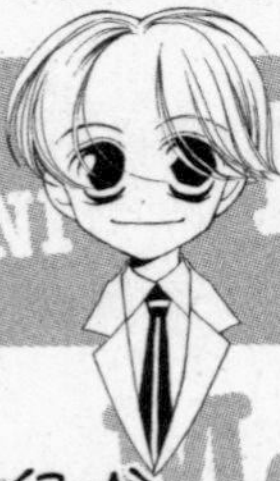

MITSUKUNI HANINOZUKA <3-A>
GOES BY THE NICKNAME "HUNNY." ALWAYS HAS HIS TOY BUNNY.

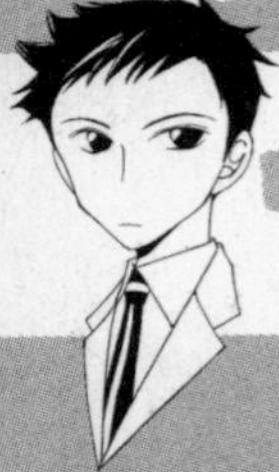

TAKASHI MORINOZUKA <3-A>
GOES BY THE NICKNAME "MORI." A MEMBER OF THE KENDO CLUB. HE QUIETLY WAITS UPON HUNNY.

STORY

THIS STORY TAKES PLACE AT OURAN INSTITUTE, AN ULTRAEXCLUSIVE PRIVATE HIGH SCHOOL. HARUHI, A SCHOLARSHIP STUDENT OF NO LINEAGE OR WEALTH, WANDERS INTO MUSIC ROOM 3 WHERE SHE ENCOUNTERS ALL SIX OF THE HANDSOME MEN OF THE HOST CLUB. UNIMPRESSED, SHE IS ABOUT TO LEAVE WHEN SHE ACCIDENTALLY BREAKS A VASE (MARKET PRICE: $80,000!) AND IS OBLIGED TO BECOME A MEMBER TO REPAY THE DEBT! ▶PREVIOUSLY, HARUHI WAS KIDNAPPED BY THE ZUKA CLUB OF ST. ROBERIA WOMEN'S INSTITUTE, A PRIVATE BOARDING SCHOOL. TO RESCUE HER, THE MEMBERS OF THE HOST CLUB SNUCK INTO A MEETING OF THE ZUKA CLUB FAITHFUL. WHAT DID TAMAKI DO WHEN HIS BELOVED "DAUGHTER" WAS IN A PINCH?

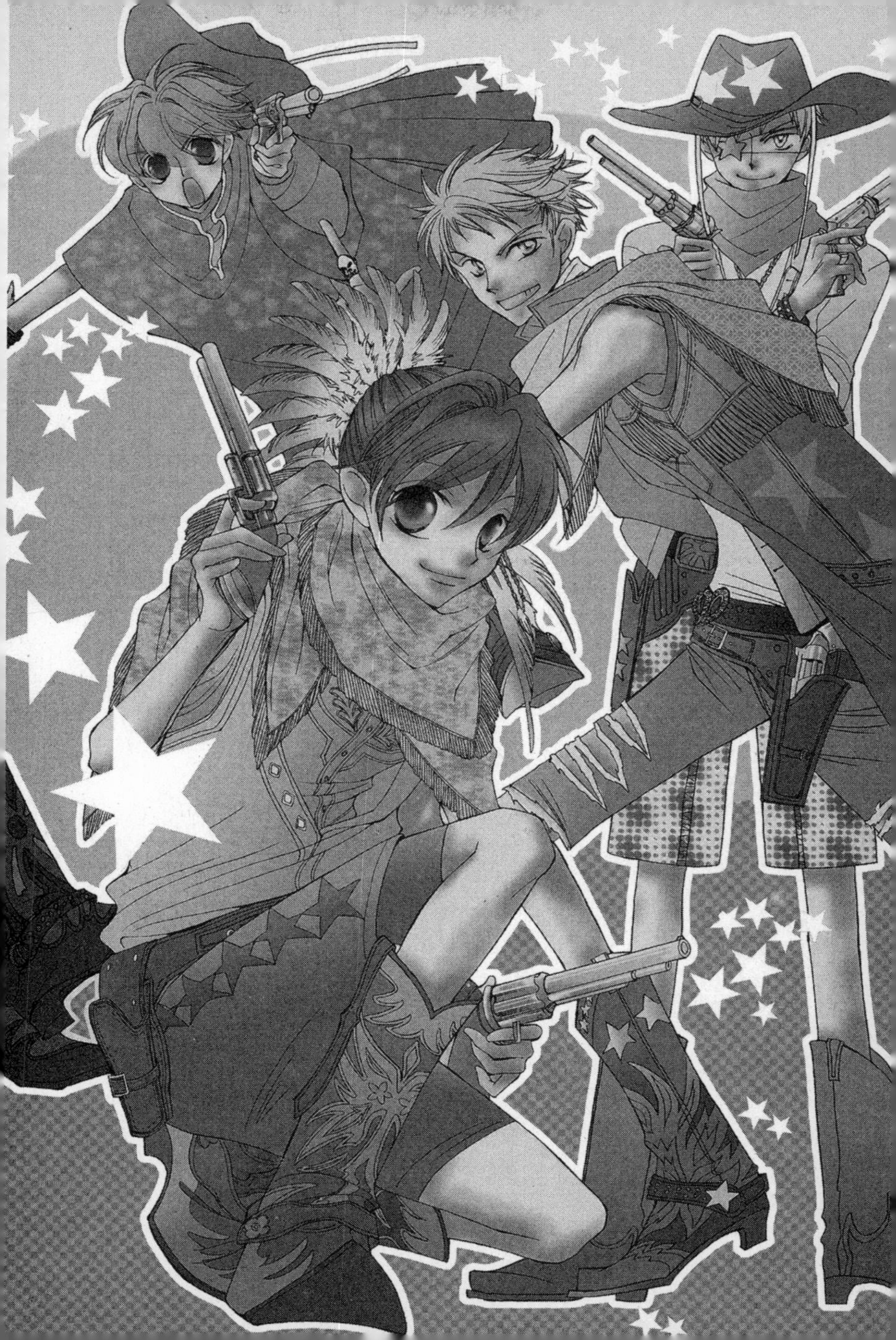

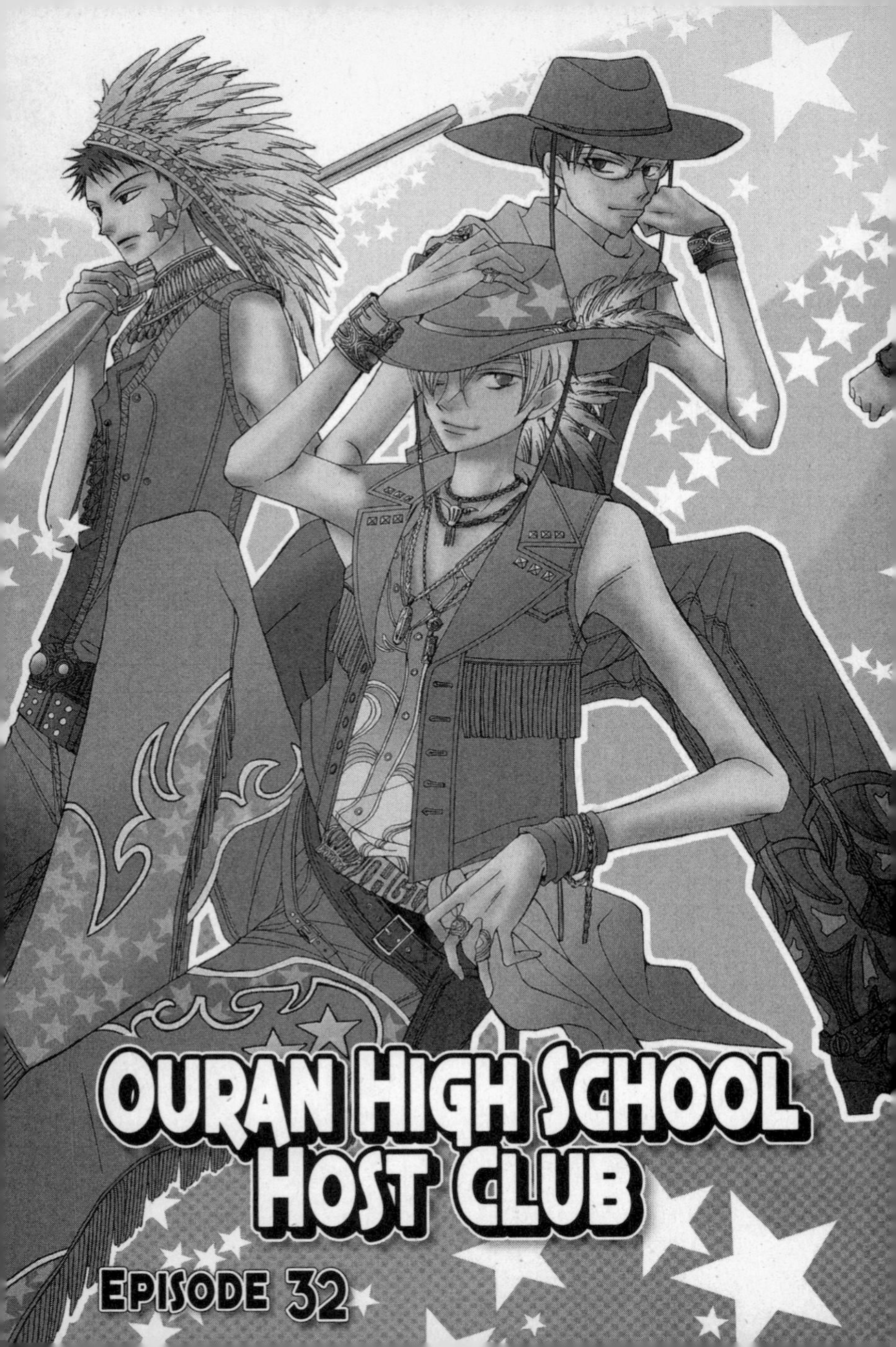
OURAN HIGH SCHOOL
HOST CLUB
EPISODE 32

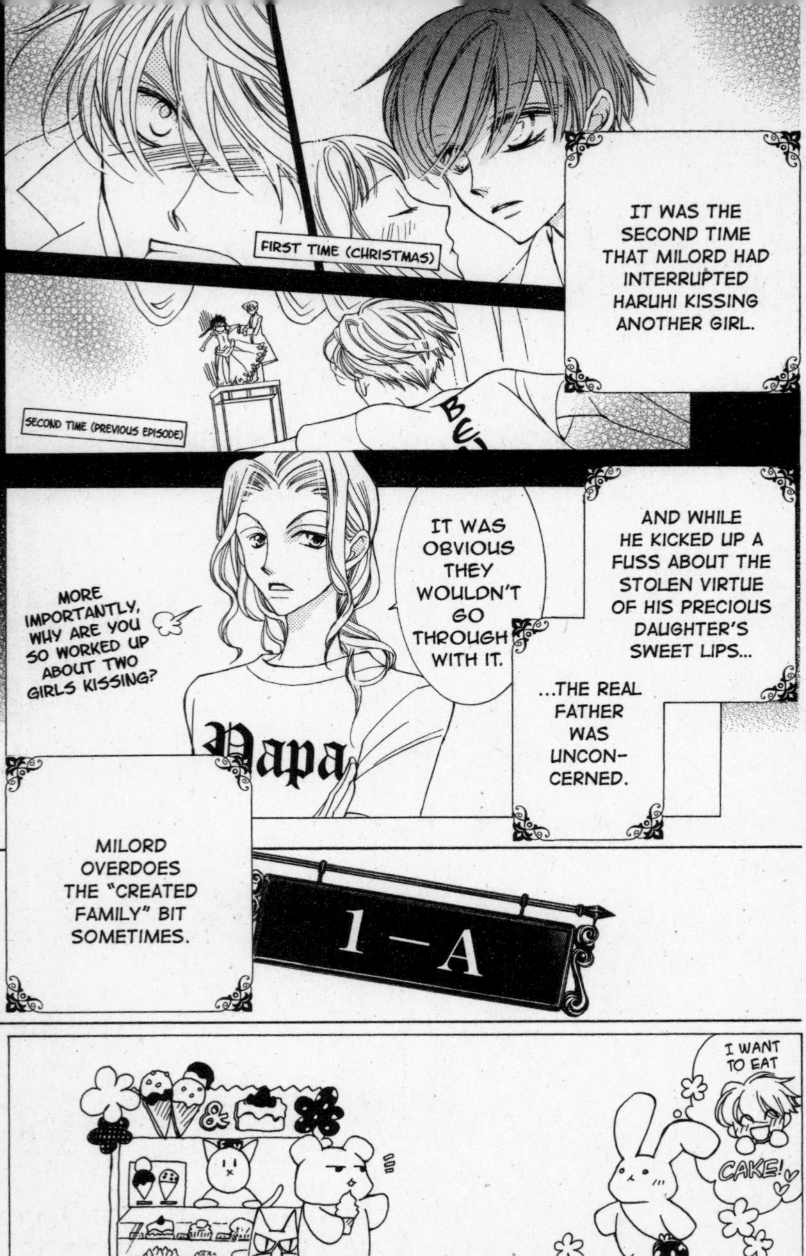
IT WAS THE SECOND TIME THAT MILORD HAD INTERRUPTED HARUHI KISSING ANOTHER GIRL.
FIRST TIME (CHRISTMAS)
SECOND TIME (PREVIOUS EPISODE)
AND WHILE HE KICKED UP A FUSS ABOUT THE STOLEN VIRTUE OF HIS PRECIOUS DAUGHTER'S SWEET LIPS...
...THE REAL FATHER WAS UNCONCERNED.
IT WAS OBVIOUS THEY WOULDN'T GO THROUGH WITH IT.
MORE IMPORTANTLY, WHY ARE YOU SO WORKED UP ABOUT TWO GIRLS KISSING?
Papa
MILORD OVERDOES THE "CREATED FAMILY" BIT SOMETIMES.
1—A
I WANT TO EAT CAKE!

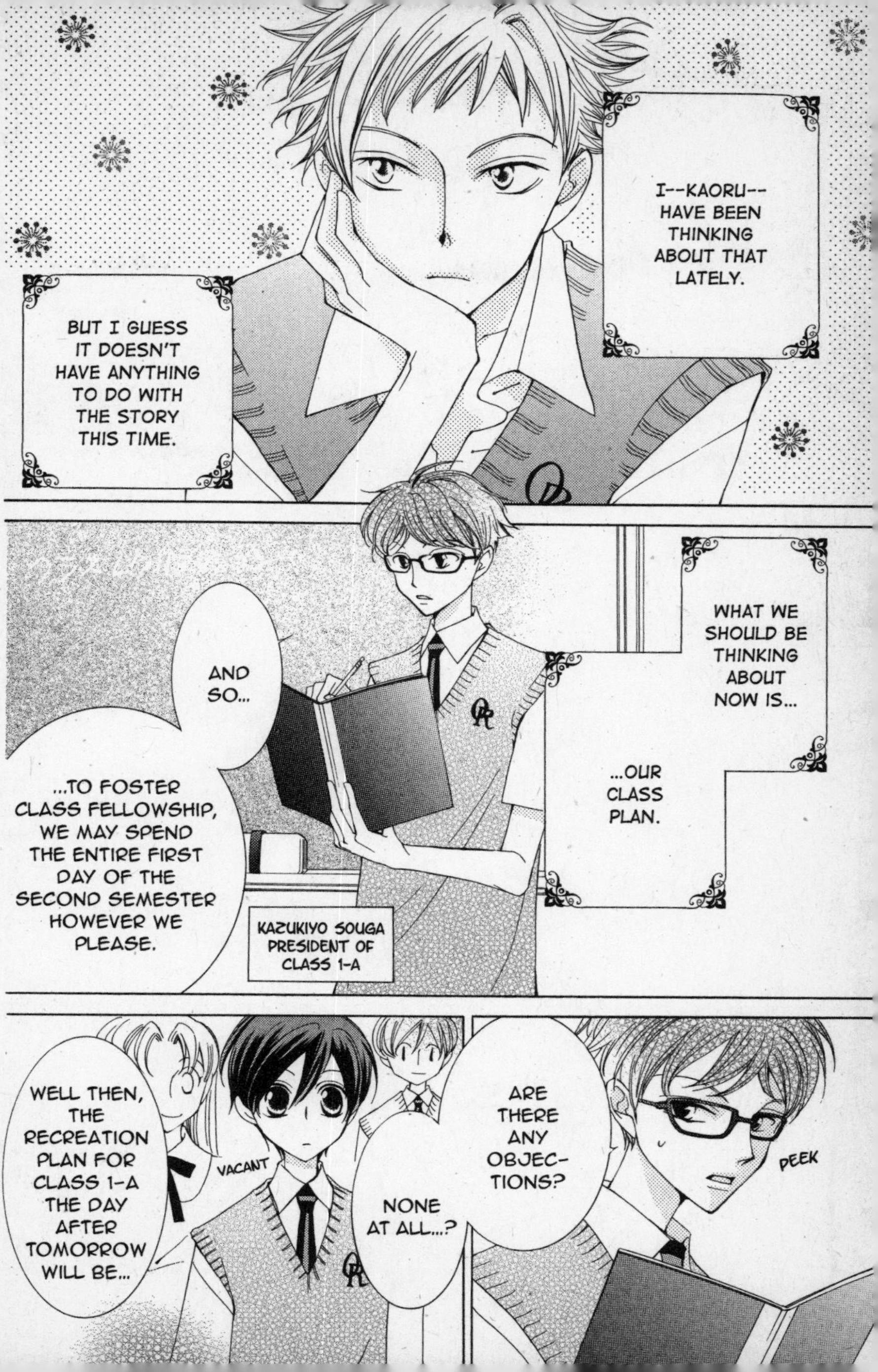
I--KAORU-- HAVE BEEN THINKING ABOUT THAT LATELY.
BUT I GUESS IT DOESN'T HAVE ANYTHING TO DO WITH THE STORY THIS TIME.
WHAT WE SHOULD BE THINKING ABOUT NOW IS...
...OUR CLASS PLAN.
AND SO...
...TO FOSTER CLASS FELLOWSHIP, WE MAY SPEND THE ENTIRE FIRST DAY OF THE SECOND SEMESTER HOWEVER WE PLEASE.
KAZUKIYO SOUGA PRESIDENT OF CLASS 1-A
ARE THERE ANY OBJEC- TIONS?
PEEK
NONE AT ALL...?
WELL THEN, THE RECREATION PLAN FOR CLASS 1-A THE DAY AFTER TOMORROW WILL BE...
VACANT

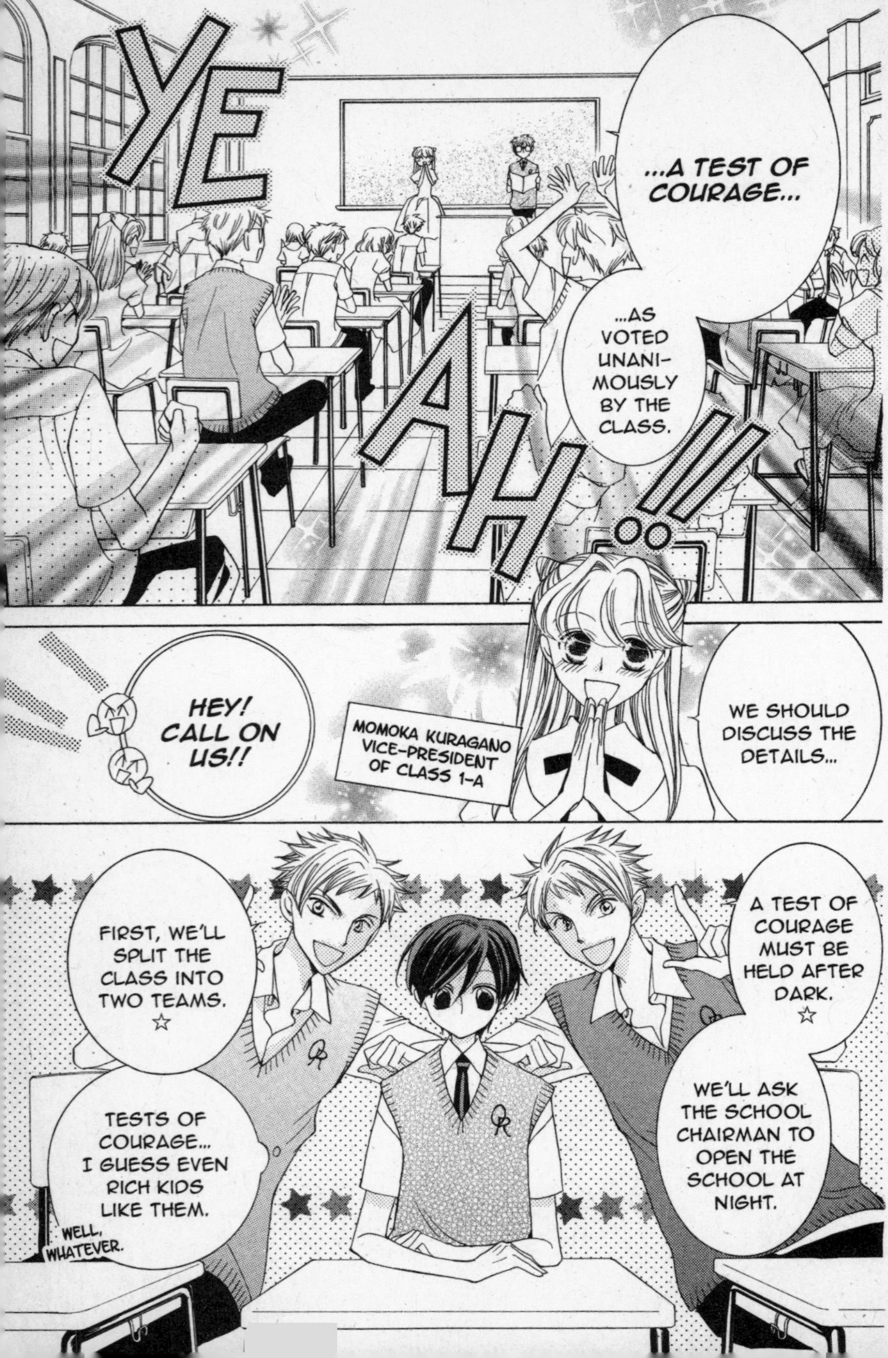
...A TEST OF COURAGE...
...AS VOTED UNANIMOUSLY BY THE CLASS.
YEAH!!
WE SHOULD DISCUSS THE DETAILS...
MOMOKA KURAGANO VICE-PRESIDENT OF CLASS 1-A
HEY! CALL ON US!!
A TEST OF COURAGE MUST BE HELD AFTER DARK. ☆
FIRST, WE'LL SPLIT THE CLASS INTO TWO TEAMS. ☆
WE'LL ASK THE SCHOOL CHAIRMAN TO OPEN THE SCHOOL AT NIGHT.
TESTS OF COURAGE... I GUESS EVEN RICH KIDS LIKE THEM.
WELL, WHATEVER.

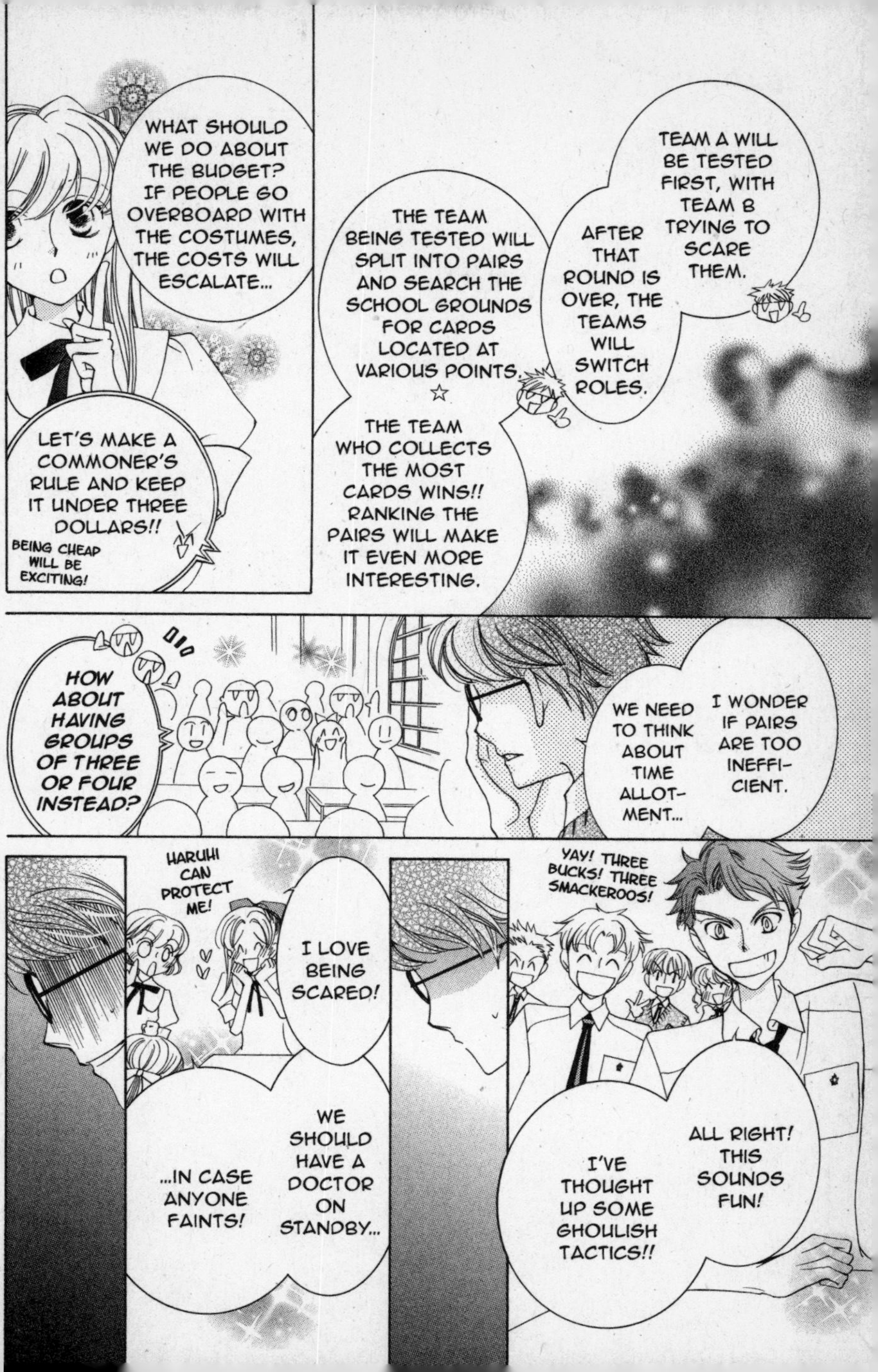
TEAM A WILL BE TESTED FIRST, WITH TEAM B TRYING TO SCARE THEM.
AFTER THAT ROUND IS OVER, THE TEAMS WILL SWITCH ROLES.
THE TEAM BEING TESTED WILL SPLIT INTO PAIRS AND SEARCH THE SCHOOL GROUNDS FOR CARDS LOCATED AT VARIOUS POINTS. ☆
THE TEAM WHO COLLECTS THE MOST CARDS WINS!! RANKING THE PAIRS WILL MAKE IT EVEN MORE INTERESTING.
WHAT SHOULD WE DO ABOUT THE BUDGET? IF PEOPLE GO OVERBOARD WITH THE COSTUMES, THE COSTS WILL ESCALATE...
LET'S MAKE A COMMONER'S RULE AND KEEP IT UNDER THREE DOLLARS!!
BEING CHEAP WILL BE EXCITING!
I WONDER IF PAIRS ARE TOO INEFFI-CIENT.
WE NEED TO THINK ABOUT TIME ALLOT-MENT...
HOW ABOUT HAVING GROUPS OF THREE OR FOUR INSTEAD?
YAY! THREE BUCKS! THREE SMACKEROOS!
ALL RIGHT! THIS SOUNDS FUN!
I'VE THOUGHT UP SOME GHOULISH TACTICS!!
I LOVE BEING SCARED!
HARUHI CAN PROTECT ME!
WE SHOULD HAVE A DOCTOR ON STANDBY...
...IN CASE ANYONE FAINTS!

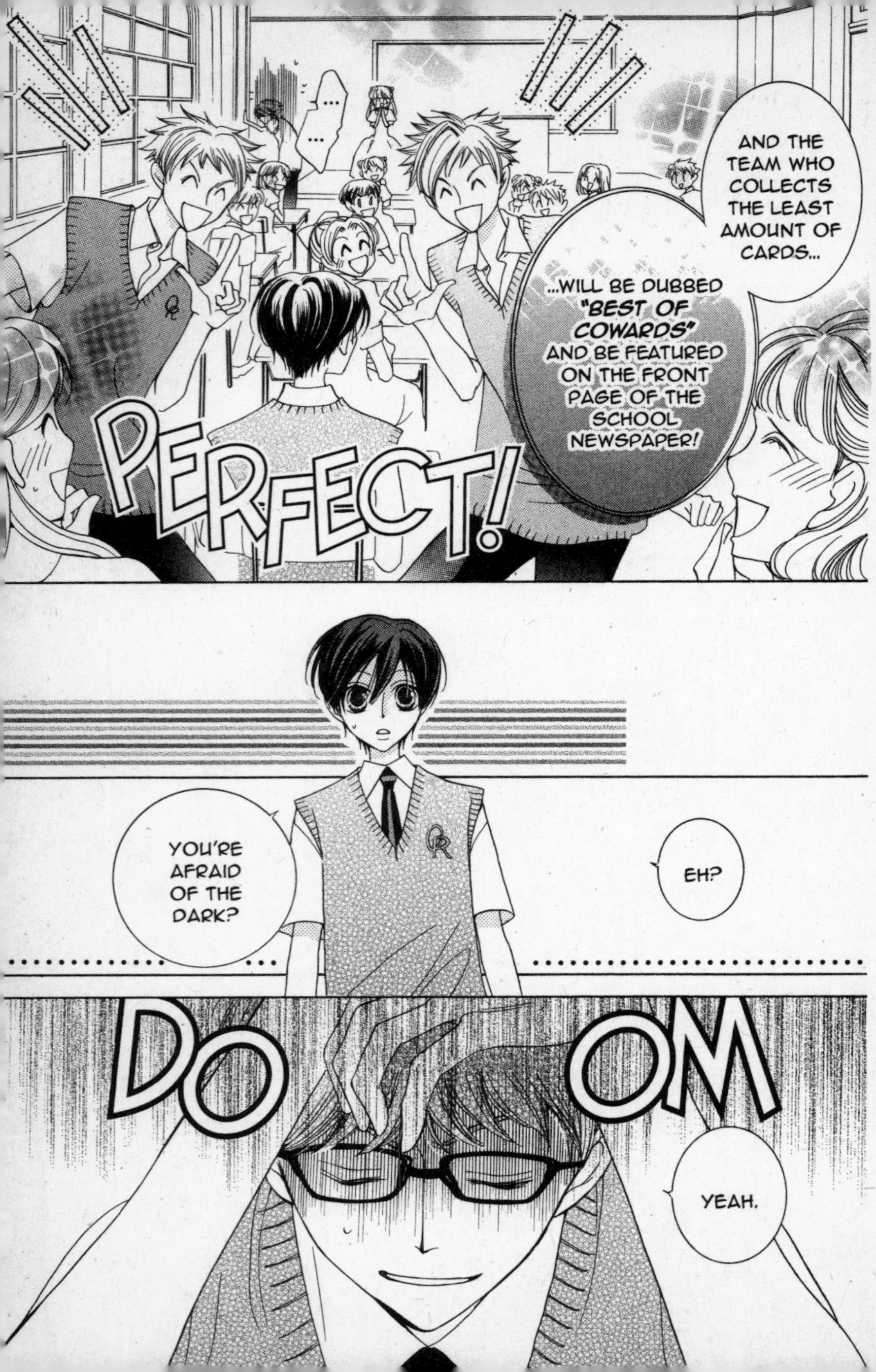
AND THE TEAM WHO COLLECTS THE LEAST AMOUNT OF CARDS...
...WILL BE DUBBED "BEST OF COWARDS" AND BE FEATURED ON THE FRONT PAGE OF THE SCHOOL NEWSPAPER!
...
...
PERFECT!
EH?
YOU'RE AFRAID OF THE DARK?
DO OM
YEAH.

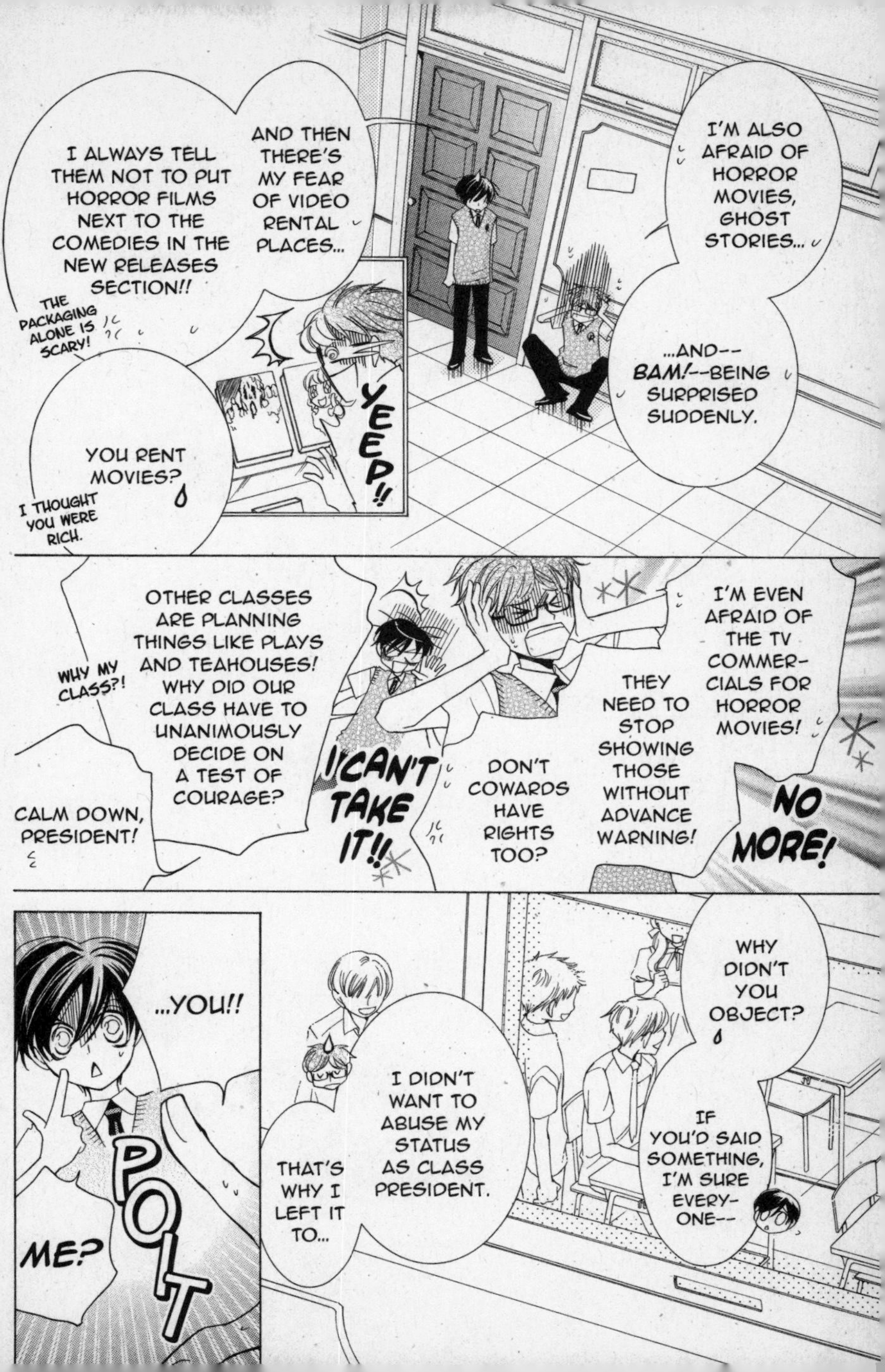

I'M ALSO AFRAID OF HORROR MOVIES, GHOST STORIES...
...AND-- BAM!--BEING SURPRISED SUDDENLY.
AND THEN THERE'S MY FEAR OF VIDEO RENTAL PLACES...
I ALWAYS TELL THEM NOT TO PUT HORROR FILMS NEXT TO THE COMEDIES IN THE NEW RELEASES SECTION!!
THE PACKAGING ALONE IS SCARY!
YEEP!!
YOU RENT MOVIES?
I THOUGHT YOU WERE RICH.
I'M EVEN AFRAID OF THE TV COMMERCIALS FOR HORROR MOVIES!
NO MORE!
THEY NEED TO STOP SHOWING THOSE WITHOUT ADVANCE WARNING!
DON'T COWARDS HAVE RIGHTS TOO?
I CAN'T TAKE IT!!
OTHER CLASSES ARE PLANNING THINGS LIKE PLAYS AND TEAHOUSES! WHY DID OUR CLASS HAVE TO UNANIMOUSLY DECIDE ON A TEST OF COURAGE?
WHY MY CLASS?!
CALM DOWN, PRESIDENT!
WHY DIDN'T YOU OBJECT?
IF YOU'D SAID SOMETHING, I'M SURE EVERY-ONE--
I DIDN'T WANT TO ABUSE MY STATUS AS CLASS PRESIDENT.
THAT'S WHY I LEFT IT TO...
...YOU!!
POIT
ME?

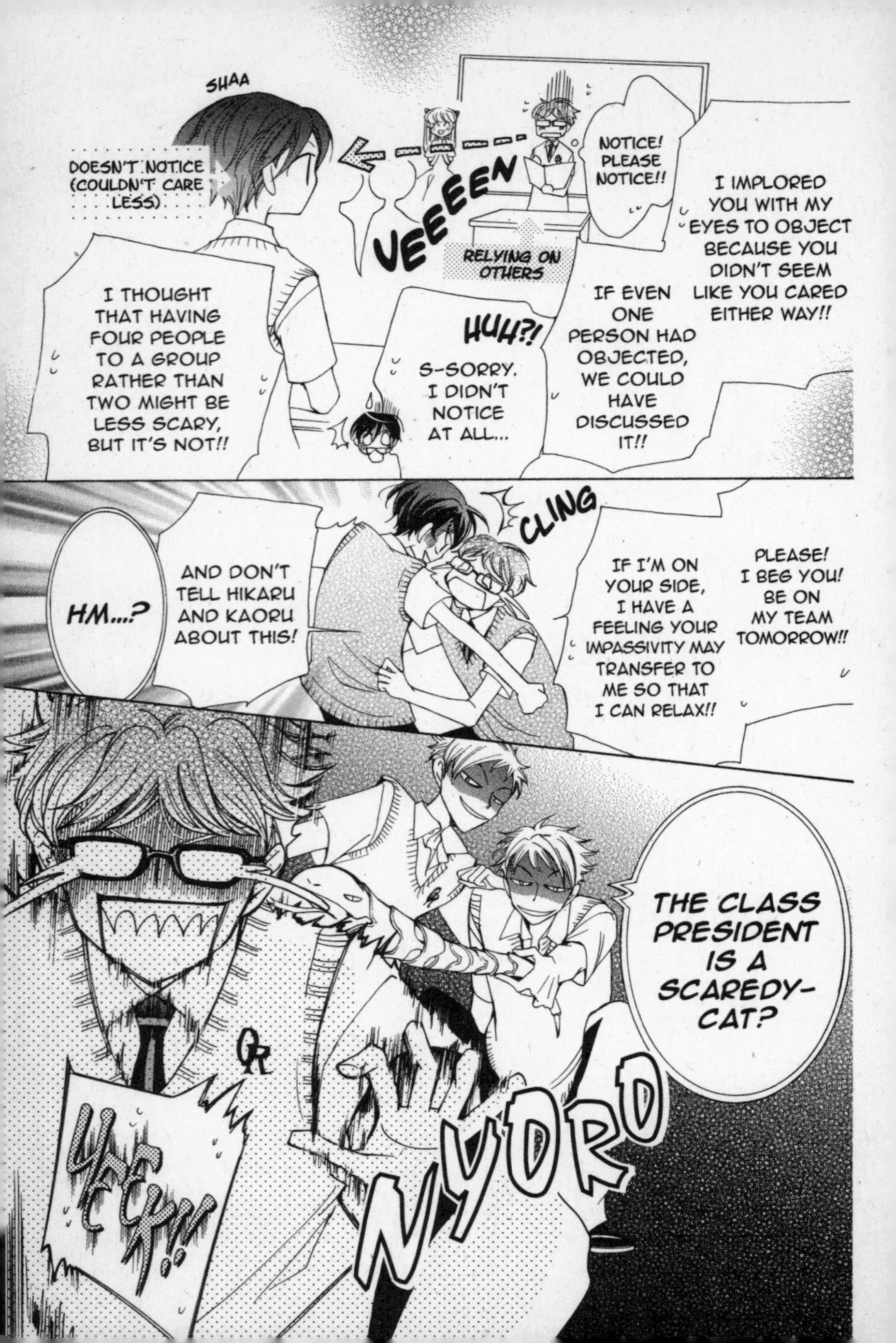
I IMPLORED YOU WITH MY EYES TO OBJECT BECAUSE YOU DIDN'T SEEM LIKE YOU CARED EITHER WAY!!
IF EVEN ONE PERSON HAD OBJECTED, WE COULD HAVE DISCUSSED IT!!
NOTICE! PLEASE NOTICE!!
RELYING ON OTHERS
VEEEEN
SHAA
DOESN'T NOTICE (COULDN'T CARE LESS)
HUH?!
S-SORRY. I DIDN'T NOTICE AT ALL...
I THOUGHT THAT HAVING FOUR PEOPLE TO A GROUP RATHER THAN TWO MIGHT BE LESS SCARY, BUT IT'S NOT!!
PLEASE! I BEG YOU! BE ON MY TEAM TOMORROW!!
IF I'M ON YOUR SIDE, I HAVE A FEELING YOUR IMPASSIVITY MAY TRANSFER TO ME SO THAT I CAN RELAX!!
CLING
AND DON'T TELL HIKARU AND KAORU ABOUT THIS!
HM...?
THE CLASS PRESIDENT IS A SCAREDY-CAT?
NYORO
YEEK!!

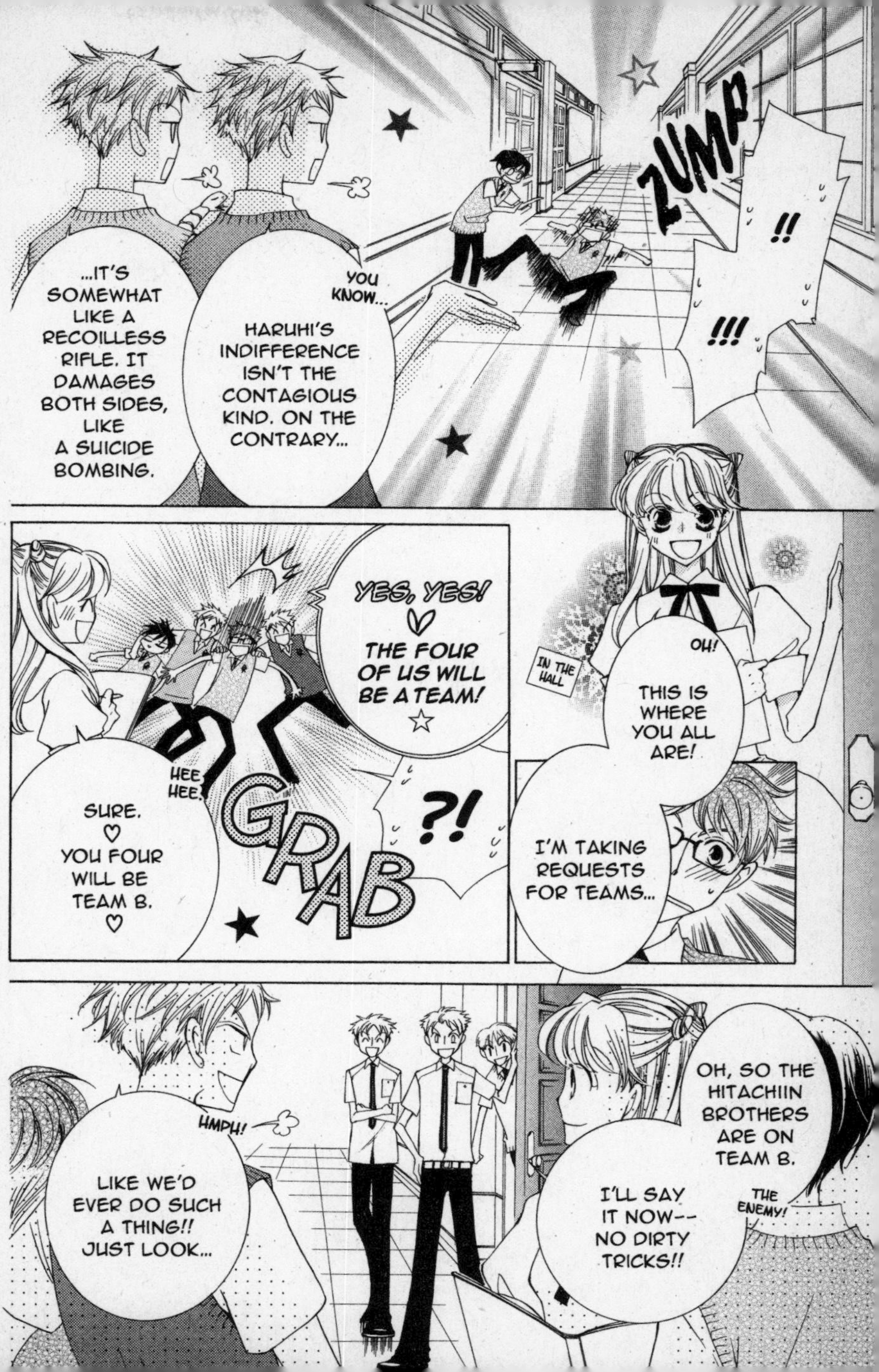
ZUMP
!!
!!!
YOU KNOW...
HARUHI'S INDIFFERENCE ISN'T THE CONTAGIOUS KIND. ON THE CONTRARY...
...IT'S SOMEWHAT LIKE A RECOILLESS RIFLE. IT DAMAGES BOTH SIDES, LIKE A SUICIDE BOMBING.
IN THE HALL
OH!
THIS IS WHERE YOU ALL ARE!
I'M TAKING REQUESTS FOR TEAMS...
YES, YES! ♡ THE FOUR OF US WILL BE A TEAM! ☆
?!
GRAB
HEE HEE
SURE. ♡ YOU FOUR WILL BE TEAM B. ♡
OH, SO THE HITACHIIN BROTHERS ARE ON TEAM B.
THE ENEMY!
I'LL SAY IT NOW-- NO DIRTY TRICKS!!
HMPH!
LIKE WE'D EVER DO SUCH A THING!! JUST LOOK...

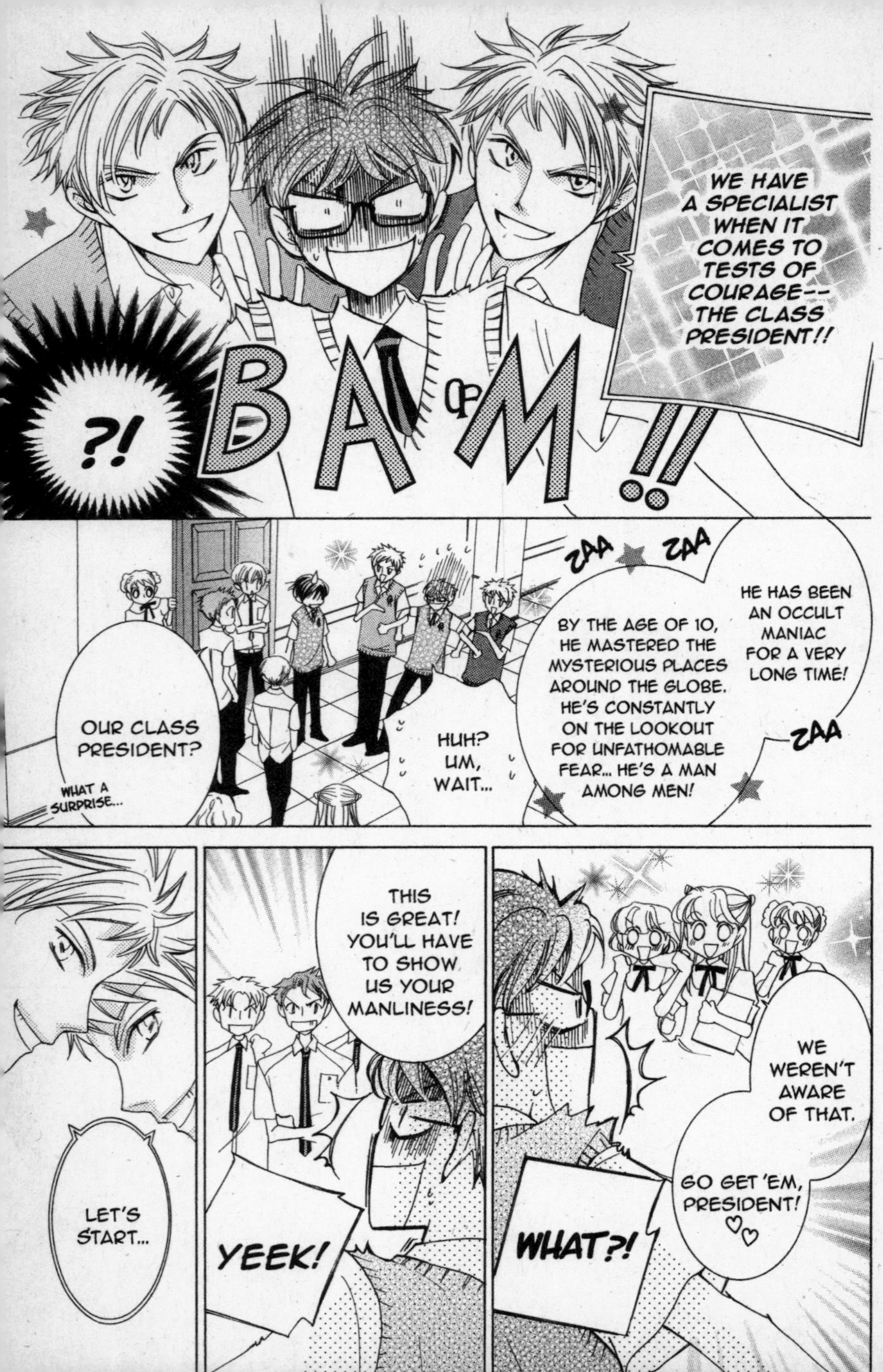
WE HAVE A SPECIALIST WHEN IT COMES TO TESTS OF COURAGE-- THE CLASS PRESIDENT!!
BAM!!
?!
ZAA ZAA
HE HAS BEEN AN OCCULT MANIAC FOR A VERY LONG TIME!
ZAA
BY THE AGE OF 10, HE MASTERED THE MYSTERIOUS PLACES AROUND THE GLOBE. HE'S CONSTANTLY ON THE LOOKOUT FOR UNFATHOMABLE FEAR... HE'S A MAN AMONG MEN!
HUH? UM, WAIT...
OUR CLASS PRESIDENT?
WHAT A SURPRISE...
WE WEREN'T AWARE OF THAT.
GO GET 'EM, PRESIDENT! ♡♡
WHAT?!
THIS IS GREAT! YOU'LL HAVE TO SHOW US YOUR MANLINESS!
YEEK!
LET'S START...

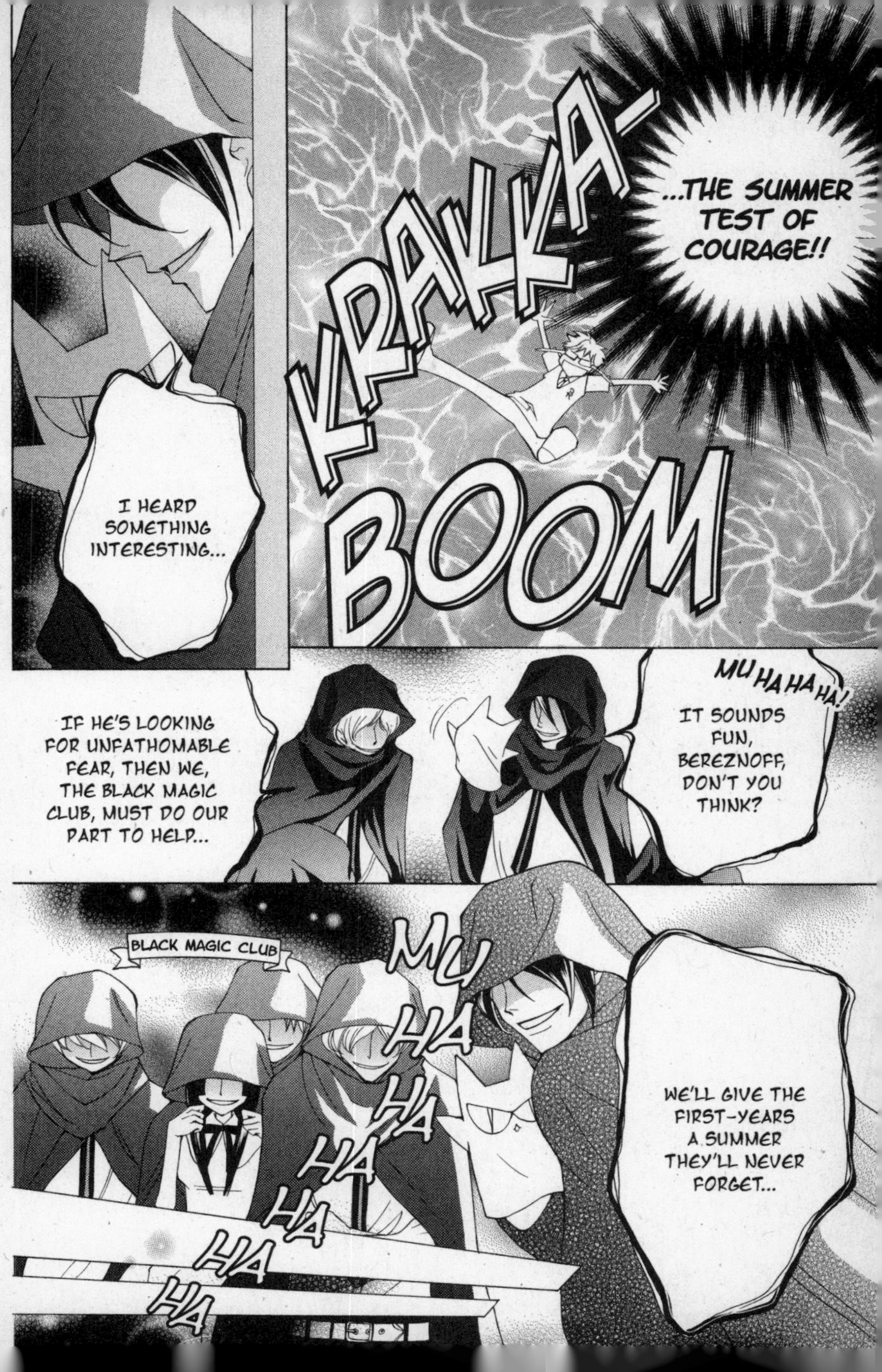
...THE SUMMER TEST OF COURAGE!!
KRAKKA-BOOM
I HEARD SOMETHING INTERESTING...
MU HA HA HA!
IT SOUNDS FUN, BEREZNOFF, DON'T YOU THINK?
IF HE'S LOOKING FOR UNFATHOMABLE FEAR, THEN WE, THE BLACK MAGIC CLUB, MUST DO OUR PART TO HELP...
WE'LL GIVE THE FIRST-YEARS A SUMMER THEY'LL NEVER FORGET...
MU HA HA HA HA HA HA
BLACK MAGIC CLUB

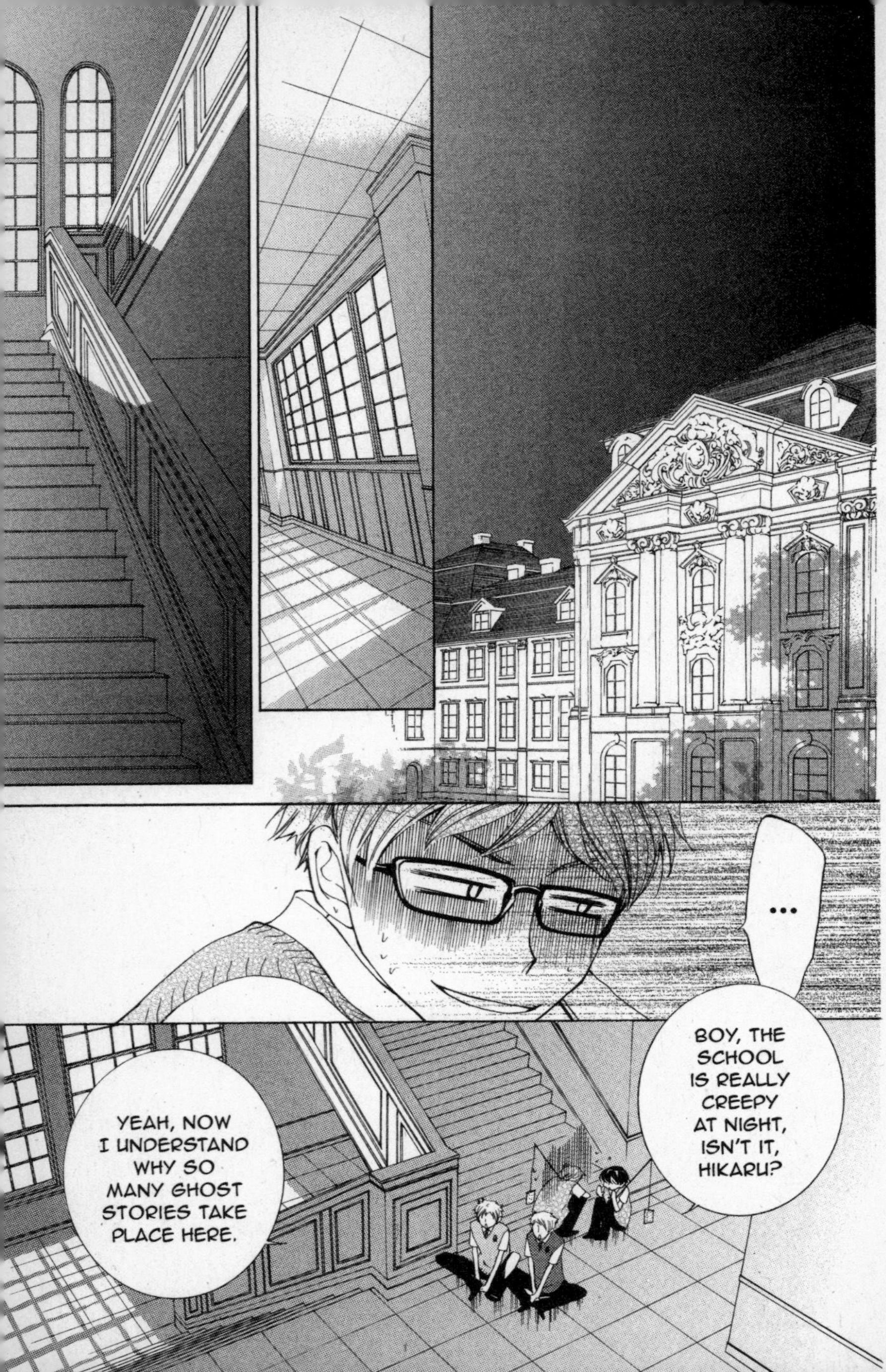
...
BOY, THE SCHOOL IS REALLY CREEPY AT NIGHT, ISN'T IT, HIKARU?
YEAH, NOW I UNDERSTAND WHY SO MANY GHOST STORIES TAKE PLACE HERE.

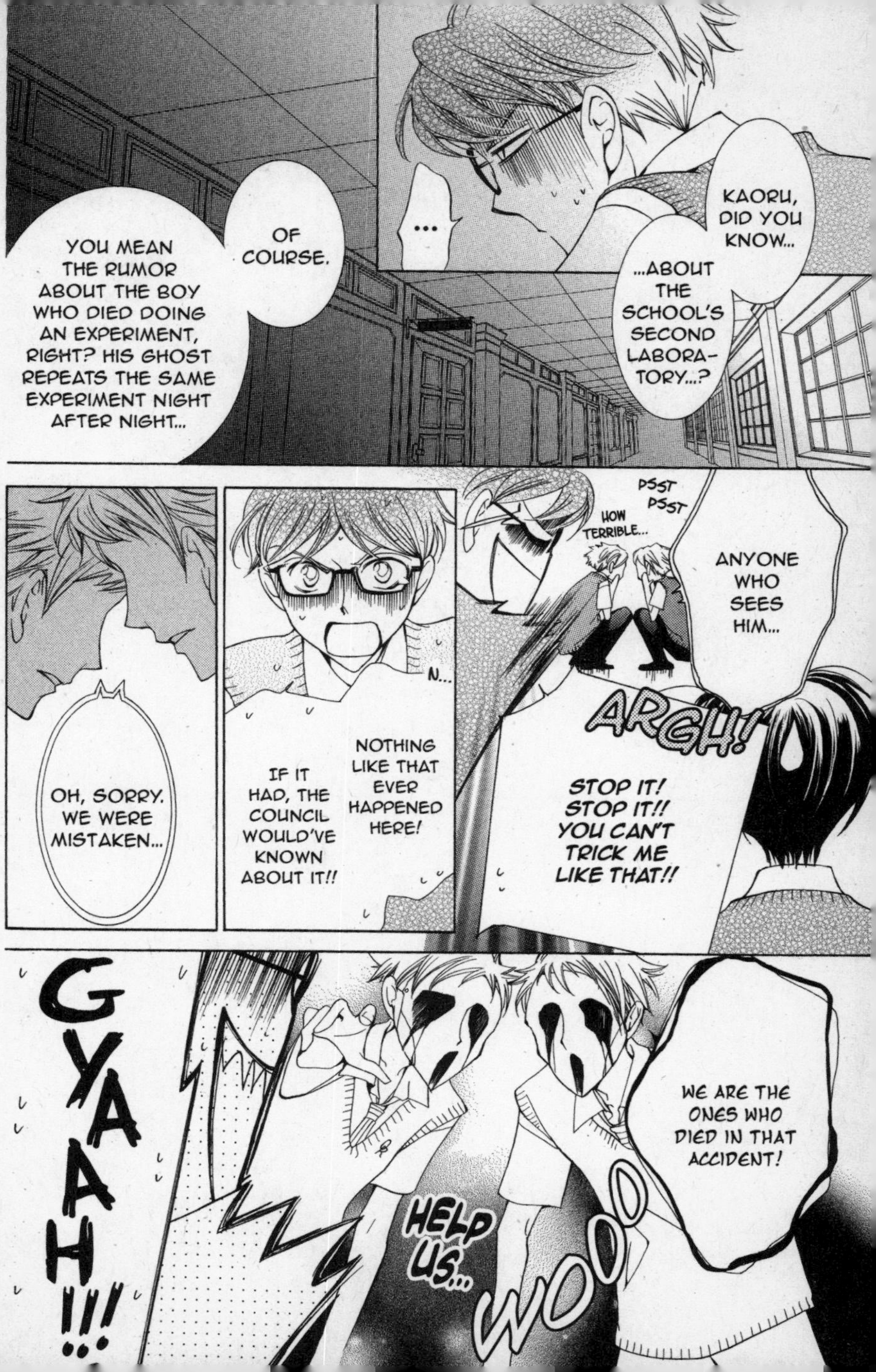
KAORU, DID YOU KNOW...
...ABOUT THE SCHOOL'S SECOND LABORATORY...?
...
OF COURSE.
YOU MEAN THE RUMOR ABOUT THE BOY WHO DIED DOING AN EXPERIMENT, RIGHT? HIS GHOST REPEATS THE SAME EXPERIMENT NIGHT AFTER NIGHT...
ANYONE WHO SEES HIM...
PSST PSST
HOW TERRIBLE...
ARGH!
STOP IT! STOP IT!! YOU CAN'T TRICK ME LIKE THAT!!
N...
NOTHING LIKE THAT EVER HAPPENED HERE!
IF IT HAD, THE COUNCIL WOULD'VE KNOWN ABOUT IT!!
OH, SORRY. WE WERE MISTAKEN...
WE ARE THE ONES WHO DIED IN THAT ACCIDENT!
WOOO
HELP US...
GYAAH!!!

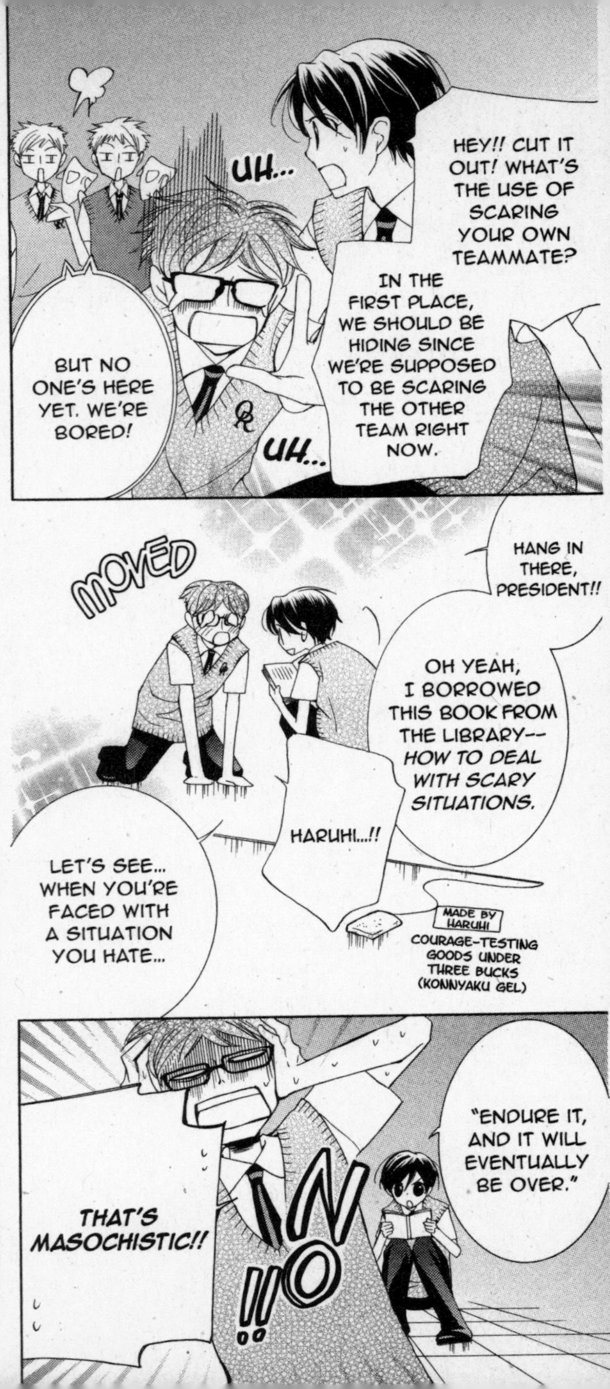
HEY!! CUT IT OUT! WHAT'S THE USE OF SCARING YOUR OWN TEAMMATE?
UH...
IN THE FIRST PLACE, WE SHOULD BE HIDING SINCE WE'RE SUPPOSED TO BE SCARING THE OTHER TEAM RIGHT NOW.
UH...
BUT NO ONE'S HERE YET. WE'RE BORED!
HANG IN THERE, PRESIDENT!!
MOVED
OH YEAH, I BORROWED THIS BOOK FROM THE LIBRARY-- *HOW TO DEAL WITH SCARY SITUATIONS.*
HARUHI...!!
MADE BY HARUHI
COURAGE-TESTING GOODS UNDER THREE BUCKS (KONNYAKU GEL)
LET'S SEE... WHEN YOU'RE FACED WITH A SITUATION YOU HATE...
"ENDURE IT, AND IT WILL EVENTUALLY BE OVER."
NO!!
THAT'S MASOCHISTIC!!

HELLO THERE!!
THIS IS BISCO. I'VE BEEN ALIVE FOR 30 YEARS AND I JUST REALIZED FOR THE FIRST TIME THAT I HAVE A VOICE FETISH. I TOLD THIS TO MY MOTHER, AND SHE SAID "ME TOO!!" SHE GAVE ME AN ENTHUSIASTIC SPEECH ABOUT HOW SHE LOVES VOICES AND WHOSE SHE LOVES MOST.

I WONDER IF I INHERITED HER FETISH?
(I DEFINITELY INHERITED HER ENTHUSIASM.)

SORRY FOR GOING ON ABOUT SOMETHING SO PERVERSE. ACTUALLY, I REWROTE THE SCRIPT FOR THIS CORNER THREE TIMES.

I'M ALWAYS IN A RUSH AT THE VERY END. I SHOULD FINISH UP SOONER SOMETIME!! THIS WAS WRITTEN AFTER VOLUME 7 WAS ALREADY ON SALE. I FORGOT I HAVE A PROCRASTINATING PERSONALITY.

AHA! TOMORROW IS THE DEADLINE!! WHAT TO DO?! (I'M A WRECK!)

ANYWAY...
ENJOY THE REST OF VOLUME 8!!!

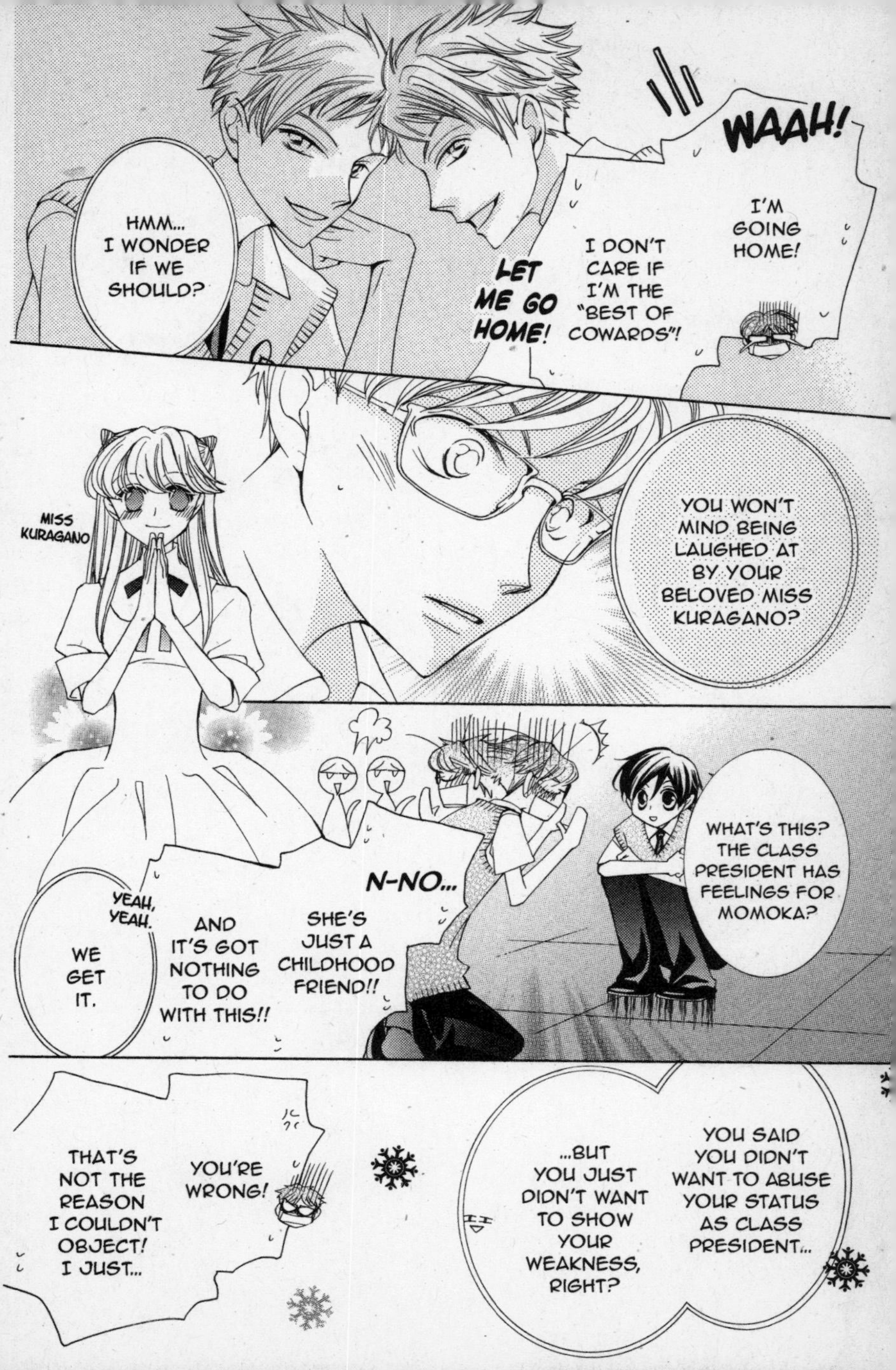
WAAH!
I'M GOING HOME!
I DON'T CARE IF I'M THE "BEST OF COWARDS"!
LET ME GO HOME!
HMM... I WONDER IF WE SHOULD?
YOU WON'T MIND BEING LAUGHED AT BY YOUR BELOVED MISS KURAGANO?
MISS KURAGANO
WHAT'S THIS? THE CLASS PRESIDENT HAS FEELINGS FOR MOMOKA?
N-NO...
SHE'S JUST A CHILDHOOD FRIEND!!
AND IT'S GOT NOTHING TO DO WITH THIS!!
YEAH, YEAH.
WE GET IT.
YOU SAID YOU DIDN'T WANT TO ABUSE YOUR STATUS AS CLASS PRESIDENT...
...BUT YOU JUST DIDN'T WANT TO SHOW YOUR WEAKNESS, RIGHT?
YOU'RE WRONG!
THAT'S NOT THE REASON I COULDN'T OBJECT! I JUST...

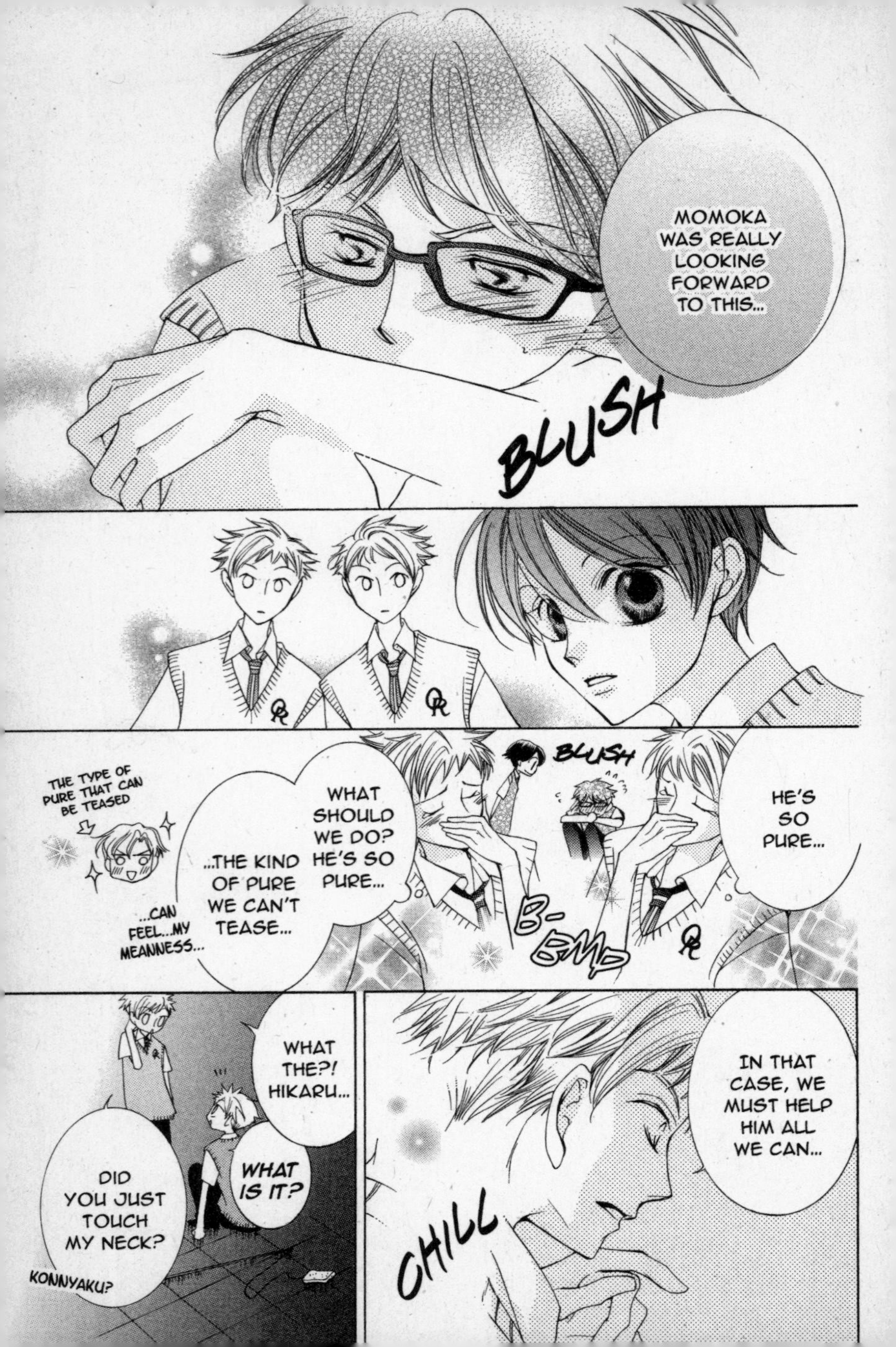
MOMOKA WAS REALLY LOOKING FORWARD TO THIS...
BLUSH
HE'S SO PURE...
BLUSH
B-BMP
WHAT SHOULD WE DO? HE'S SO PURE...
...THE KIND OF PURE WE CAN'T TEASE...
...CAN FEEL...MY MEANNESS...
THE TYPE OF PURE THAT CAN BE TEASED
IN THAT CASE, WE MUST HELP HIM ALL WE CAN...
CHILL
WHAT THE?! HIKARU...
WHAT IS IT?
DID YOU JUST TOUCH MY NECK?
KONNYAKU?

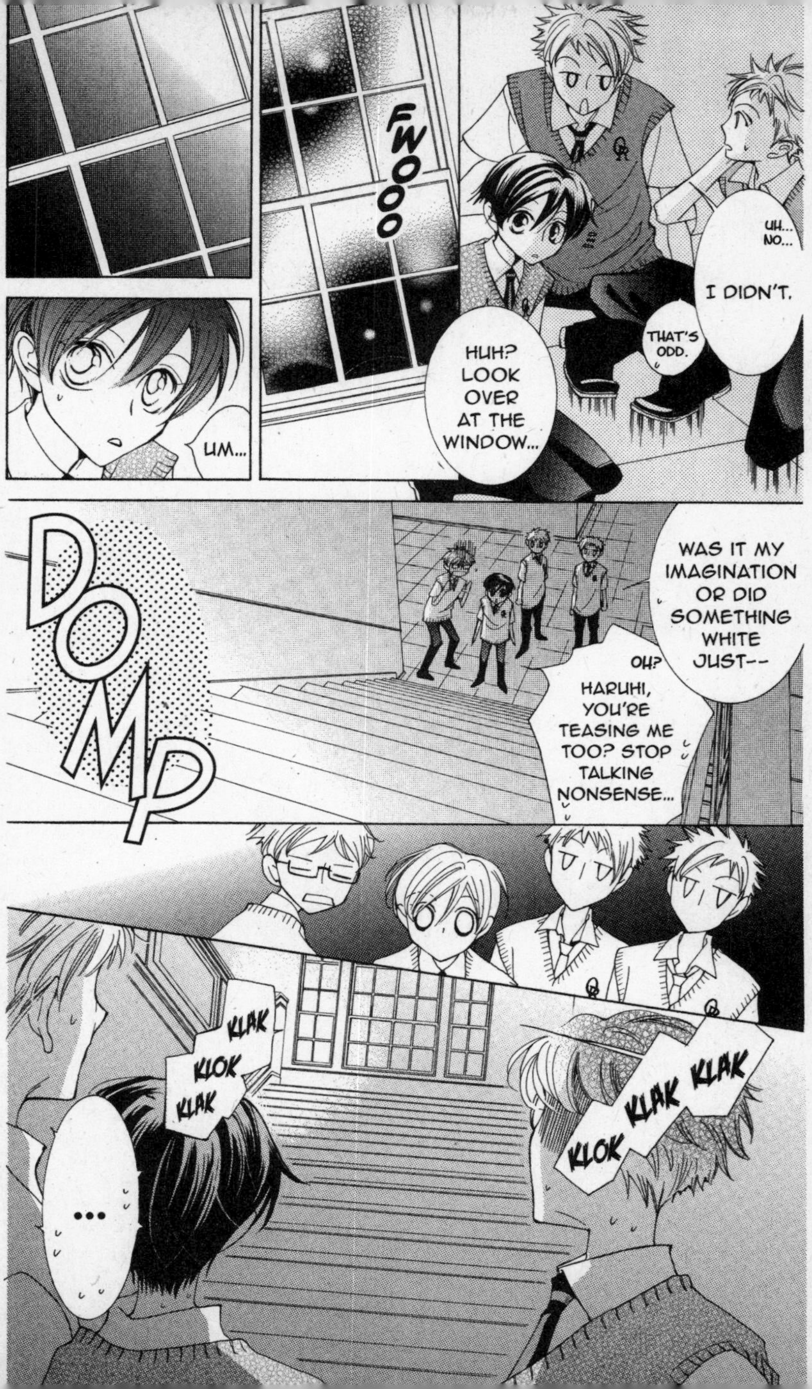
UH... NO...
I DIDN'T.
THAT'S ODD.
HUH? LOOK OVER AT THE WINDOW...
FWOOOO
UM...
WAS IT MY IMAGINATION OR DID SOMETHING WHITE JUST--
OH?
HARUHI, YOU'RE TEASING ME TOO? STOP TALKING NONSENSE...
DOMP
KLOK KLAK KLAK
KLAK KLOK KLAK
...

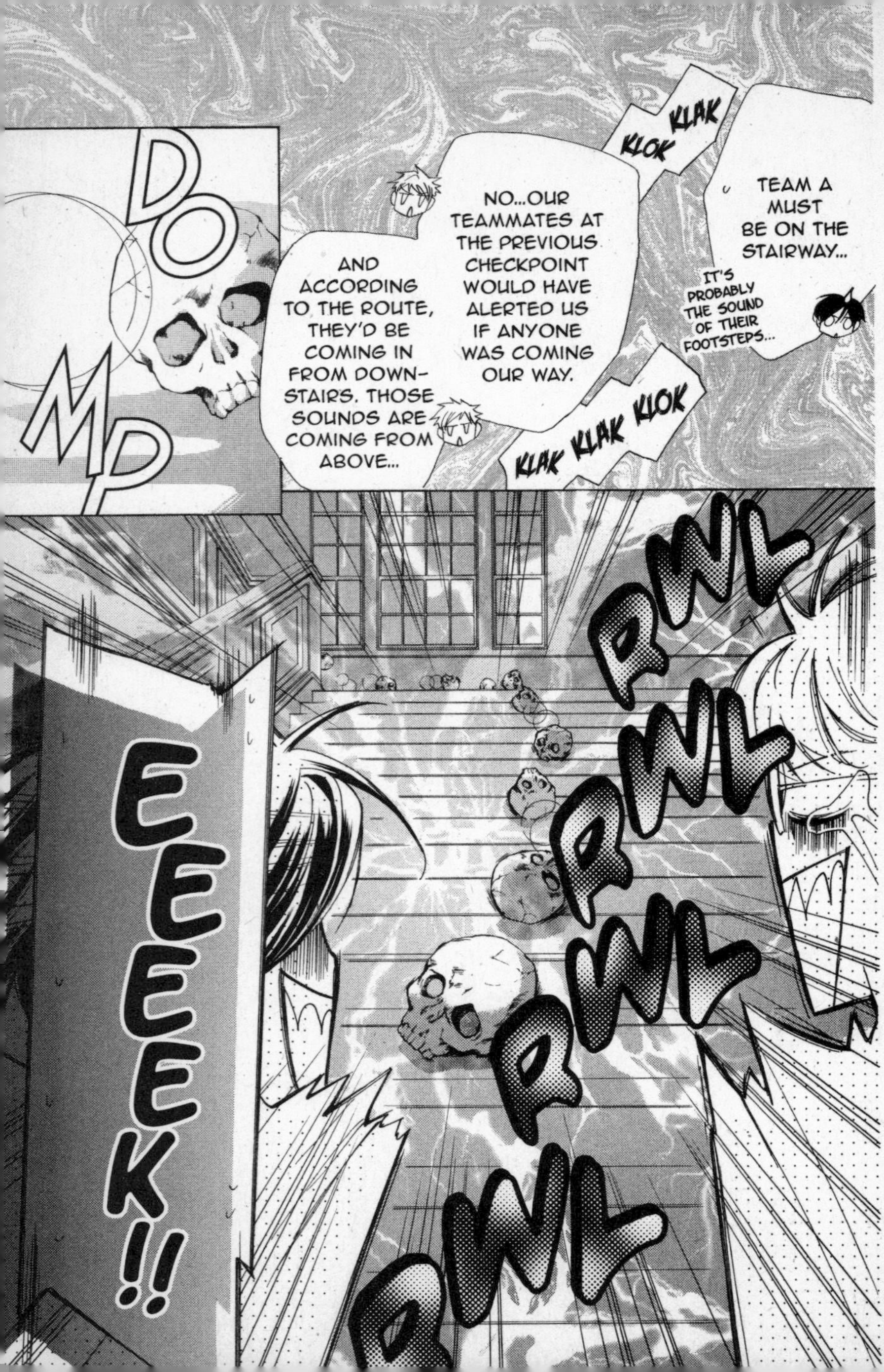
KLOK KLAK
TEAM A MUST BE ON THE STAIRWAY...
IT'S PROBABLY THE SOUND OF THEIR FOOTSTEPS...
NO...OUR TEAMMATES AT THE PREVIOUS CHECKPOINT WOULD HAVE ALERTED US IF ANYONE WAS COMING OUR WAY.
AND ACCORDING TO THE ROUTE, THEY'D BE COMING IN FROM DOWN-STAIRS. THOSE SOUNDS ARE COMING FROM ABOVE...
KLAK KLAK KLOK
DOMP
RWL RWL RWL RWL RWL
EEEEEK!!

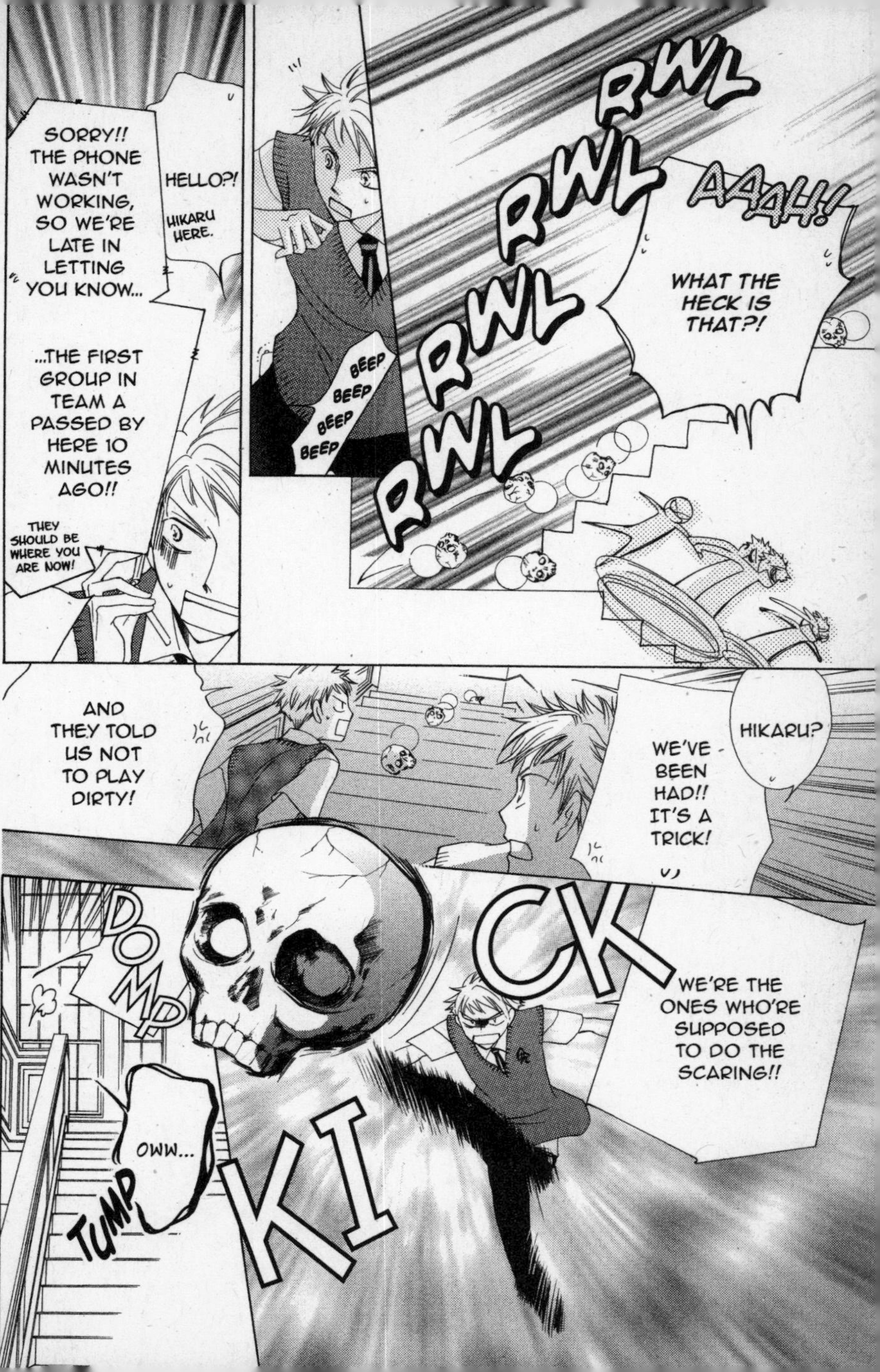
RWL RWL RWL RWL
AAAH!
WHAT THE HECK IS THAT?!
HELLO?!
HIKARU HERE.
BEEP BEEP BEEP BEEP
SORRY!! THE PHONE WASN'T WORKING, SO WE'RE LATE IN LETTING YOU KNOW...
...THE FIRST GROUP IN TEAM A PASSED BY HERE 10 MINUTES AGO!!
THEY SHOULD BE WHERE YOU ARE NOW!
HIKARU?
WE'VE BEEN HAD!! IT'S A TRICK!
AND THEY TOLD US NOT TO PLAY DIRTY!
WE'RE THE ONES WHO'RE SUPPOSED TO DO THE SCARING!!
KICK
DOMP
OWW...
TUMP

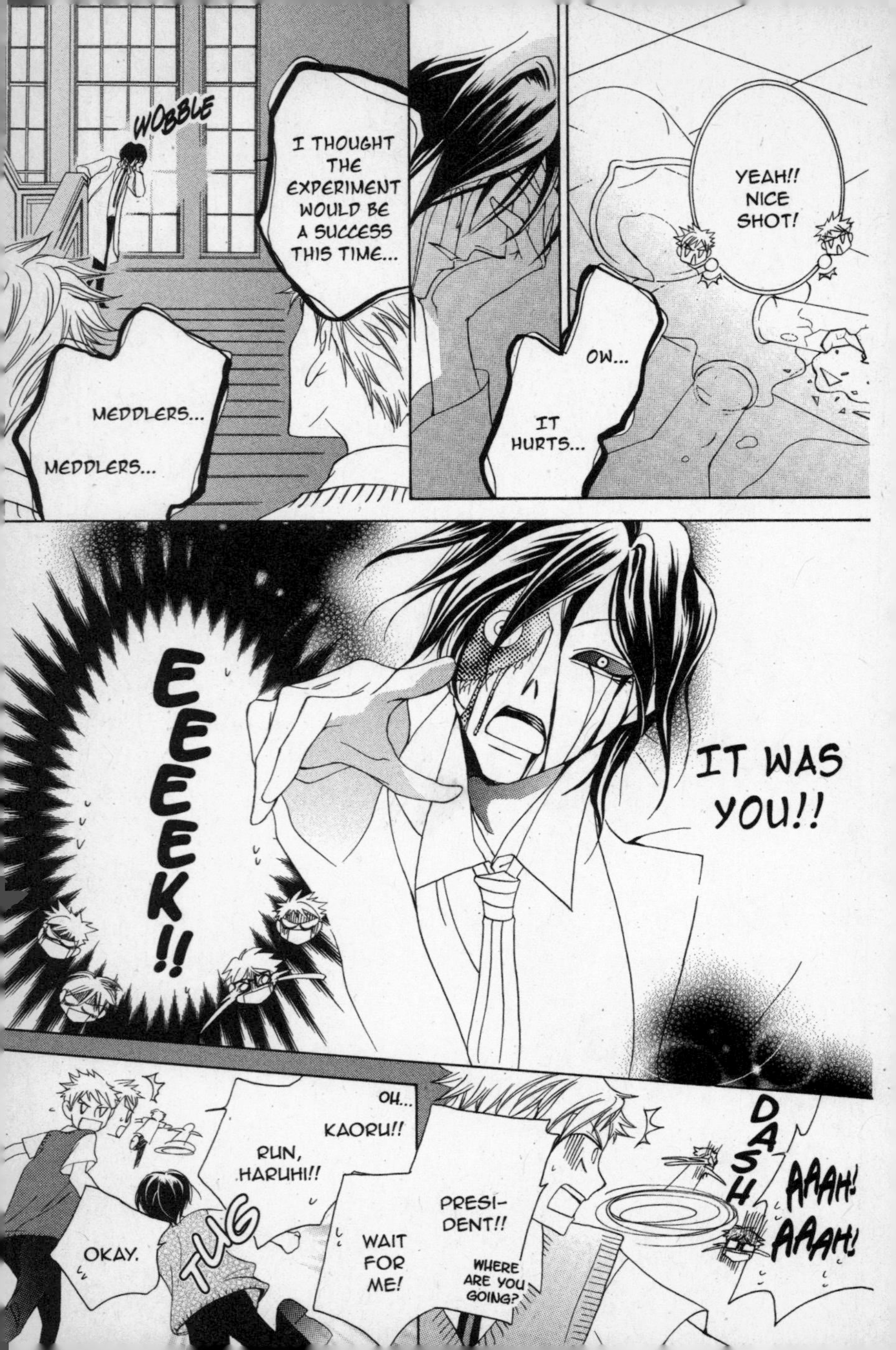
YEAH!! NICE SHOT!
OW...
IT HURTS...
WOBBLE
I THOUGHT THE EXPERIMENT WOULD BE A SUCCESS THIS TIME...
MEDDLERS...
MEDDLERS...
IT WAS YOU!!
EEEEEK!!
DASH
AAAH! AAAH!
PRESI-DENT!!
WHERE ARE YOU GOING?
WAIT FOR ME!
OH... KAORU!!
RUN, HARUHI!!
TUG
OKAY.

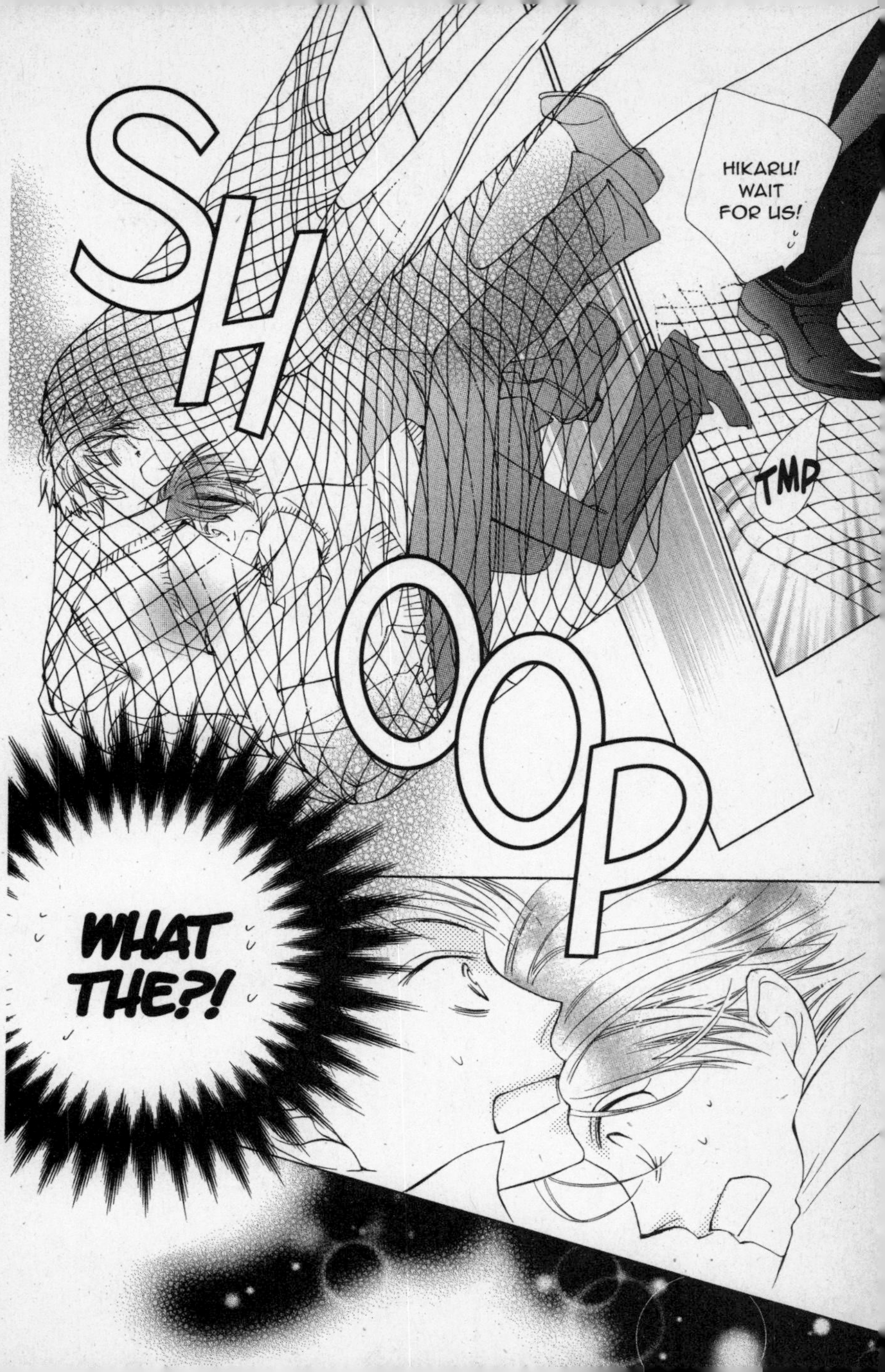
HIKARU! WAIT FOR US!
TMP
SHOOOP
WHAT THE?!

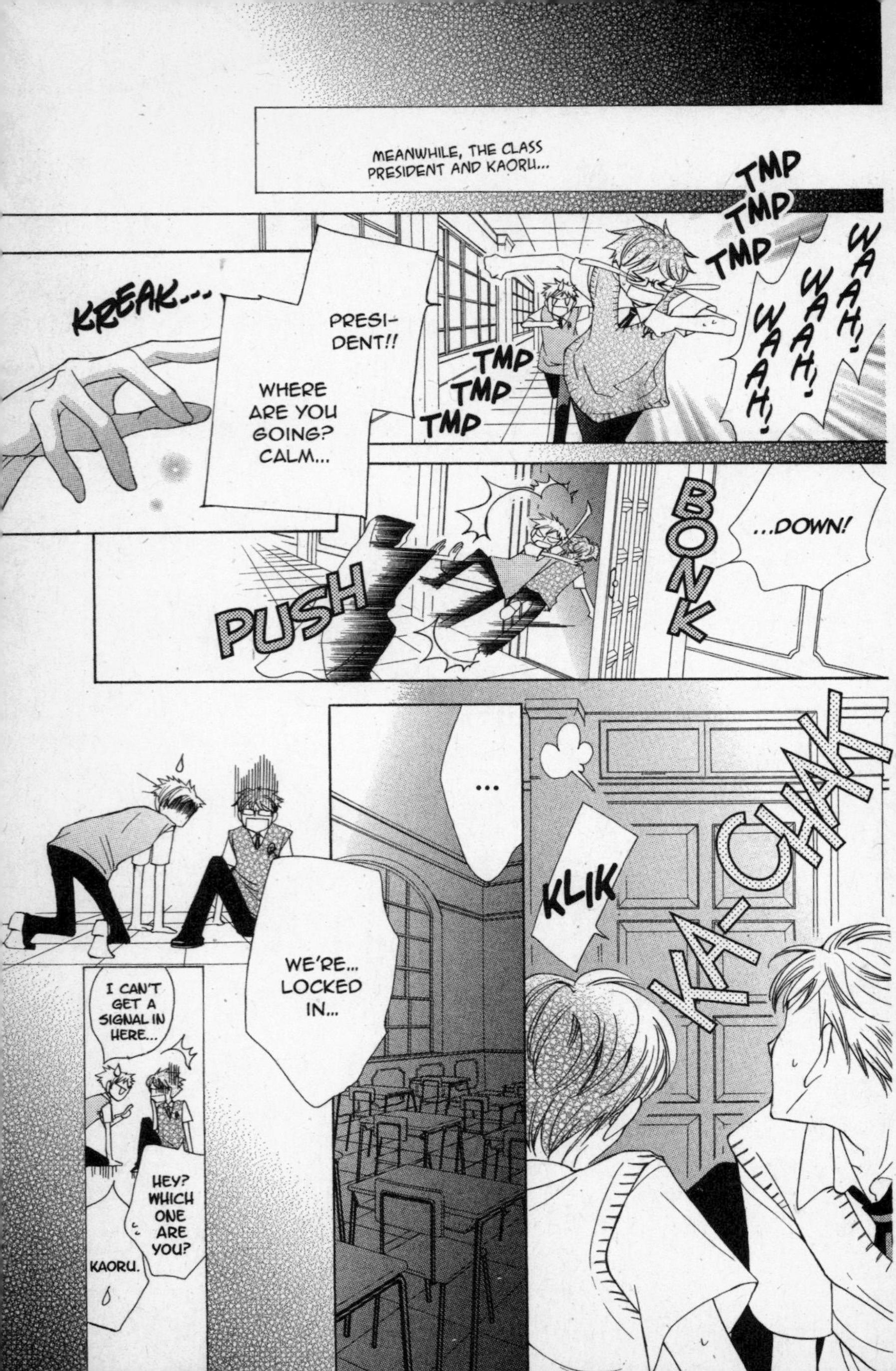
MEANWHILE, THE CLASS PRESIDENT AND KAORU...
TMP TMP TMP
WAAH! WAAH! WAAH!
TMP TMP TMP
KREAK...
PRESIDENT!!
WHERE ARE YOU GOING? CALM...
...DOWN!
BONK
PUSH
KA-CHAK
KLIK
...
WE'RE... LOCKED IN...
I CAN'T GET A SIGNAL IN HERE...
HEY? WHICH ONE ARE YOU?
KAORU.

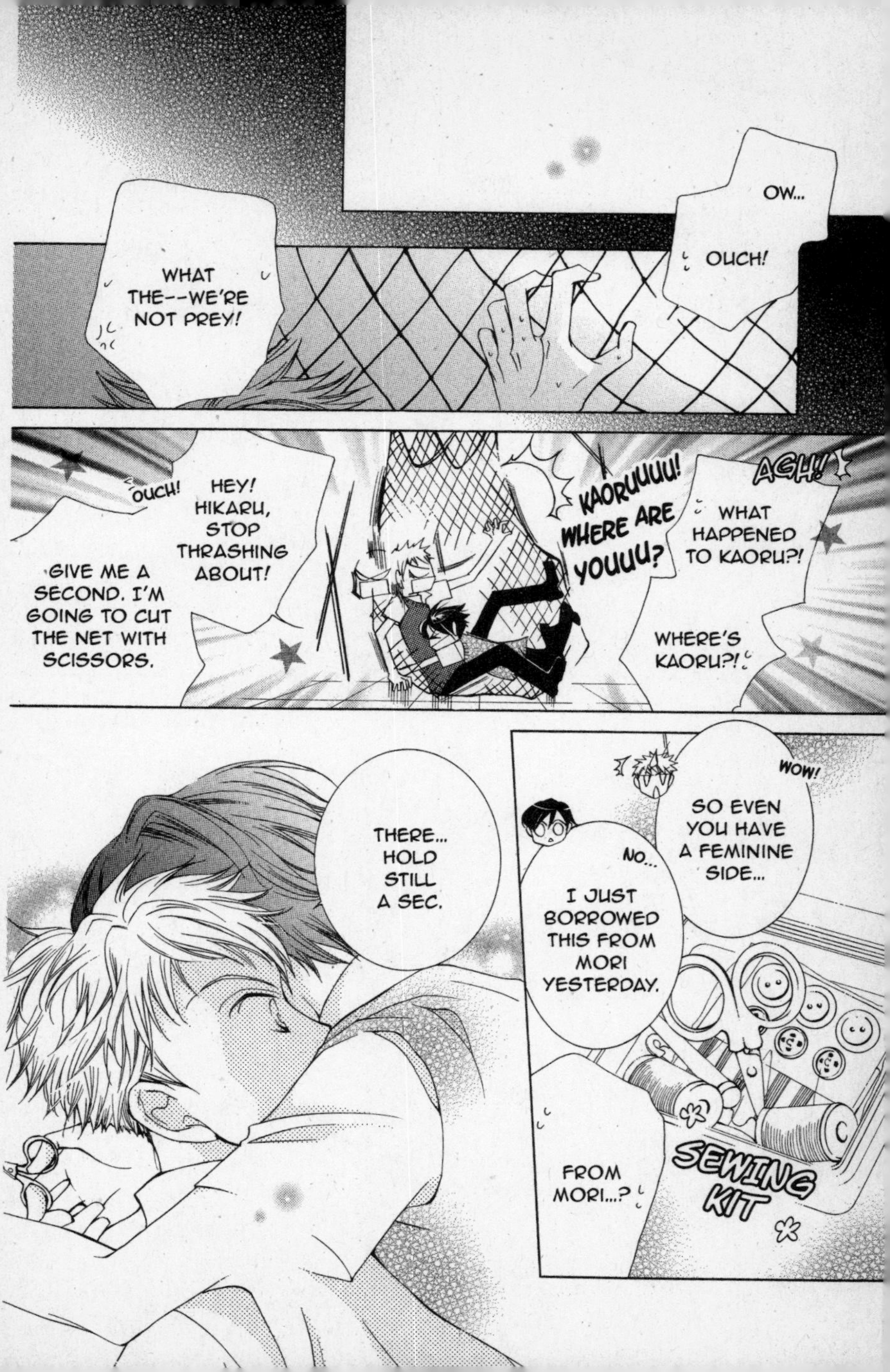
OW...
OUCH!
WHAT THE--WE'RE NOT PREY!
AGH!
WHAT HAPPENED TO KAORU?!
WHERE'S KAORU?!
KAORUUUU! WHERE ARE YOUUU?
HEY! HIKARU, STOP THRASHING ABOUT!
OUCH!
GIVE ME A SECOND. I'M GOING TO CUT THE NET WITH SCISSORS.
WOW!
SO EVEN YOU HAVE A FEMININE SIDE...
NO...
I JUST BORROWED THIS FROM MORI YESTERDAY.
FROM MORI...?
SEWING KIT
THERE... HOLD STILL A SEC.

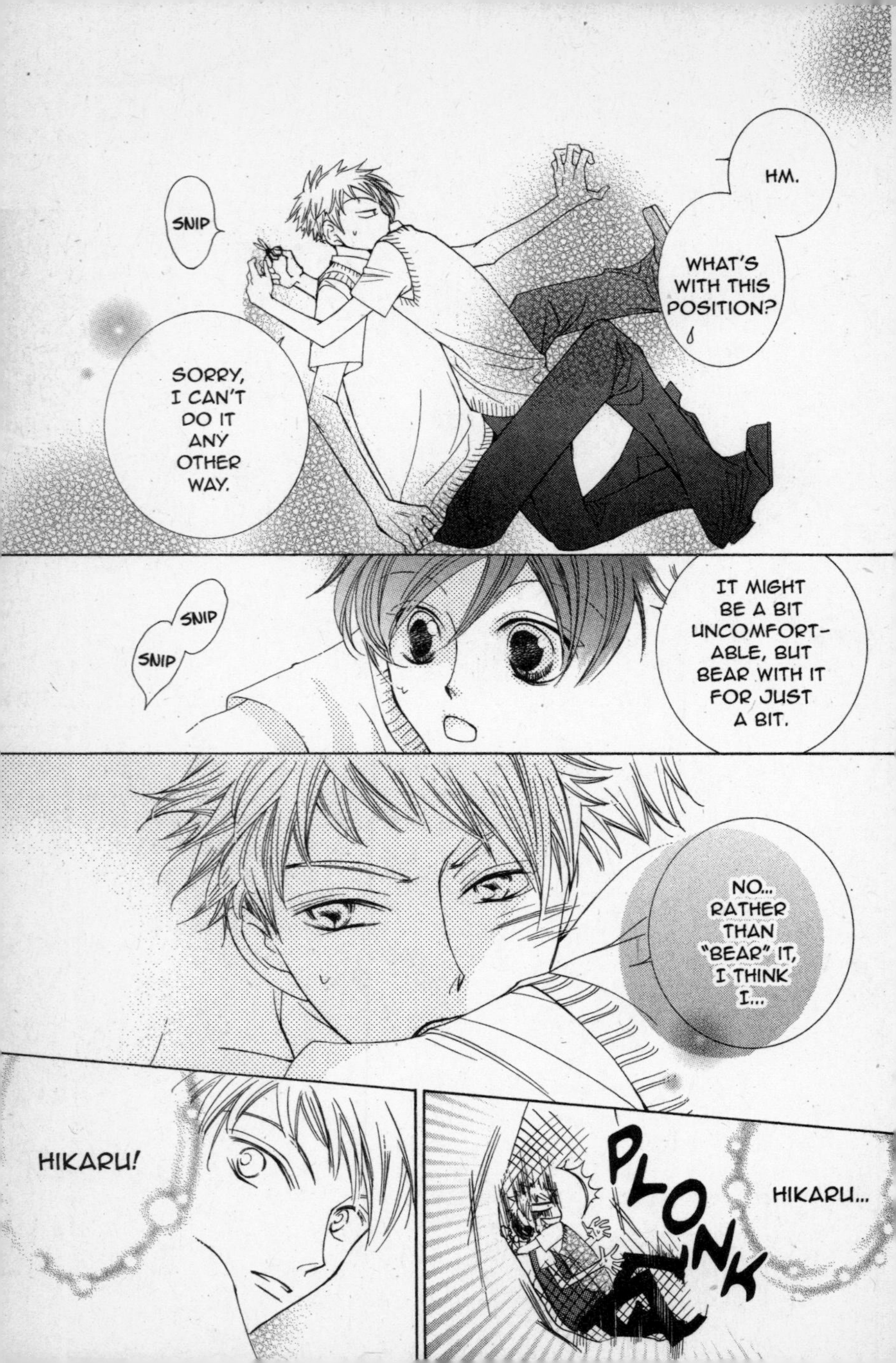
HM.
WHAT'S WITH THIS POSITION?
SNIP
SORRY, I CAN'T DO IT ANY OTHER WAY.
IT MIGHT BE A BIT UNCOMFORT-ABLE, BUT BEAR WITH IT FOR JUST A BIT.
SNIP
SNIP
NO... RATHER THAN "BEAR" IT, I THINK I...
HIKARU...
PLONK
HIKARU!

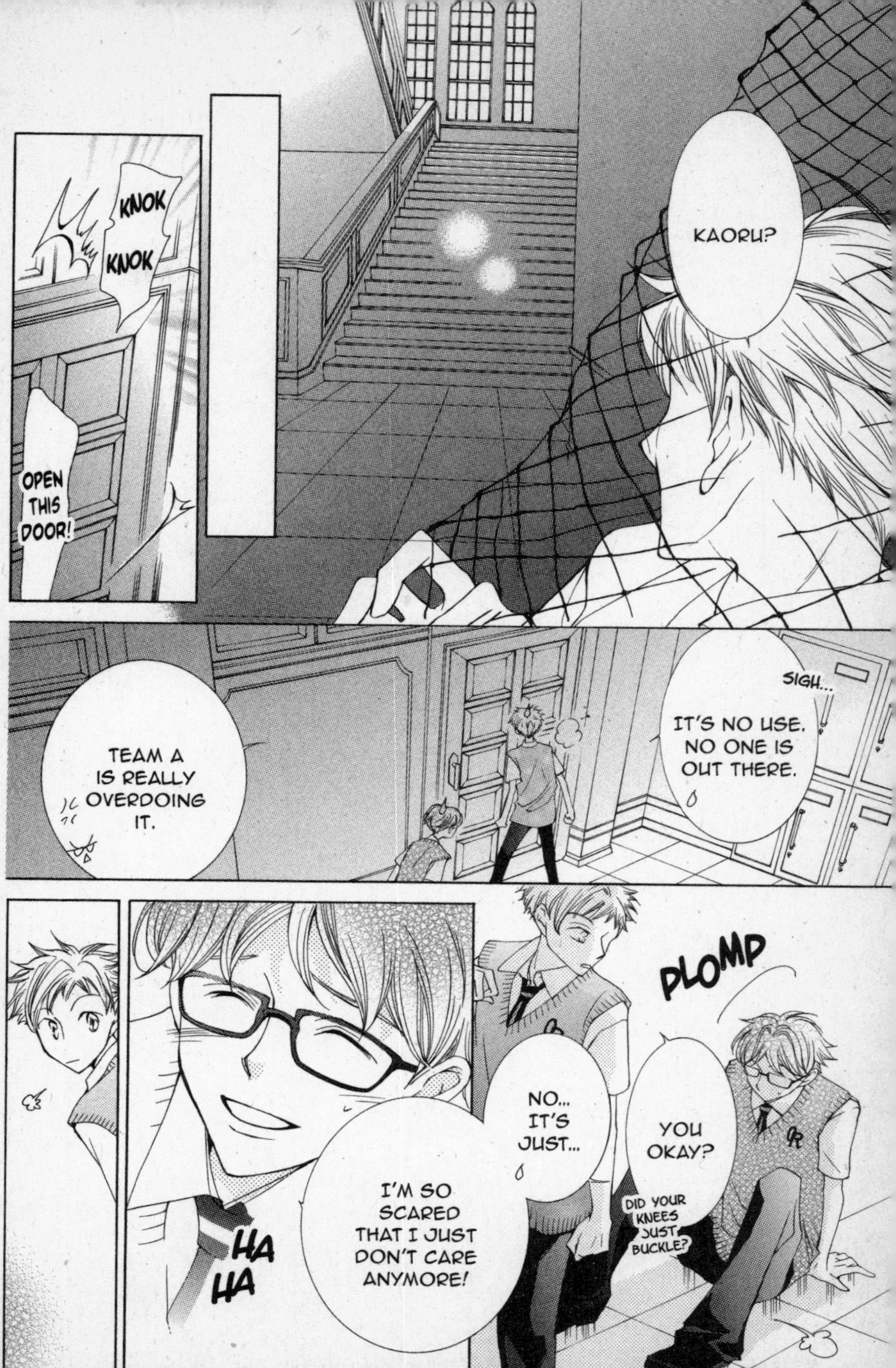
KAORU?
KNOK
KNOK
OPEN THIS DOOR!
SIGH...
IT'S NO USE. NO ONE IS OUT THERE.
TEAM A IS REALLY OVERDOING IT.
PLOMP
YOU OKAY?
DID YOUR KNEES JUST BUCKLE?
NO... IT'S JUST...
I'M SO SCARED THAT I JUST DON'T CARE ANYMORE!
HA HA

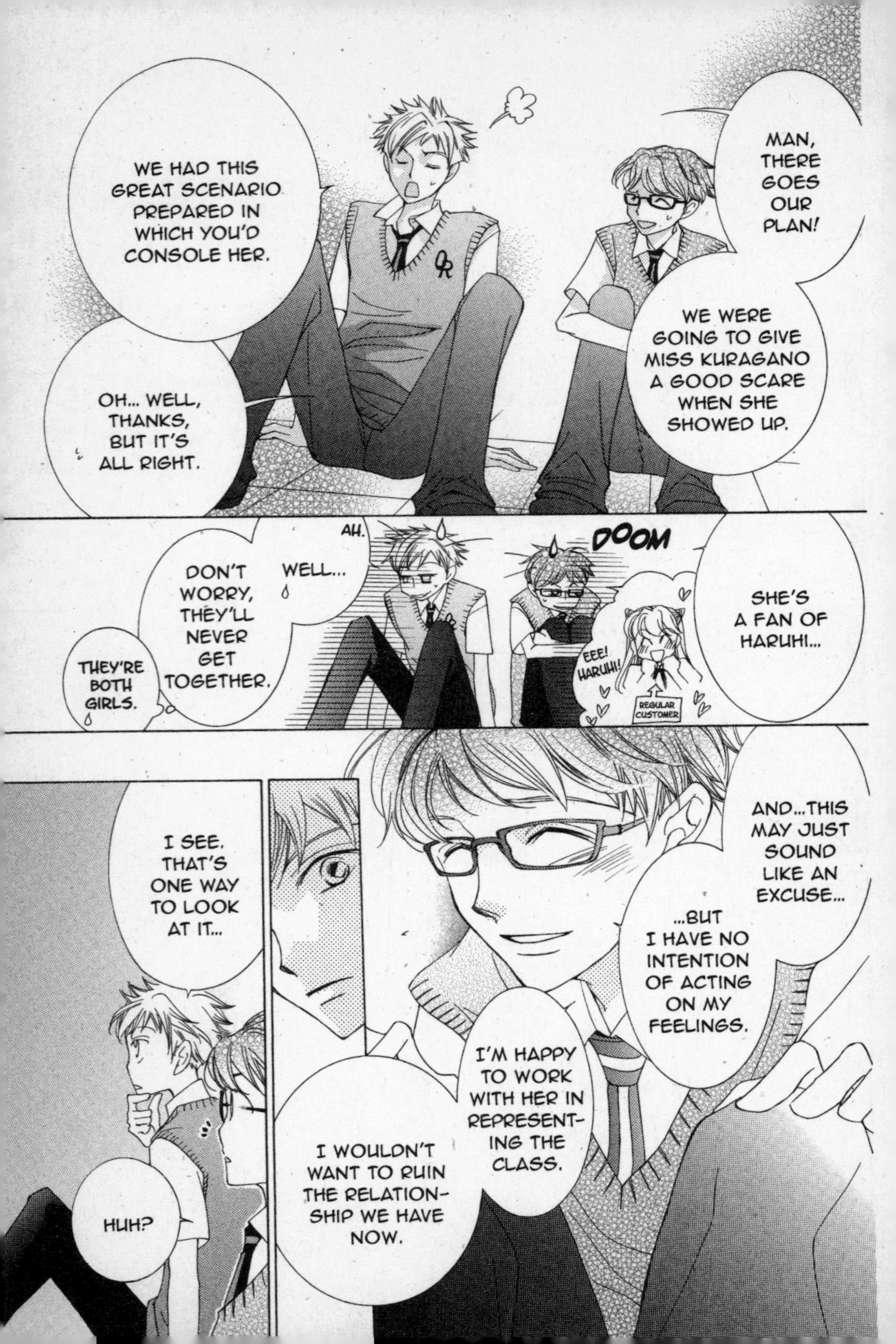
MAN, THERE GOES OUR PLAN!
WE WERE GOING TO GIVE MISS KURAGANO A GOOD SCARE WHEN SHE SHOWED UP.
WE HAD THIS GREAT SCENARIO PREPARED IN WHICH YOU'D CONSOLE HER.
OH... WELL, THANKS, BUT IT'S ALL RIGHT.
SHE'S A FAN OF HARUHI...
DOOM
EEE! HARUHI!
REGULAR CUSTOMER
AH.
WELL...
DON'T WORRY, THEY'LL NEVER GET TOGETHER.
THEY'RE BOTH GIRLS.
AND...THIS MAY JUST SOUND LIKE AN EXCUSE...
...BUT I HAVE NO INTENTION OF ACTING ON MY FEELINGS.
I'M HAPPY TO WORK WITH HER IN REPRESENTING THE CLASS.
I WOULDN'T WANT TO RUIN THE RELATIONSHIP WE HAVE NOW.
I SEE. THAT'S ONE WAY TO LOOK AT IT...
HUH?

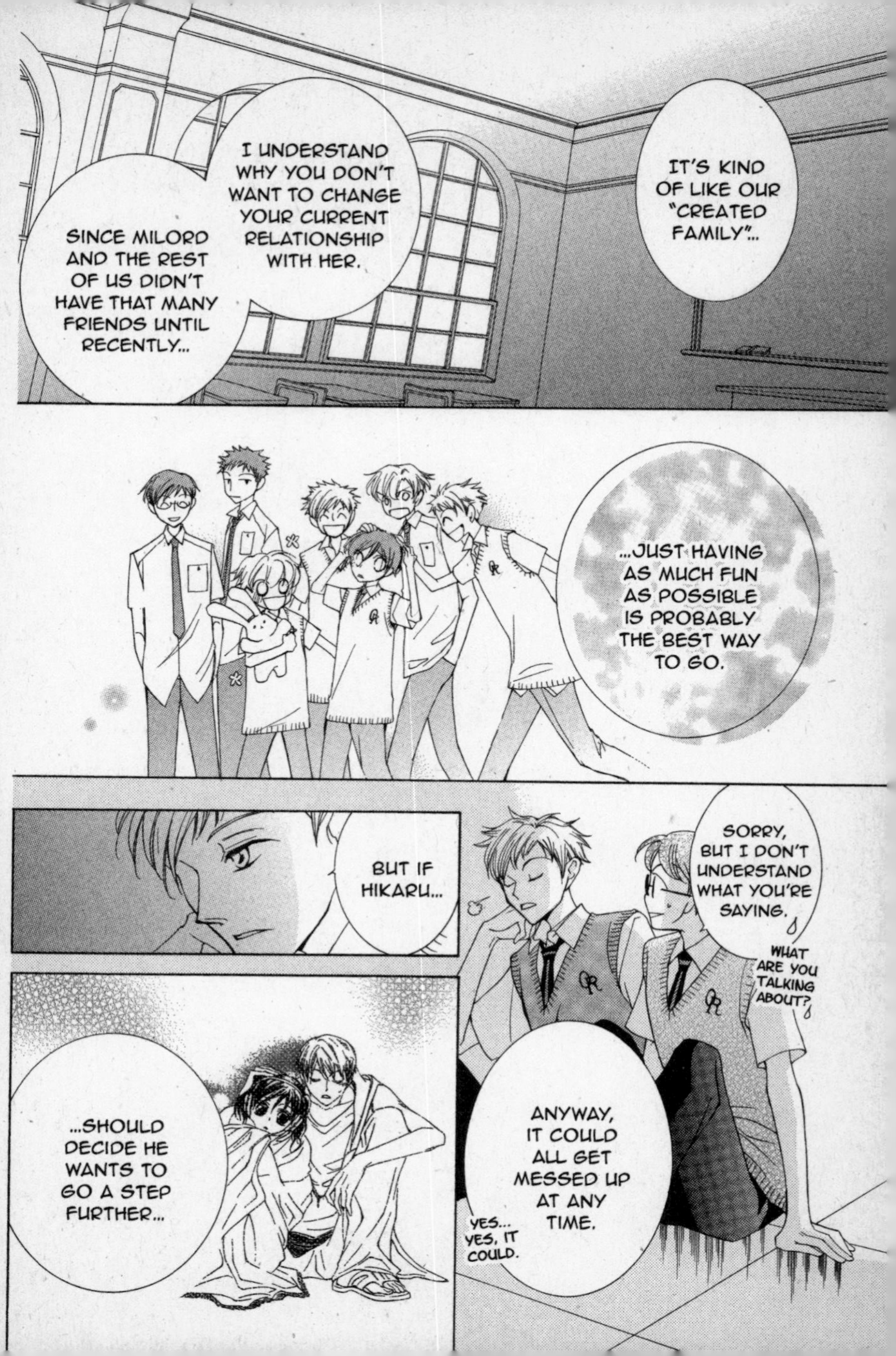
IT'S KIND OF LIKE OUR "CREATED FAMILY"...
I UNDERSTAND WHY YOU DON'T WANT TO CHANGE YOUR CURRENT RELATIONSHIP WITH HER.
SINCE MILORD AND THE REST OF US DIDN'T HAVE THAT MANY FRIENDS UNTIL RECENTLY...
...JUST HAVING AS MUCH FUN AS POSSIBLE IS PROBABLY THE BEST WAY TO GO.
SORRY, BUT I DON'T UNDERSTAND WHAT YOU'RE SAYING.
WHAT ARE YOU TALKING ABOUT?
ANYWAY, IT COULD ALL GET MESSED UP AT ANY TIME.
YES... YES, IT COULD.
BUT IF HIKARU...
...SHOULD DECIDE HE WANTS TO GO A STEP FURTHER...

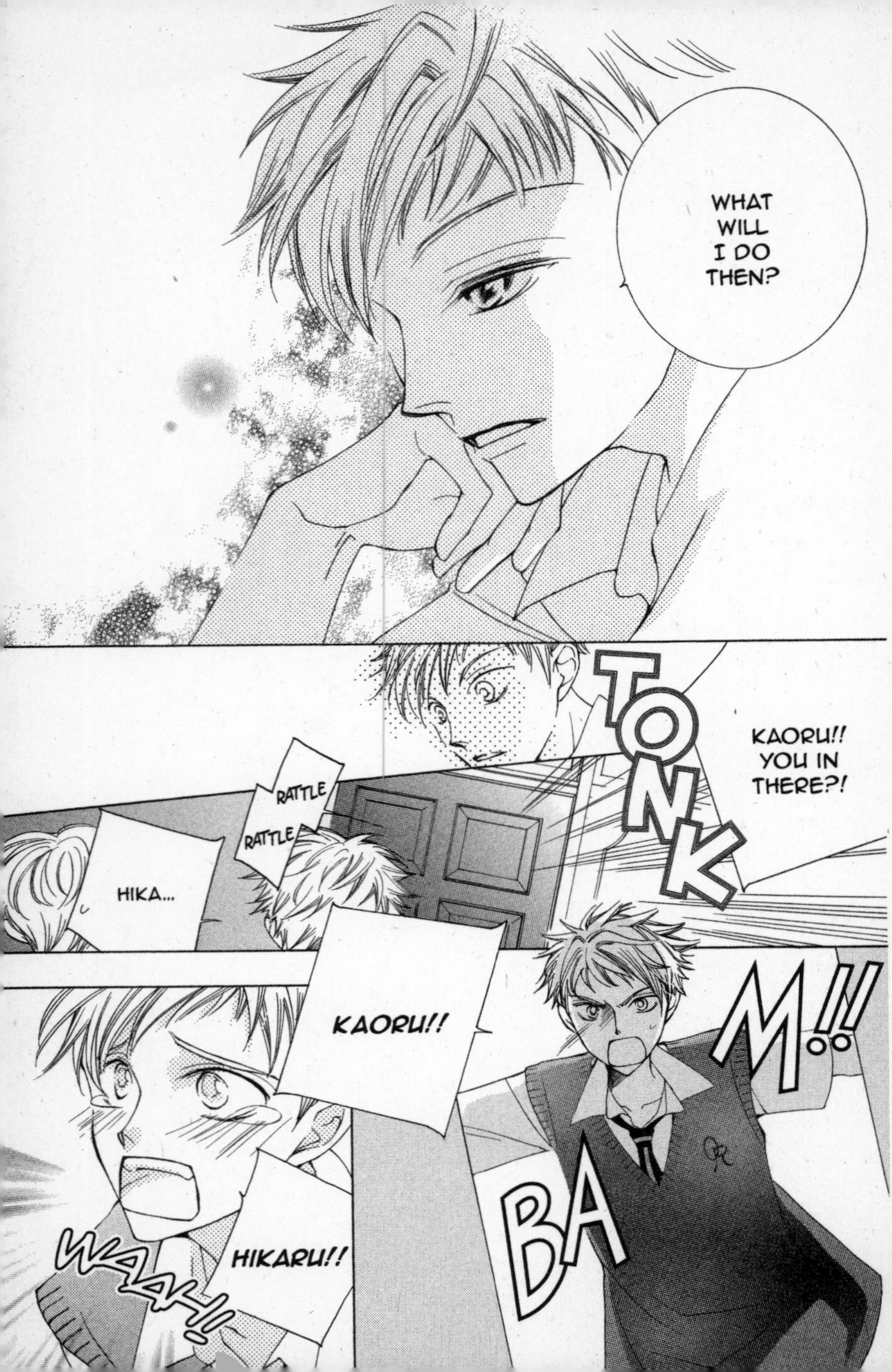
WHAT WILL I DO THEN?
KAORU!! YOU IN THERE?!
TONK
RATTLE
RATTLE
HIKA...
BAM!!
KAORU!!
HIKARU!!
WAAH!!

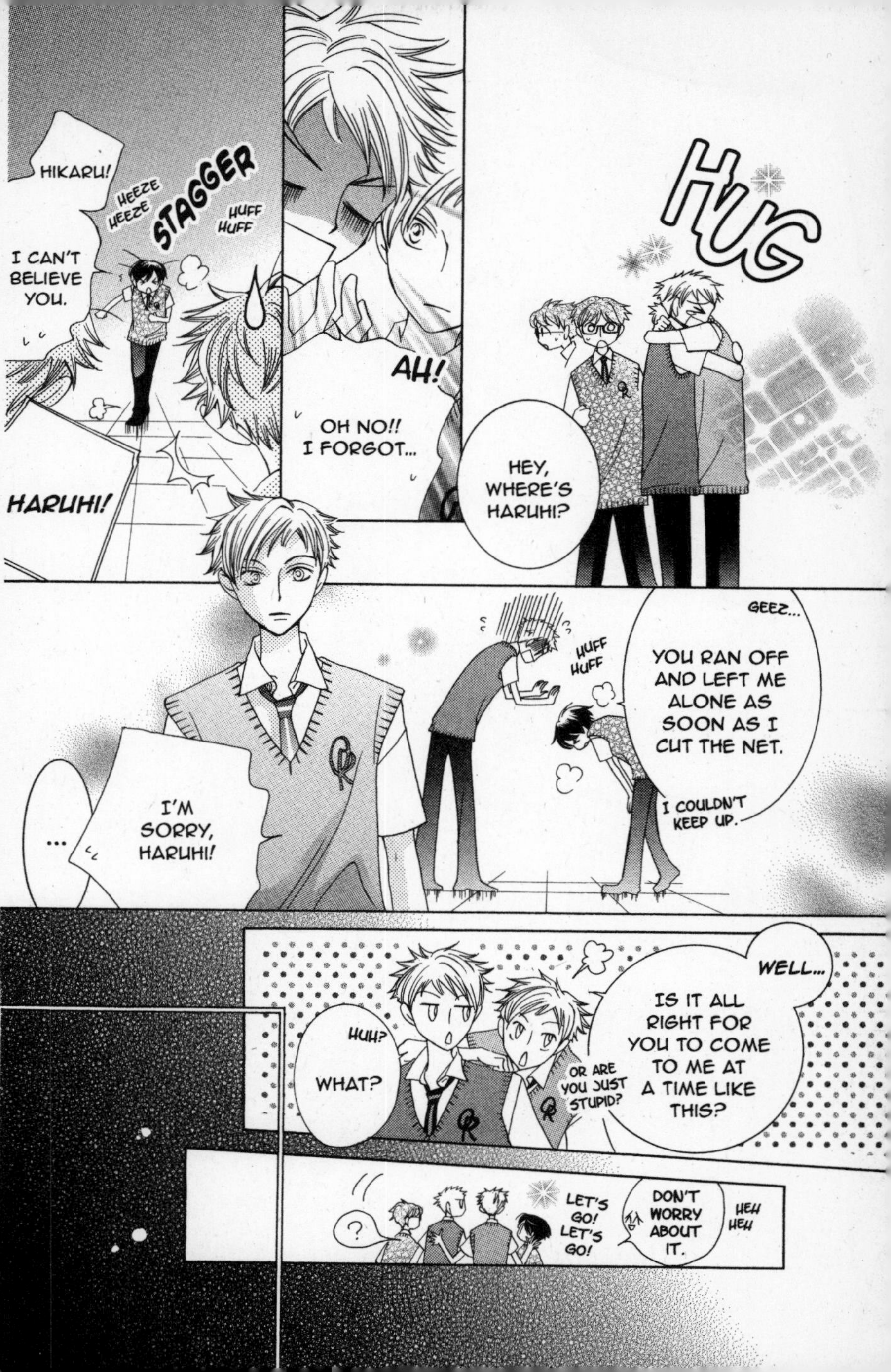
HUG
HEY, WHERE'S HARUHI?
AH!
OH NO!! I FORGOT...
HIKARU!
HEEZE HEEZE
STAGGER
HUFF HUFF
I CAN'T BELIEVE YOU.
HARUHI!
GEEZ...
YOU RAN OFF AND LEFT ME ALONE AS SOON AS I CUT THE NET.
HUFF HUFF
I COULDN'T KEEP UP.
I'M SORRY, HARUHI!
...
WELL...
IS IT ALL RIGHT FOR YOU TO COME TO ME AT A TIME LIKE THIS?
OR ARE YOU JUST STUPID?
HUH?
WHAT?
HEH HEH
DON'T WORRY ABOUT IT.
LET'S GO! LET'S GO!
?

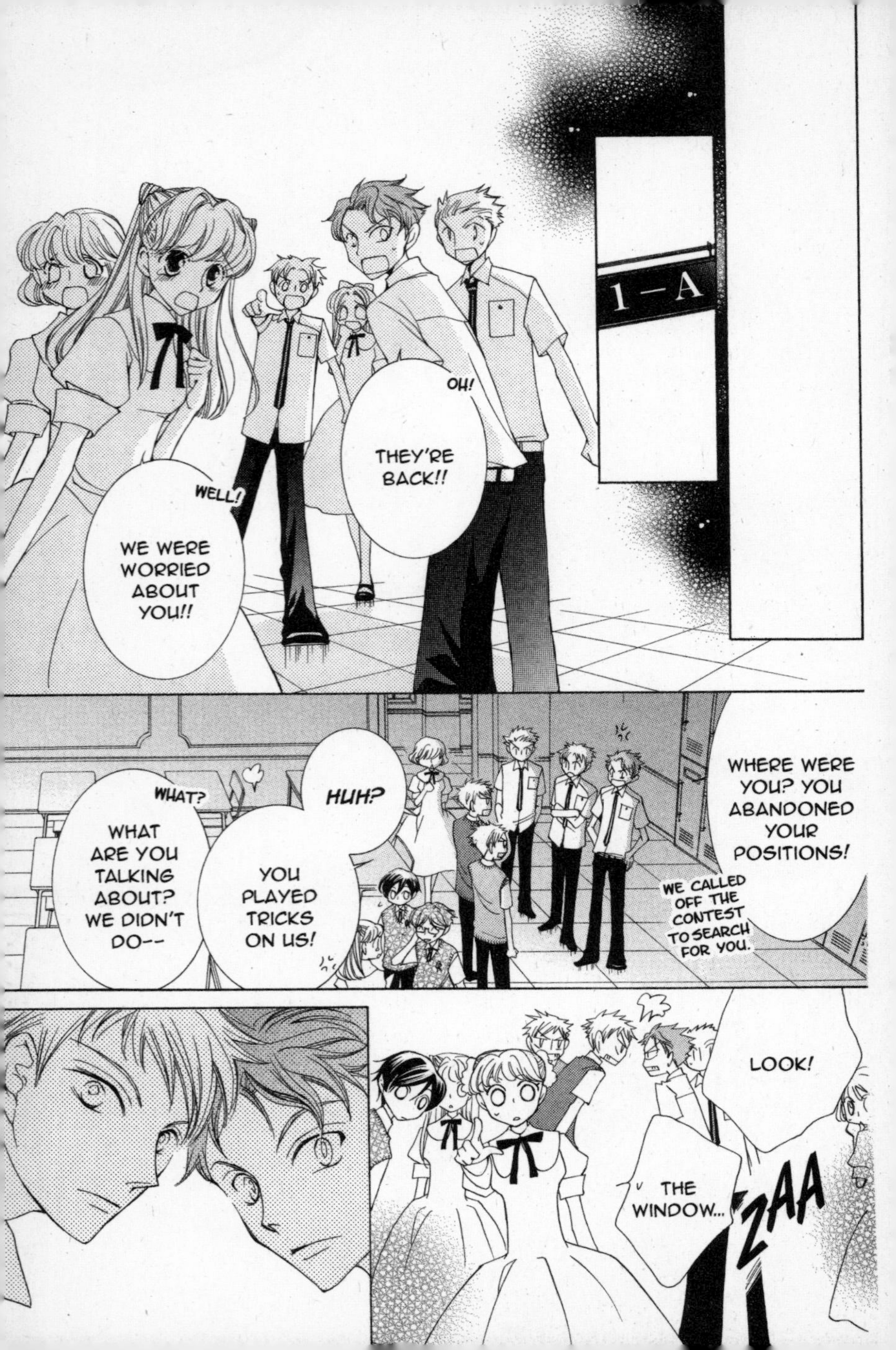
1-A
OH! THEY'RE BACK!!
WELL! WE WERE WORRIED ABOUT YOU!!
WHERE WERE YOU? YOU ABANDONED YOUR POSITIONS!
WE CALLED OFF THE CONTEST TO SEARCH FOR YOU.
HUH? YOU PLAYED TRICKS ON US!
WHAT? WHAT ARE YOU TALKING ABOUT? WE DIDN'T DO--
LOOK!
THE WINDOW...
ZAA

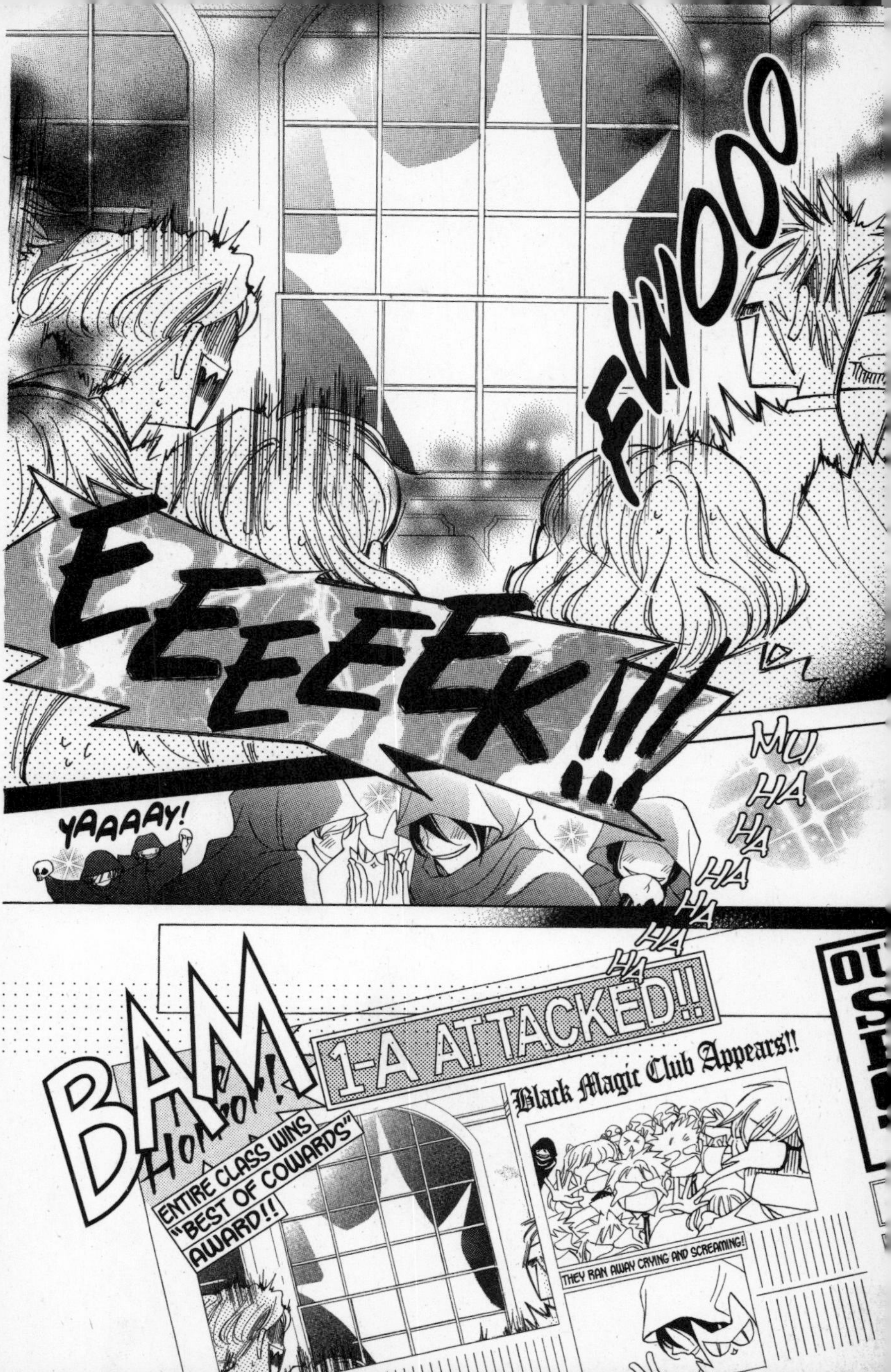
FWOOO
EEEEK!!!
MU HA HA HA HA HA HA
YAAAAY!
1-A ATTACKED!!
Black Magic Club Appears!!
THEY RAN AWAY CRYING AND SCREAMING!
ENTIRE CLASS WINS "BEST OF COWARDS" AWARD!!
BAM

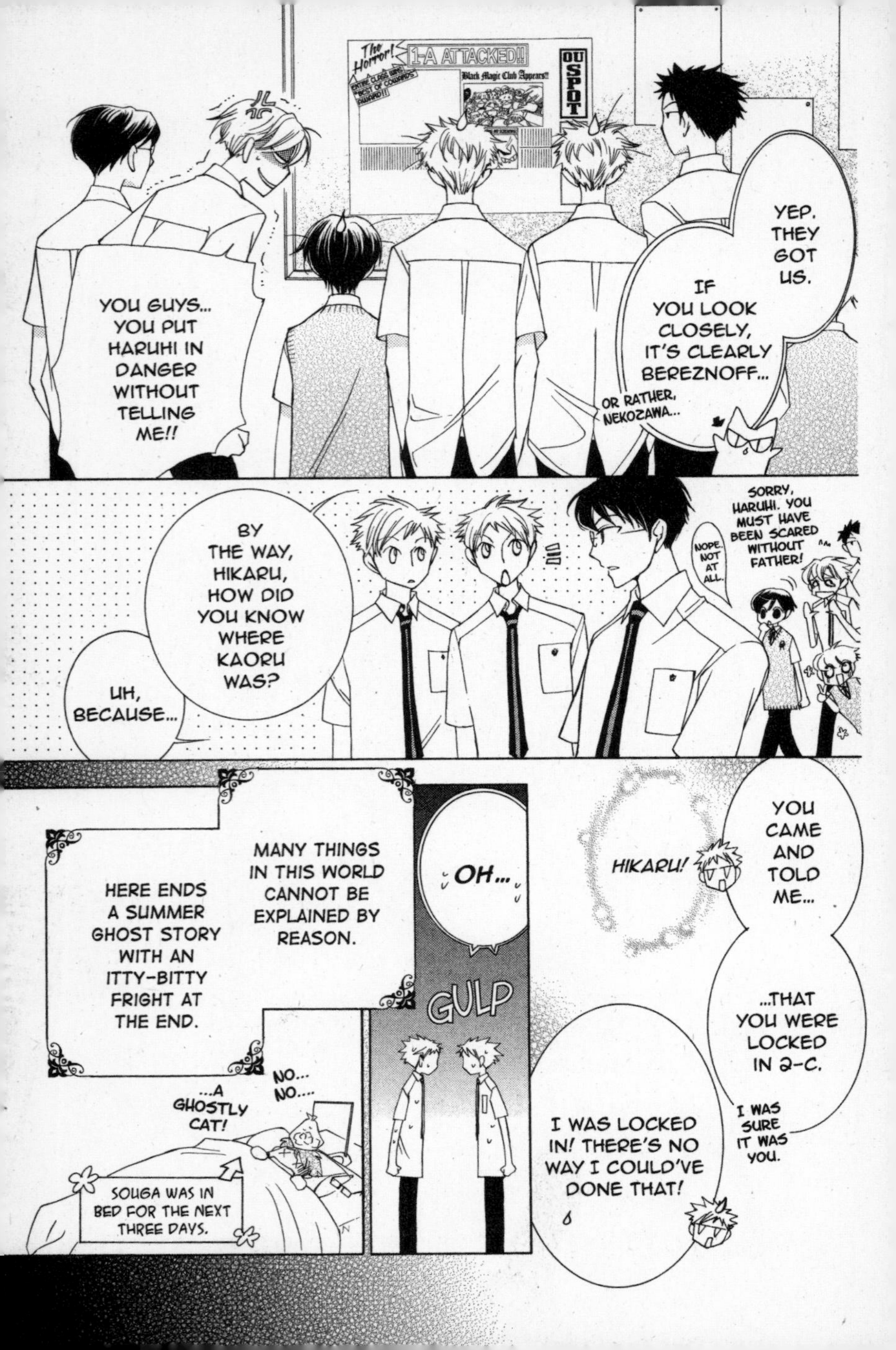
The Horror!
1-A ATTACKED!!
ENTIRE CLASS WINS "BEST OF COWARDS" AWARD!!
Black Magic Club Appears!!
OU SPOT
YEP. THEY GOT US.
IF YOU LOOK CLOSELY, IT'S CLEARLY BEREZNOFF...
OR RATHER, NEKOZAWA...
YOU GUYS... YOU PUT HARUHI IN DANGER WITHOUT TELLING ME!!
SORRY, HARUHI. YOU MUST HAVE BEEN SCARED WITHOUT FATHER!
NOPE. NOT AT ALL.
BY THE WAY, HIKARU, HOW DID YOU KNOW WHERE KAORU WAS?
UH, BECAUSE...
YOU CAME AND TOLD ME...
HIKARU!
...THAT YOU WERE LOCKED IN 2-C.
I WAS SURE IT WAS YOU.
I WAS LOCKED IN! THERE'S NO WAY I COULD'VE DONE THAT!
OH...
GULP
MANY THINGS IN THIS WORLD CANNOT BE EXPLAINED BY REASON.
HERE ENDS A SUMMER GHOST STORY WITH AN ITTY-BITTY FRIGHT AT THE END.
NO... NO....
...A GHOSTLY CAT!
SOUGA WAS IN BED FOR THE NEXT THREE DAYS.

GUEST ROOM: FAXES

SPECIAL THANKS TO
HARI TOKEINO!!

I LOVE THIS!!

ESPECIALLY HIM!
↓

HARI TOKEINO

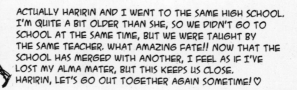

"...I CAN STILL CARRY HIM!"

I GOT THIS PICTURE BY FAX FROM HARIRIN (HARI TOKEINO)
A CHILDHOOD FRIEND AND AUTHOR OF HANA TO YUME'S
ONIICHAN TO ISSHO NI! (WITH MY OLDER BROTHER!) HOW
BEAUTIFUL!! I LOVE HER SENSE.

ACTUALLY HARIRIN AND I WENT TO THE SAME HIGH SCHOOL.
I'M QUITE A BIT OLDER THAN SHE, SO WE DIDN'T GO TO
SCHOOL AT THE SAME TIME, BUT WE WERE TAUGHT BY
THE SAME TEACHER. WHAT AMAZING FATE!! NOW THAT THE
SCHOOL HAS MERGED WITH ANOTHER, I FEEL AS IF I'VE
LOST MY ALMA MATER, BUT THIS KEEPS US CLOSE.
HARIRIN, LET'S GO OUT TOGETHER AGAIN SOMETIME! ♡

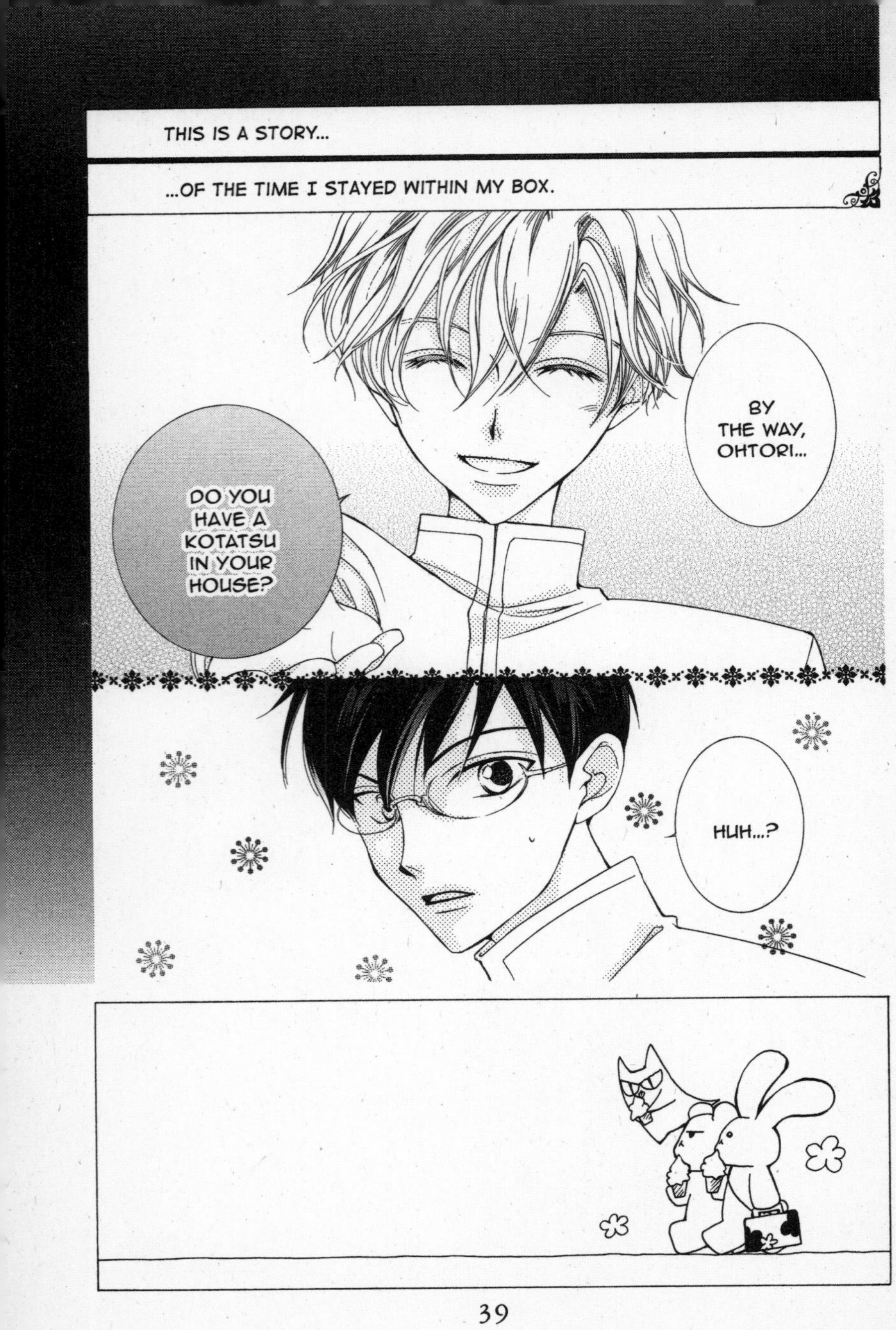
THIS IS A STORY...
...OF THE TIME I STAYED WITHIN MY BOX.
BY THE WAY, OHTORI...
DO YOU HAVE A KOTATSU IN YOUR HOUSE?
HUH...?

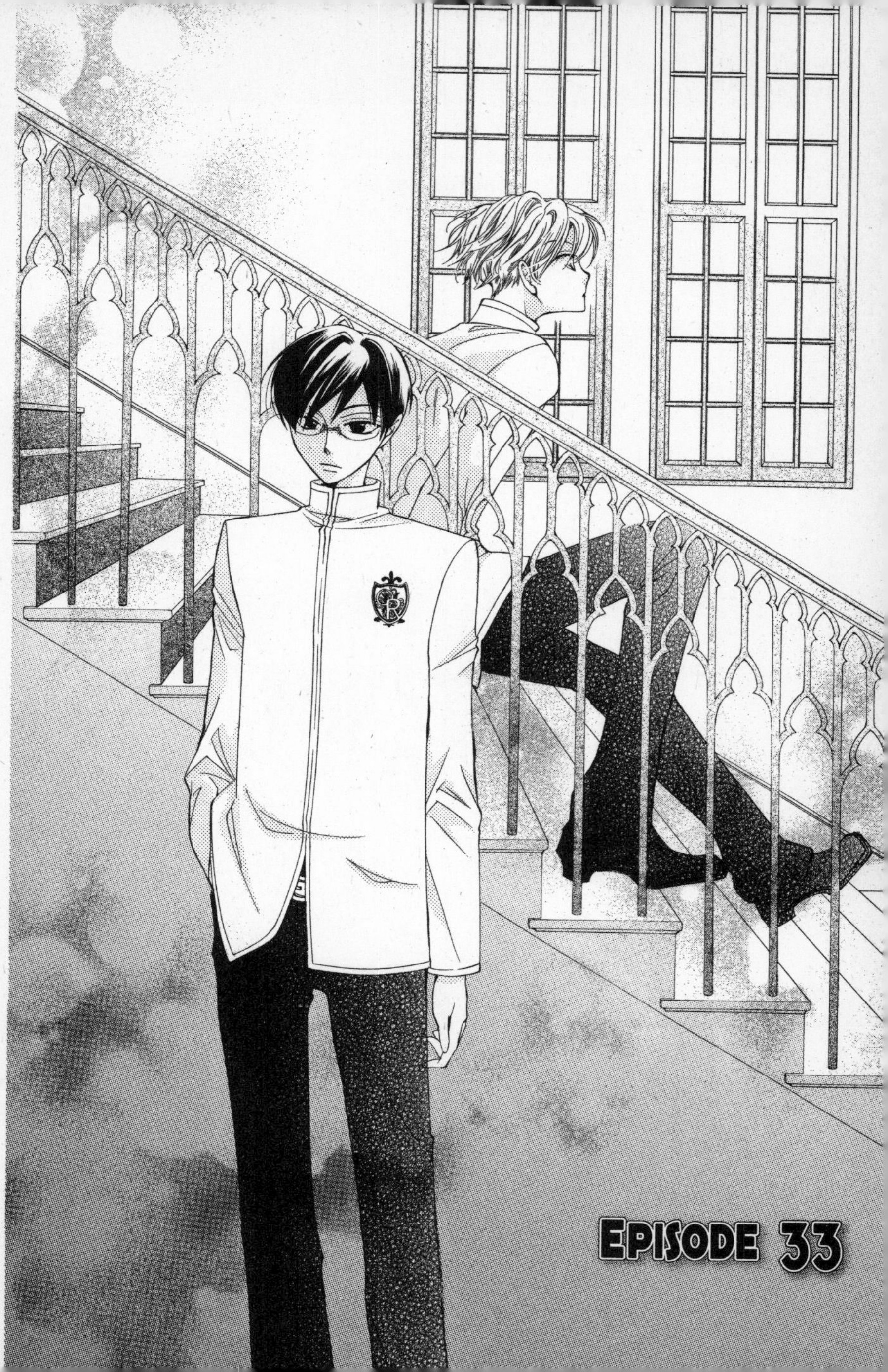
Episode 33

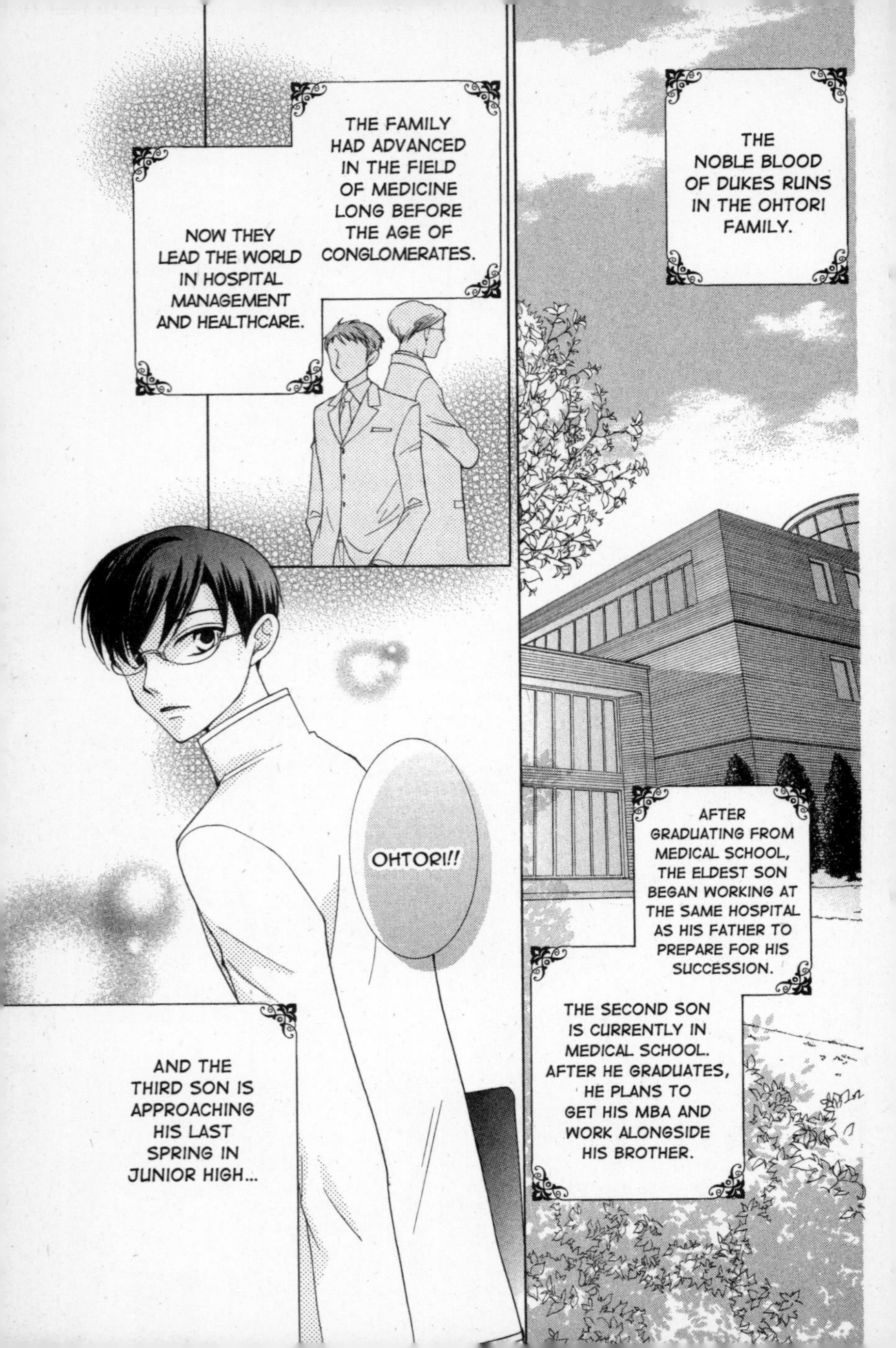
THE NOBLE BLOOD OF DUKES RUNS IN THE OHTORI FAMILY.
AFTER GRADUATING FROM MEDICAL SCHOOL, THE ELDEST SON BEGAN WORKING AT THE SAME HOSPITAL AS HIS FATHER TO PREPARE FOR HIS SUCCESSION.
THE SECOND SON IS CURRENTLY IN MEDICAL SCHOOL. AFTER HE GRADUATES, HE PLANS TO GET HIS MBA AND WORK ALONGSIDE HIS BROTHER.
THE FAMILY HAD ADVANCED IN THE FIELD OF MEDICINE LONG BEFORE THE AGE OF CONGLOMERATES.
NOW THEY LEAD THE WORLD IN HOSPITAL MANAGEMENT AND HEALTHCARE.
OHTORI!!
AND THE THIRD SON IS APPROACHING HIS LAST SPRING IN JUNIOR HIGH...

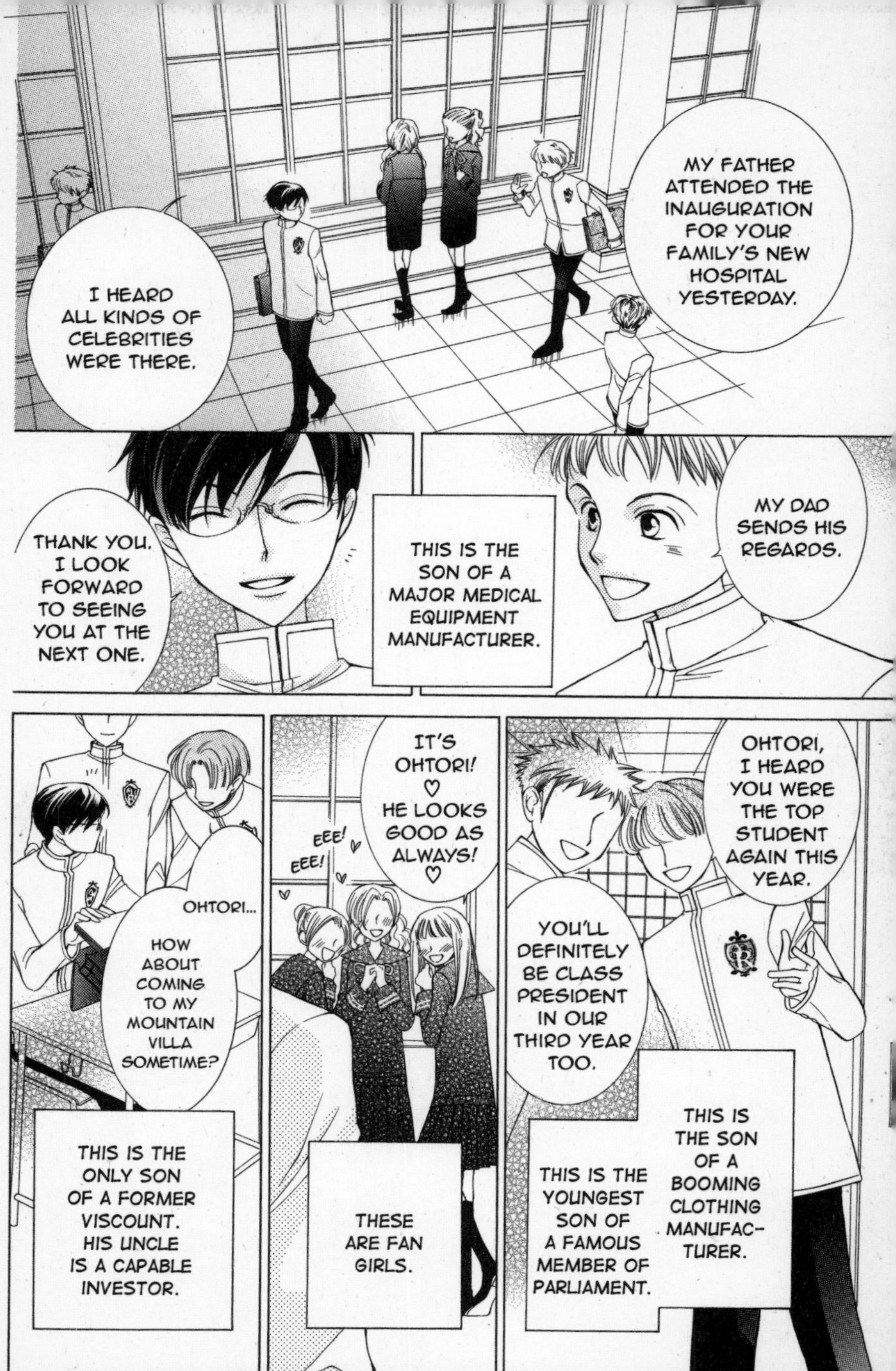
MY FATHER ATTENDED THE INAUGURATION FOR YOUR FAMILY'S NEW HOSPITAL YESTERDAY.
I HEARD ALL KINDS OF CELEBRITIES WERE THERE.
MY DAD SENDS HIS REGARDS.
THIS IS THE SON OF A MAJOR MEDICAL EQUIPMENT MANUFACTURER.
THANK YOU. I LOOK FORWARD TO SEEING YOU AT THE NEXT ONE.
OHTORI, I HEARD YOU WERE THE TOP STUDENT AGAIN THIS YEAR.
YOU'LL DEFINITELY BE CLASS PRESIDENT IN OUR THIRD YEAR TOO.
THIS IS THE SON OF A BOOMING CLOTHING MANUFAC-TURER.
THIS IS THE YOUNGEST SON OF A FAMOUS MEMBER OF PARLIAMENT.
IT'S OHTORI! ♡ HE LOOKS GOOD AS ALWAYS! ♡
EEE! EEE!
THESE ARE FAN GIRLS.
OHTORI... HOW ABOUT COMING TO MY MOUNTAIN VILLA SOMETIME?
THIS IS THE ONLY SON OF A FORMER VISCOUNT. HIS UNCLE IS A CAPABLE INVESTOR.

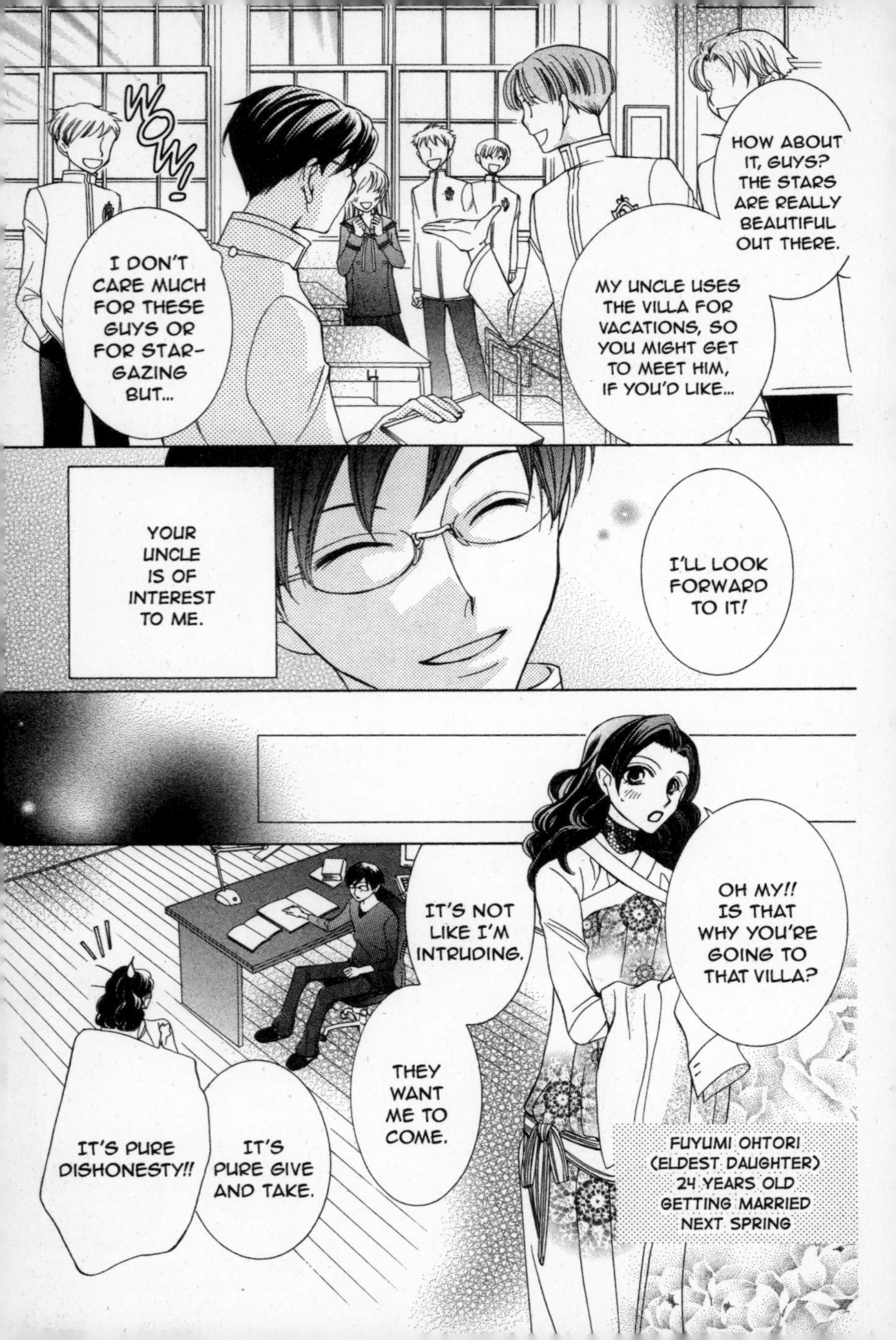
HOW ABOUT IT, GUYS? THE STARS ARE REALLY BEAUTIFUL OUT THERE.
MY UNCLE USES THE VILLA FOR VACATIONS, SO YOU MIGHT GET TO MEET HIM, IF YOU'D LIKE...
WOW!
I DON'T CARE MUCH FOR THESE GUYS OR FOR STAR-GAZING BUT...
I'LL LOOK FORWARD TO IT!
YOUR UNCLE IS OF INTEREST TO ME.
OH MY!! IS THAT WHY YOU'RE GOING TO THAT VILLA?
FUYUMI OHTORI (ELDEST DAUGHTER) 24 YEARS OLD GETTING MARRIED NEXT SPRING
IT'S NOT LIKE I'M INTRUDING.
THEY WANT ME TO COME.
IT'S PURE GIVE AND TAKE.
IT'S PURE DISHONESTY!!

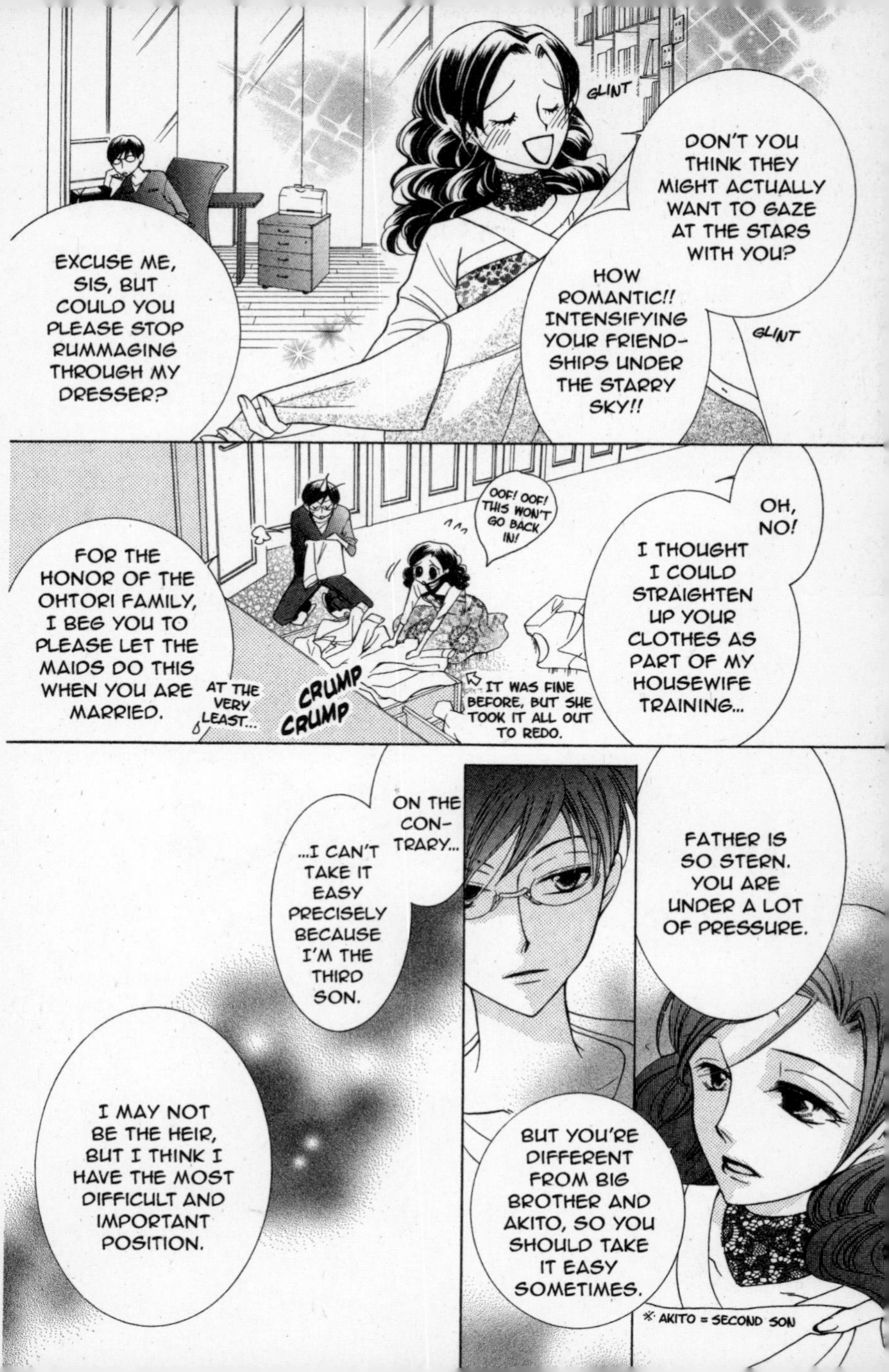
DON'T YOU THINK THEY MIGHT ACTUALLY WANT TO GAZE AT THE STARS WITH YOU?
GLINT
HOW ROMANTIC!! INTENSIFYING YOUR FRIEND-SHIPS UNDER THE STARRY SKY!!
GLINT
EXCUSE ME, SIS, BUT COULD YOU PLEASE STOP RUMMAGING THROUGH MY DRESSER?
OH, NO! I THOUGHT I COULD STRAIGHTEN UP YOUR CLOTHES AS PART OF MY HOUSEWIFE TRAINING...
OOF! OOF! THIS WON'T GO BACK IN!
IT WAS FINE BEFORE, BUT SHE TOOK IT ALL OUT TO REDO.
CRUMP CRUMP
FOR THE HONOR OF THE OHTORI FAMILY, I BEG YOU TO PLEASE LET THE MAIDS DO THIS WHEN YOU ARE MARRIED.
AT THE VERY LEAST...
FATHER IS SO STERN. YOU ARE UNDER A LOT OF PRESSURE.
BUT YOU'RE DIFFERENT FROM BIG BROTHER AND AKITO, SO YOU SHOULD TAKE IT EASY SOMETIMES.
※ AKITO = SECOND SON
ON THE CON-TRARY...
...I CAN'T TAKE IT EASY PRECISELY BECAUSE I'M THE THIRD SON.
I MAY NOT BE THE HEIR, BUT I THINK I HAVE THE MOST DIFFICULT AND IMPORTANT POSITION.

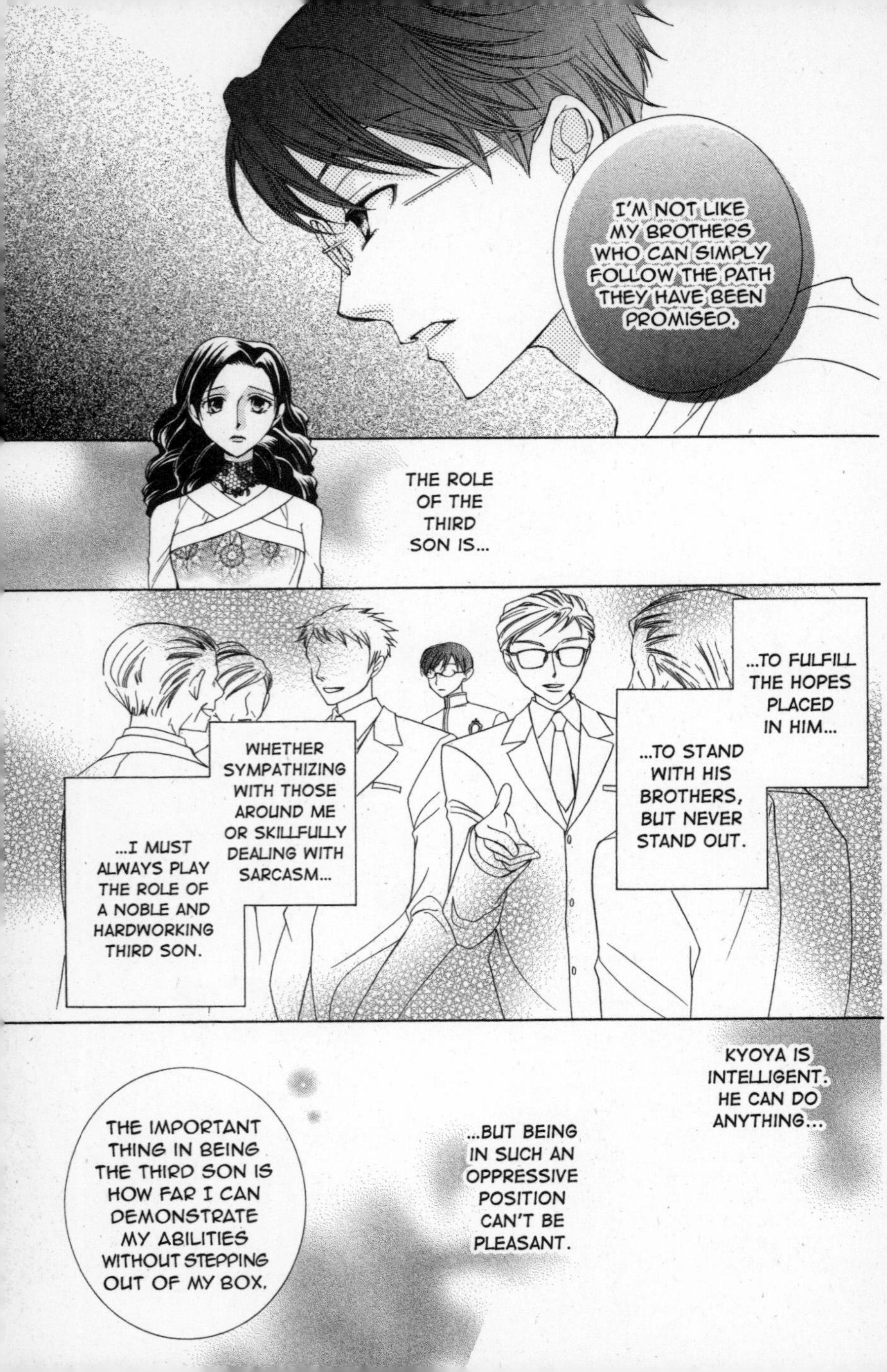
I'M NOT LIKE MY BROTHERS WHO CAN SIMPLY FOLLOW THE PATH THEY HAVE BEEN PROMISED.
THE ROLE OF THE THIRD SON IS...
...TO FULFILL THE HOPES PLACED IN HIM...
...TO STAND WITH HIS BROTHERS, BUT NEVER STAND OUT.
WHETHER SYMPATHIZING WITH THOSE AROUND ME OR SKILLFULLY DEALING WITH SARCASM...
...I MUST ALWAYS PLAY THE ROLE OF A NOBLE AND HARDWORKING THIRD SON.
KYOYA IS INTELLIGENT. HE CAN DO ANYTHING...
...BUT BEING IN SUCH AN OPPRESSIVE POSITION CAN'T BE PLEASANT.
THE IMPORTANT THING IN BEING THE THIRD SON IS HOW FAR I CAN DEMONSTRATE MY ABILITIES WITHOUT STEPPING OUT OF MY BOX.

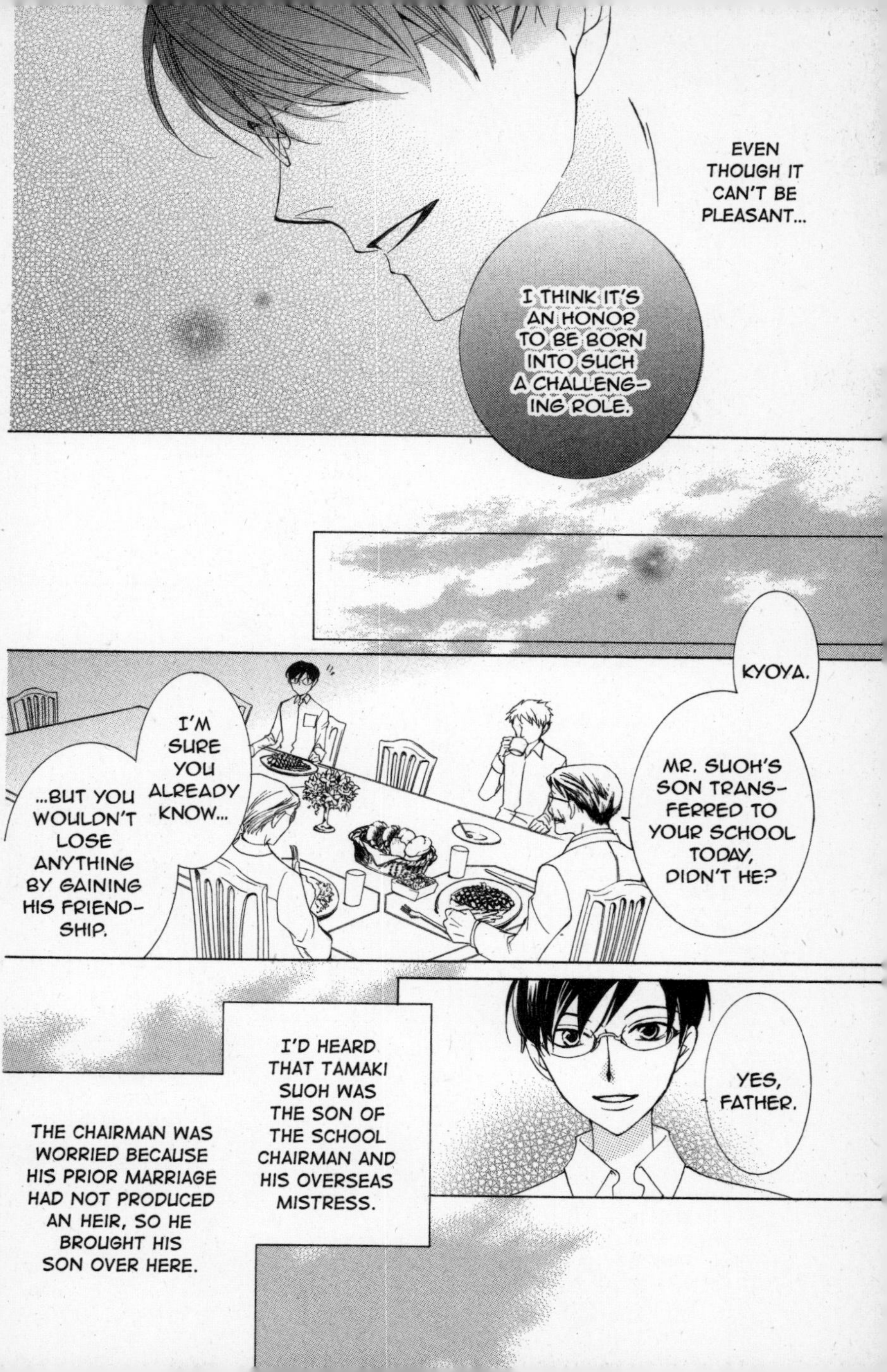
EVEN THOUGH IT CAN'T BE PLEASANT...
I THINK IT'S AN HONOR TO BE BORN INTO SUCH A CHALLENG-ING ROLE.
KYOYA.
MR. SUOH'S SON TRANS-FERRED TO YOUR SCHOOL TODAY, DIDN'T HE?
I'M SURE YOU ALREADY KNOW...
...BUT YOU WOULDN'T LOSE ANYTHING BY GAINING HIS FRIEND-SHIP.
YES, FATHER.
I'D HEARD THAT TAMAKI SUOH WAS THE SON OF THE SCHOOL CHAIRMAN AND HIS OVERSEAS MISTRESS.
THE CHAIRMAN WAS WORRIED BECAUSE HIS PRIOR MARRIAGE HAD NOT PRODUCED AN HEIR, SO HE BROUGHT HIS SON OVER HERE.

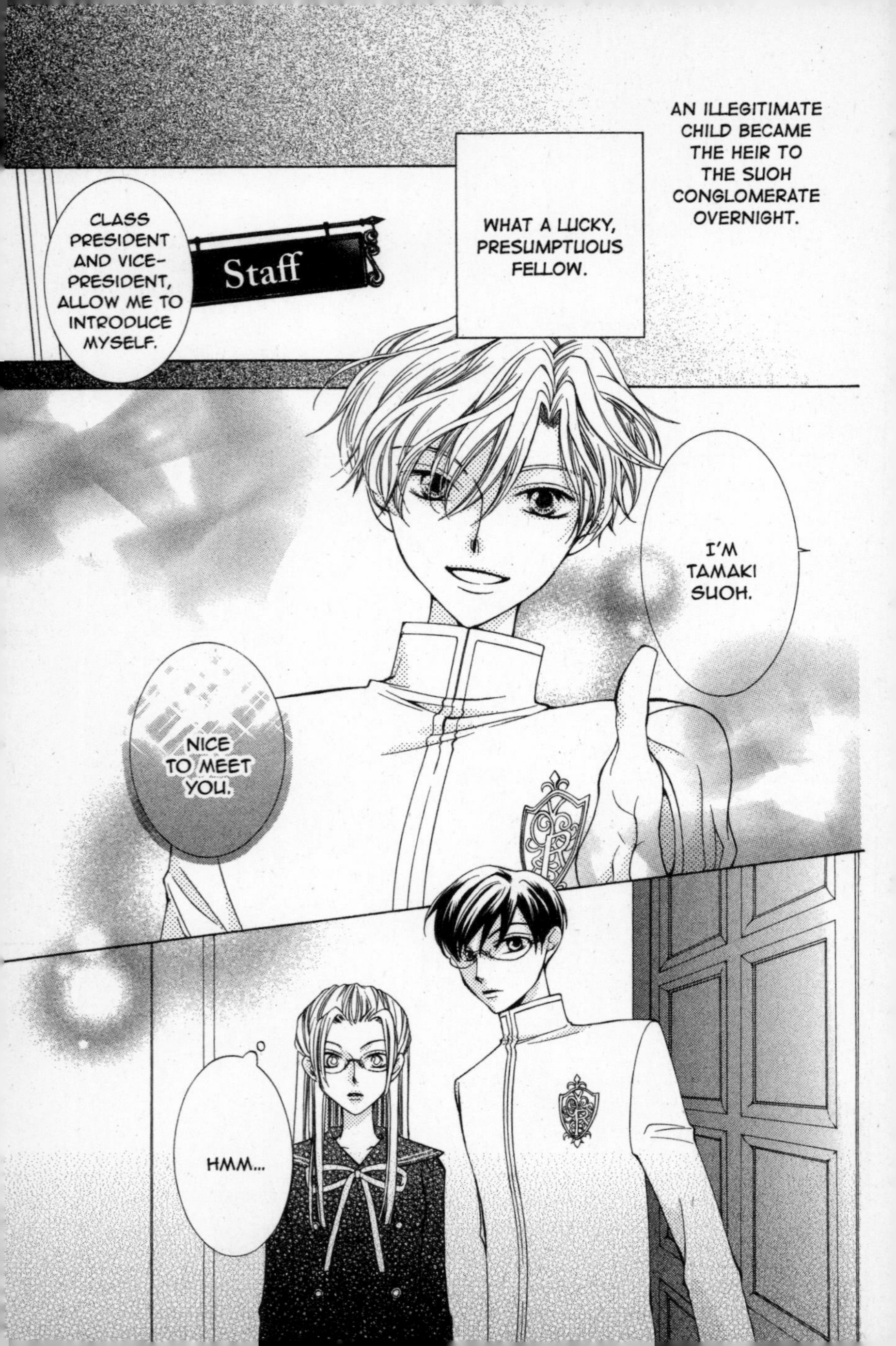

AN ILLEGITIMATE CHILD BECAME THE HEIR TO THE SUOH CONGLOMERATE OVERNIGHT.
WHAT A LUCKY, PRESUMPTUOUS FELLOW.
Staff
CLASS PRESIDENT AND VICE-PRESIDENT, ALLOW ME TO INTRODUCE MYSELF.
I'M TAMAKI SUOH.
NICE TO MEET YOU.
HMM...

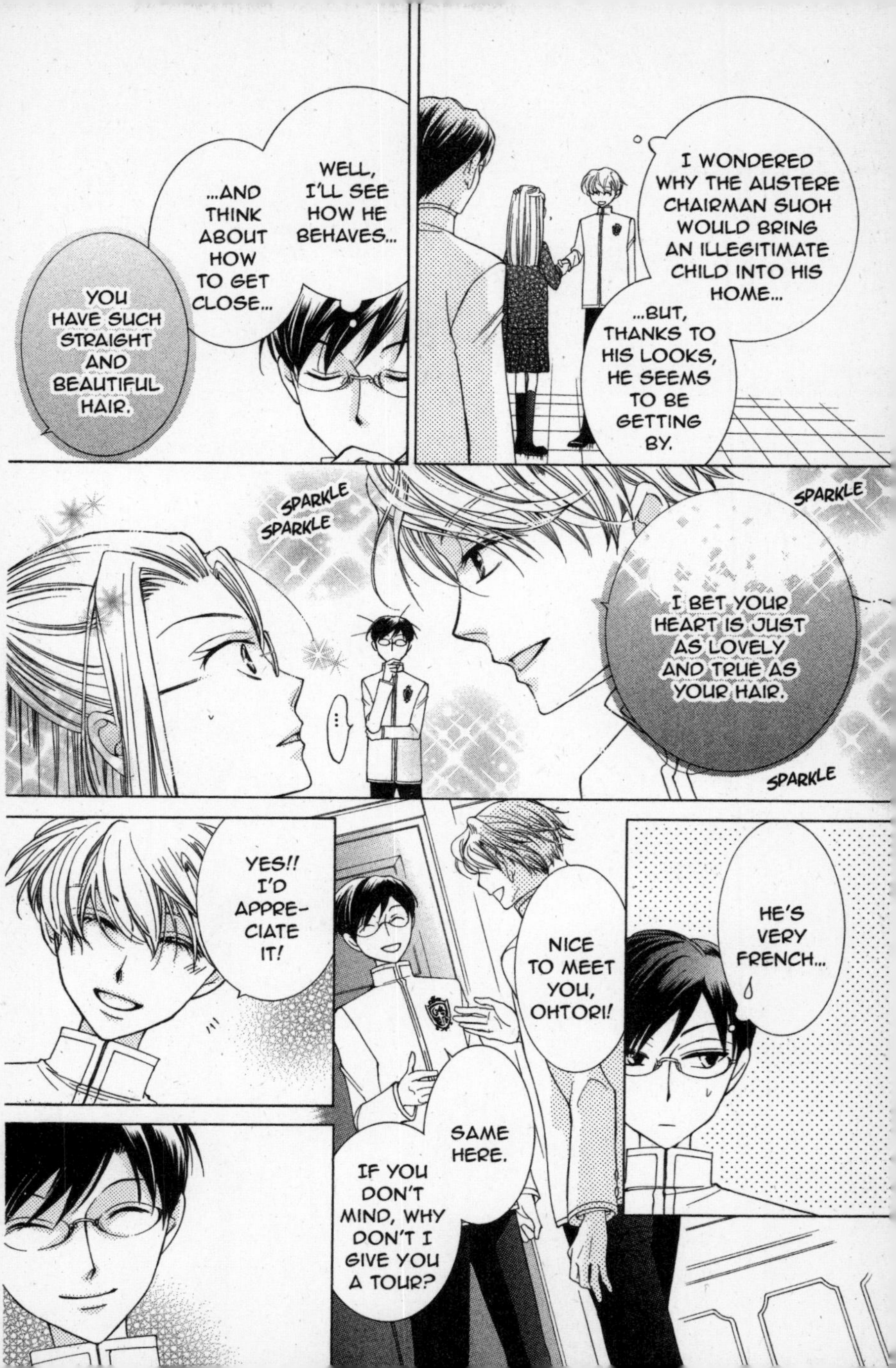
I WONDERED WHY THE AUSTERE CHAIRMAN SUOH WOULD BRING AN ILLEGITIMATE CHILD INTO HIS HOME...
...BUT, THANKS TO HIS LOOKS, HE SEEMS TO BE GETTING BY.
WELL, I'LL SEE HOW HE BEHAVES...
...AND THINK ABOUT HOW TO GET CLOSE...
YOU HAVE SUCH STRAIGHT AND BEAUTIFUL HAIR.
SPARKLE
I BET YOUR HEART IS JUST AS LOVELY AND TRUE AS YOUR HAIR.
SPARKLE
SPARKLE
...
SPARKLE
HE'S VERY FRENCH...
NICE TO MEET YOU, OHTORI!
SAME HERE.
IF YOU DON'T MIND, WHY DON'T I GIVE YOU A TOUR?
YES!! I'D APPRECIATE IT!

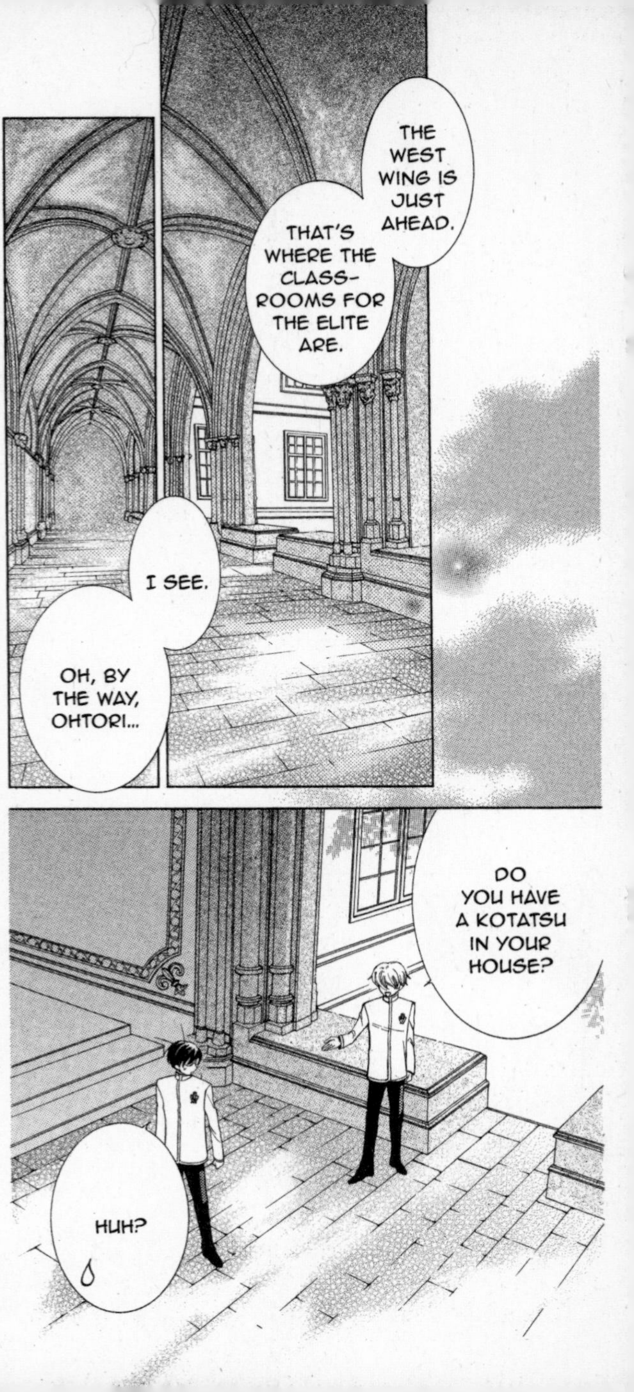
THE WEST WING IS JUST AHEAD.
THAT'S WHERE THE CLASS-ROOMS FOR THE ELITE ARE.
I SEE.
OH, BY THE WAY, OHTORI...
DO YOU HAVE A KOTATSU IN YOUR HOUSE?
HUH?

✿SOMETIMES I GET LETTERS ASKING ME WHICH MEMBER OF THE HOST CLUB I AM LIKE.

I GUESS I HAVE A BIT OF ALL OF THEM IN ME, EXCEPT FOR HUNNY AND MORI.

YET!! THE CLASS PRESIDENT IN THE "TEST OF COURAGE" EPISODE IS ALSO A VERSION OF MYSELF. YES... EVERYONE--MYSELF INCLUDED--ACKNOWLEDGES THAT I'M AN EXTREME COWARD!

YUI, A STAFF MEMBER AT MY STUDIO, TELLS ME MY COWARDICE IS FOUND IN ONLY ONE OUT OF EVERY THOUSAND PEOPLE. YOU KNOW... SHE'S ABSOLUTELY RIGHT.

EVEN THOUGH I'M THE ONE WHO CREATES THIS MANGA, I'VE NEVER HATED THE TWINS SO MUCH... IF YOU HAVE FRIENDS LIKE THE CLASS PRESIDENT, PLEASE DON'T AMUSE YOURSELF BY FRIGHTENING THEM!!

HEY, I MEAN IT! (DEEPLY FELT)

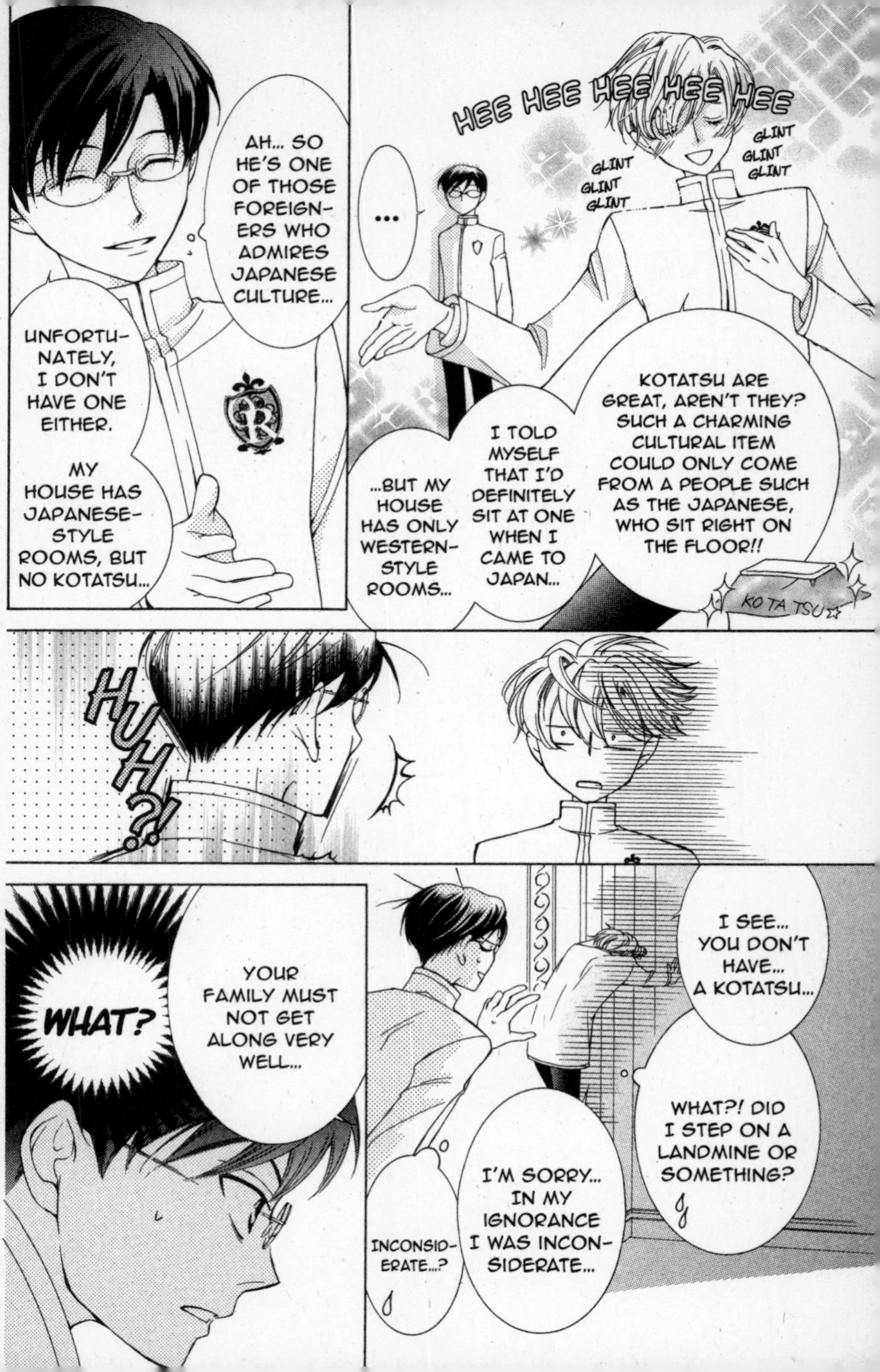
HEE HEE HEE HEE HEE
GLINT GLINT GLINT
GLINT GLINT GLINT
KOTATSU ARE GREAT, AREN'T THEY? SUCH A CHARMING CULTURAL ITEM COULD ONLY COME FROM A PEOPLE SUCH AS THE JAPANESE, WHO SIT RIGHT ON THE FLOOR!!
I TOLD MYSELF THAT I'D DEFINITELY SIT AT ONE WHEN I CAME TO JAPAN...
...BUT MY HOUSE HAS ONLY WESTERN-STYLE ROOMS...
KOTATSU☆
...
AH... SO HE'S ONE OF THOSE FOREIGNERS WHO ADMIRES JAPANESE CULTURE...
UNFORTUNATELY, I DON'T HAVE ONE EITHER.
MY HOUSE HAS JAPANESE-STYLE ROOMS, BUT NO KOTATSU...
HUH?!
I SEE... YOU DON'T HAVE... A KOTATSU...
WHAT?! DID I STEP ON A LANDMINE OR SOMETHING?
I'M SORRY... IN MY IGNORANCE I WAS INCONSIDERATE...
INCONSIDERATE...?
WHAT?
YOUR FAMILY MUST NOT GET ALONG VERY WELL...

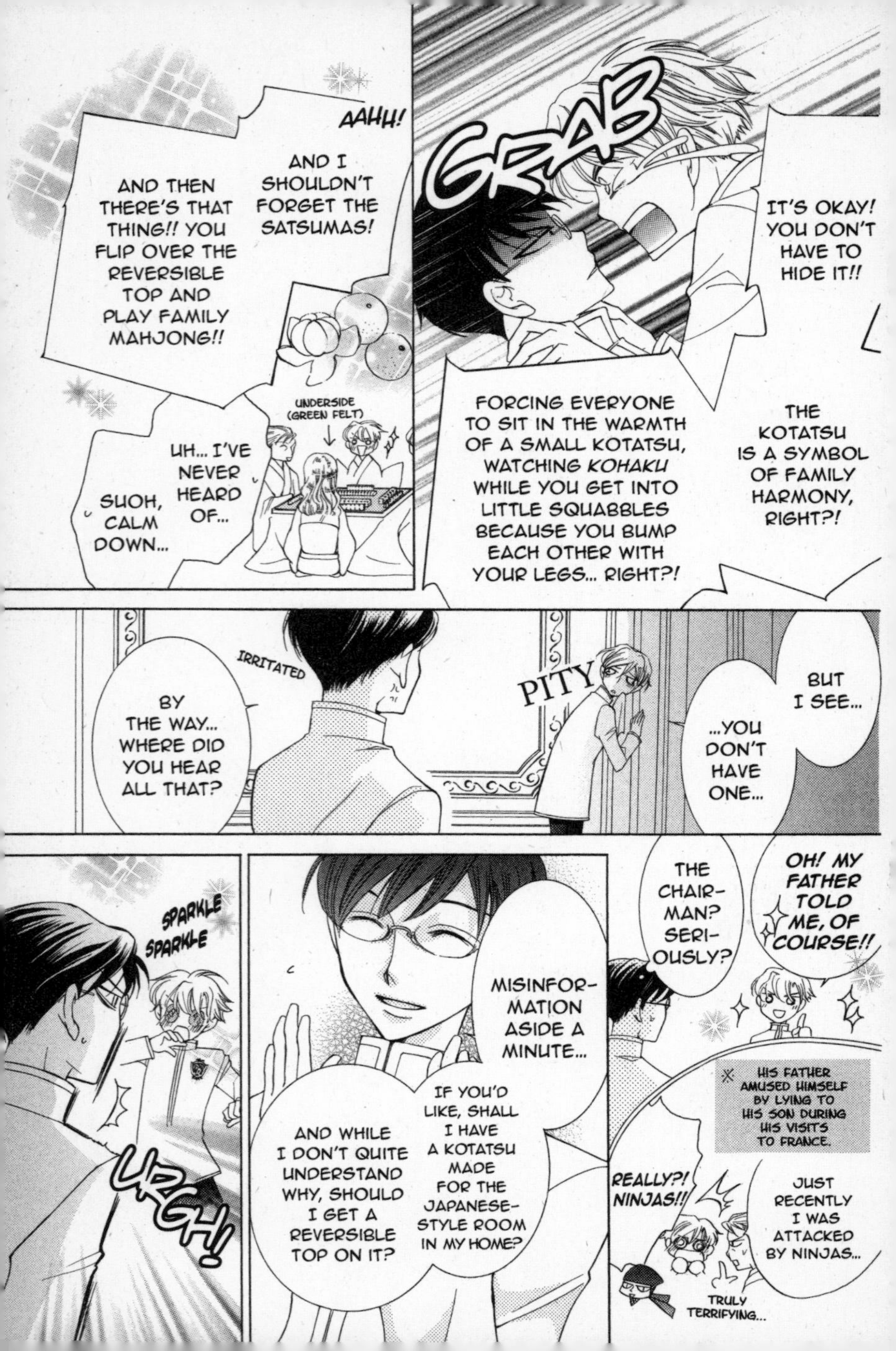
IT'S OKAY! YOU DON'T HAVE TO HIDE IT!!
GRAB
THE KOTATSU IS A SYMBOL OF FAMILY HARMONY, RIGHT?!
FORCING EVERYONE TO SIT IN THE WARMTH OF A SMALL KOTATSU, WATCHING *KOHAKU* WHILE YOU GET INTO LITTLE SQUABBLES BECAUSE YOU BUMP EACH OTHER WITH YOUR LEGS... RIGHT?!
AAHH!
AND I SHOULDN'T FORGET THE SATSUMAS!
AND THEN THERE'S THAT THING!! YOU FLIP OVER THE REVERSIBLE TOP AND PLAY FAMILY MAHJONG!!
UNDERSIDE (GREEN FELT)
UH... I'VE NEVER HEARD OF...
SUOH, CALM DOWN...
BUT I SEE...
...YOU DON'T HAVE ONE...
PITY
IRRITATED
BY THE WAY... WHERE DID YOU HEAR ALL THAT?
OH! MY FATHER TOLD ME, OF COURSE!!
THE CHAIRMAN? SERIOUSLY?
※ HIS FATHER AMUSED HIMSELF BY LYING TO HIS SON DURING HIS VISITS TO FRANCE.
JUST RECENTLY I WAS ATTACKED BY NINJAS...
REALLY?! NINJAS!!
TRULY TERRIFYING...
MISINFORMATION ASIDE A MINUTE...
IF YOU'D LIKE, SHALL I HAVE A KOTATSU MADE FOR THE JAPANESE-STYLE ROOM IN MY HOME?
AND WHILE I DON'T QUITE UNDERSTAND WHY, SHOULD I GET A REVERSIBLE TOP ON IT?
SPARKLE SPARKLE
URGH!

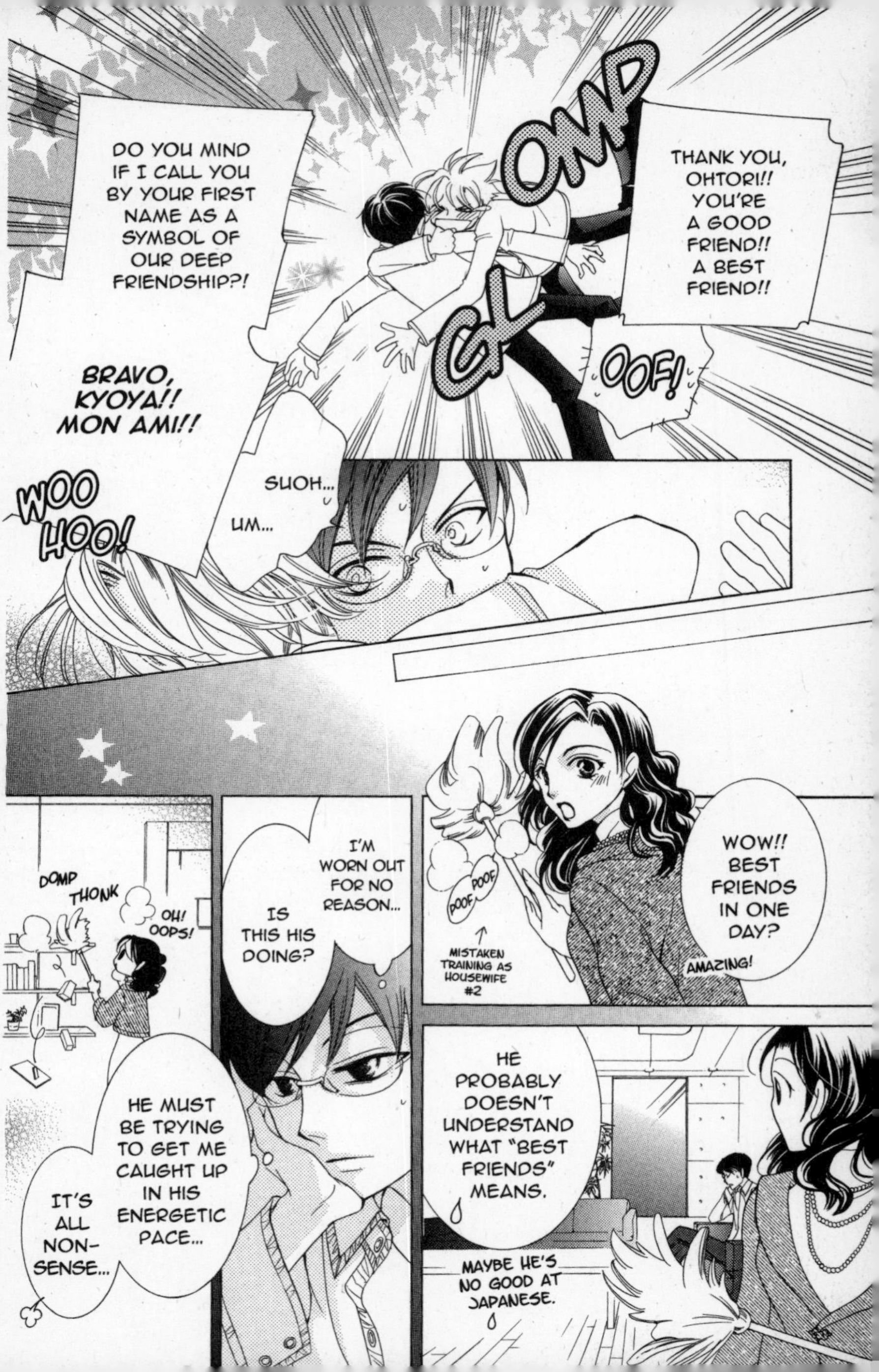

THANK YOU, OHTORI!! YOU'RE A GOOD FRIEND!! A BEST FRIEND!!
GLOMP
OOF!
DO YOU MIND IF I CALL YOU BY YOUR FIRST NAME AS A SYMBOL OF OUR DEEP FRIENDSHIP?!
BRAVO, KYOYA!! MON AMI!!
SUOH...
UM...
WOO HOO!
WOW!! BEST FRIENDS IN ONE DAY?
AMAZING!
POOF POOF
MISTAKEN TRAINING AS HOUSEWIFE #2
I'M WORN OUT FOR NO REASON...
IS THIS HIS DOING?
DOMP
THONK
OH! OOPS!
HE PROBABLY DOESN'T UNDERSTAND WHAT "BEST FRIENDS" MEANS.
MAYBE HE'S NO GOOD AT JAPANESE.
HE MUST BE TRYING TO GET ME CAUGHT UP IN HIS ENERGETIC PACE...
IT'S ALL NON-SENSE...

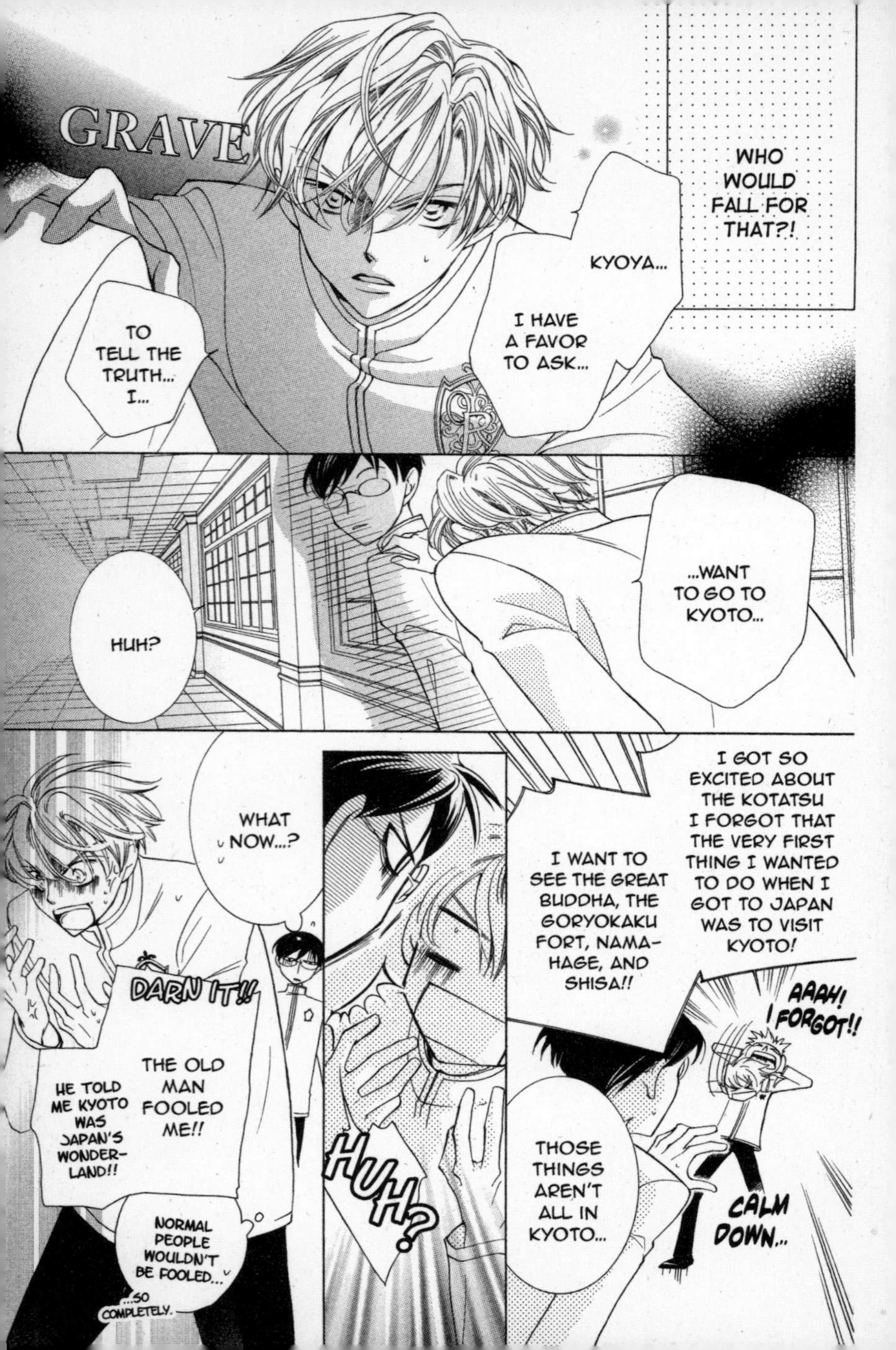
WHO WOULD FALL FOR THAT?!
KYOYA...
I HAVE A FAVOR TO ASK...
GRAVE
TO TELL THE TRUTH... I...
...WANT TO GO TO KYOTO...
HUH?
I GOT SO EXCITED ABOUT THE KOTATSU I FORGOT THAT THE VERY FIRST THING I WANTED TO DO WHEN I GOT TO JAPAN WAS TO VISIT KYOTO!
AAAH! I FORGOT!!
I WANT TO SEE THE GREAT BUDDHA, THE GORYOKAKU FORT, NAMA-HAGE, AND SHISA!!
CALM DOWN...
THOSE THINGS AREN'T ALL IN KYOTO...
HUH?
WHAT NOW...?
DARN IT!!
THE OLD MAN FOOLED ME!!
HE TOLD ME KYOTO WAS JAPAN'S WONDER-LAND!!
NORMAL PEOPLE WOULDN'T BE FOOLED...
...SO COMPLETELY.

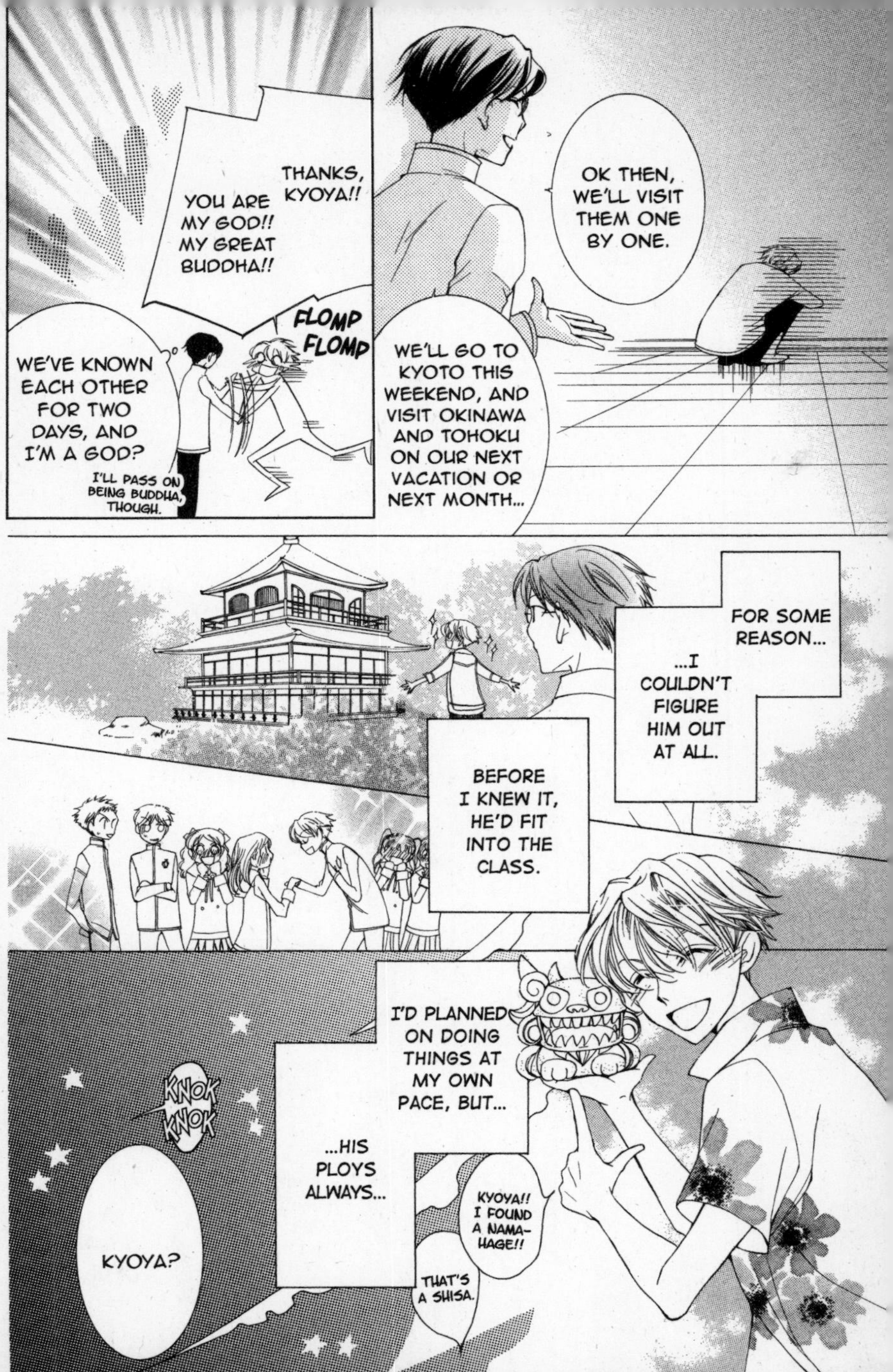
OK THEN, WE'LL VISIT THEM ONE BY ONE.
WE'LL GO TO KYOTO THIS WEEKEND, AND VISIT OKINAWA AND TOHOKU ON OUR NEXT VACATION OR NEXT MONTH...
THANKS, KYOYA!!
YOU ARE MY GOD!! MY GREAT BUDDHA!!
FLOMP FLOMP
WE'VE KNOWN EACH OTHER FOR TWO DAYS, AND I'M A GOD?
I'LL PASS ON BEING BUDDHA, THOUGH.
FOR SOME REASON...
...I COULDN'T FIGURE HIM OUT AT ALL.
BEFORE I KNEW IT, HE'D FIT INTO THE CLASS.
I'D PLANNED ON DOING THINGS AT MY OWN PACE, BUT...
...HIS PLOYS ALWAYS...
KYOYA!! I FOUND A NAMA-HAGE!!
THAT'S A SHISA.
KNOK KNOK
KYOYA?

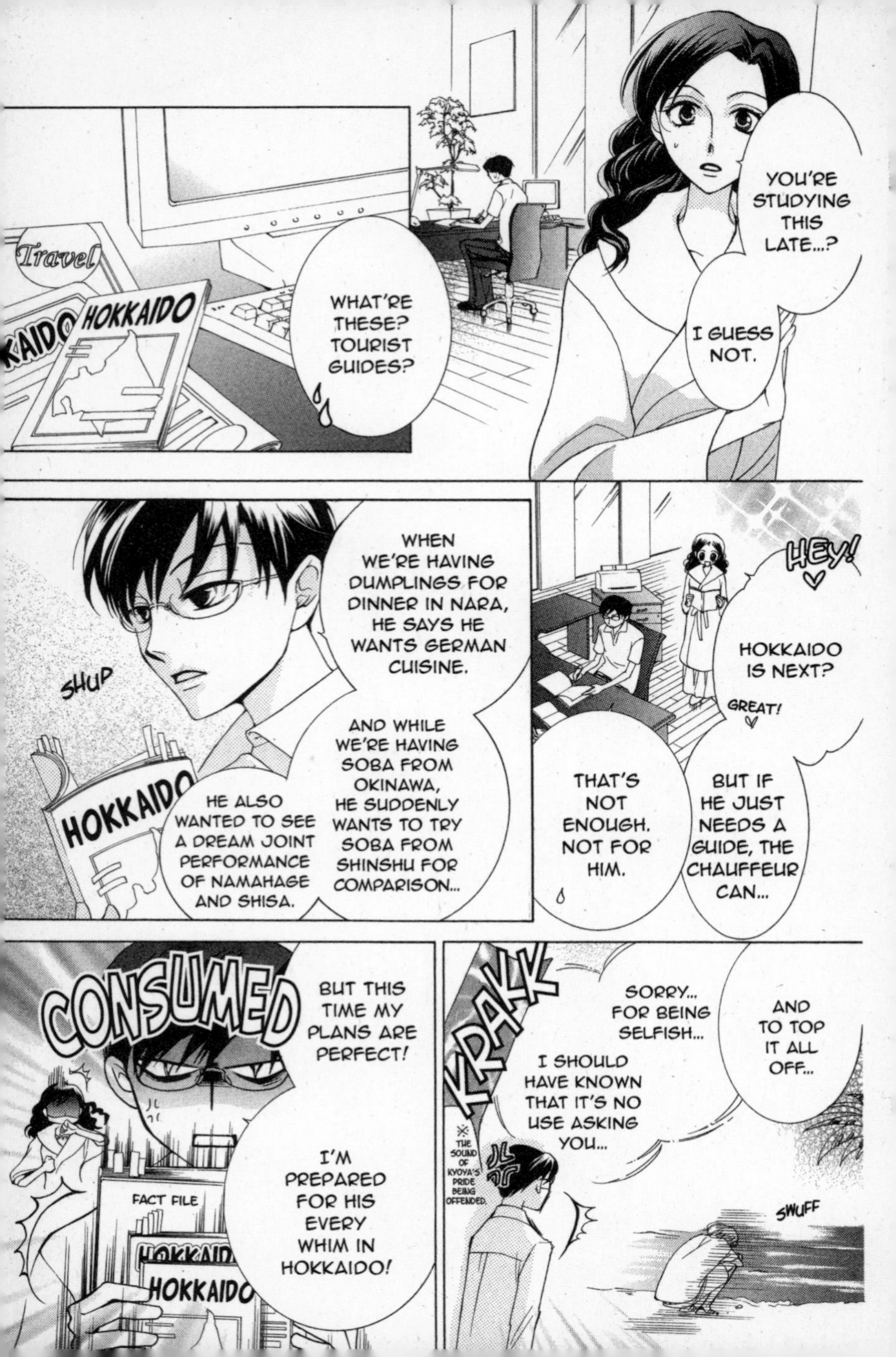
YOU'RE STUDYING THIS LATE...?
I GUESS NOT.
Travel
HOKKAIDO
KAIDO
WHAT'RE THESE? TOURIST GUIDES?
HEY!
HOKKAIDO IS NEXT?
GREAT!
BUT IF HE JUST NEEDS A GUIDE, THE CHAUFFEUR CAN...
THAT'S NOT ENOUGH. NOT FOR HIM.
WHEN WE'RE HAVING DUMPLINGS FOR DINNER IN NARA, HE SAYS HE WANTS GERMAN CUISINE.
AND WHILE WE'RE HAVING SOBA FROM OKINAWA, HE SUDDENLY WANTS TO TRY SOBA FROM SHINSHU FOR COMPARISON...
HE ALSO WANTED TO SEE A DREAM JOINT PERFORMANCE OF NAMAHAGE AND SHISA.
SHUP
HOKKAIDO
AND TO TOP IT ALL OFF...
SORRY... FOR BEING SELFISH...
I SHOULD HAVE KNOWN THAT IT'S NO USE ASKING YOU...
KRAKK
※THE SOUND OF KYOYA'S PRIDE BEING OFFENDED.
SWUFF
CONSUMED
BUT THIS TIME MY PLANS ARE PERFECT!
I'M PREPARED FOR HIS EVERY WHIM IN HOKKAIDO!
FACT FILE
HOKKAIDO
HOKKAIDO

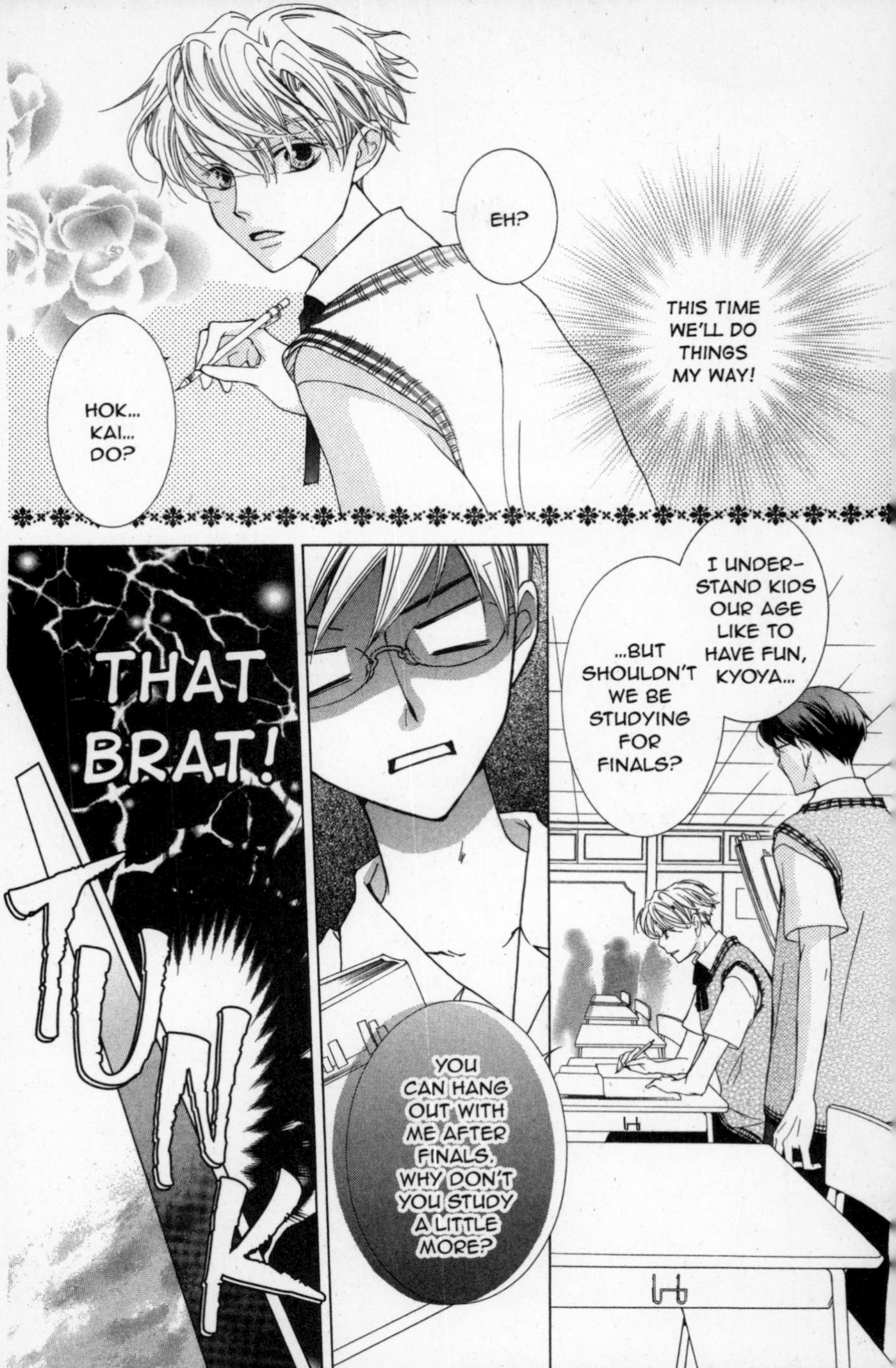
THIS TIME WE'LL DO THINGS MY WAY!
EH?
HOK... KAI... DO?
I UNDER-STAND KIDS OUR AGE LIKE TO HAVE FUN, KYOYA...
...BUT SHOULDN'T WE BE STUDYING FOR FINALS?
YOU CAN HANG OUT WITH ME AFTER FINALS. WHY DON'T YOU STUDY A LITTLE MORE?
THAT BRAT!
TUNK

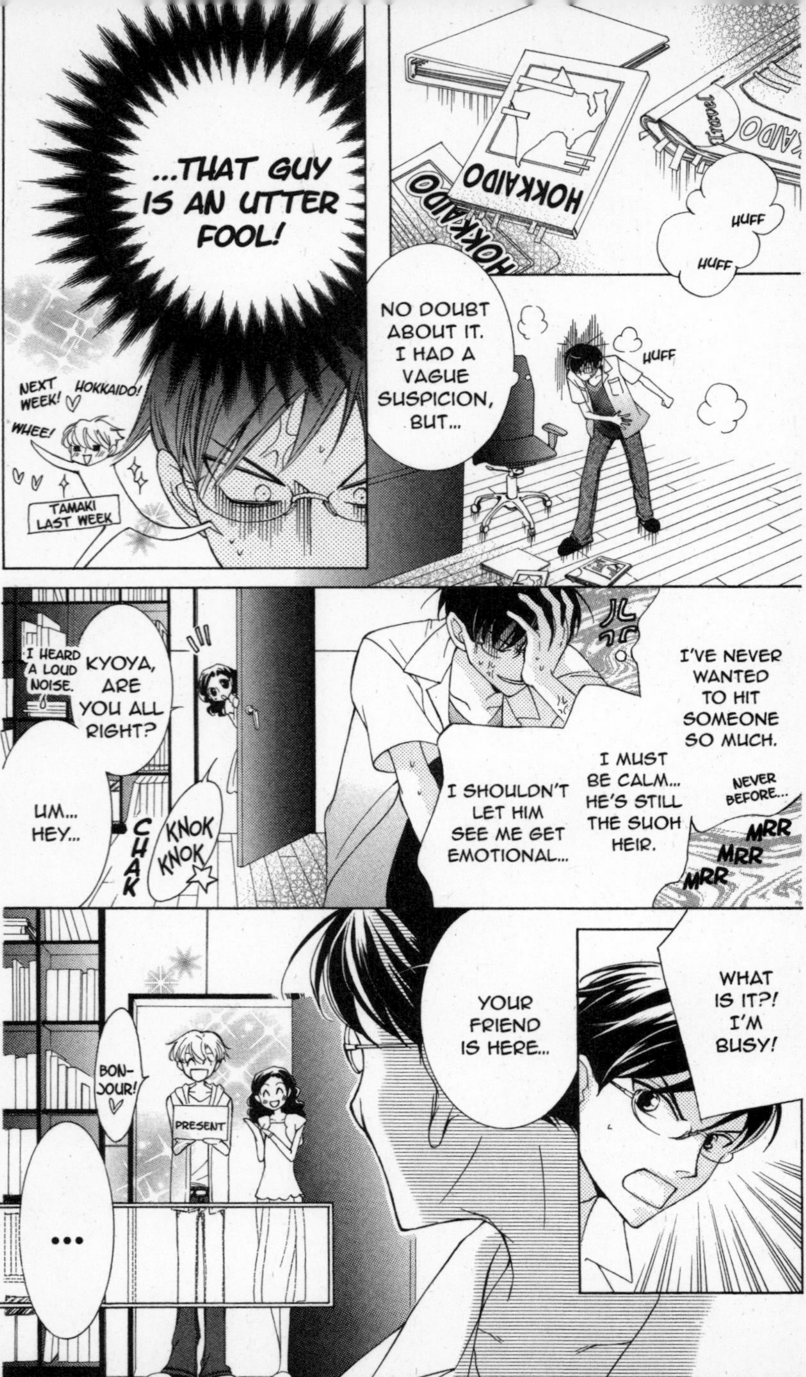
HOKKAIDO
HOKKAIDO
Travel
HUFF
HUFF
NO DOUBT ABOUT IT. I HAD A VAGUE SUSPICION, BUT...
HUFF
...THAT GUY IS AN UTTER FOOL!
NEXT WEEK!
HOKKAIDO!
WHEE!
TAMAKI LAST WEEK
I'VE NEVER WANTED TO HIT SOMEONE SO MUCH.
NEVER BEFORE...
MRR
MRR
MRR
I MUST BE CALM... HE'S STILL THE SUOH HEIR.
I SHOULDN'T LET HIM SEE ME GET EMOTIONAL...
KYOYA, ARE YOU ALL RIGHT?
I HEARD A LOUD NOISE.
KNOK KNOK
CHAK
UM... HEY...
WHAT IS IT?! I'M BUSY!
YOUR FRIEND IS HERE...
BON-JOUR!
PRESENT
...

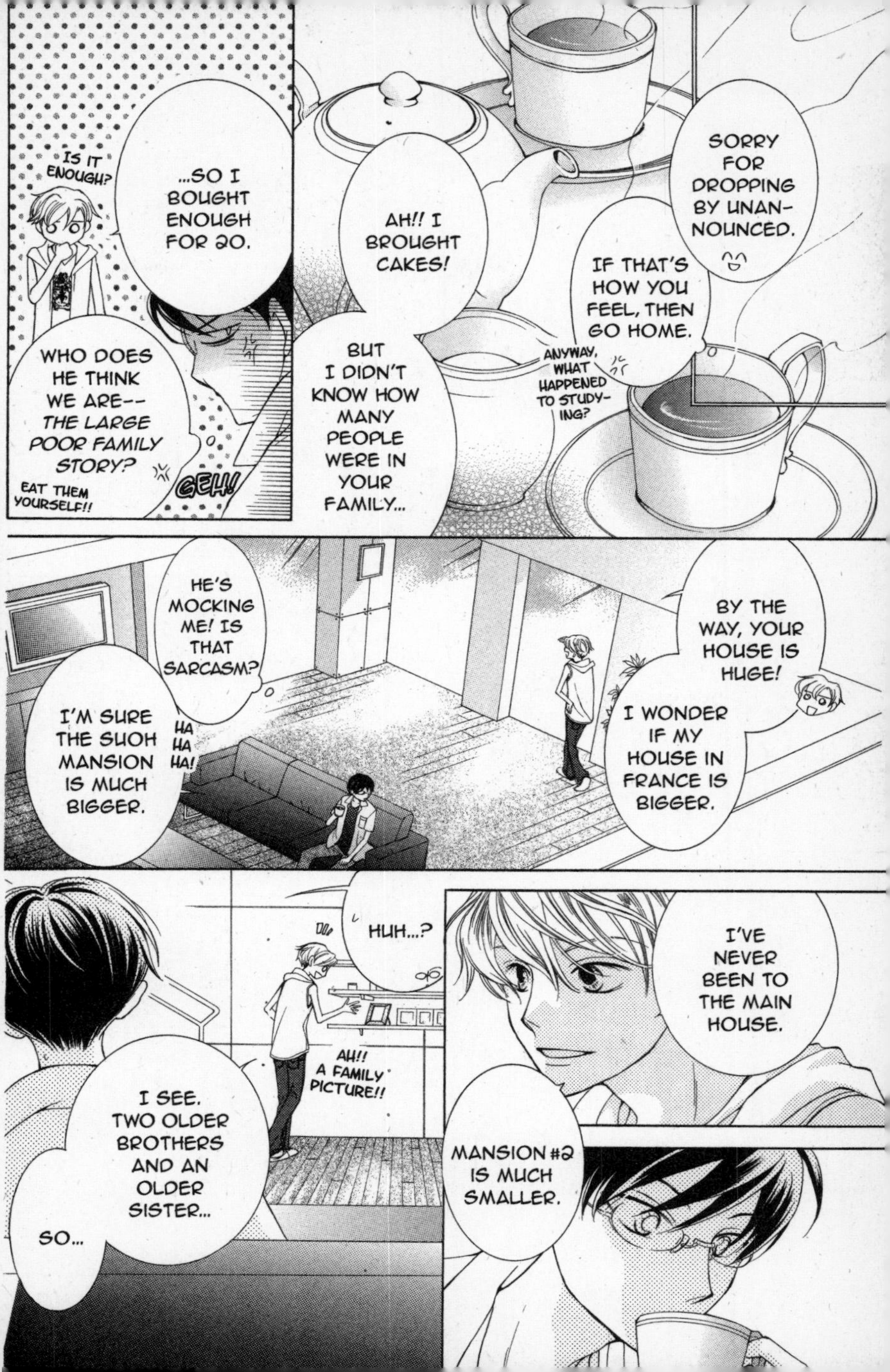
SORRY FOR DROPPING BY UNANNOUNCED.
IF THAT'S HOW YOU FEEL, THEN GO HOME.
AH!! I BROUGHT CAKES!
ANYWAY, WHAT HAPPENED TO STUDYING?
BUT I DIDN'T KNOW HOW MANY PEOPLE WERE IN YOUR FAMILY...
...SO I BOUGHT ENOUGH FOR 20.
IS IT ENOUGH?
WHO DOES HE THINK WE ARE-- THE LARGE POOR FAMILY STORY?
GEH!
EAT THEM YOURSELF!!
BY THE WAY, YOUR HOUSE IS HUGE!
I WONDER IF MY HOUSE IN FRANCE IS BIGGER.
HE'S MOCKING ME! IS THAT SARCASM?
HA HA HA!
I'M SURE THE SUOH MANSION IS MUCH BIGGER.
I'VE NEVER BEEN TO THE MAIN HOUSE.
MANSION #2 IS MUCH SMALLER.
HUH...?
AH!! A FAMILY PICTURE!!
I SEE. TWO OLDER BROTHERS AND AN OLDER SISTER...
SO...

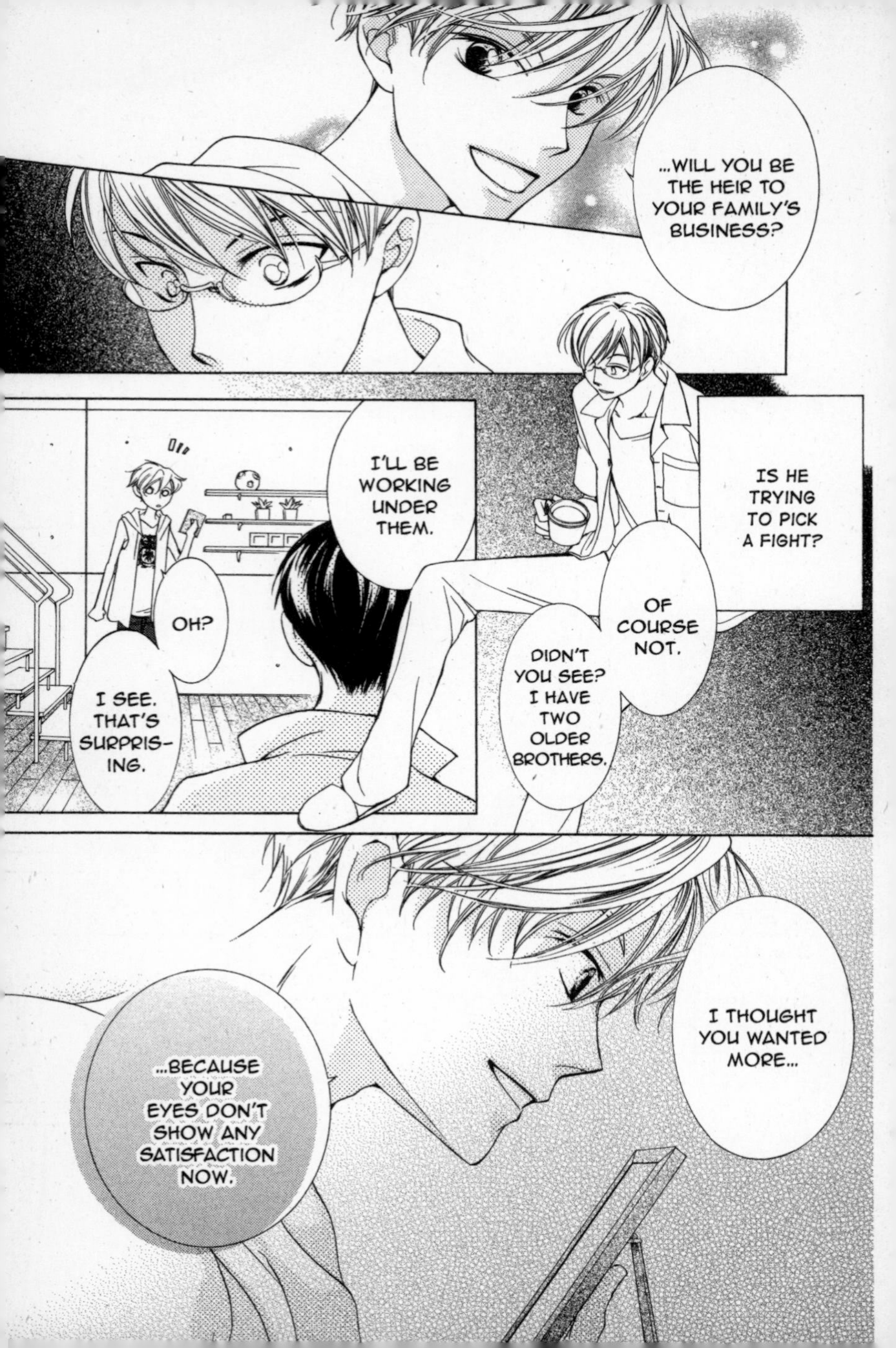
...WILL YOU BE THE HEIR TO YOUR FAMILY'S BUSINESS?
IS HE TRYING TO PICK A FIGHT?
OF COURSE NOT.
DIDN'T YOU SEE? I HAVE TWO OLDER BROTHERS.
I'LL BE WORKING UNDER THEM.
OH?
I SEE. THAT'S SURPRIS-ING.
I THOUGHT YOU WANTED MORE...
...BECAUSE YOUR EYES DON'T SHOW ANY SATISFACTION NOW.

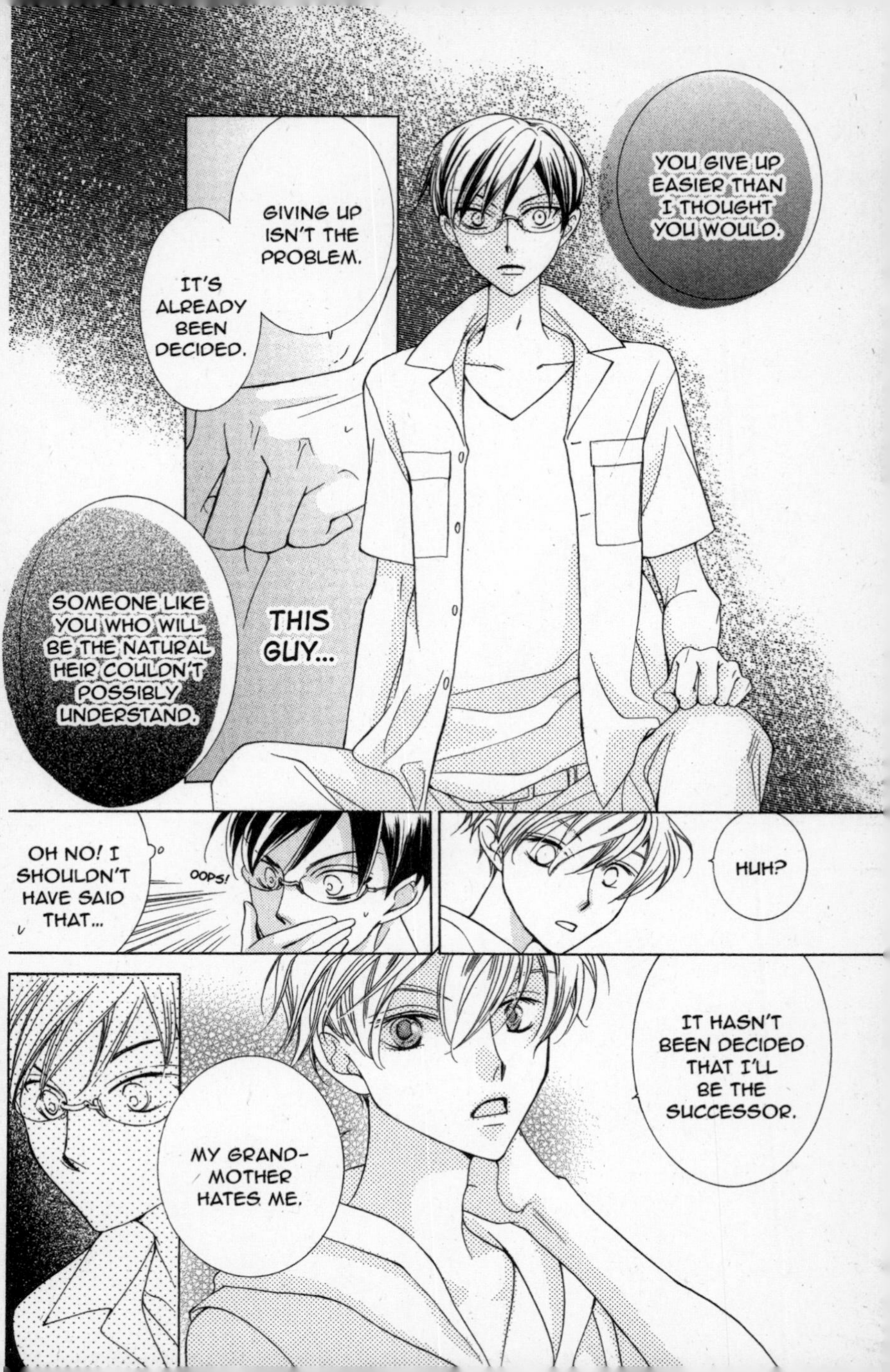
YOU GIVE UP EASIER THAN I THOUGHT YOU WOULD.
GIVING UP ISN'T THE PROBLEM.
IT'S ALREADY BEEN DECIDED.
THIS GUY...
SOMEONE LIKE YOU WHO WILL BE THE NATURAL HEIR COULDN'T POSSIBLY UNDERSTAND.
HUH?
OOPS!
OH NO! I SHOULDN'T HAVE SAID THAT...
IT HASN'T BEEN DECIDED THAT I'LL BE THE SUCCESSOR.
MY GRAND-MOTHER HATES ME.

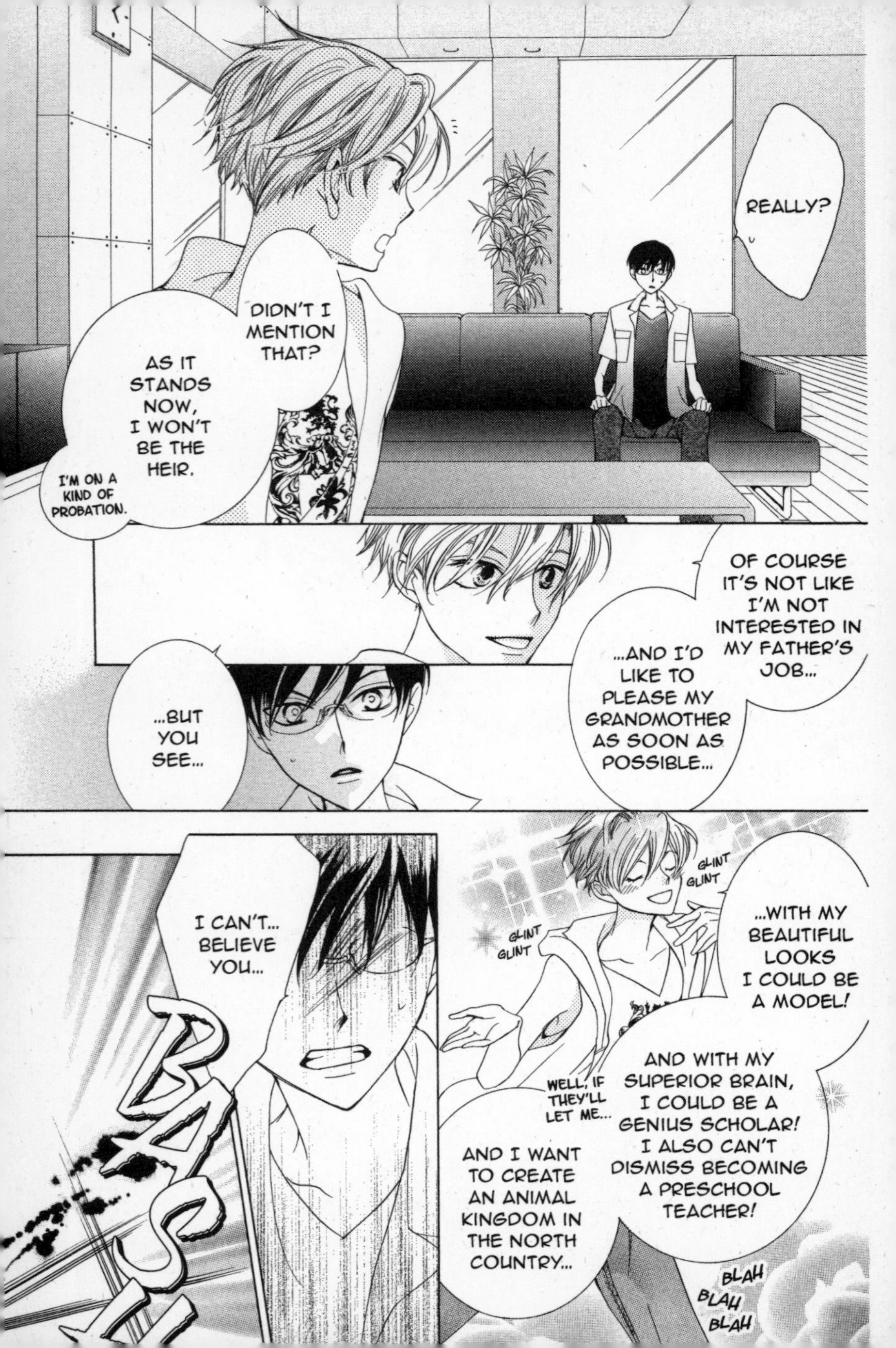
REALLY?
DIDN'T I MENTION THAT?
AS IT STANDS NOW, I WON'T BE THE HEIR.
I'M ON A KIND OF PROBATION.
OF COURSE IT'S NOT LIKE I'M NOT INTERESTED IN MY FATHER'S JOB...
...AND I'D LIKE TO PLEASE MY GRANDMOTHER AS SOON AS POSSIBLE...
...BUT YOU SEE...
GLINT GLINT
...WITH MY BEAUTIFUL LOOKS I COULD BE A MODEL!
GLINT GLINT
AND WITH MY SUPERIOR BRAIN, I COULD BE A GENIUS SCHOLAR! I ALSO CAN'T DISMISS BECOMING A PRESCHOOL TEACHER!
WELL, IF THEY'LL LET ME...
AND I WANT TO CREATE AN ANIMAL KINGDOM IN THE NORTH COUNTRY...
BLAH BLAH BLAH
I CAN'T... BELIEVE YOU...
BASH

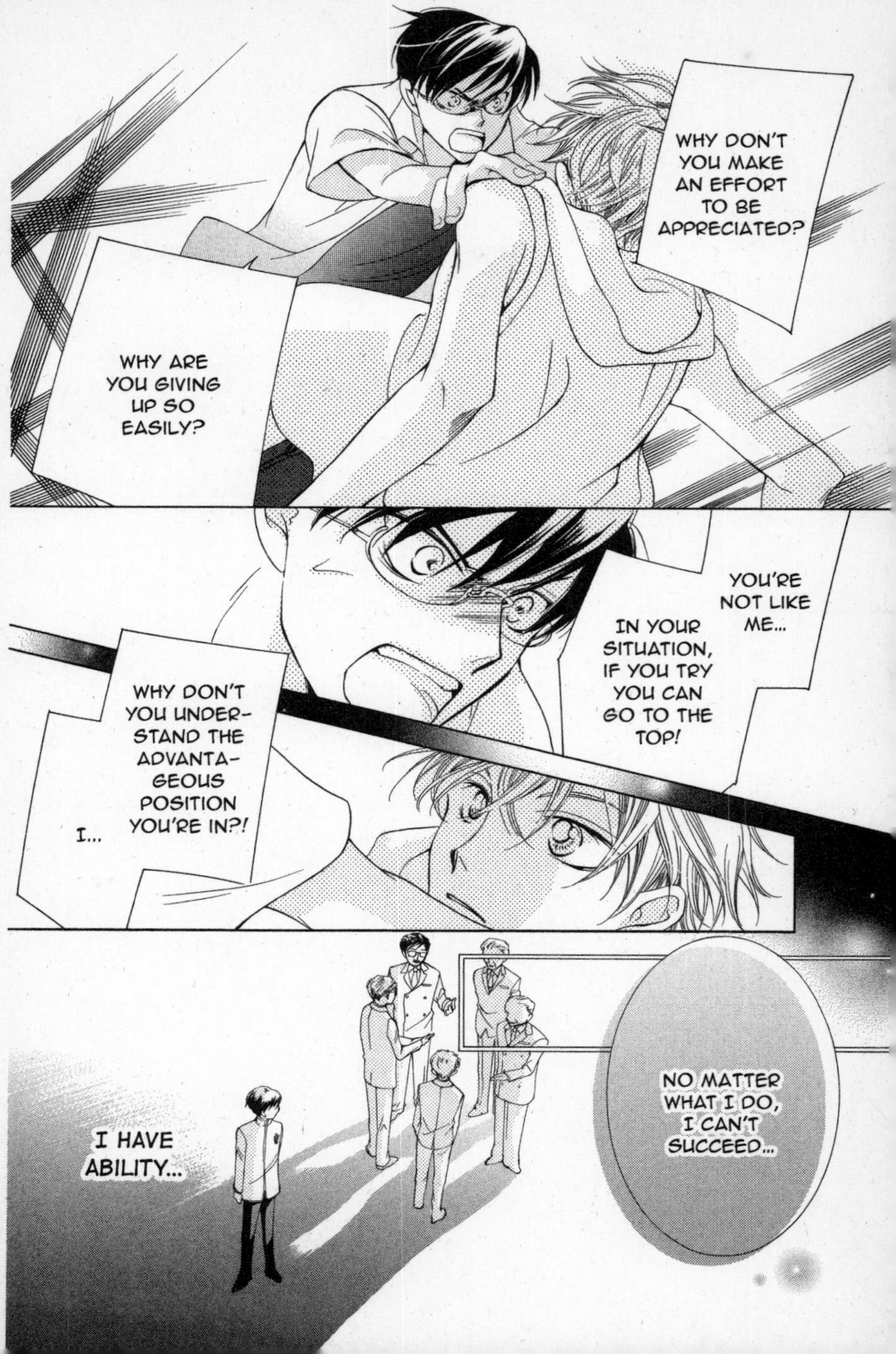
WHY DON'T YOU MAKE AN EFFORT TO BE APPRECIATED?
WHY ARE YOU GIVING UP SO EASILY?
YOU'RE NOT LIKE ME...
IN YOUR SITUATION, IF YOU TRY YOU CAN GO TO THE TOP!
WHY DON'T YOU UNDER-STAND THE ADVANTA-GEOUS POSITION YOU'RE IN?!
I...
NO MATTER WHAT I DO, I CAN'T SUCCEED...
I HAVE ABILITY...

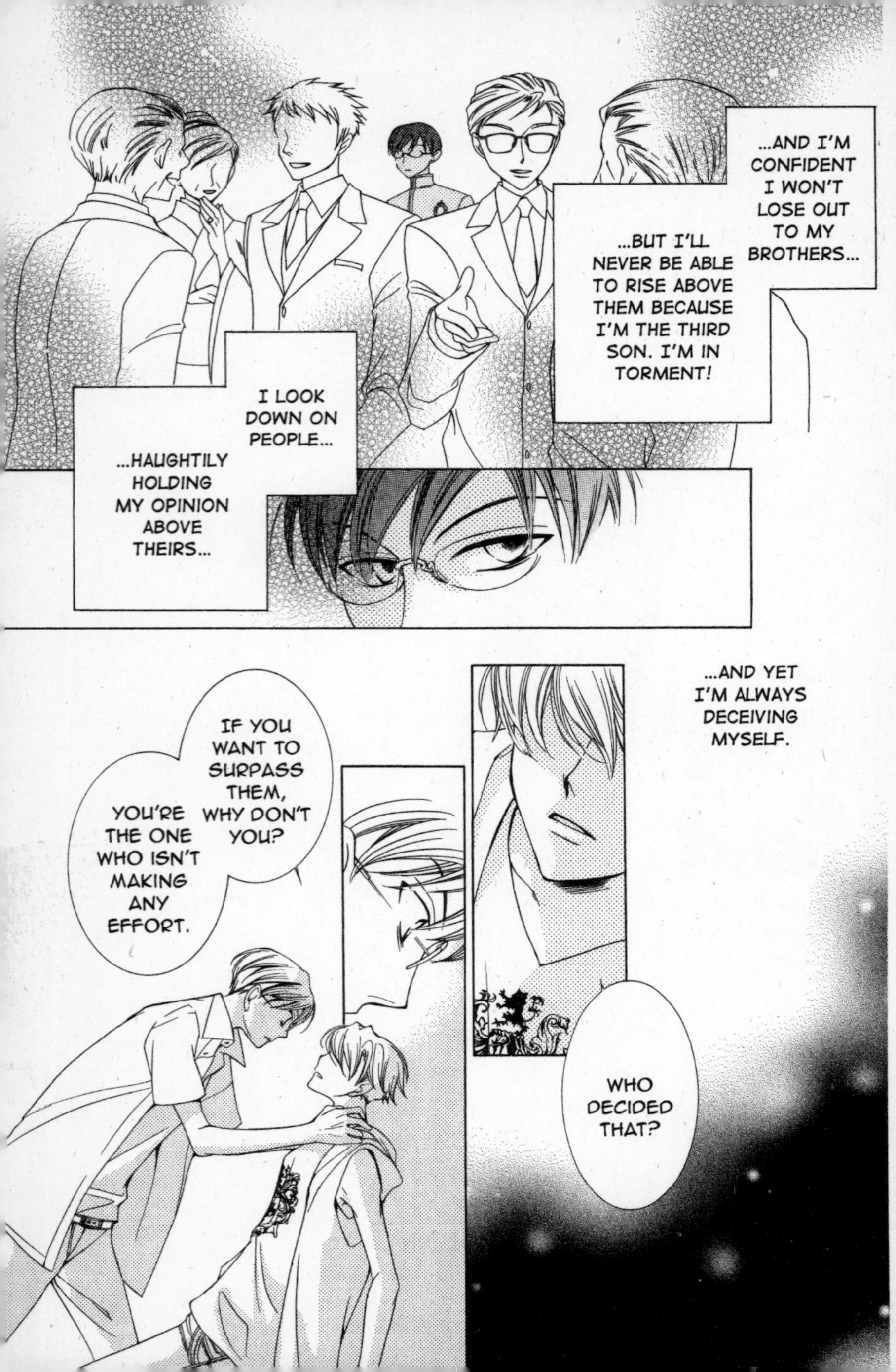
...AND I'M CONFIDENT I WON'T LOSE OUT TO MY BROTHERS...
...BUT I'LL NEVER BE ABLE TO RISE ABOVE THEM BECAUSE I'M THE THIRD SON. I'M IN TORMENT!
I LOOK DOWN ON PEOPLE...
...HAUGHTILY HOLDING MY OPINION ABOVE THEIRS...
...AND YET I'M ALWAYS DECEIVING MYSELF.
WHO DECIDED THAT?
IF YOU WANT TO SURPASS THEM, WHY DON'T YOU?
YOU'RE THE ONE WHO ISN'T MAKING ANY EFFORT.

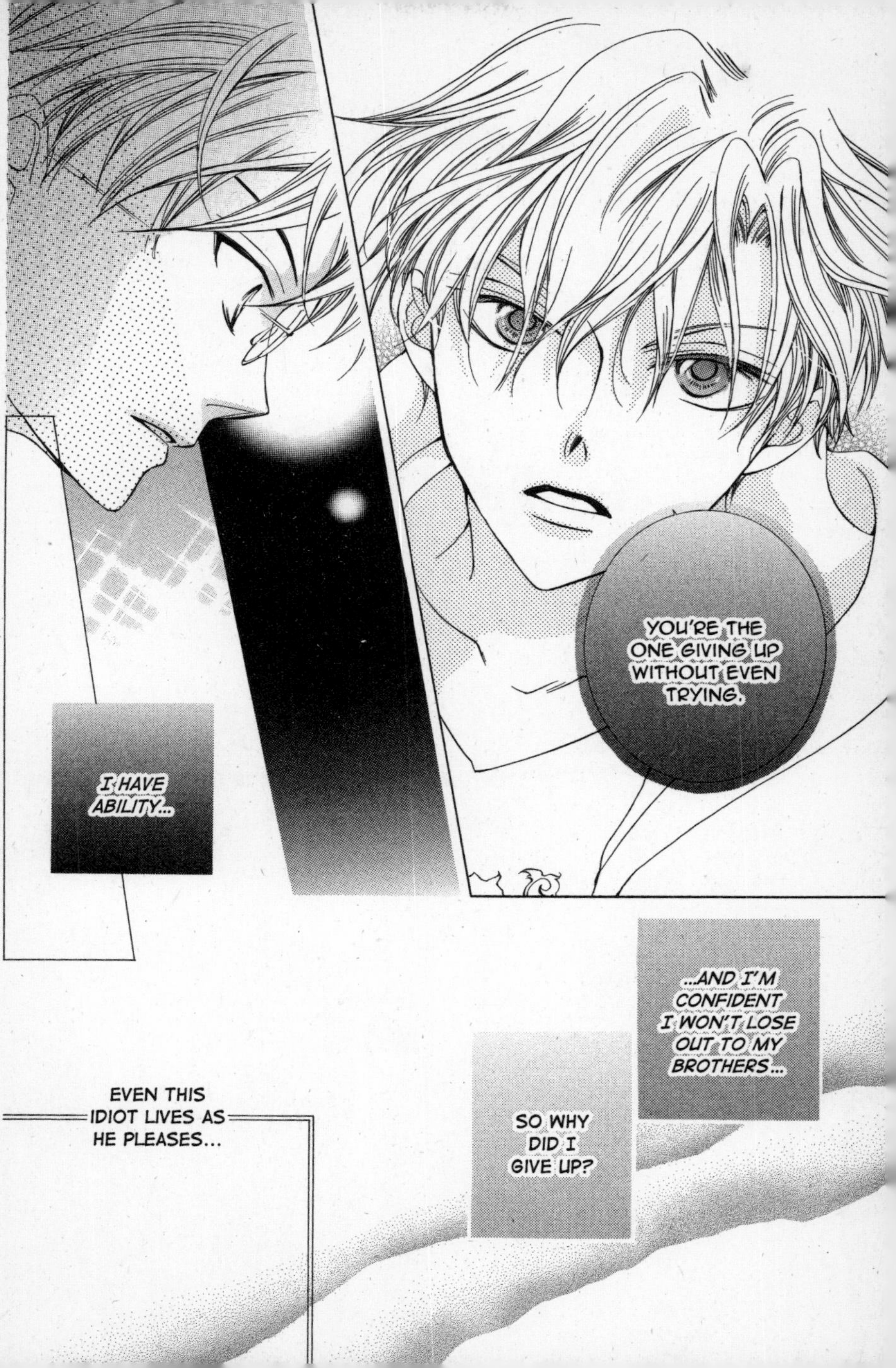
YOU'RE THE ONE GIVING UP WITHOUT EVEN TRYING.
I HAVE ABILITY...
...AND I'M CONFIDENT I WON'T LOSE OUT TO MY BROTHERS...
SO WHY DID I GIVE UP?
EVEN THIS IDIOT LIVES AS HE PLEASES...

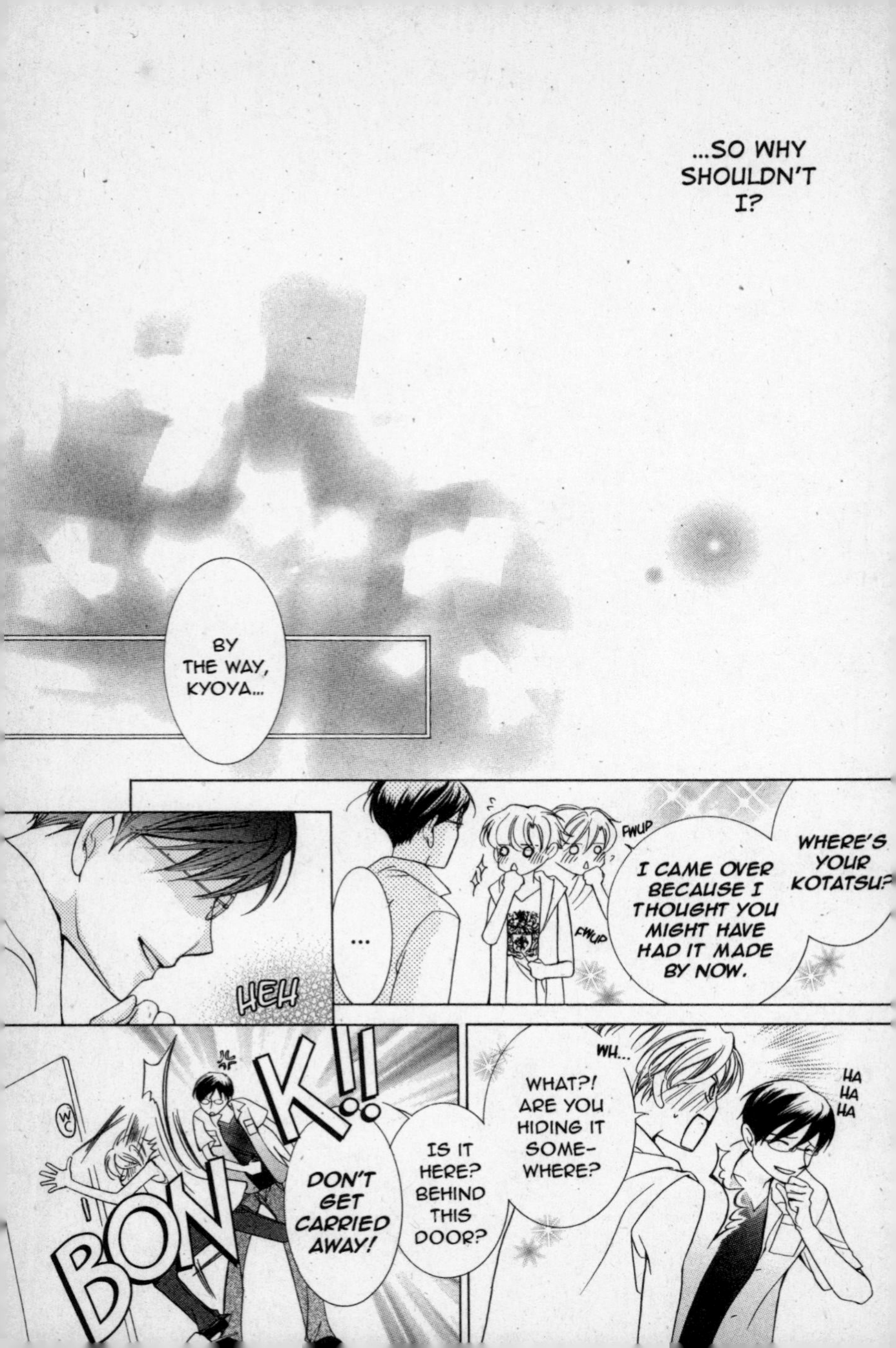
...SO WHY SHOULDN'T I?
BY THE WAY, KYOYA...
WHERE'S YOUR KOTATSU?
I CAME OVER BECAUSE I THOUGHT YOU MIGHT HAVE HAD IT MADE BY NOW.
FWUP
FWUP
...
HEH
HA HA HA
WH...
WHAT?! ARE YOU HIDING IT SOME-WHERE?
IS IT HERE? BEHIND THIS DOOR?
DON'T GET CARRIED AWAY!
BONK!!
WC

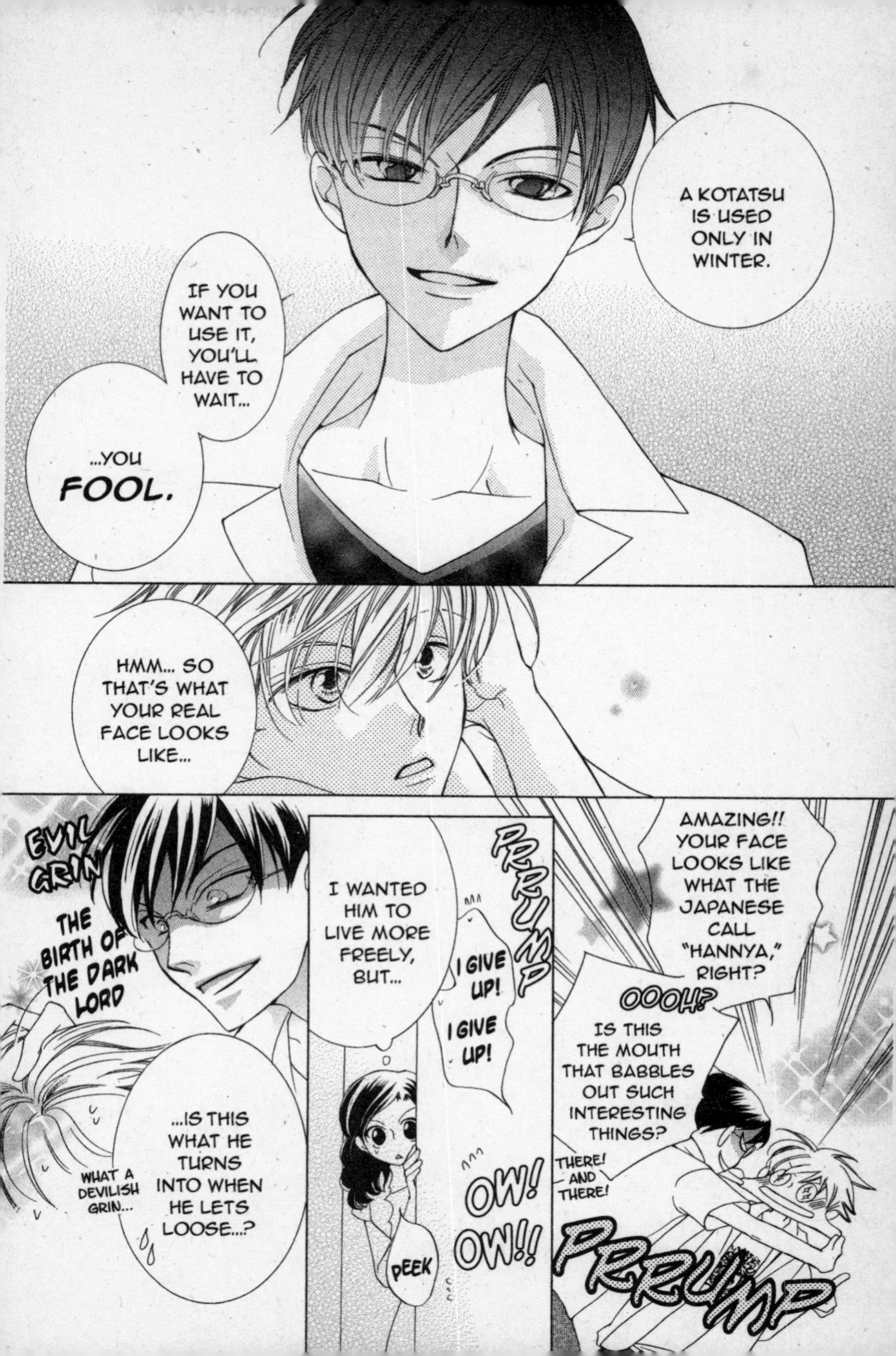
A KOTATSU IS USED ONLY IN WINTER.
IF YOU WANT TO USE IT, YOU'LL HAVE TO WAIT...
...YOU FOOL.
HMM... SO THAT'S WHAT YOUR REAL FACE LOOKS LIKE...
AMAZING!! YOUR FACE LOOKS LIKE WHAT THE JAPANESE CALL "HANNYA," RIGHT?
OOOH?
IS THIS THE MOUTH THAT BABBLES OUT SUCH INTERESTING THINGS?
THERE! AND THERE!
PRRUMP
PRRUMP
I GIVE UP! I GIVE UP!
I WANTED HIM TO LIVE MORE FREELY, BUT...
OW! OW!!
PEEK
EVIL GRIN
THE BIRTH OF THE DARK LORD
...IS THIS WHAT HE TURNS INTO WHEN HE LETS LOOSE...?
WHAT A DEVILISH GRIN...

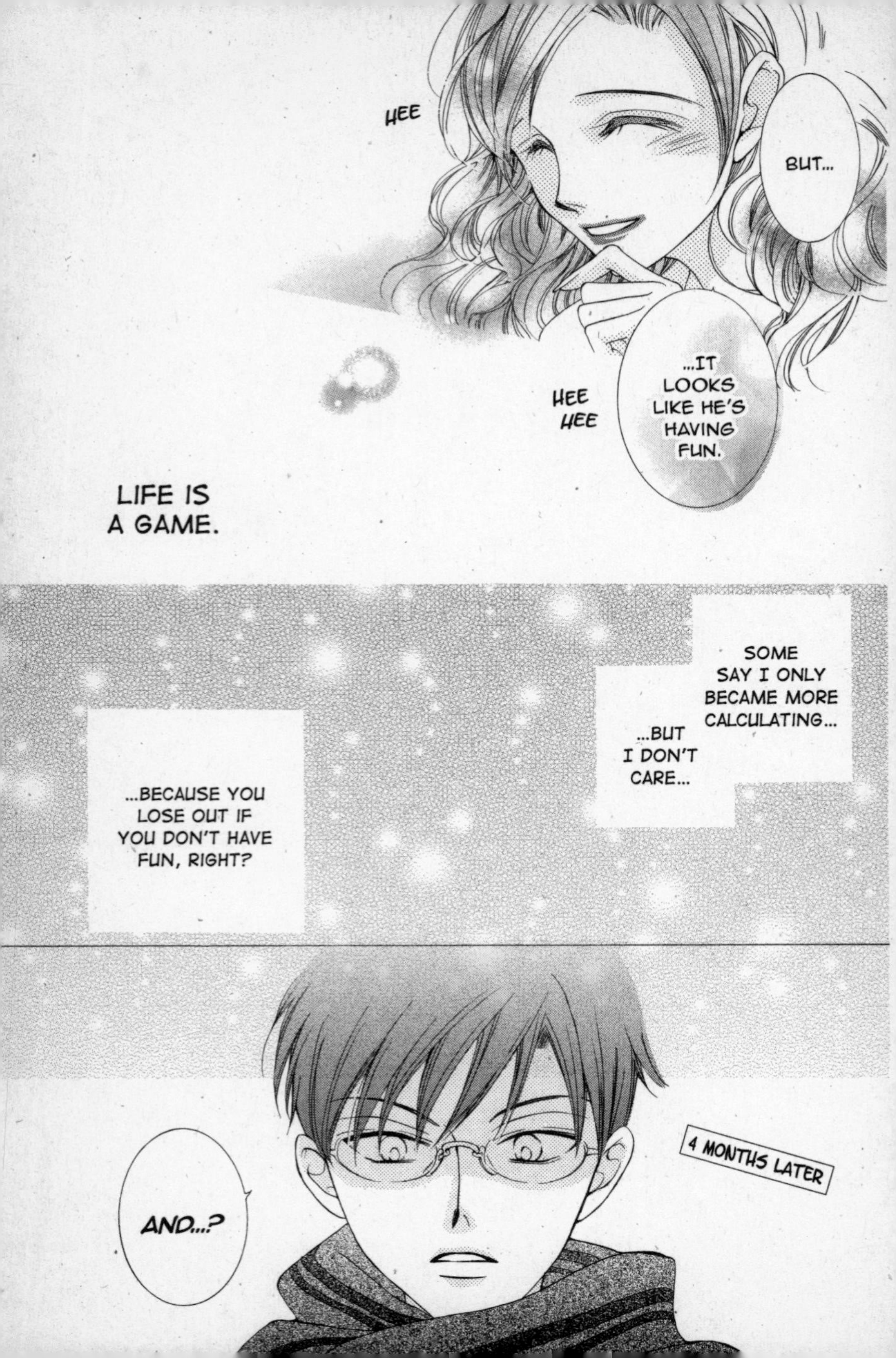

BUT...
HEE
...IT LOOKS LIKE HE'S HAVING FUN.
HEE HEE
LIFE IS A GAME.
SOME SAY I ONLY BECAME MORE CALCULATING...
...BUT I DON'T CARE...
...BECAUSE YOU LOSE OUT IF YOU DON'T HAVE FUN, RIGHT?
4 MONTHS LATER
AND...?

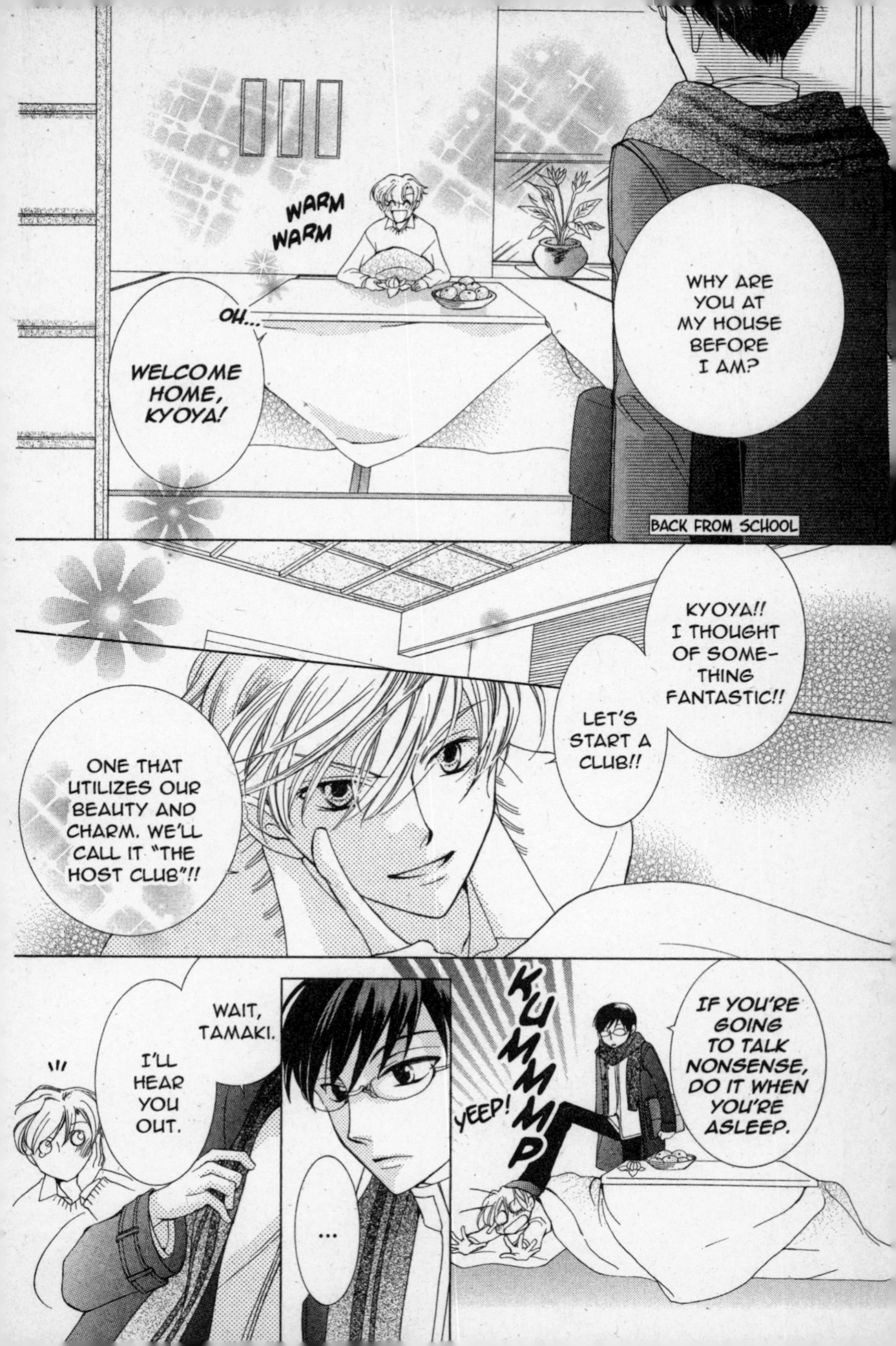
BACK FROM SCHOOL
WHY ARE YOU AT MY HOUSE BEFORE I AM?
WARM WARM
OH...
WELCOME HOME, KYOYA!
KYOYA!! I THOUGHT OF SOME-THING FANTASTIC!!
LET'S START A CLUB!!
ONE THAT UTILIZES OUR BEAUTY AND CHARM. WE'LL CALL IT "THE HOST CLUB"!!
IF YOU'RE GOING TO TALK NONSENSE, DO IT WHEN YOU'RE ASLEEP.
KUMMMMP
YEEP!
...
WAIT, TAMAKI.
I'LL HEAR YOU OUT.

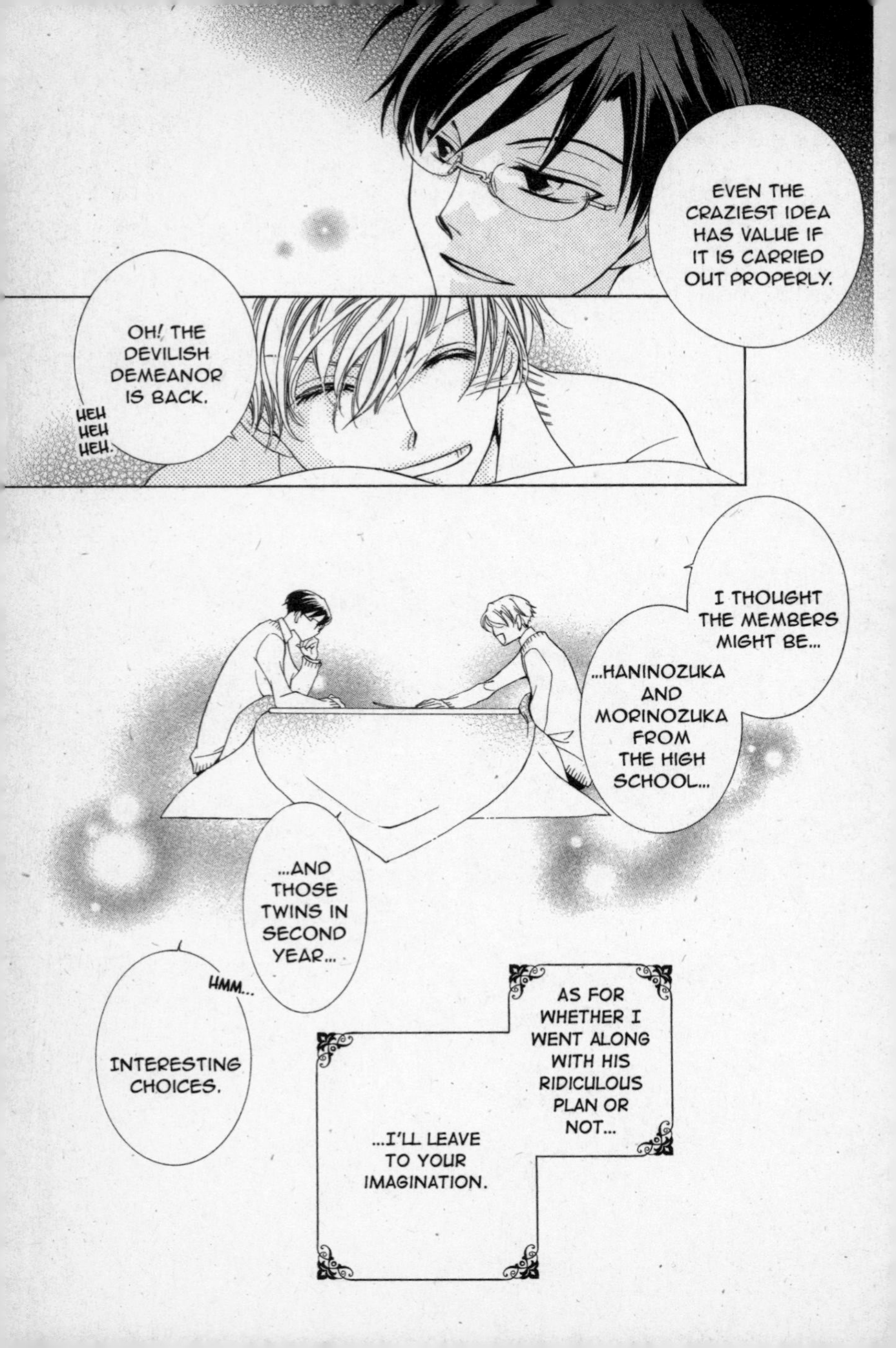
EVEN THE CRAZIEST IDEA HAS VALUE IF IT IS CARRIED OUT PROPERLY.
OH! THE DEVILISH DEMEANOR IS BACK.
HEH HEH HEH.
I THOUGHT THE MEMBERS MIGHT BE...
...HANINOZUKA AND MORINOZUKA FROM THE HIGH SCHOOL...
...AND THOSE TWINS IN SECOND YEAR...
HMM...
INTERESTING CHOICES.
AS FOR WHETHER I WENT ALONG WITH HIS RIDICULOUS PLAN OR NOT...
...I'LL LEAVE TO YOUR IMAGINATION.

✿HOST CLUB OVERSEAS✿

I'M REALLY THANKFUL THAT *HOST CLUB* IS PUBLISHED IN COUNTRIES OTHER THAN JAPAN, BUT I WONDER HOW FOREIGN READERS CAN ENJOY IT WITH SO MANY JOKES MEANT FOR THE JAPANESE COMMON FOLK AND MANGA LOVERS.

SOMETIMES I GET LETTERS FROM FOREIGN READERS. SOME ARE IN REALLY GOOD JAPANESE, AND OTHERS I CAN'T READ AT ALL... (SORRY!), BUT YOUR LOVE IS DEFINITELY CONVEYED!! I'M VERY HAPPY! THANK YOU!!!

I HOPE THIS MESSAGE IS TRANSLATED TO REACH YOU OVERSEAS READERS!!! (LAUGH)

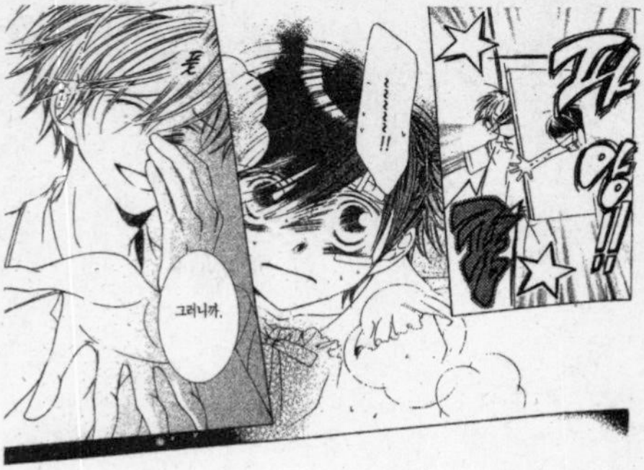
그러니까.

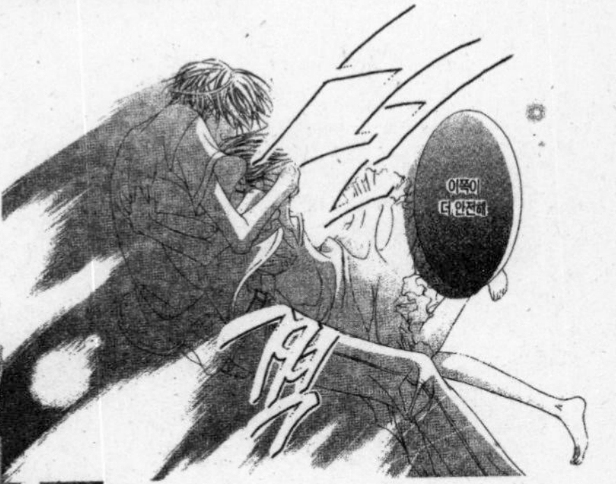
이쪽이 더 안전해

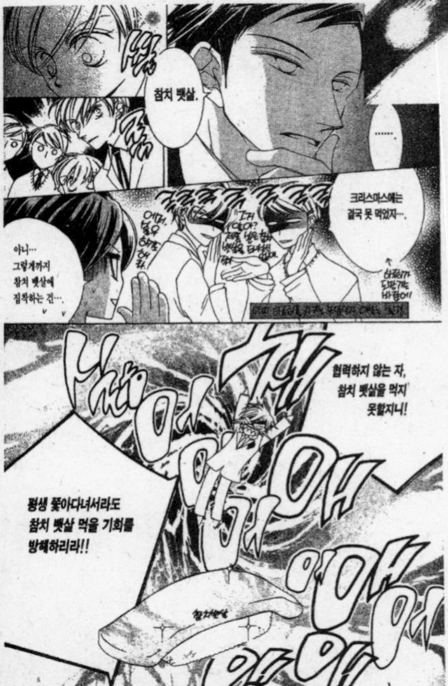
참치 뱃살.
......
크리스마스에는 결국 못 먹었지….
아니… 그렇게까지 참치 뱃살에 집착하는 건…
협력하지 않는 자, 참치 뱃살을 먹지 못할지니!
평생 쫓아다녀서라도 참치 뱃살 먹을 기회를 방해하리라!!

✿KOREAN VERSION✿

THE SOUND EFFECTS ARE AMAZING!! VERY IMPRESSIVE!!! I THINK THE EDITOR MUST HAVE REMOVED THE EFFECTS I DREW, INSERTED NEW ONES, AND THEN TOUCHED UP THE PICTURES WITH A COMPUTER... WHAT TALENT!!

HOST CLUB HAS A LOT OF HANDWRITTEN WORDS, SO IT MUST BE HARD WORK. THANK YOU!!

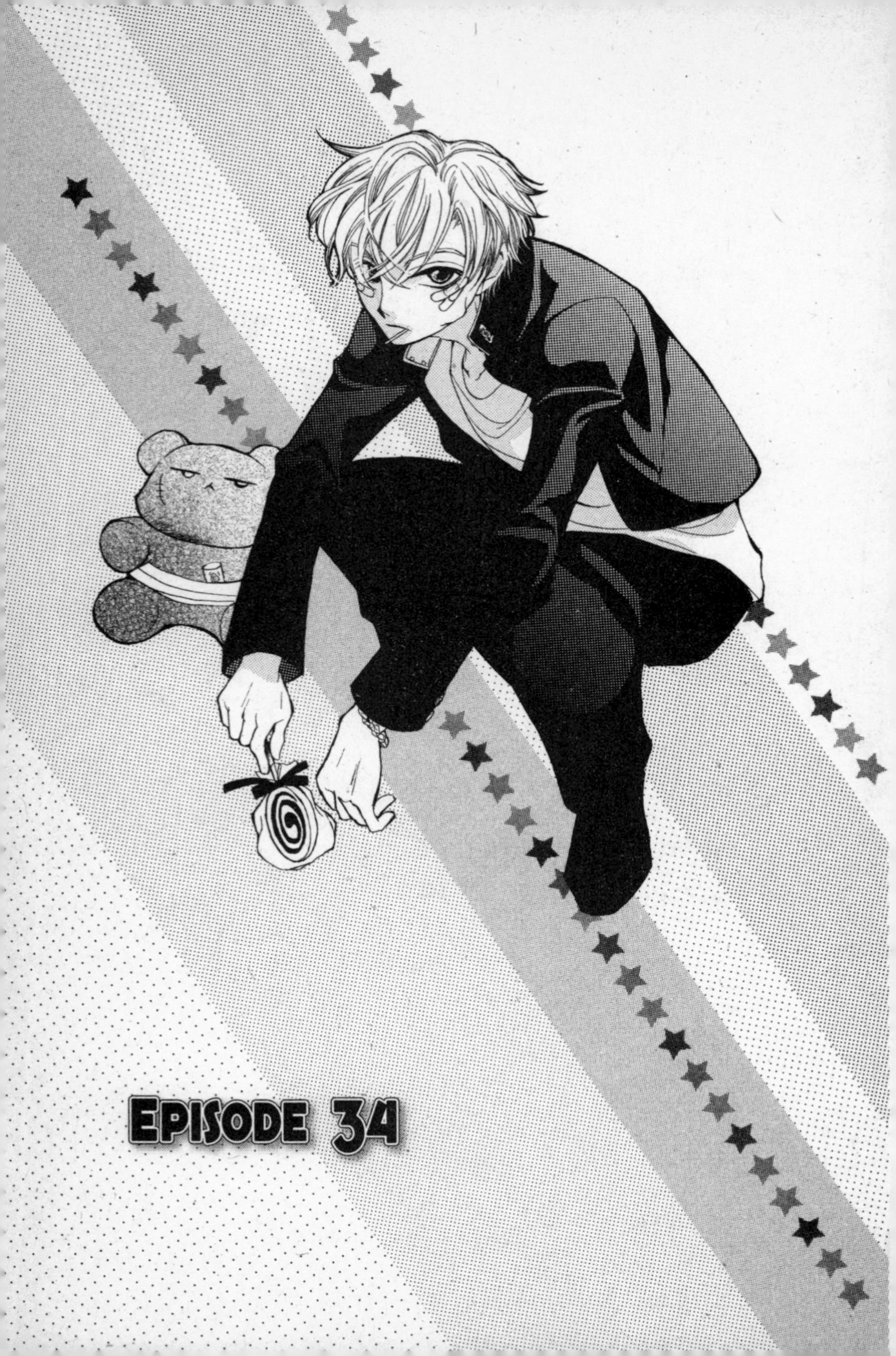
EPISODE 34

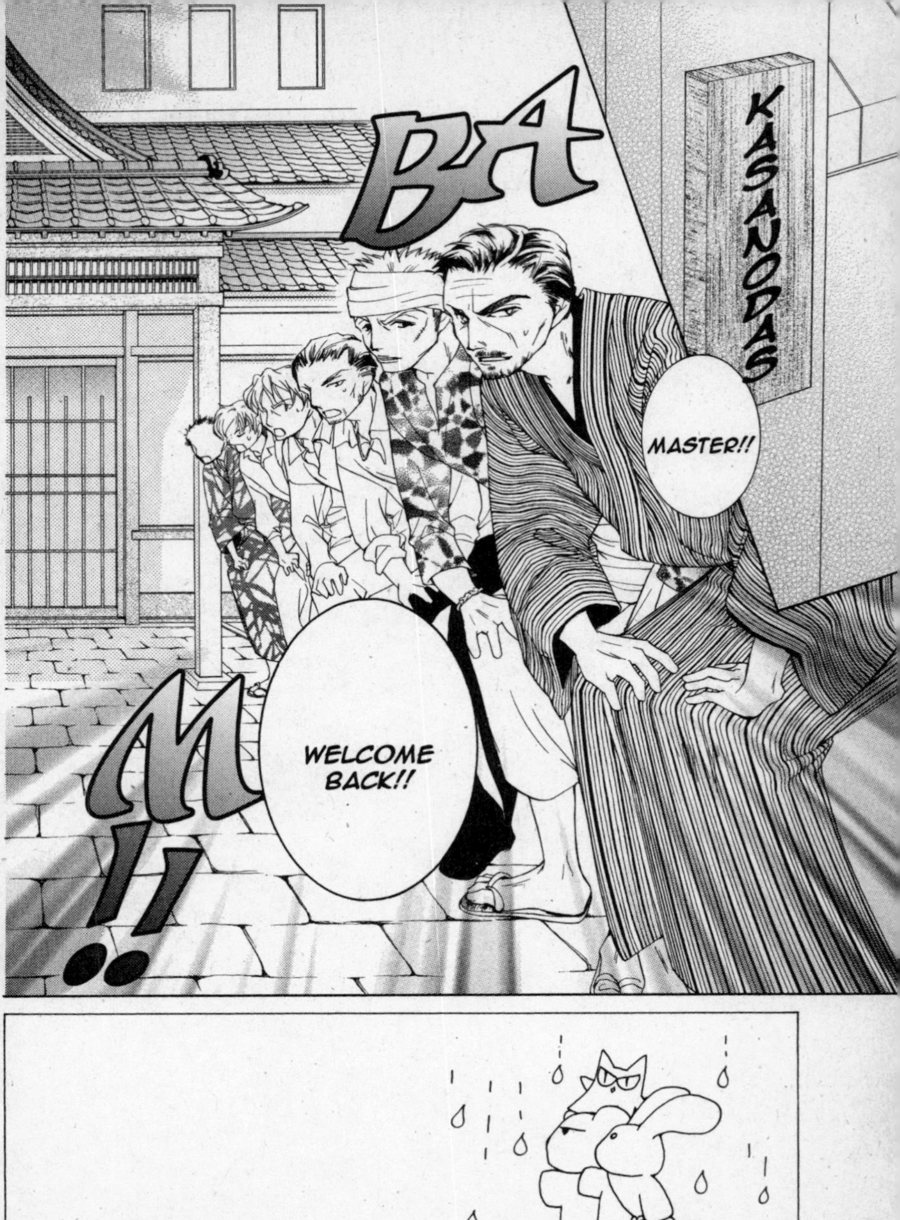
KASANODAS
BA
MASTER!!
WELCOME BACK!!
M!!

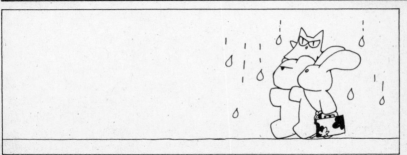

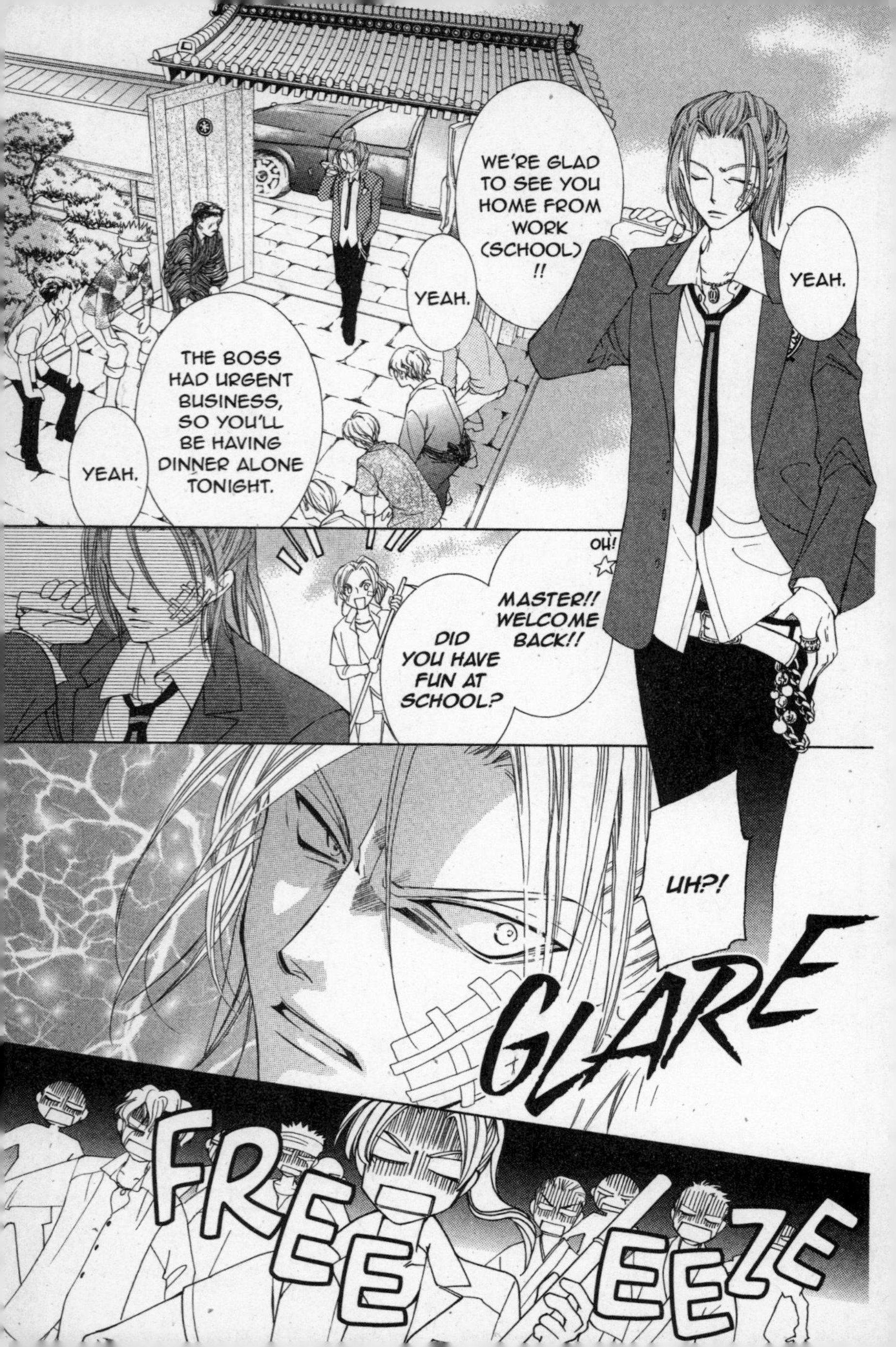

WE'RE GLAD TO SEE YOU HOME FROM WORK (SCHOOL) !!
YEAH.
YEAH.
THE BOSS HAD URGENT BUSINESS, SO YOU'LL BE HAVING DINNER ALONE TONIGHT.
YEAH.
OH!
MASTER!! WELCOME BACK!!
DID YOU HAVE FUN AT SCHOOL?
UH?!
GLARE
FREE EEZE

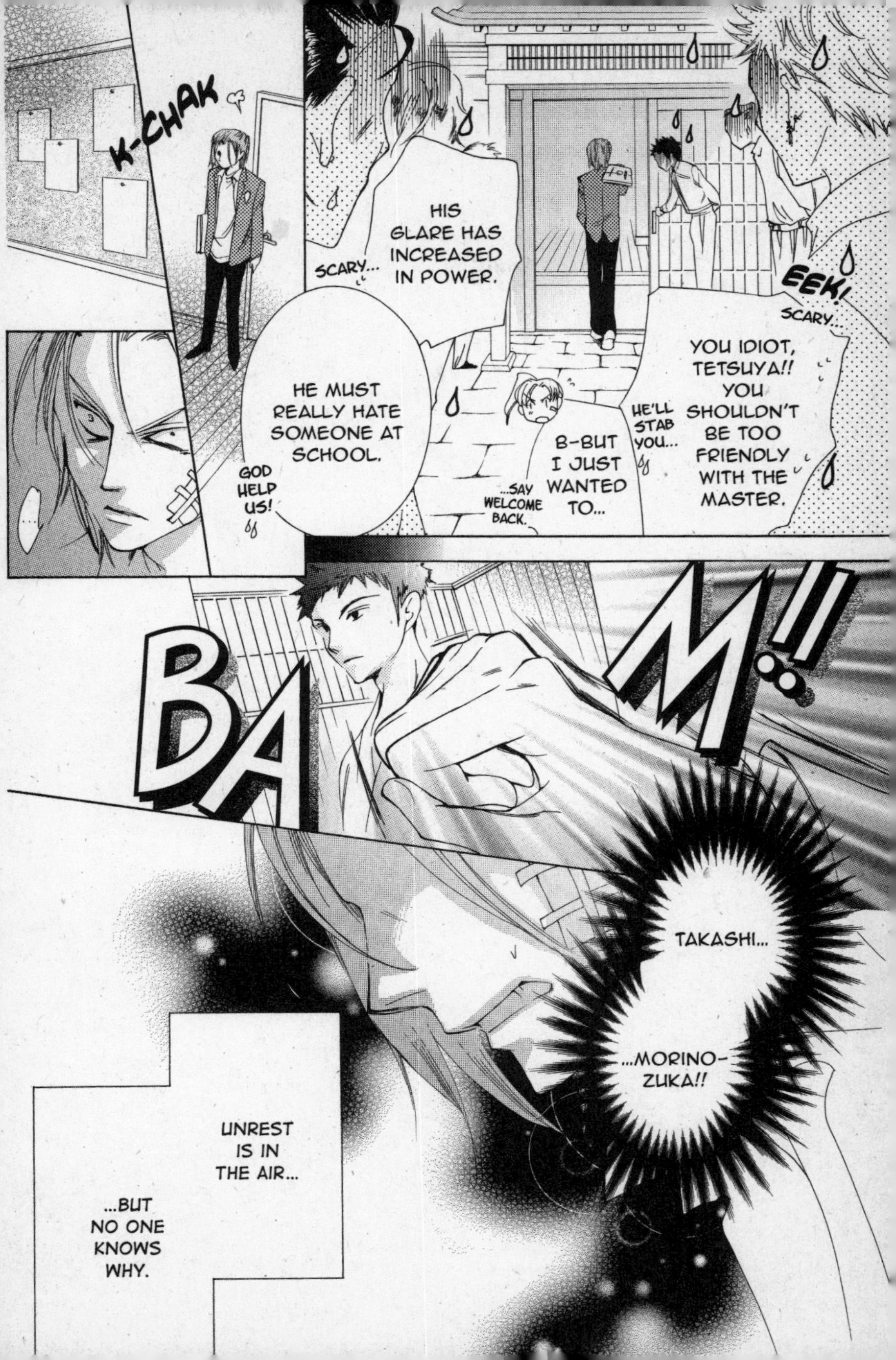
EEK!
SCARY...
YOU IDIOT, TETSUYA!! YOU SHOULDN'T BE TOO FRIENDLY WITH THE MASTER.
HE'LL STAB YOU...
B-BUT I JUST WANTED TO...
...SAY WELCOME BACK.
HIS GLARE HAS INCREASED IN POWER.
SCARY...
HE MUST REALLY HATE SOMEONE AT SCHOOL.
GOD HELP US!
K-CHAK
...
BAM!!
TAKASHI...
...MORINO-ZUKA!!
UNREST IS IN THE AIR...
...BUT NO ONE KNOWS WHY.

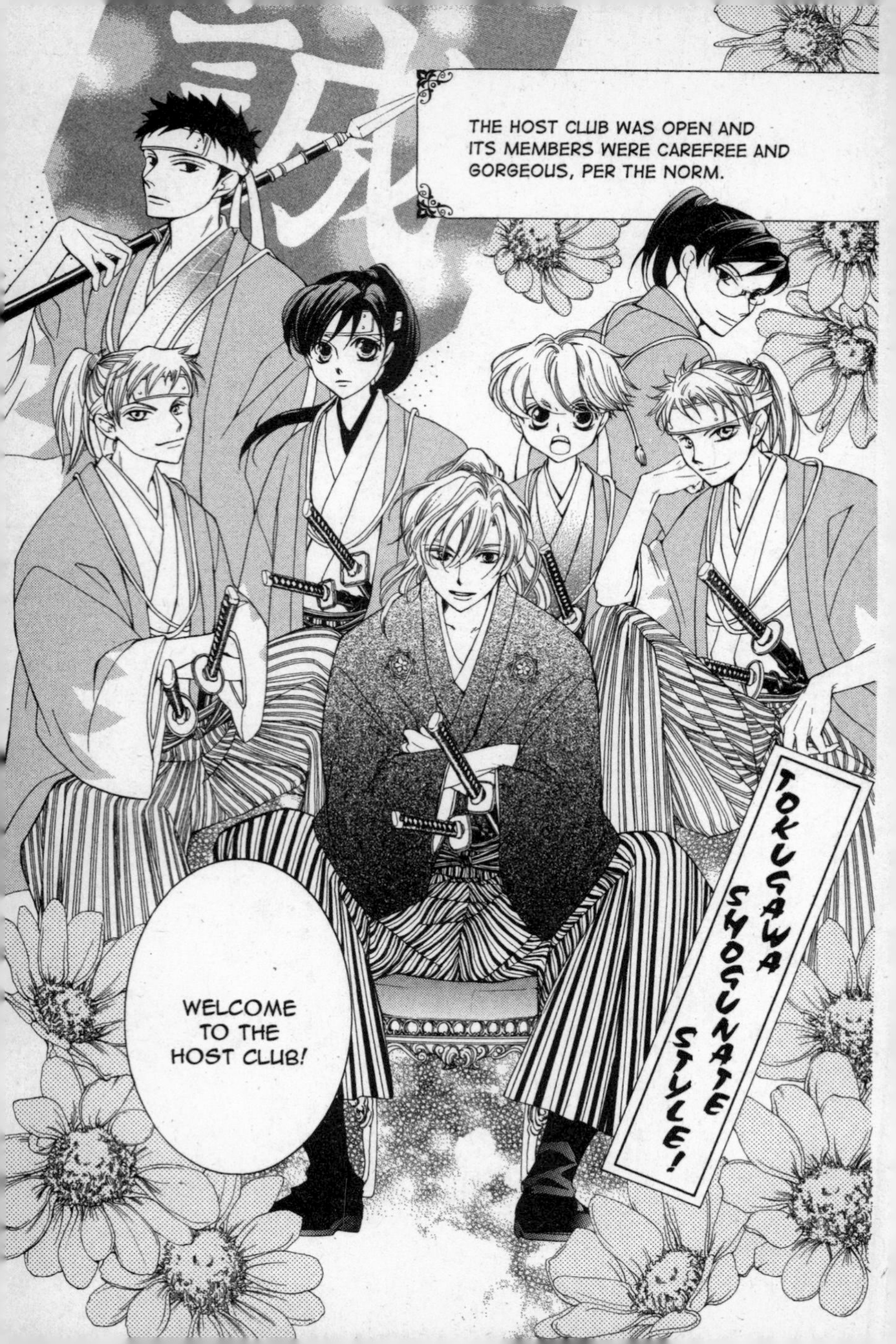
THE HOST CLUB WAS OPEN AND ITS MEMBERS WERE CAREFREE AND GORGEOUS, PER THE NORM.
TOKUGAWA SHOGUNATE STYLE!
WELCOME TO THE HOST CLUB!

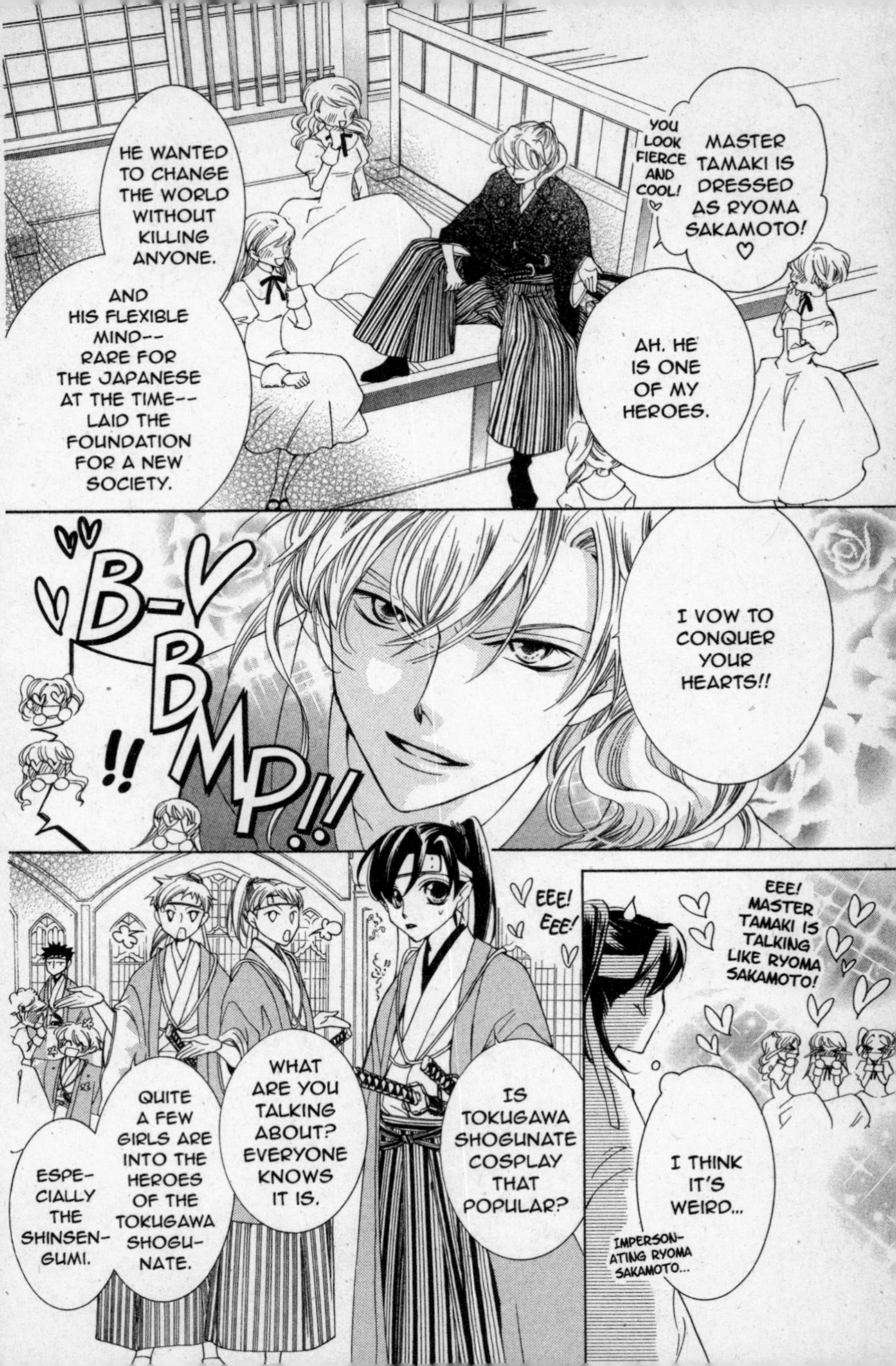
MASTER TAMAKI IS DRESSED AS RYOMA SAKAMOTO! ♡
YOU LOOK FIERCE AND COOL! ♡
AH. HE IS ONE OF MY HEROES.
HE WANTED TO CHANGE THE WORLD WITHOUT KILLING ANYONE.
AND HIS FLEXIBLE MIND-- RARE FOR THE JAPANESE AT THE TIME-- LAID THE FOUNDATION FOR A NEW SOCIETY.
I VOW TO CONQUER YOUR HEARTS!!
B-BMP!!
!!
EEE! MASTER TAMAKI IS TALKING LIKE RYOMA SAKAMOTO!
I THINK IT'S WEIRD...
IMPERSONATING RYOMA SAKAMOTO...
EEE! EEE!
IS TOKUGAWA SHOGUNATE COSPLAY THAT POPULAR?
WHAT ARE YOU TALKING ABOUT? EVERYONE KNOWS IT IS.
QUITE A FEW GIRLS ARE INTO THE HEROES OF THE TOKUGAWA SHOGUNATE.
ESPECIALLY THE SHINSENGUMI.

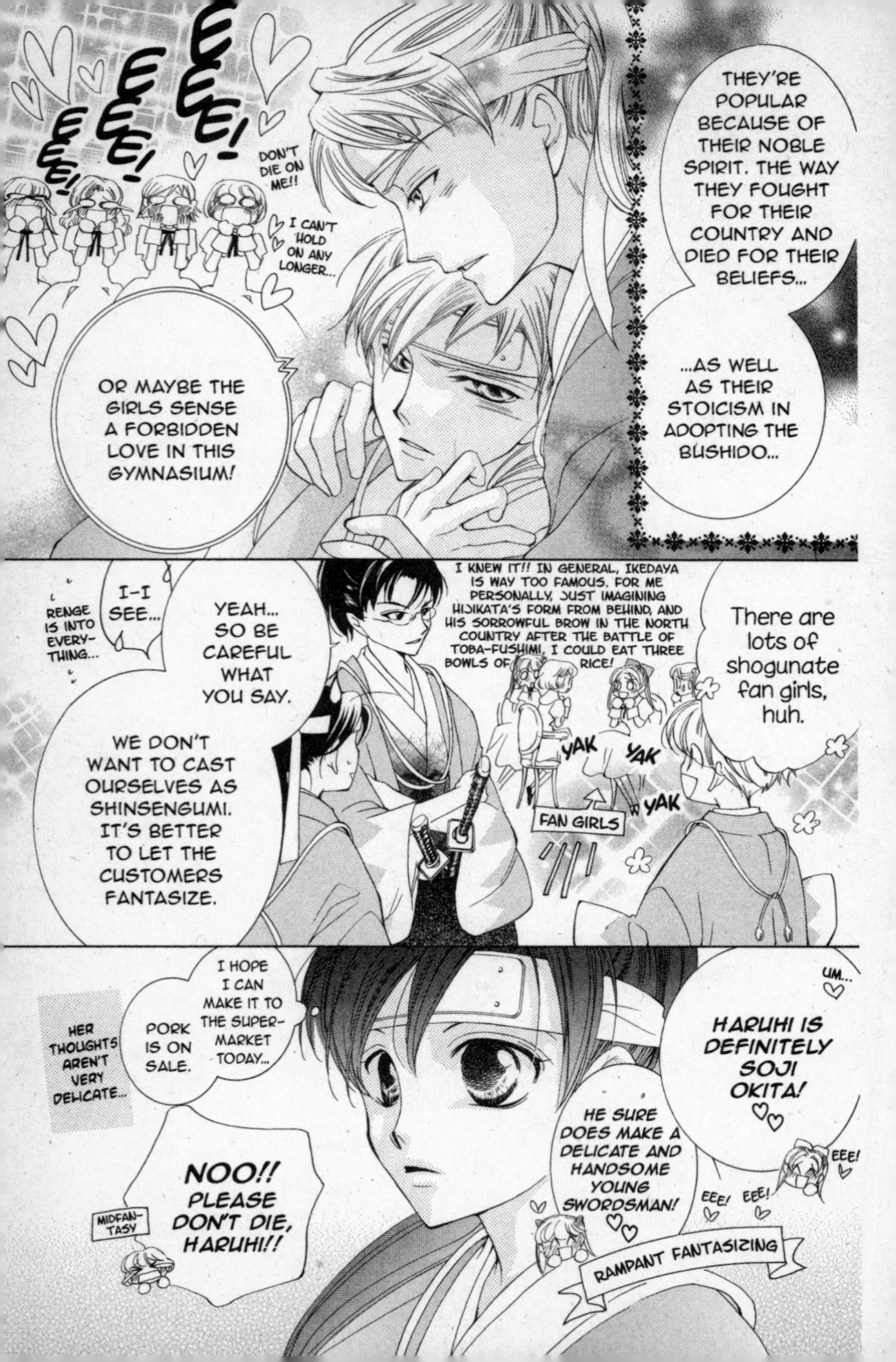

THEY'RE POPULAR BECAUSE OF THEIR NOBLE SPIRIT. THE WAY THEY FOUGHT FOR THEIR COUNTRY AND DIED FOR THEIR BELIEFS...
...AS WELL AS THEIR STOICISM IN ADOPTING THE BUSHIDO...
EEEE!
EEEE!
EEEE!
DON'T DIE ON ME!!
I CAN'T HOLD ON ANY LONGER...
OR MAYBE THE GIRLS SENSE A FORBIDDEN LOVE IN THIS GYMNASIUM!
There are lots of shogunate fan girls, huh.
I KNEW IT!! IN GENERAL, IKEDAYA IS WAY TOO FAMOUS. FOR ME PERSONALLY, JUST IMAGINING HIJIKATA'S FORM FROM BEHIND, AND HIS SORROWFUL BROW IN THE NORTH COUNTRY AFTER THE BATTLE OF TOBA-FUSHIMI, I COULD EAT THREE BOWLS OF RICE!
YAK
YAK
YAK
FAN GIRLS
YEAH... SO BE CAREFUL WHAT YOU SAY.
I-I SEE...
RENGE IS INTO EVERYTHING...
WE DON'T WANT TO CAST OURSELVES AS SHINSENGUMI. IT'S BETTER TO LET THE CUSTOMERS FANTASIZE.
UM...
HARUHI IS DEFINITELY SOJI OKITA!
EEE!
HE SURE DOES MAKE A DELICATE AND HANDSOME YOUNG SWORDSMAN!
EEE!
EEE!
RAMPANT FANTASIZING
I HOPE I CAN MAKE IT TO THE SUPER-MARKET TODAY...
PORK IS ON SALE.
HER THOUGHTS AREN'T VERY DELICATE...
NOO!! PLEASE DON'T DIE, HARUHI!!
MIDFANTASY

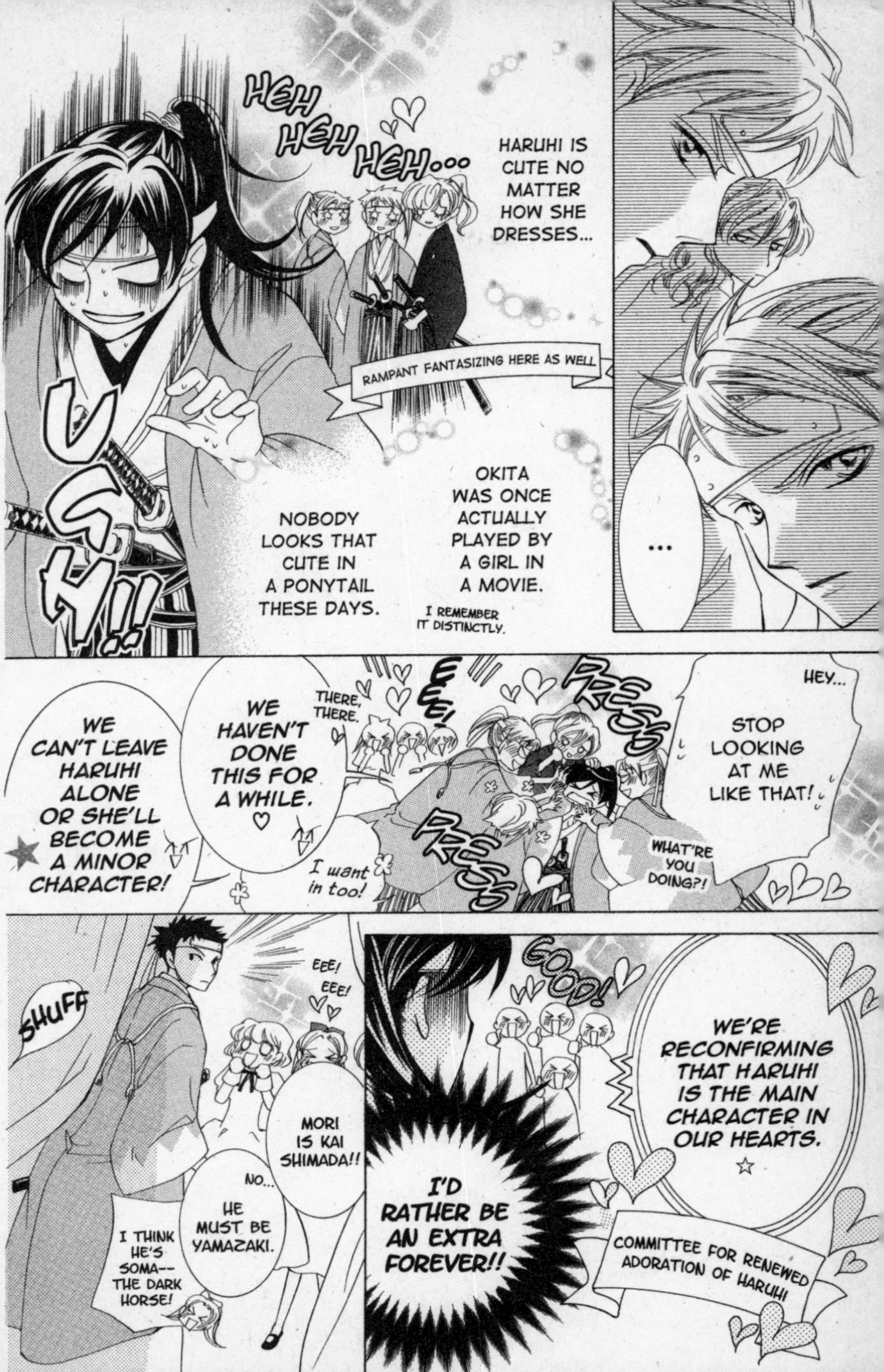
...
HARUHI IS CUTE NO MATTER HOW SHE DRESSES...
HEH HEH HEH...
RAMPANT FANTASIZING HERE AS WELL
OKITA WAS ONCE ACTUALLY PLAYED BY A GIRL IN A MOVIE.
I REMEMBER IT DISTINCTLY.
NOBODY LOOKS THAT CUTE IN A PONYTAIL THESE DAYS.
UGH!!
HEY...
STOP LOOKING AT ME LIKE THAT!
PRESS
WHAT'RE YOU DOING?!
EEE!
PRESS
THERE, THERE.
WE HAVEN'T DONE THIS FOR A WHILE. ♡
I want in too!
WE CAN'T LEAVE HARUHI ALONE OR SHE'LL BECOME A MINOR CHARACTER!
GOOD!
WE'RE RECONFIRMING THAT HARUHI IS THE MAIN CHARACTER IN OUR HEARTS. ☆
I'D RATHER BE AN EXTRA FOREVER!!
COMMITTEE FOR RENEWED ADORATION OF HARUHI
EEE! EEE!
MORI IS KAI SHIMADA!!
NO... HE MUST BE YAMAZAKI.
SHUFF
I THINK HE'S SOMA-- THE DARK HORSE!

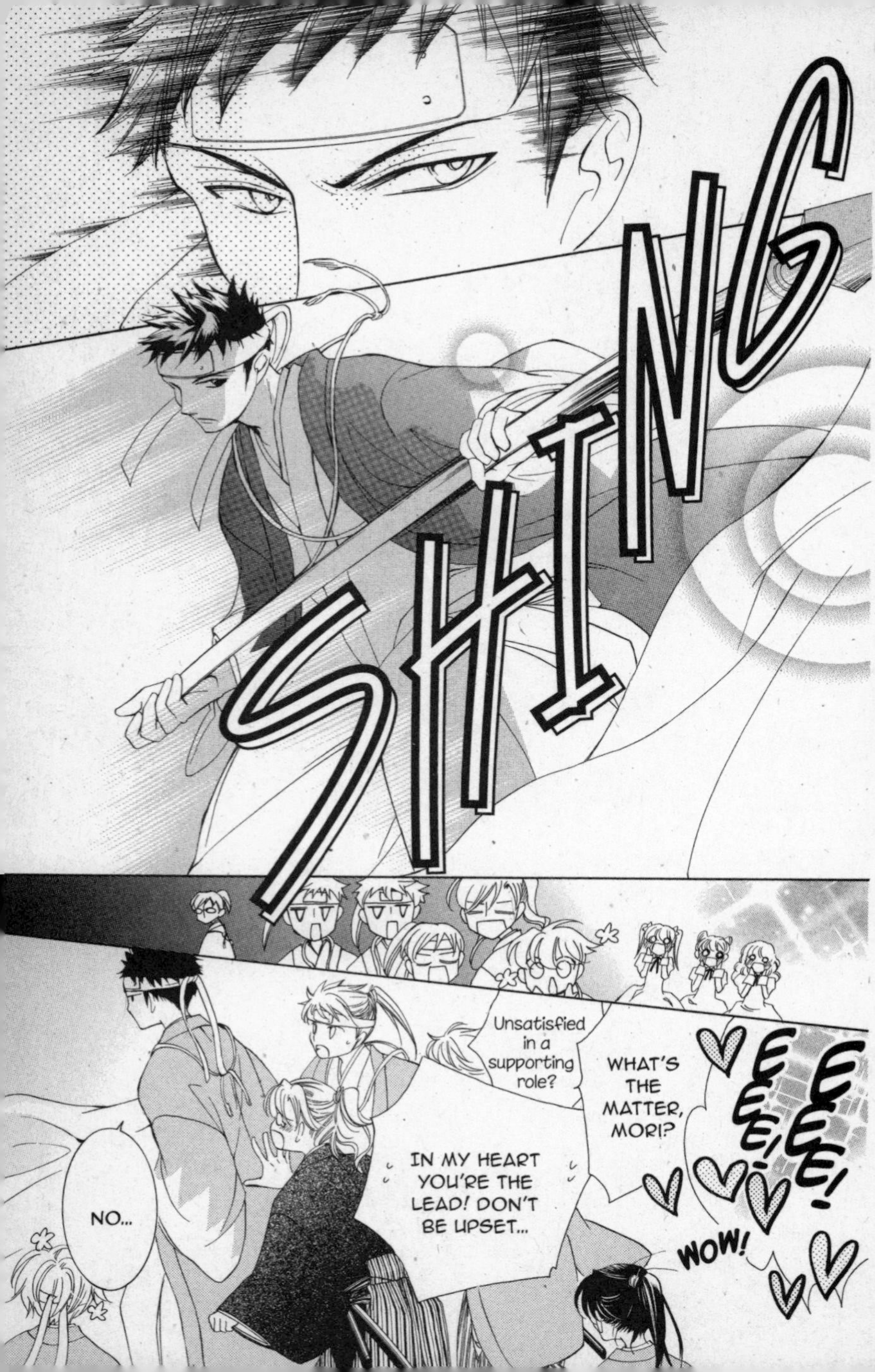
SHING
EEEE!
EEE!
WOW!
WHAT'S THE MATTER, MORI?
Unsatisfied in a supporting role?
IN MY HEART YOU'RE THE LEAD! DON'T BE UPSET...
NO...

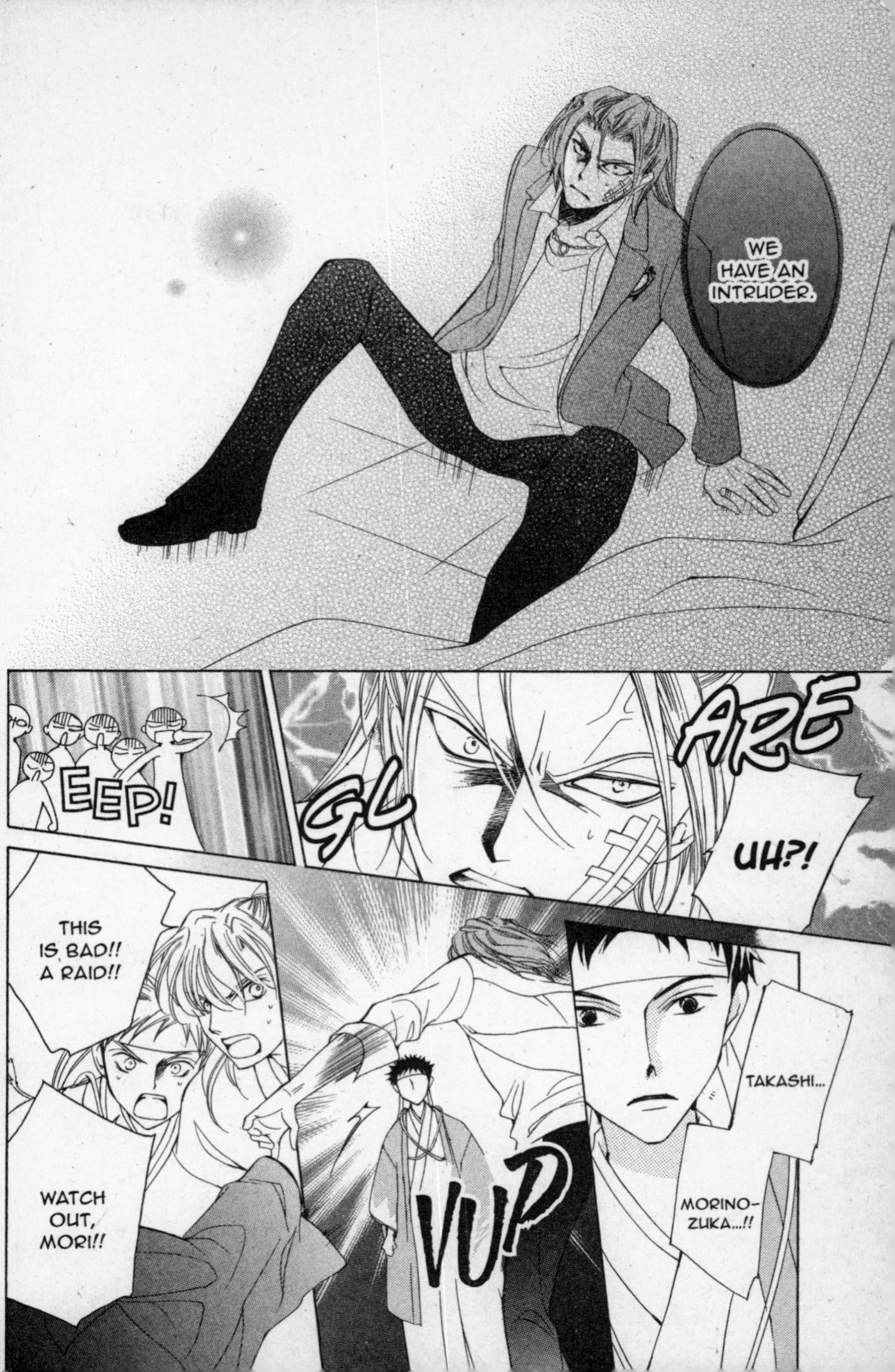
WE HAVE AN INTRUDER.
GLARE
UH?!
EEP!
TAKASHI...
MORINO-ZUKA...!!
VUP
THIS IS BAD!! A RAID!!
WATCH OUT, MORI!!

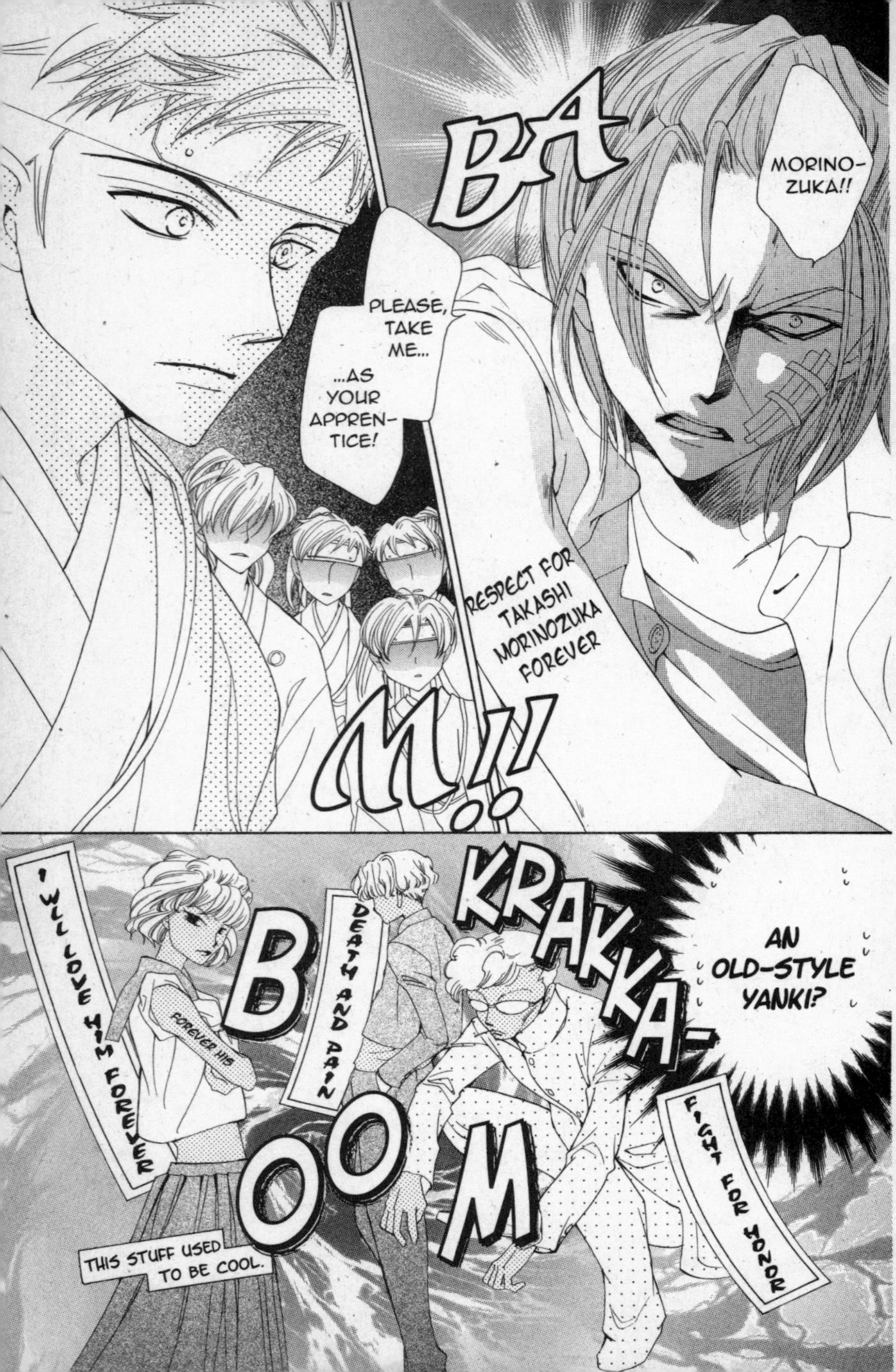
BA
MORINO-ZUKA!!
PLEASE, TAKE ME... ...AS YOUR APPRENTICE!
M!!
RESPECT FOR TAKASHI MORINOZUKA FOREVER
KRAKKA-
AN OLD-STYLE YANKI?
FIGHT FOR HONOR
BOOOM
DEATH AND PAIN
I WILL LOVE HIM FOREVER
FOREVER HIS
THIS STUFF USED TO BE COOL.

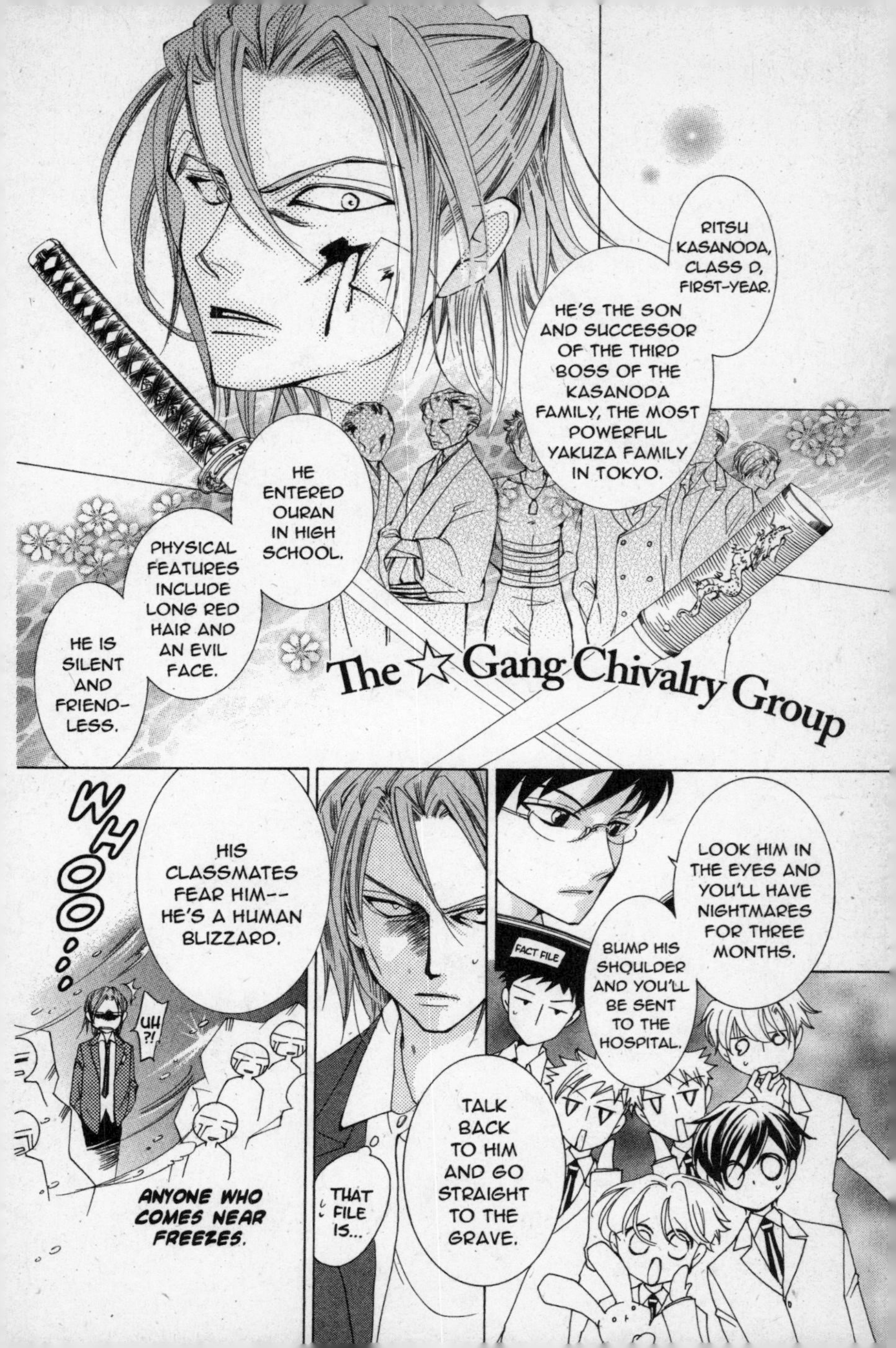

RITSU KASANODA, CLASS D, FIRST-YEAR.
HE'S THE SON AND SUCCESSOR OF THE THIRD BOSS OF THE KASANODA FAMILY, THE MOST POWERFUL YAKUZA FAMILY IN TOKYO.
HE ENTERED OURAN IN HIGH SCHOOL.
PHYSICAL FEATURES INCLUDE LONG RED HAIR AND AN EVIL FACE.
HE IS SILENT AND FRIEND-LESS.
The ☆ Gang Chivalry Group
LOOK HIM IN THE EYES AND YOU'LL HAVE NIGHTMARES FOR THREE MONTHS.
FACT FILE
BUMP HIS SHOULDER AND YOU'LL BE SENT TO THE HOSPITAL.
TALK BACK TO HIM AND GO STRAIGHT TO THE GRAVE.
THAT FILE IS...
HIS CLASSMATES FEAR HIM--HE'S A HUMAN BLIZZARD.
WHOOO...
UH ?!
ANYONE WHO COMES NEAR FREEZES.

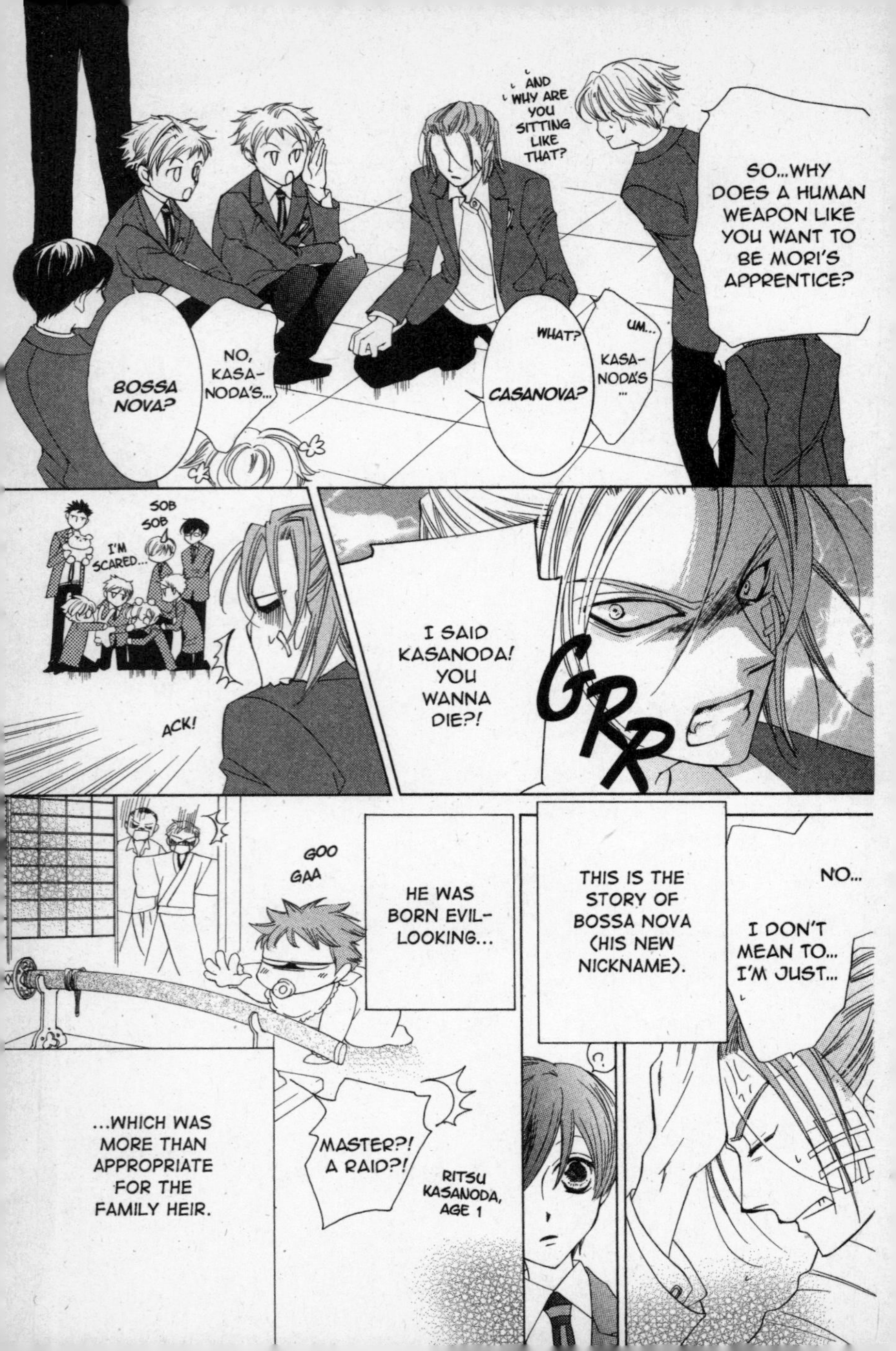
SO...WHY DOES A HUMAN WEAPON LIKE YOU WANT TO BE MORI'S APPRENTICE?
AND WHY ARE YOU SITTING LIKE THAT?
UM... KASANODA'S...
WHAT? CASANOVA?
NO, KASANODA'S...
BOSSA NOVA?
GRR
I SAID KASANODA! YOU WANNA DIE?!
ACK!
SOB SOB
I'M SCARED...
NO... I DON'T MEAN TO... I'M JUST...
THIS IS THE STORY OF BOSSA NOVA (HIS NEW NICKNAME).
HE WAS BORN EVIL-LOOKING...
GOO GAA
MASTER?! A RAID?!
RITSU KASANODA, AGE 1
...WHICH WAS MORE THAN APPROPRIATE FOR THE FAMILY HEIR.

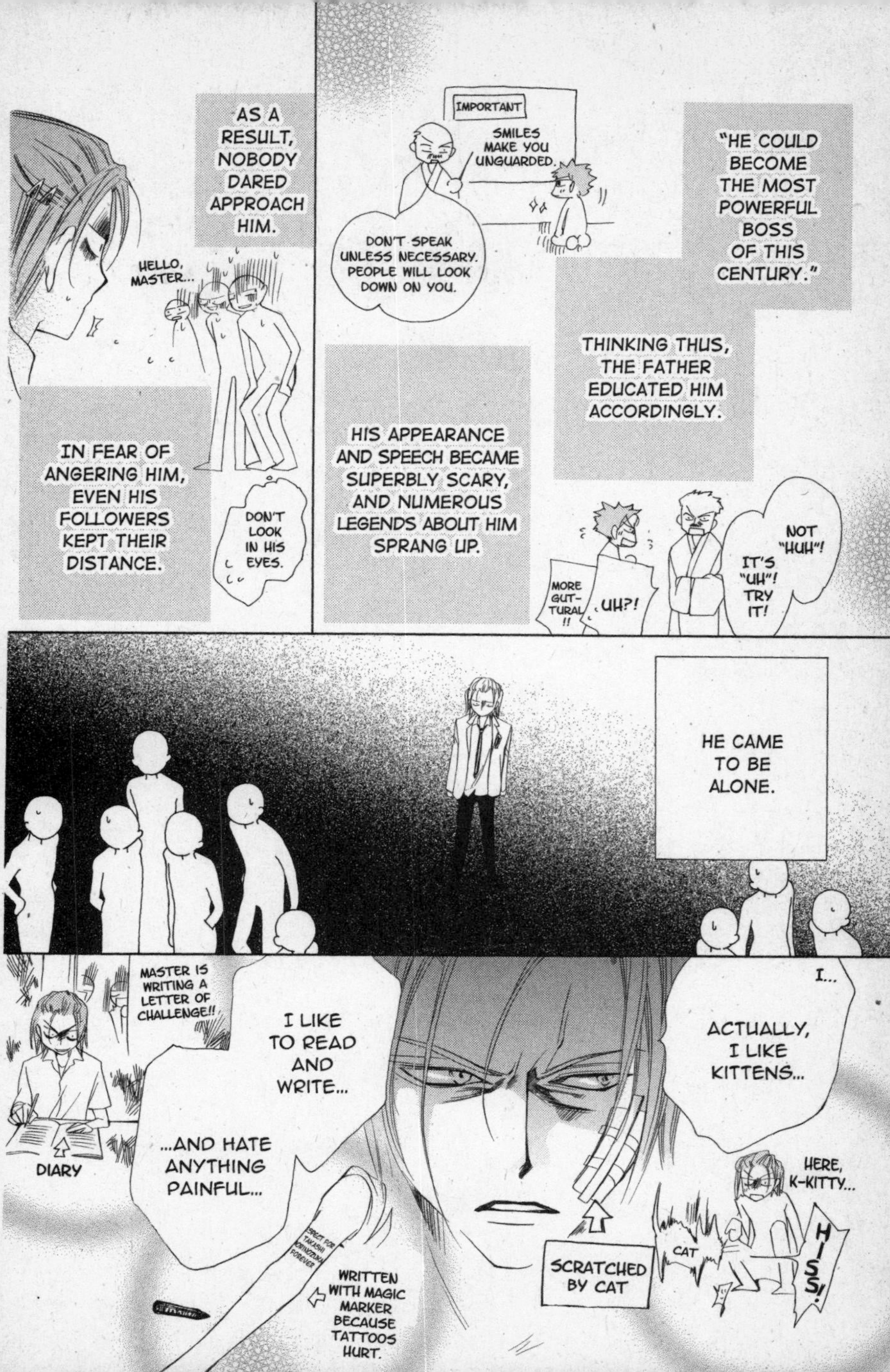
"HE COULD BECOME THE MOST POWERFUL BOSS OF THIS CENTURY."
IMPORTANT
SMILES MAKE YOU UNGUARDED.
DON'T SPEAK UNLESS NECESSARY. PEOPLE WILL LOOK DOWN ON YOU.
THINKING THUS, THE FATHER EDUCATED HIM ACCORDINGLY.
HIS APPEARANCE AND SPEECH BECAME SUPERBLY SCARY, AND NUMEROUS LEGENDS ABOUT HIM SPRANG UP.
NOT "HUH"! IT'S "UH"! TRY IT!
UH?!
MORE GUT-TURAL!!
AS A RESULT, NOBODY DARED APPROACH HIM.
HELLO, MASTER...
IN FEAR OF ANGERING HIM, EVEN HIS FOLLOWERS KEPT THEIR DISTANCE.
DON'T LOOK IN HIS EYES.
HE CAME TO BE ALONE.
I...
ACTUALLY, I LIKE KITTENS...
HERE, K-KITTY...
HISS!
CAT
SCRATCHED BY CAT
I LIKE TO READ AND WRITE...
...AND HATE ANYTHING PAINFUL...
WRITTEN WITH MAGIC MARKER BECAUSE TATTOOS HURT.
MASTER IS WRITING A LETTER OF CHALLENGE!!
DIARY

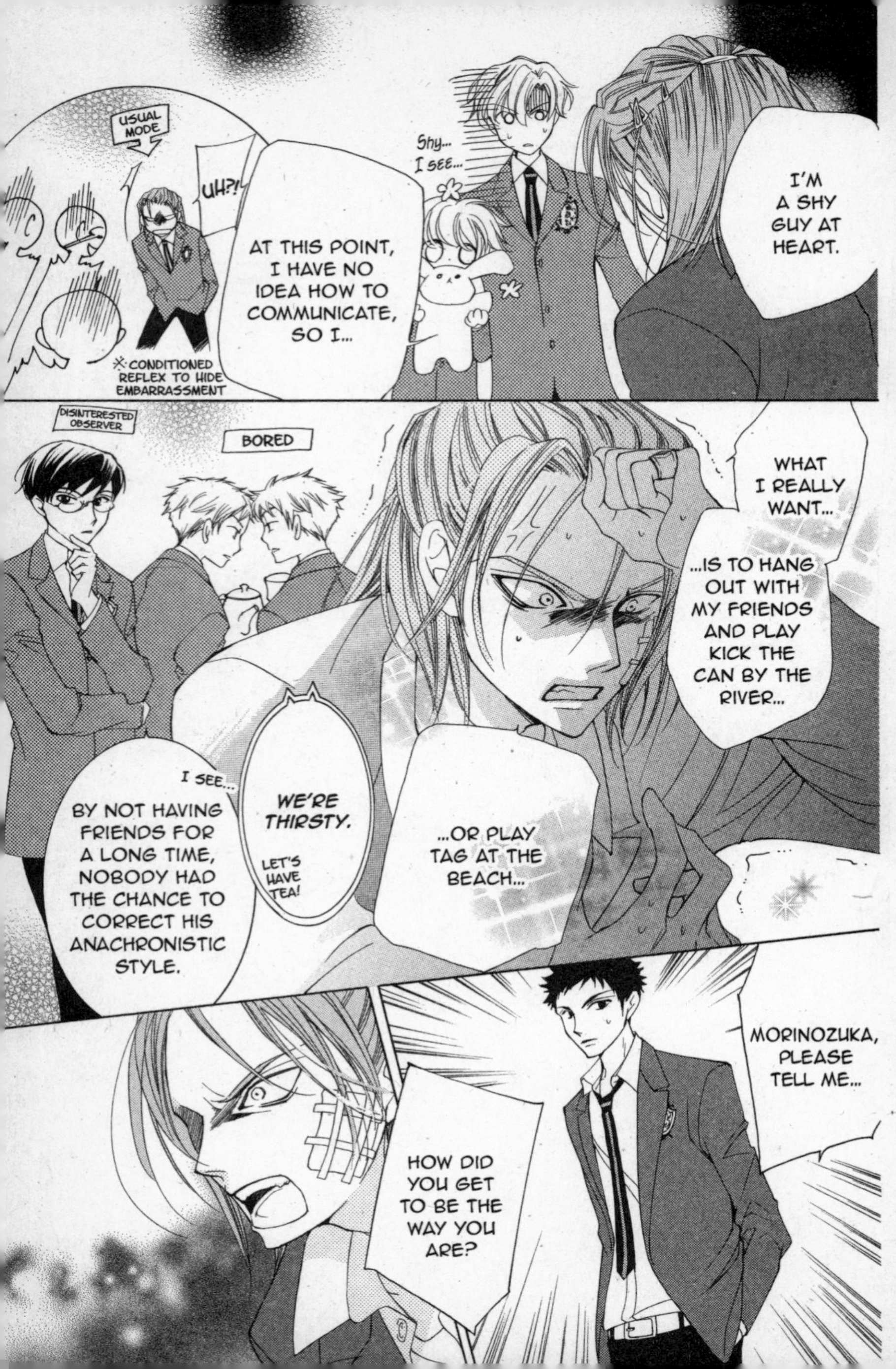
I'M A SHY GUY AT HEART.
Shy... I see...
AT THIS POINT, I HAVE NO IDEA HOW TO COMMUNICATE, SO I...
UH?!
USUAL MODE
※CONDITIONED REFLEX TO HIDE EMBARRASSMENT
WHAT I REALLY WANT...
...IS TO HANG OUT WITH MY FRIENDS AND PLAY KICK THE CAN BY THE RIVER...
...OR PLAY TAG AT THE BEACH...
...
WE'RE THIRSTY.
LET'S HAVE TEA!
BORED
DISINTERESTED OBSERVER
I SEE...
BY NOT HAVING FRIENDS FOR A LONG TIME, NOBODY HAD THE CHANCE TO CORRECT HIS ANACHRONISTIC STYLE.
MORINOZUKA, PLEASE TELL ME...
HOW DID YOU GET TO BE THE WAY YOU ARE?

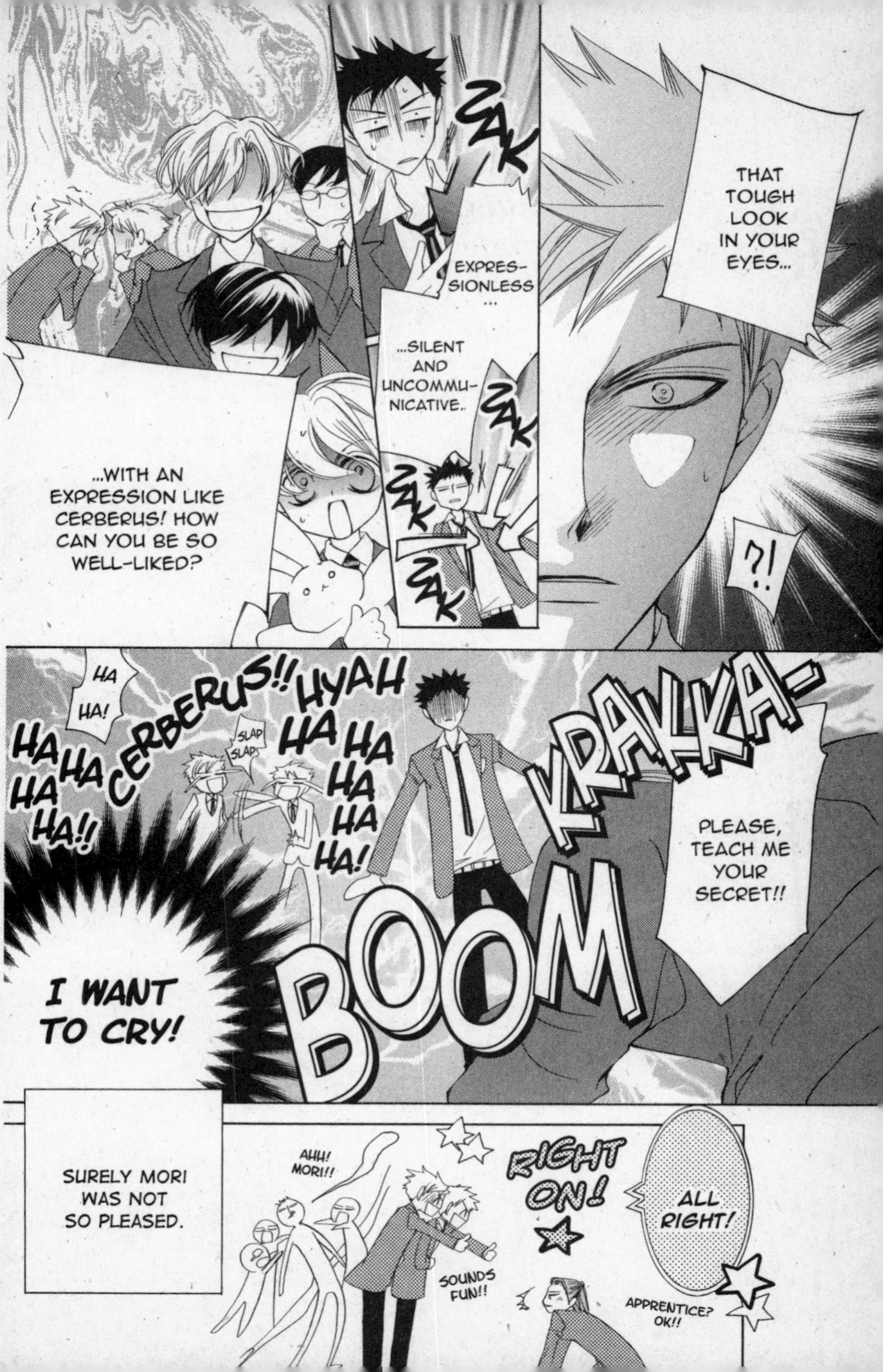
THAT TOUGH LOOK IN YOUR EYES...
?!
ZAK
EXPRES-SIONLESS ...
...SILENT AND UNCOMMU-NICATIVE..
ZAK
ZAK
ZAK
...WITH AN EXPRESSION LIKE CERBERUS! HOW CAN YOU BE SO WELL-LIKED?
PLEASE, TEACH ME YOUR SECRET!!
KRAKKA-
BOOM
HYAH HA HA HA HA HA HA HA!
CERBERUS!!
HA HA!
SLAP SLAP
HA HA HA HA HA!!
I WANT TO CRY!
ALL RIGHT!
RIGHT ON!
APPRENTICE? OK!!
SOUNDS FUN!!
AHH! MORI!!
SURELY MORI WAS NOT SO PLEASED.

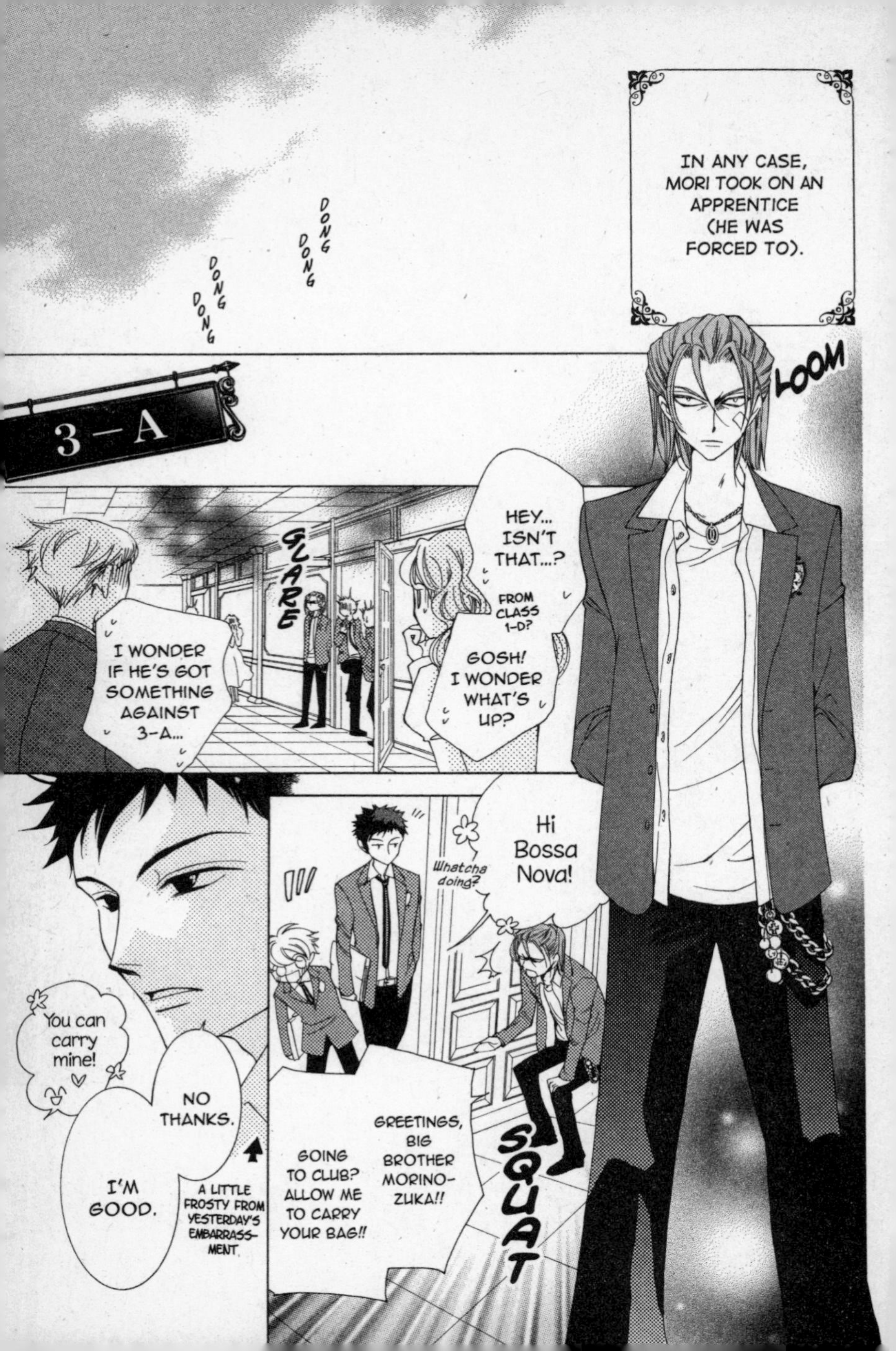
IN ANY CASE, MORI TOOK ON AN APPRENTICE (HE WAS FORCED TO).
DONG DONG
DONG DONG
LOOM
3-A
HEY... ISN'T THAT...?
FROM CLASS 1-D?
GOSH! I WONDER WHAT'S UP?
GLARE
I WONDER IF HE'S GOT SOMETHING AGAINST 3-A...
Hi Bossa Nova!
Whatcha doing?
SQUAT
GREETINGS, BIG BROTHER MORINO-ZUKA!!
GOING TO CLUB? ALLOW ME TO CARRY YOUR BAG!!
NO THANKS.
I'M GOOD.
A LITTLE FROSTY FROM YESTERDAY'S EMBARRASS-MENT.
You can carry mine!

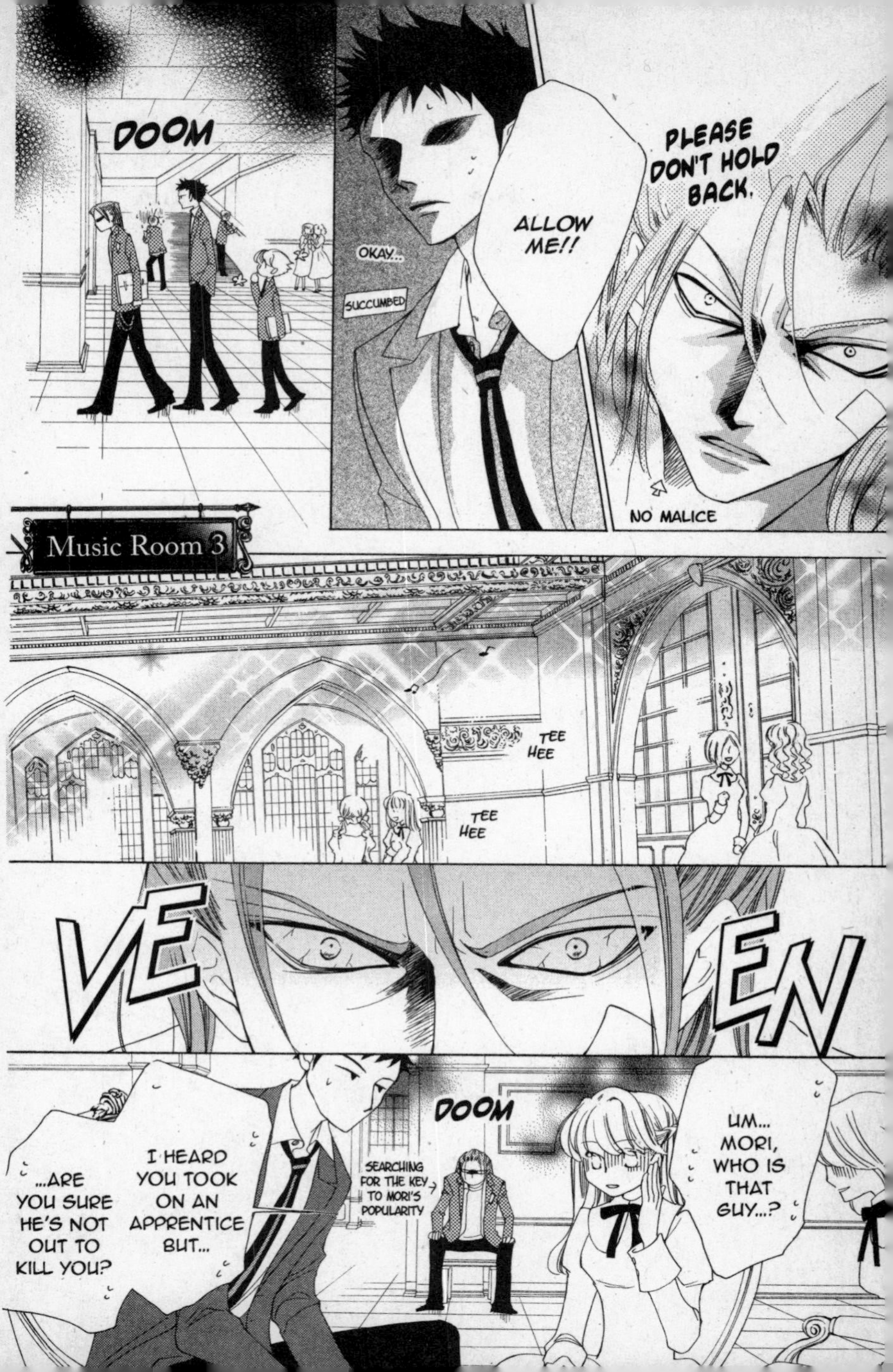
PLEASE DON'T HOLD BACK.
NO MALICE
ALLOW ME!!
OKAY...
SUCCUMBED
DOOM
Music Room 3
TEE HEE
TEE HEE
VEEN
UM... MORI, WHO IS THAT GUY...?
DOOM
SEARCHING FOR THE KEY TO MORI'S POPULARITY
I HEARD YOU TOOK ON AN APPRENTICE BUT...
...ARE YOU SURE HE'S NOT OUT TO KILL YOU?

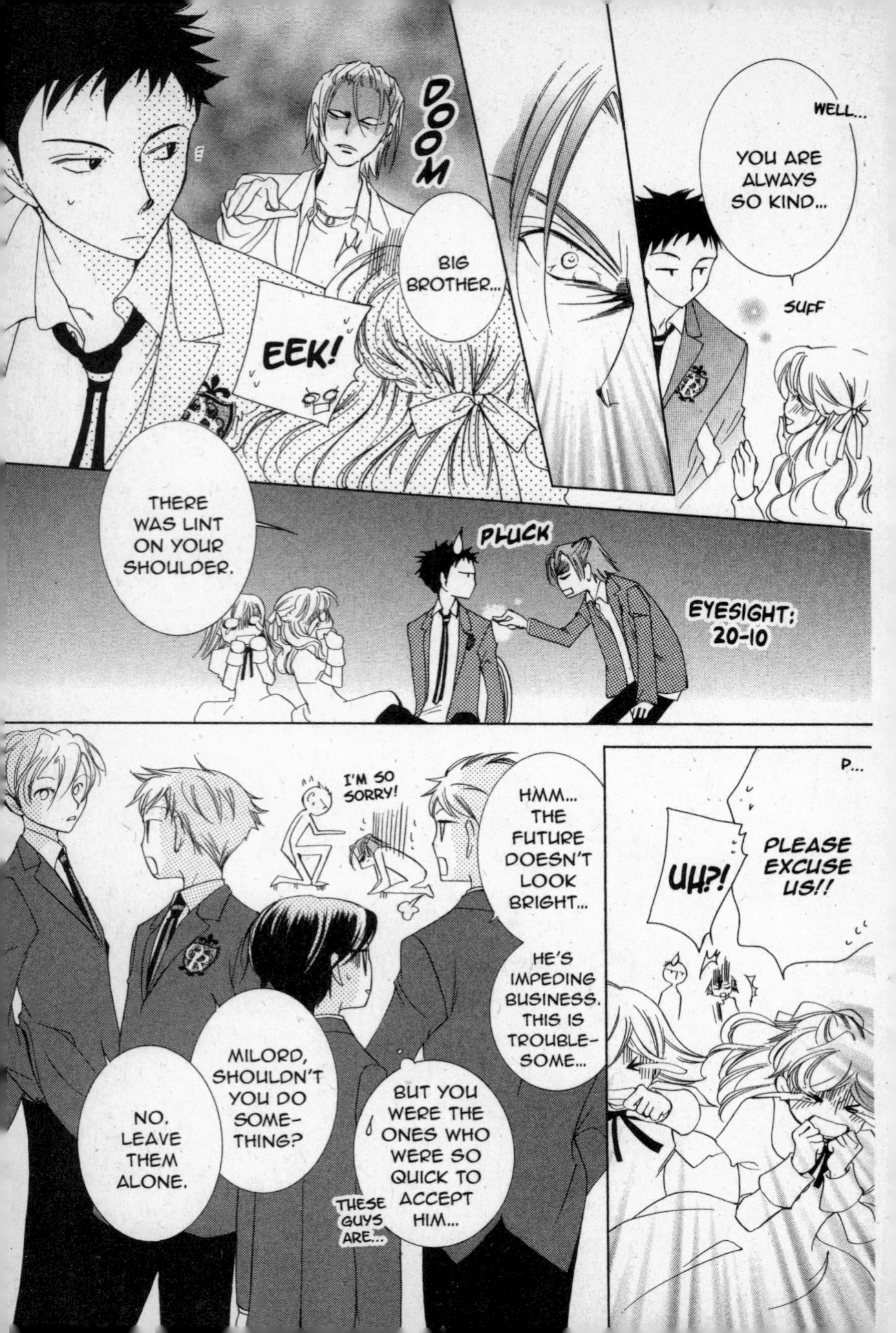
WELL...
YOU ARE ALWAYS SO KIND...
SUFF
BIG BROTHER...
DOOM
EEK!
EYESIGHT: 20-10
PLUCK
THERE WAS LINT ON YOUR SHOULDER.
P...
PLEASE EXCUSE US!!
UH?!
HMM... THE FUTURE DOESN'T LOOK BRIGHT...
HE'S IMPEDING BUSINESS. THIS IS TROUBLE-SOME...
I'M SO SORRY!
BUT YOU WERE THE ONES WHO WERE SO QUICK TO ACCEPT HIM...
THESE GUYS ARE...
MILORD, SHOULDN'T YOU DO SOME-THING?
NO. LEAVE THEM ALONE.

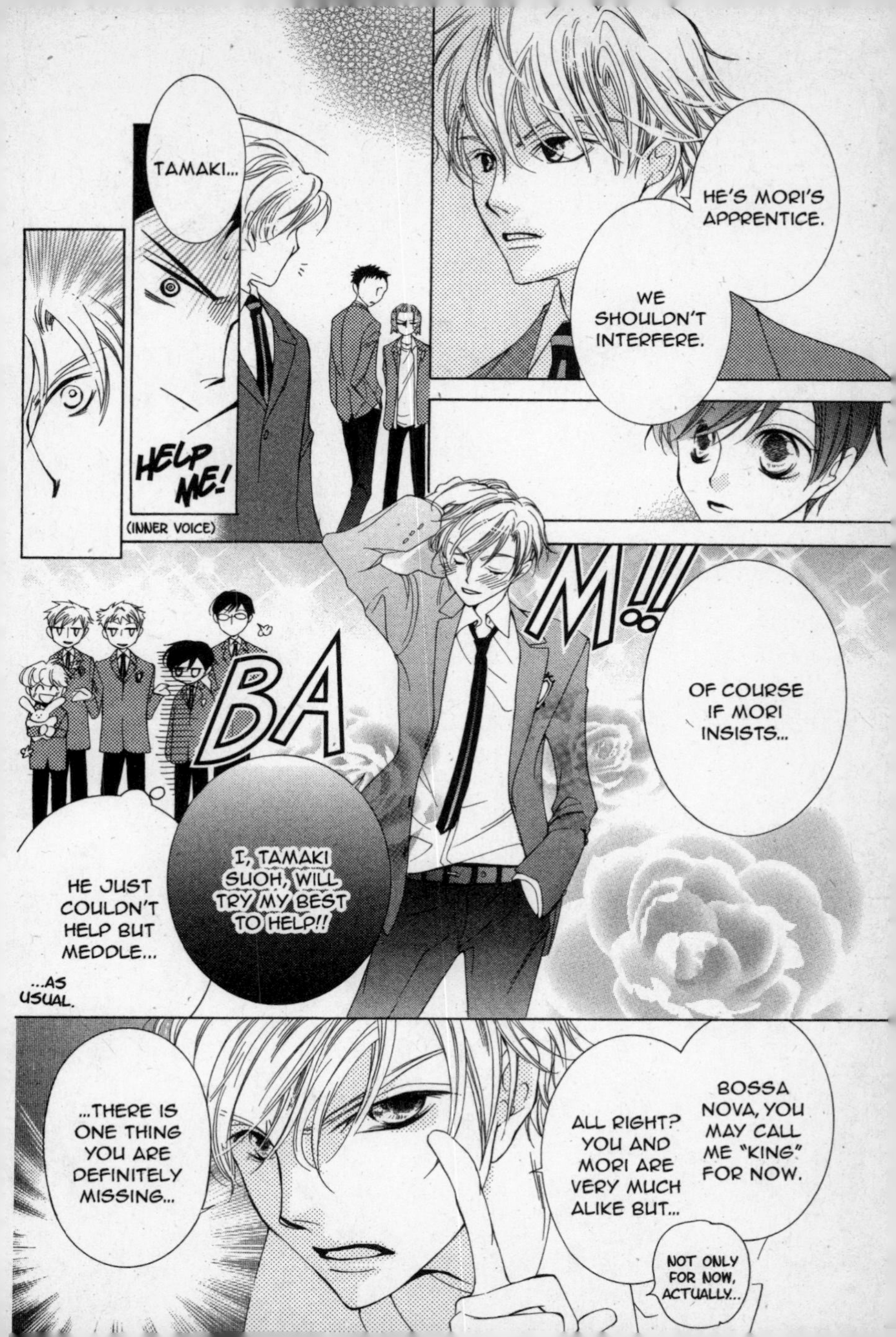
HE'S MORI'S APPRENTICE.
WE SHOULDN'T INTERFERE.
TAMAKI...
HELP ME!
(INNER VOICE)
BAM!!
OF COURSE IF MORI INSISTS...
I, TAMAKI SUOH, WILL TRY MY BEST TO HELP!!
HE JUST COULDN'T HELP BUT MEDDLE...
...AS USUAL.
BOSSA NOVA, YOU MAY CALL ME "KING" FOR NOW.
NOT ONLY FOR NOW, ACTUALLY...
ALL RIGHT? YOU AND MORI ARE VERY MUCH ALIKE BUT...
...THERE IS ONE THING YOU ARE DEFINITELY MISSING...

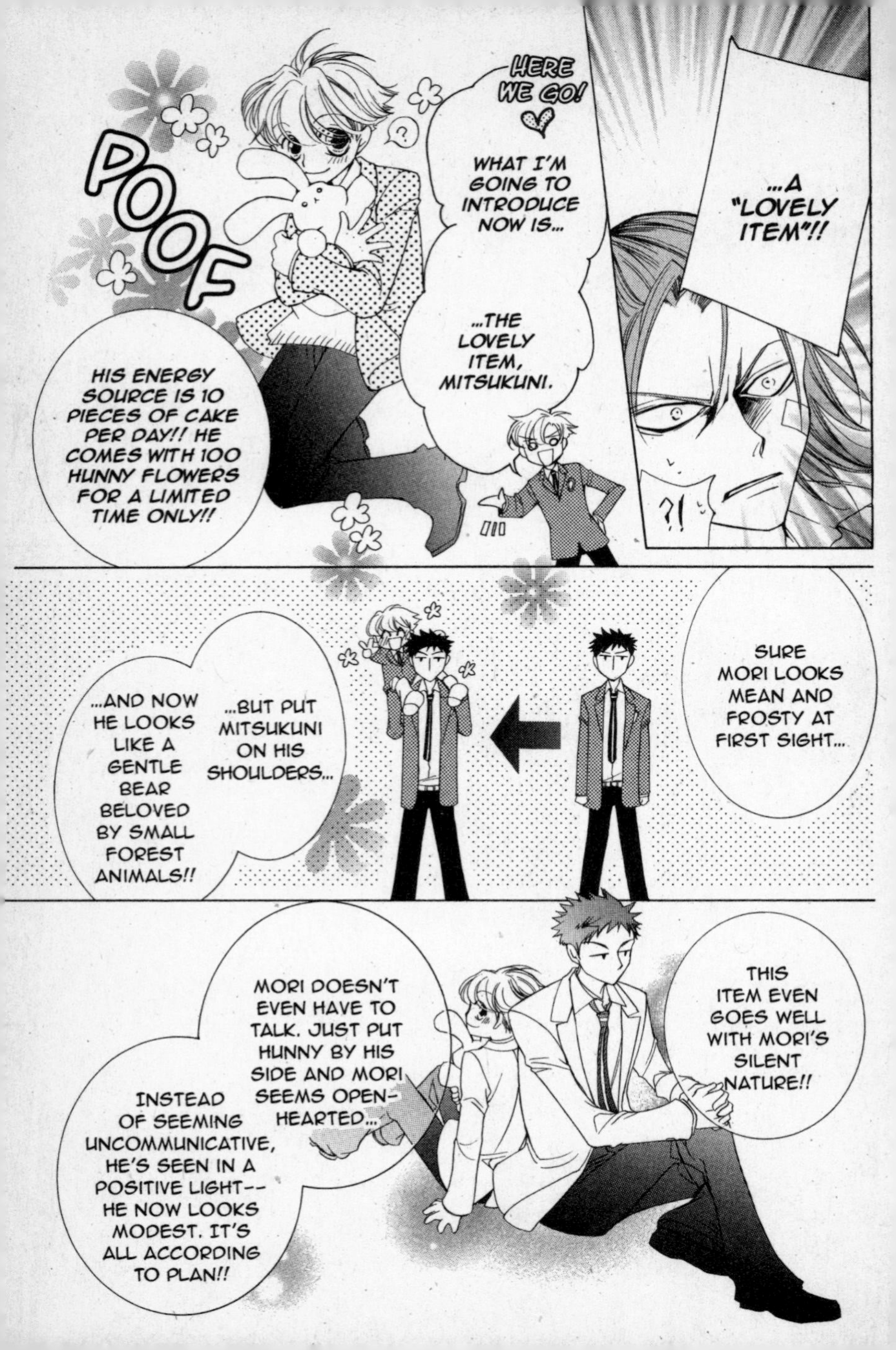
...A "LOVELY ITEM"!!
?!
HERE WE GO! ♥
WHAT I'M GOING TO INTRODUCE NOW IS...
...THE LOVELY ITEM, MITSUKUNI.
?
POOF
POOF
HIS ENERGY SOURCE IS 10 PIECES OF CAKE PER DAY!! HE COMES WITH 100 HUNNY FLOWERS FOR A LIMITED TIME ONLY!!
SURE MORI LOOKS MEAN AND FROSTY AT FIRST SIGHT...
...BUT PUT MITSUKUNI ON HIS SHOULDERS...
...AND NOW HE LOOKS LIKE A GENTLE BEAR BELOVED BY SMALL FOREST ANIMALS!!
THIS ITEM EVEN GOES WELL WITH MORI'S SILENT NATURE!!
MORI DOESN'T EVEN HAVE TO TALK. JUST PUT HUNNY BY HIS SIDE AND MORI SEEMS OPEN-HEARTED...
INSTEAD OF SEEMING UNCOMMUNICATIVE, HE'S SEEN IN A POSITIVE LIGHT-- HE NOW LOOKS MODEST. IT'S ALL ACCORDING TO PLAN!!

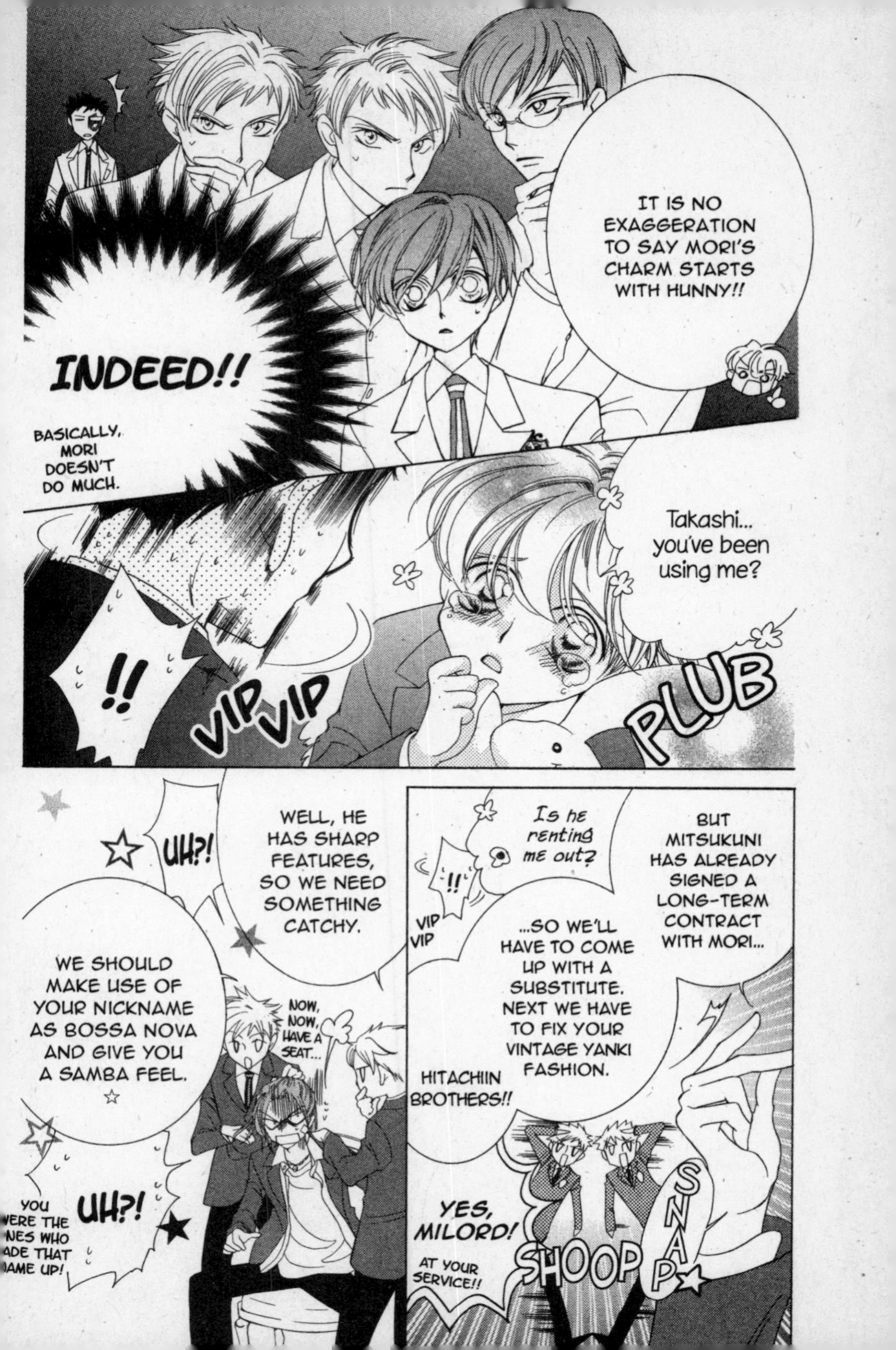
IT IS NO EXAGGERATION TO SAY MORI'S CHARM STARTS WITH HUNNY!!
INDEED!!
BASICALLY, MORI DOESN'T DO MUCH.
Takashi... you've been using me?
PLUB
!!
VIP VIP
BUT MITSUKUNI HAS ALREADY SIGNED A LONG-TERM CONTRACT WITH MORI...
Is he renting me out?
!!
VIP VIP
...SO WE'LL HAVE TO COME UP WITH A SUBSTITUTE. NEXT WE HAVE TO FIX YOUR VINTAGE YANKI FASHION.
HITACHIIN BROTHERS!!
SNAP
SHOOP
YES, MILORD!
AT YOUR SERVICE!!
WELL, HE HAS SHARP FEATURES, SO WE NEED SOMETHING CATCHY.
UH?!
WE SHOULD MAKE USE OF YOUR NICKNAME AS BOSSA NOVA AND GIVE YOU A SAMBA FEEL.
NOW, NOW, HAVE A SEAT...
UH?!
YOU ERE THE NES WHO ADE THAT AME UP!

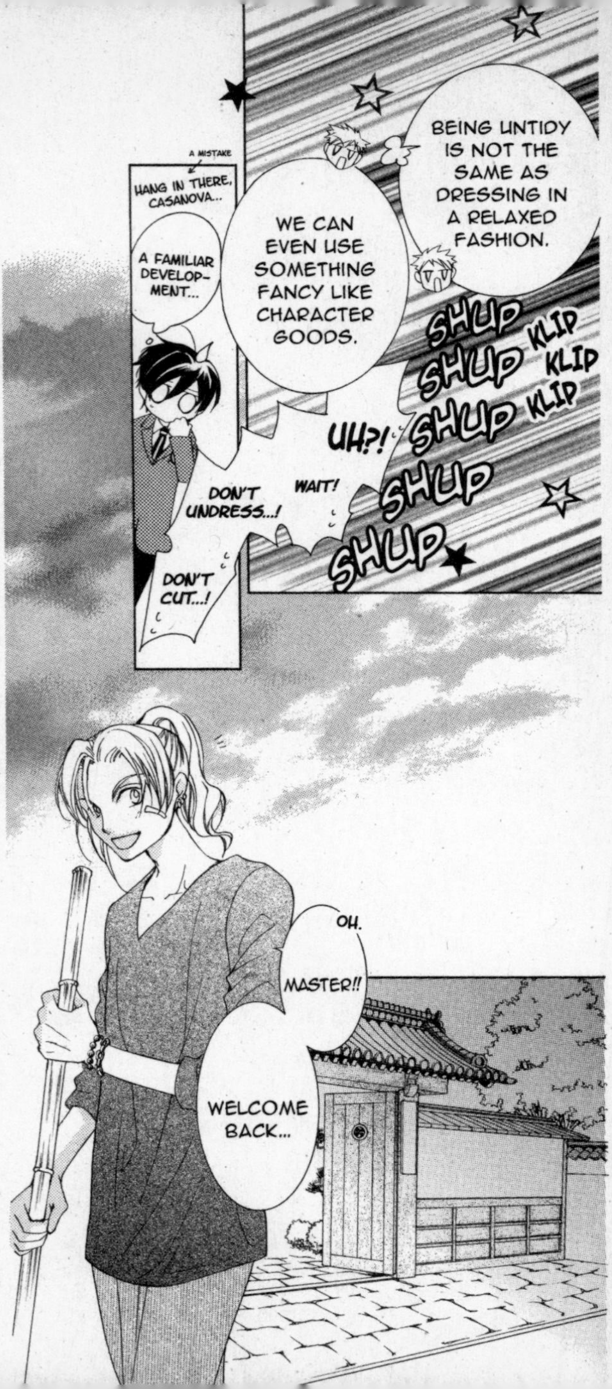
BEING UNTIDY IS NOT THE SAME AS DRESSING IN A RELAXED FASHION.
WE CAN EVEN USE SOMETHING FANCY LIKE CHARACTER GOODS.
SHUP SHUP SHUP SHUP SHUP
KLIP KLIP KLIP
UH?!
WAIT!
DON'T UNDRESS...!
DON'T CUT...!
A MISTAKE
HANG IN THERE, CASANOVA...
A FAMILIAR DEVELOPMENT...
OH.
MASTER!!
WELCOME BACK...

WELCOME BACK...

I'D LIKE TO SAY A LITTLE MORE ABOUT ME BEING A COWARD. ALL VIDEO RENTAL PLACES, PLEASE PAY ATTENTION! PLEASE DO NOT PUT HORROR MOVIES OUT ON DISPLAY EVEN WHEN THEY ARE NEW RELEASES...

IF YOU HAPPEN TO SEE A SUSPICIOUS WOMAN IN A COLD SWEAT WALKING AROUND THE SHOP, IT'S PROBABLY ME.

WHEN I ACCIDENTALLY SEE THE HORROR MOVIE PACKAGING, I RUN TO THE COMEDY SECTION AS FAST AS I CAN. THE COMEDY AND ANIME AREAS ARE MY SAFETY ZONES (BECAUSE THERE AREN'T ANY HORROR MOVIES MIXED IN THERE.)

THE OTHER DAY, I WENT TO BORROW *DENSHA OTOKO* (I'M SO INTO YAMADA IN *WHITE NIGHTS*) AND I HAPPENED TO SEE A HORROR MOVIE... I ENDED UP RENTING FOUR COMEDIES ON DVD...

BUT I DIDN'T HAVE ENOUGH TIME TO WATCH THAT MANY AT ONCE SO I JUST RETURNED THEM... SILLY ME.

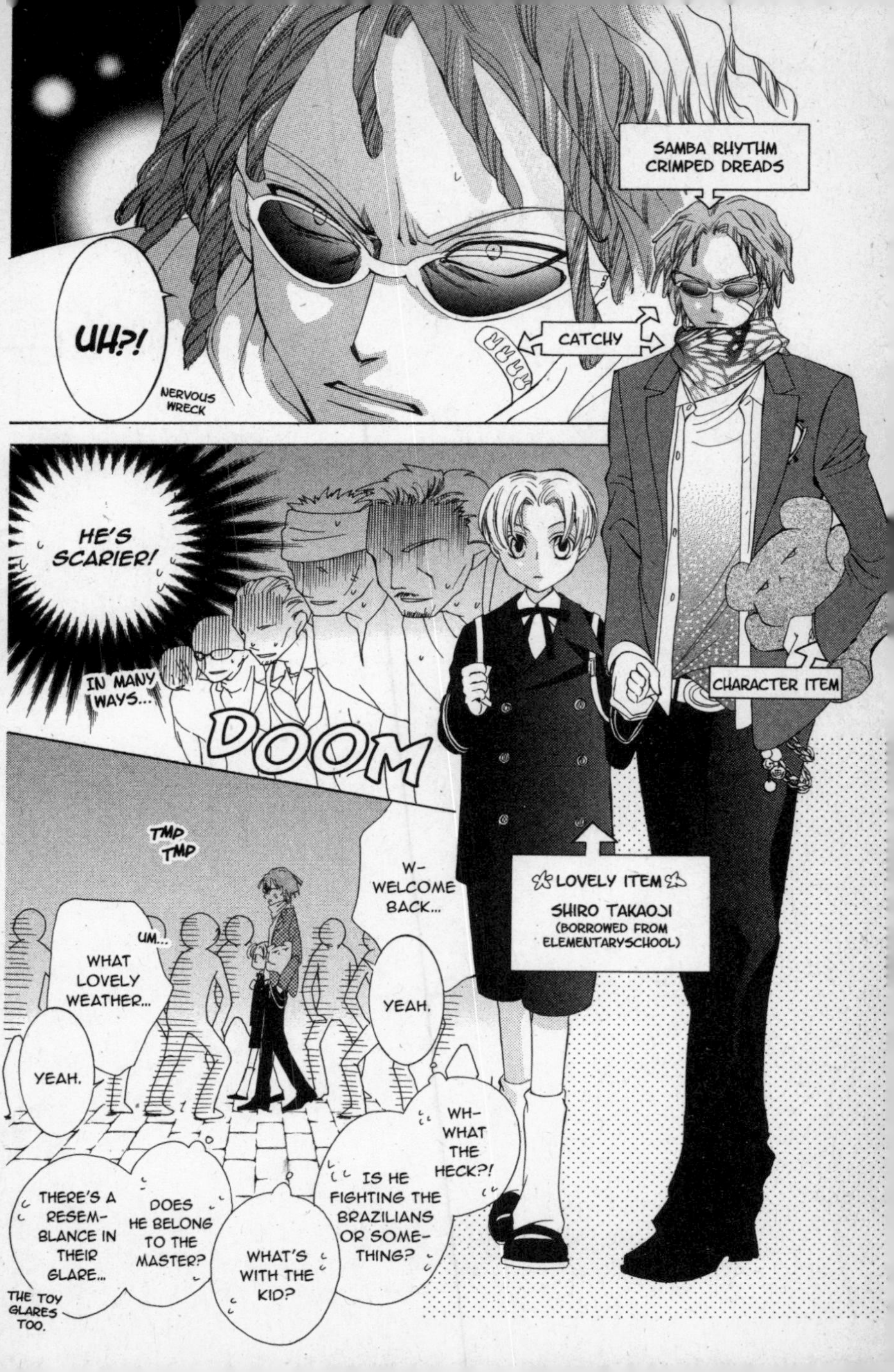
SAMBA RHYTHM CRIMPED DREADS
CATCHY
CHARACTER ITEM
LOVELY ITEM
SHIRO TAKAOJI
(BORROWED FROM ELEMENTARYSCHOOL)
UH?!
NERVOUS WRECK
HE'S SCARIER!
IN MANY WAYS...
DOOM
TMP TMP
W- WELCOME BACK...
UM...
WHAT LOVELY WEATHER...
YEAH.
YEAH.
WH- WHAT THE HECK?!
IS HE FIGHTING THE BRAZILIANS OR SOME-THING?
WHAT'S WITH THE KID?
DOES HE BELONG TO THE MASTER?
THERE'S A RESEM-BLANCE IN THEIR GLARE...
THE TOY GLARES TOO.

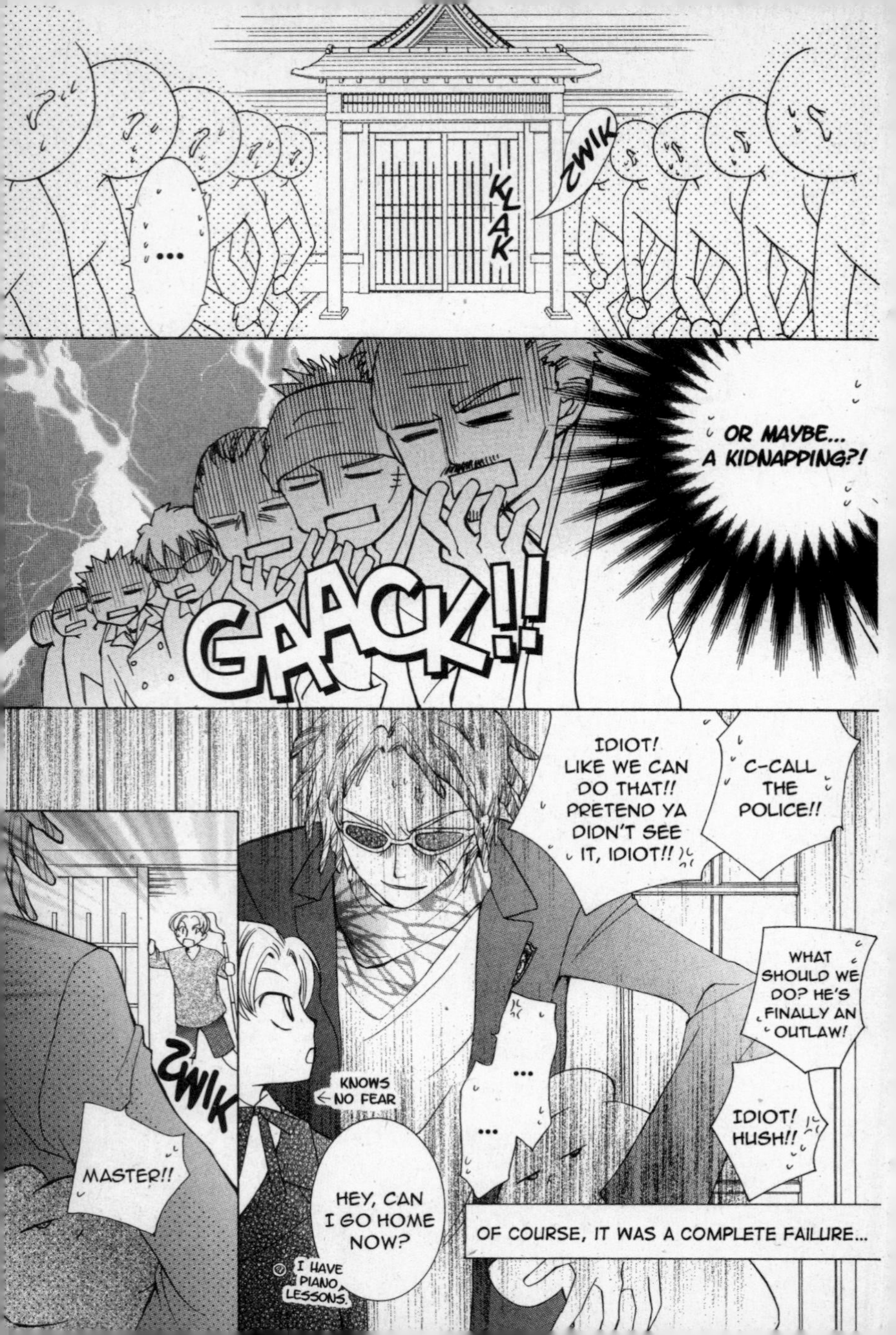
ZWIK
KLAK
...
OR MAYBE... A KIDNAPPING?!
GAACK!!
C-CALL THE POLICE!!
IDIOT! LIKE WE CAN DO THAT!! PRETEND YA DIDN'T SEE IT, IDIOT!!
WHAT SHOULD WE DO? HE'S FINALLY AN OUTLAW!
IDIOT! HUSH!!
...
...
OF COURSE, IT WAS A COMPLETE FAILURE...
KNOWS ← NO FEAR
HEY, CAN I GO HOME NOW?
I HAVE PIANO LESSONS.
ZWIK
MASTER!!

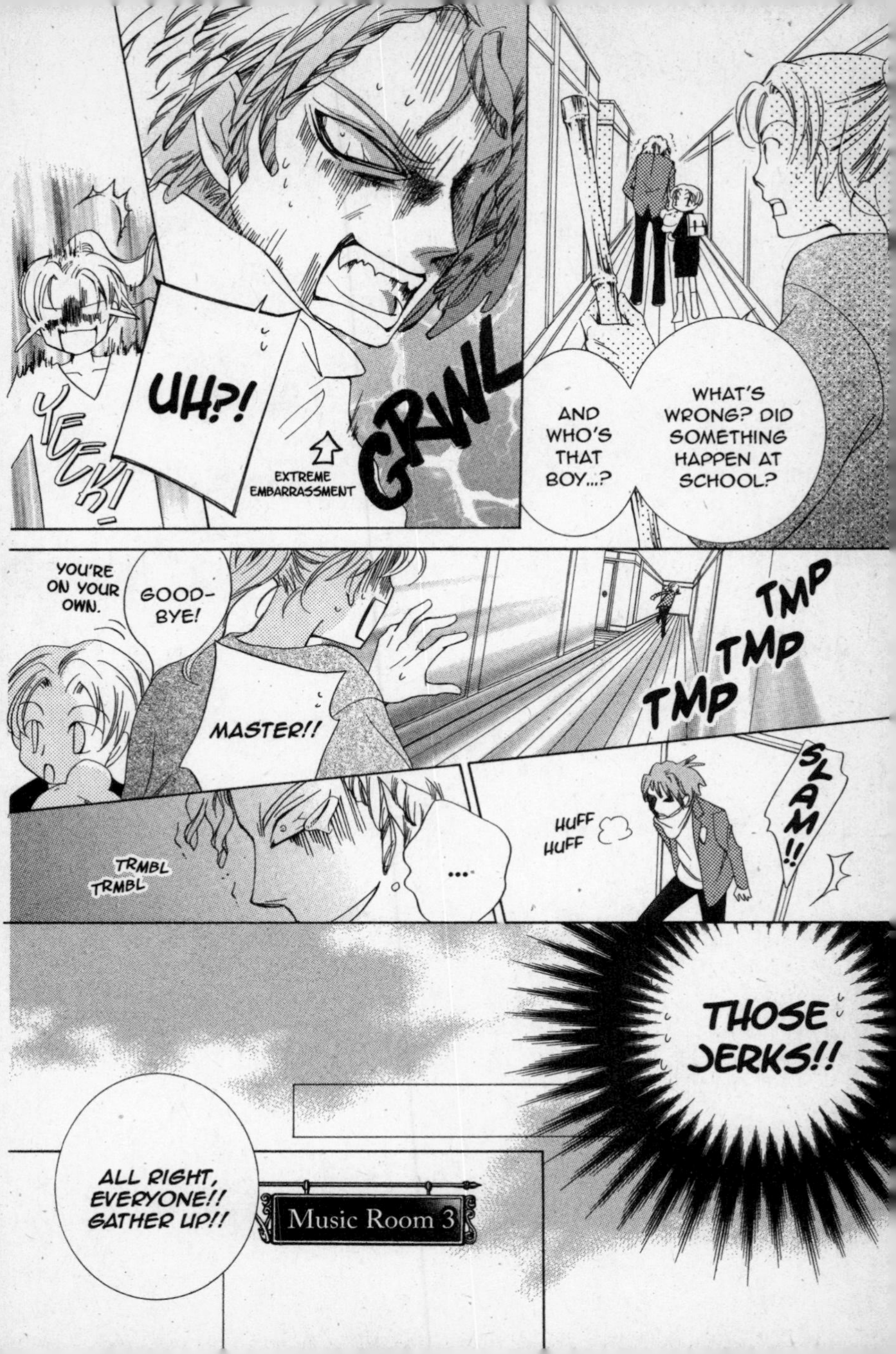
WHAT'S WRONG? DID SOMETHING HAPPEN AT SCHOOL?
AND WHO'S THAT BOY...?
GRWL
UH?!
EXTREME EMBARRASSMENT
YEEEK!
TMP TMP TMP
GOOD-BYE!
YOU'RE ON YOUR OWN.
MASTER!!
SLAM!!
HUFF HUFF
...
TRMBL TRMBL
THOSE JERKS!!
Music Room 3
ALL RIGHT, EVERYONE!! GATHER UP!!

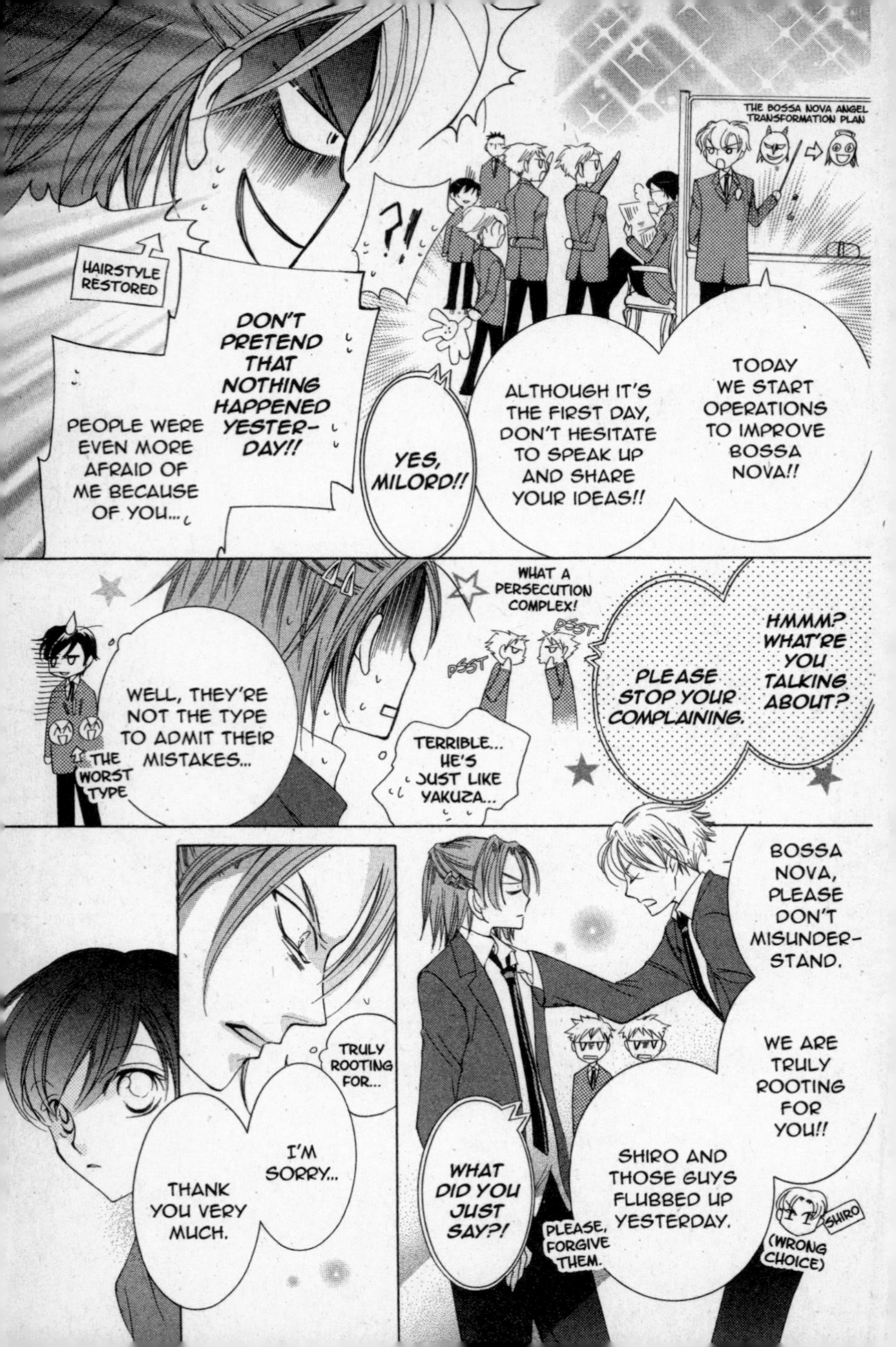
THE BOSSA NOVA ANGEL TRANSFORMATION PLAN
TODAY WE START OPERATIONS TO IMPROVE BOSSA NOVA!!
ALTHOUGH IT'S THE FIRST DAY, DON'T HESITATE TO SPEAK UP AND SHARE YOUR IDEAS!!
YES, MILORD!!
?!
DON'T PRETEND THAT NOTHING HAPPENED YESTERDAY!!
PEOPLE WERE EVEN MORE AFRAID OF ME BECAUSE OF YOU...
HAIRSTYLE RESTORED
HMMM? WHAT'RE YOU TALKING ABOUT?
PLEASE STOP YOUR COMPLAINING.
WHAT A PERSECUTION COMPLEX!
PSST
PSST
TERRIBLE... HE'S JUST LIKE YAKUZA...
WELL, THEY'RE NOT THE TYPE TO ADMIT THEIR MISTAKES...
THE WORST TYPE
BOSSA NOVA, PLEASE DON'T MISUNDERSTAND.
WE ARE TRULY ROOTING FOR YOU!!
SHIRO AND THOSE GUYS FLUBBED UP YESTERDAY.
SHIRO
(WRONG CHOICE)
PLEASE, FORGIVE THEM.
WHAT DID YOU JUST SAY?!
TRULY ROOTING FOR...
I'M SORRY...
THANK YOU VERY MUCH.

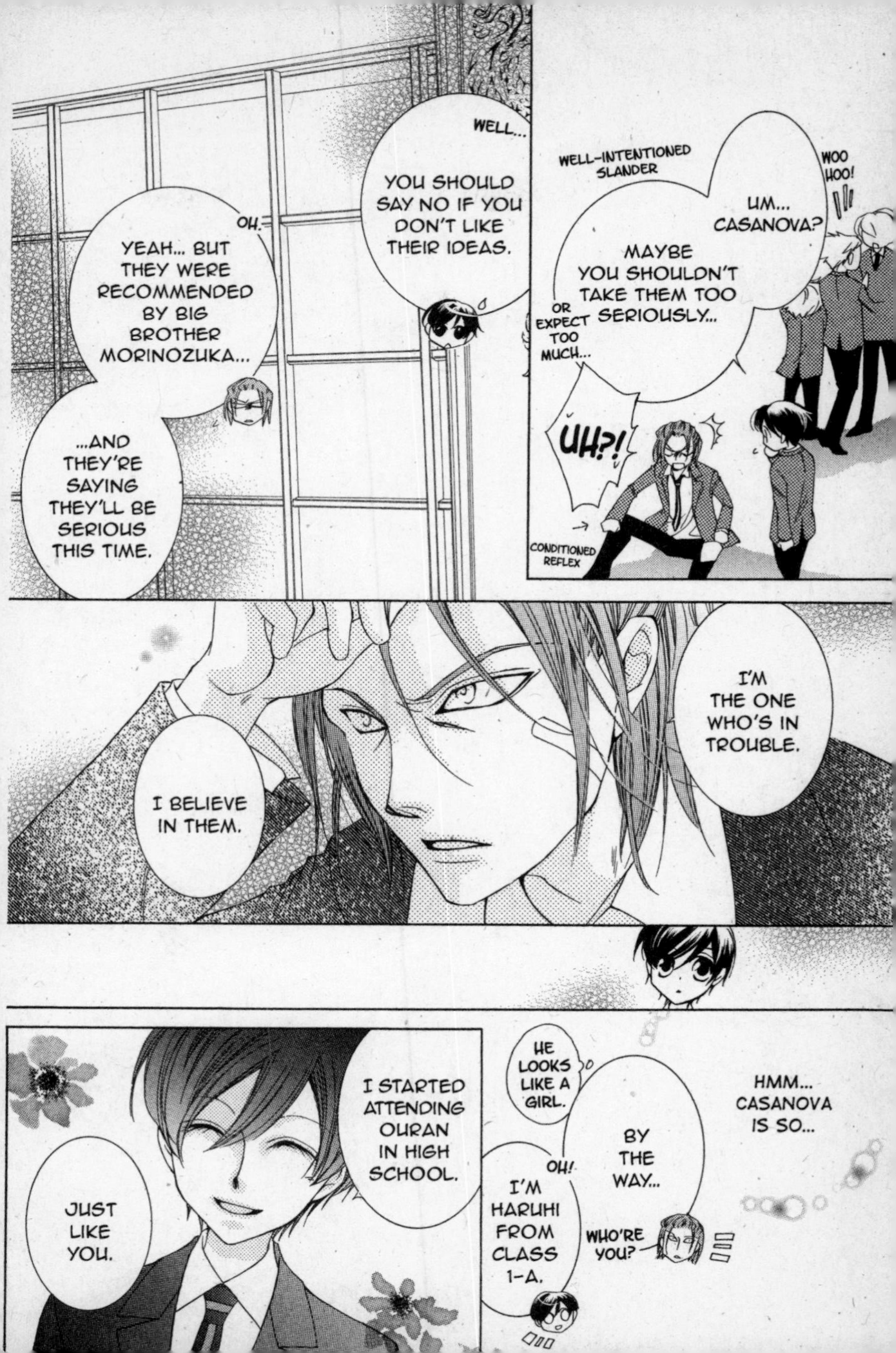
WOO HOO!
WELL-INTENTIONED SLANDER
UM... CASANOVA?
MAYBE YOU SHOULDN'T TAKE THEM TOO SERIOUSLY...
OR EXPECT TOO MUCH...
UH?!
CONDITIONED REFLEX
WELL...
YOU SHOULD SAY NO IF YOU DON'T LIKE THEIR IDEAS.
OH.
YEAH... BUT THEY WERE RECOMMENDED BY BIG BROTHER MORINOZUKA...
...AND THEY'RE SAYING THEY'LL BE SERIOUS THIS TIME.
I'M THE ONE WHO'S IN TROUBLE.
I BELIEVE IN THEM.
HMM... CASANOVA IS SO...
BY THE WAY...
HE LOOKS LIKE A GIRL.
WHO'RE YOU?
OH!
I'M HARUHI FROM CLASS 1-A.
I STARTED ATTENDING OURAN IN HIGH SCHOOL.
JUST LIKE YOU.

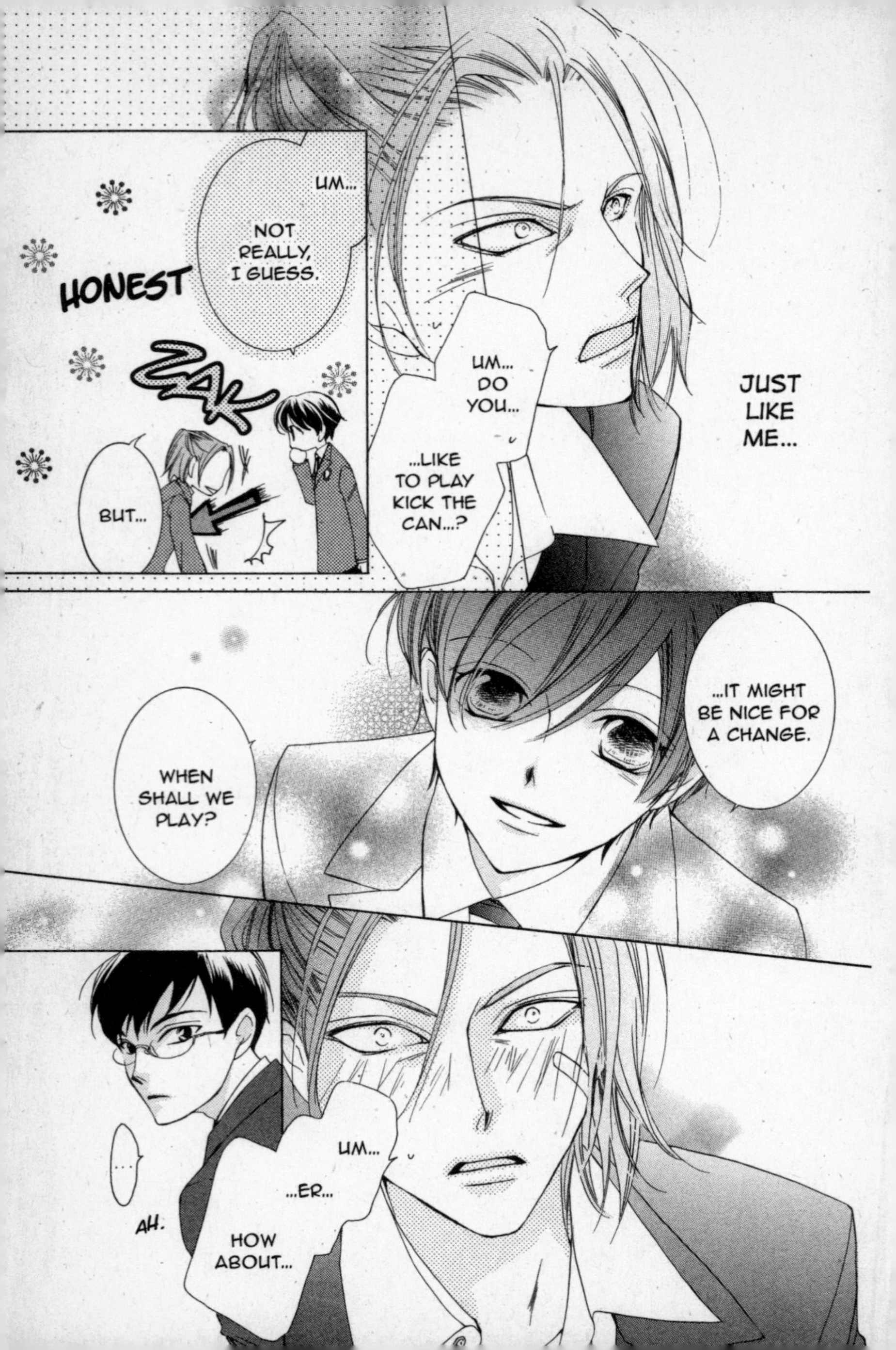
JUST LIKE ME...
UM... DO YOU...
...LIKE TO PLAY KICK THE CAN...?
UM...
NOT REALLY, I GUESS.
HONEST
ZAK
BUT...
...IT MIGHT BE NICE FOR A CHANGE.
WHEN SHALL WE PLAY?
UM...
...ER...
HOW ABOUT...
...
AH.

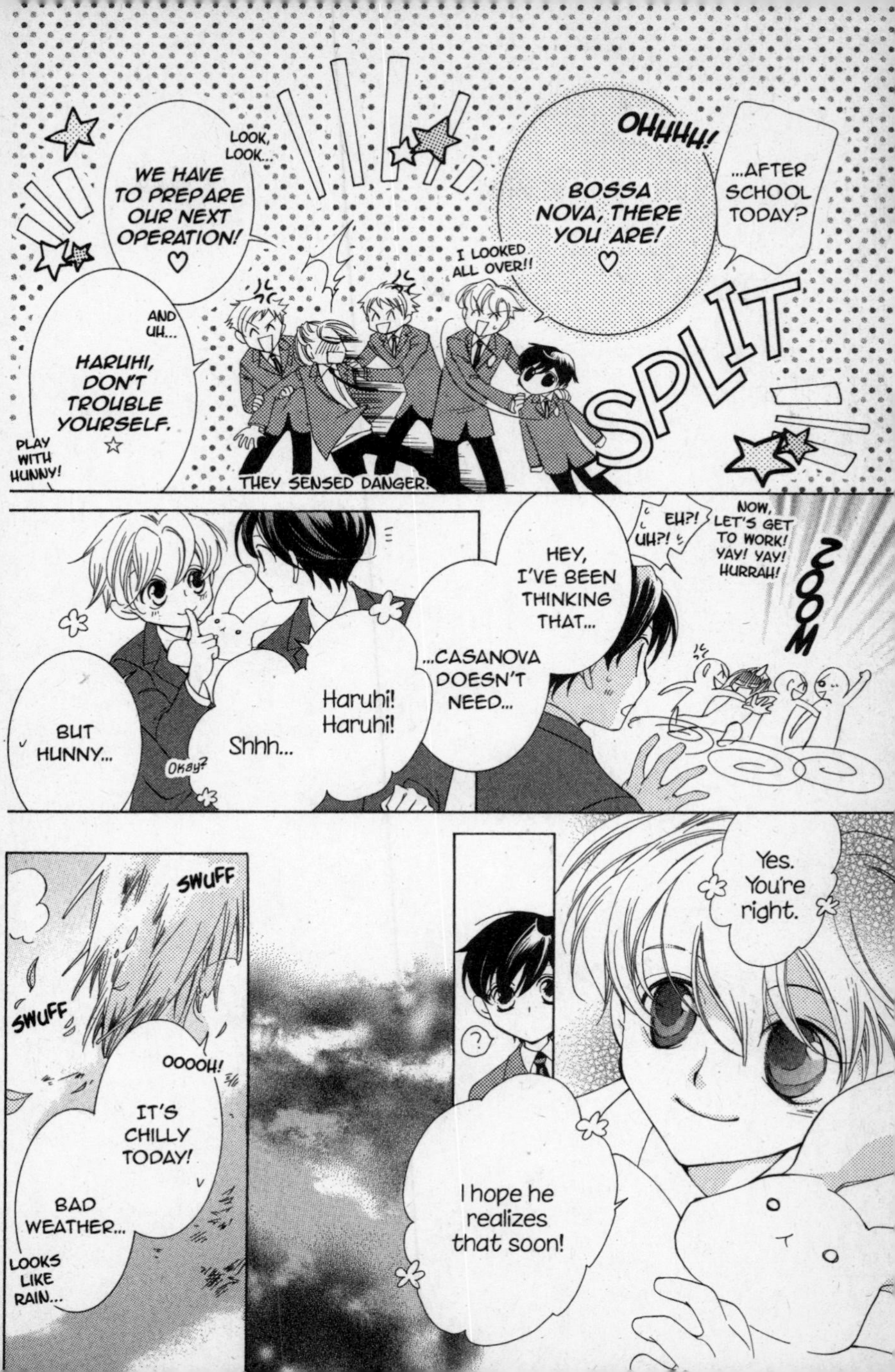
...AFTER SCHOOL TODAY?
OHHHH!
BOSSA NOVA, THERE YOU ARE! ♡
I LOOKED ALL OVER!!
SPLIT
LOOK, LOOK...
WE HAVE TO PREPARE OUR NEXT OPERATION! ♡
AND UH...
HARUHI, DON'T TROUBLE YOURSELF. ☆
PLAY WITH HUNNY!
THEY SENSED DANGER.
NOW, LET'S GET TO WORK! YAY! YAY! HURRAH!
ZOOM
EH?!
UH?!
HEY, I'VE BEEN THINKING THAT...
...CASANOVA DOESN'T NEED...
Haruhi! Haruhi!
Shhh...
Okay?
BUT HUNNY...
Yes. You're right.
I hope he realizes that soon!
SWUFF
SWUFF
OOOOH!
IT'S CHILLY TODAY!
BAD WEATHER...
LOOKS LIKE RAIN...

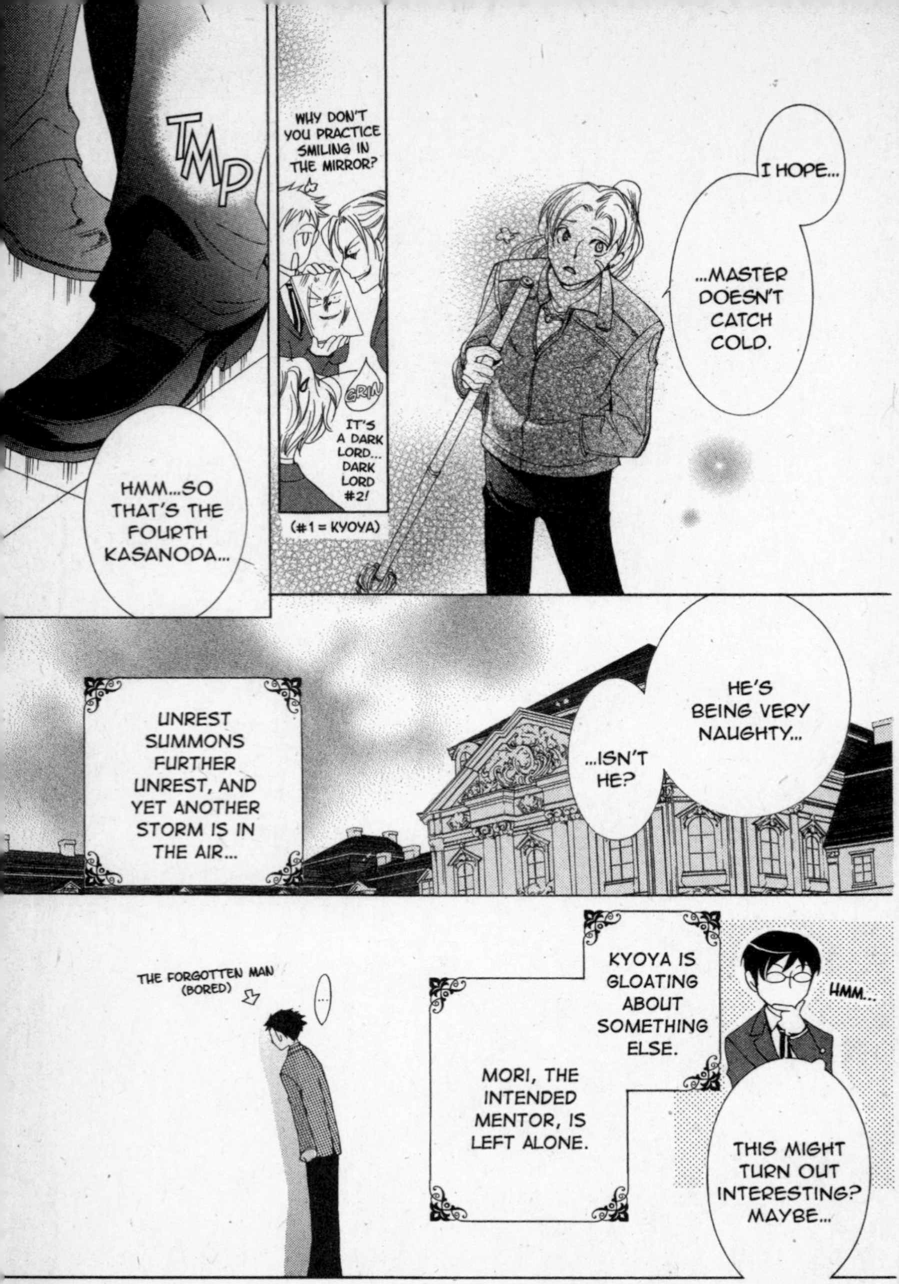
I HOPE...
...MASTER DOESN'T CATCH COLD.
WHY DON'T YOU PRACTICE SMILING IN THE MIRROR?
GRIN
IT'S A DARK LORD... DARK LORD #2!
(#1 = KYOYA)
TMP
HMM...SO THAT'S THE FOURTH KASANODA...
HE'S BEING VERY NAUGHTY...
...ISN'T HE?
UNREST SUMMONS FURTHER UNREST, AND YET ANOTHER STORM IS IN THE AIR...
HMM...
THIS MIGHT TURN OUT INTERESTING? MAYBE...
KYOYA IS GLOATING ABOUT SOMETHING ELSE.
MORI, THE INTENDED MENTOR, IS LEFT ALONE.
THE FORGOTTEN MAN (BORED)
...

✿SINGAPORE VERSION✿ ➜

YOU MAY BE ABLE TO UNDERSTAND SOME OF THE TEXT. NOTICE THAT THE TITLE IS "櫻蘭高校♂公關部."

↑
LOOK! (LAUGH)

THE AUTHOR'S NAME IS "葉鳥 鏃子." I ASKED FOR MY NAME TO BE WRITTEN THIS WAY BECAUSE THE "BIS" MEANS "RIVET." ✩ I CHOSE THAT MYSELF.

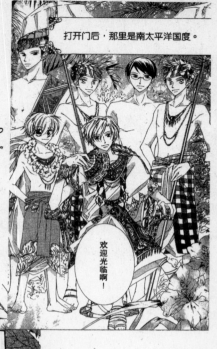

打开门后，那里是南太平洋国度。
欢迎光临啊！

บทเรียนที่ 2 ในการเป็นสุภาพบุรุษ
ต้องเป็นผู้ที่มีความคิดเป็นของตัวเอง
เรา จะทำการกล่าวถึงสุซุชิมะกับคุณหนูคาสึงะ!!
ท่านผู้มีเกียรติทุกท่าน
ต่อไป เดี๋ยวนะ!! รายงานเรื่องของสุซุชิมะมาซิ!!
และได้รับการหมั้นหมายโดยผู้ใหญ่ทั้งสองฝ่าย!!
ทั้งสองคนเป็นเพื่อนกันมาตั้งแต่เด็ก
ครับ
ก่อนอื่นพี่น้องฮิตาจิอิง!!
แล้วเรื่องซ้อมเต้นล่ะ..

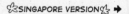

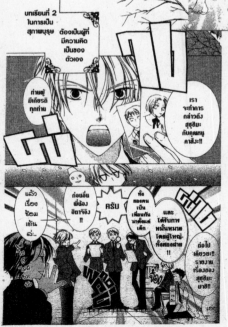

➜ ✿THAI VERSION✿

THE REVERSED PAGES ARE HORRIFYING! MY LOW-QUALITY SKETCHES GET EVEN WORSE...

THIS IS ONE OF THE BETTER ONES...YEAH.

THE EFFECTS LETTERING IN THAI ARE SO CUTE...!!!

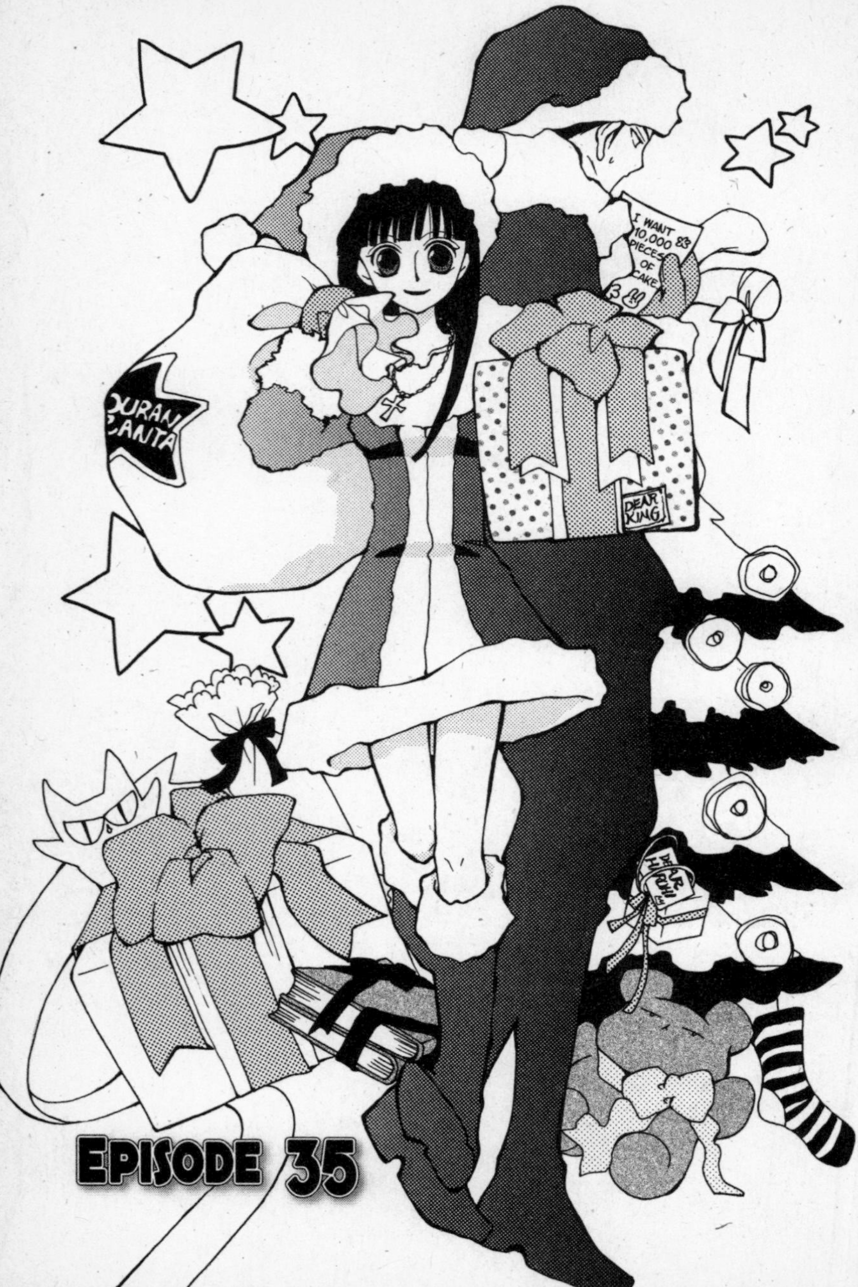
I WANT 10,000 PIECES OF CAKE
OURAN SANTA
DEAR KING
DEAR HARUHI
EPISODE 35

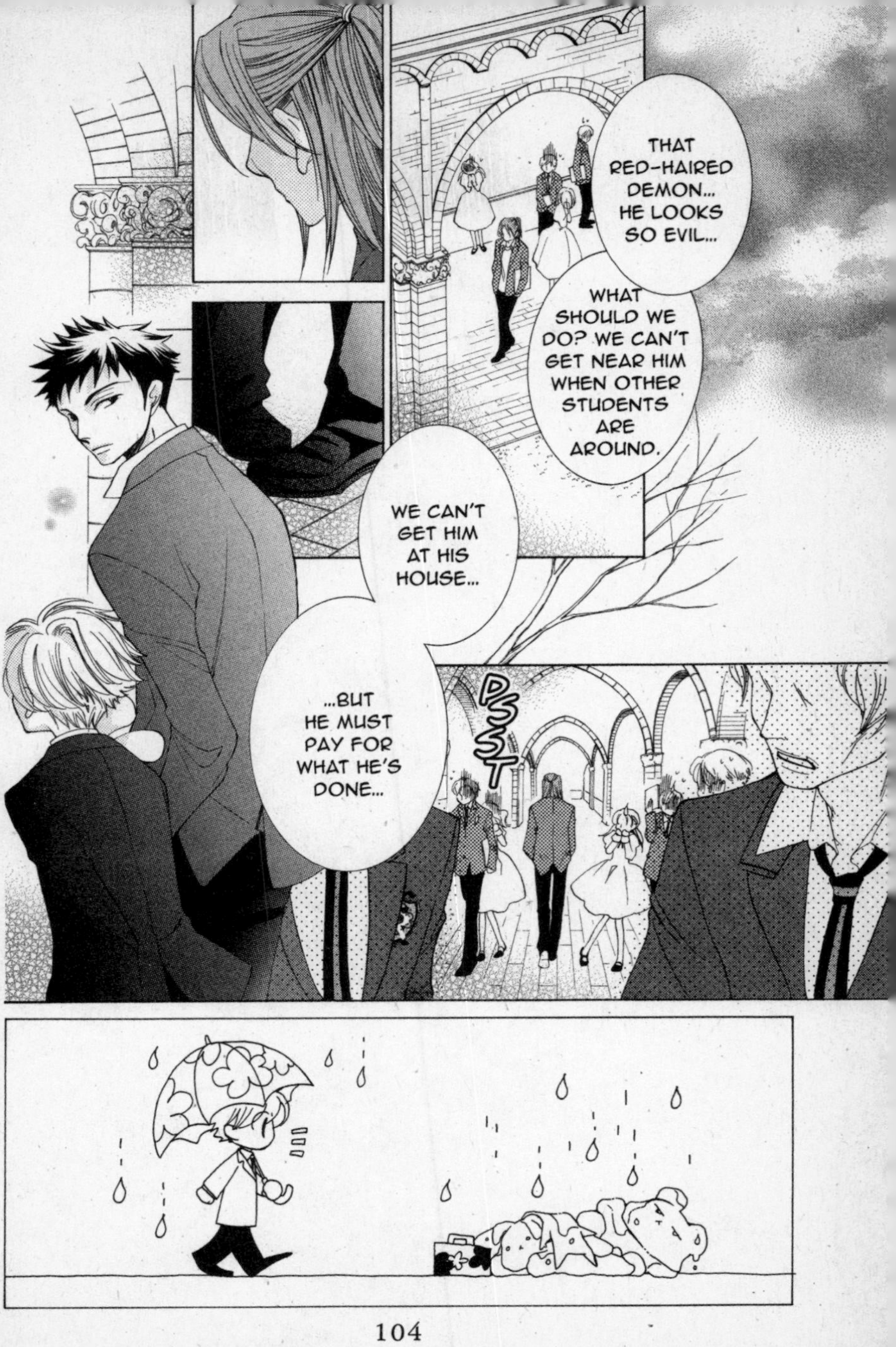
THAT RED-HAIRED DEMON... HE LOOKS SO EVIL...
WHAT SHOULD WE DO? WE CAN'T GET NEAR HIM WHEN OTHER STUDENTS ARE AROUND.
WE CAN'T GET HIM AT HIS HOUSE...
...BUT HE MUST PAY FOR WHAT HE'S DONE...
PSST

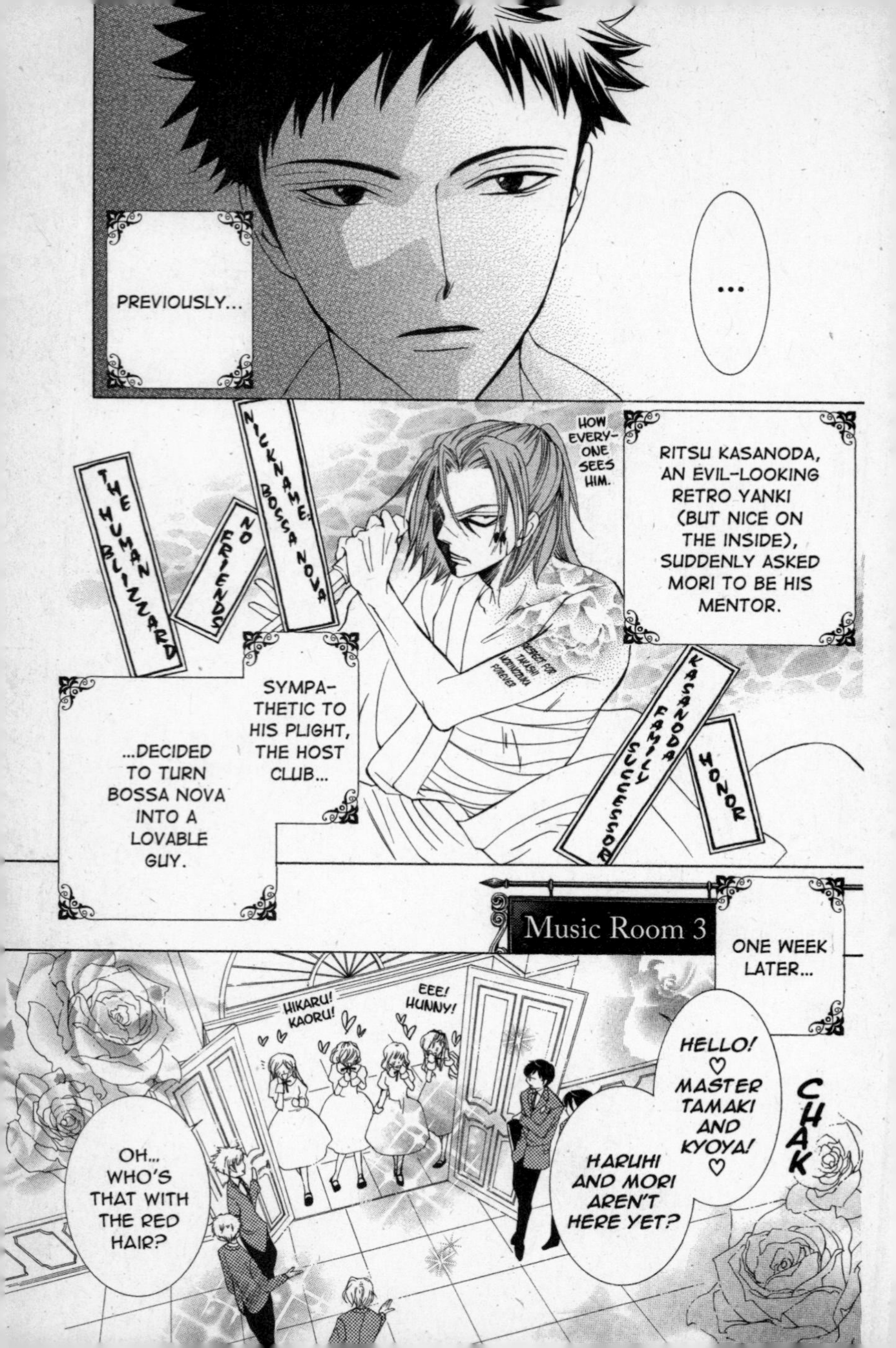
...
PREVIOUSLY...
RITSU KASANODA, AN EVIL-LOOKING RETRO YANKI (BUT NICE ON THE INSIDE), SUDDENLY ASKED MORI TO BE HIS MENTOR.
HOW EVERY-ONE SEES HIM.
HONOR
KASANODA FAMILY SUCCESSOR
RESPECT FOR TAKASHI MORINOZUKA FOREVER
NICKNAME: BOSSA NOVA
NO FRIENDS
THE HUMAN BLIZZARD
SYMPA-THETIC TO HIS PLIGHT, THE HOST CLUB...
...DECIDED TO TURN BOSSA NOVA INTO A LOVABLE GUY.
ONE WEEK LATER...
Music Room 3
CHAK
HELLO! ♡ MASTER TAMAKI AND KYOYA! ♡
EEE! HUNNY!
HIKARU! KAORU!
HARUHI AND MORI AREN'T HERE YET?
OH... WHO'S THAT WITH THE RED HAIR?

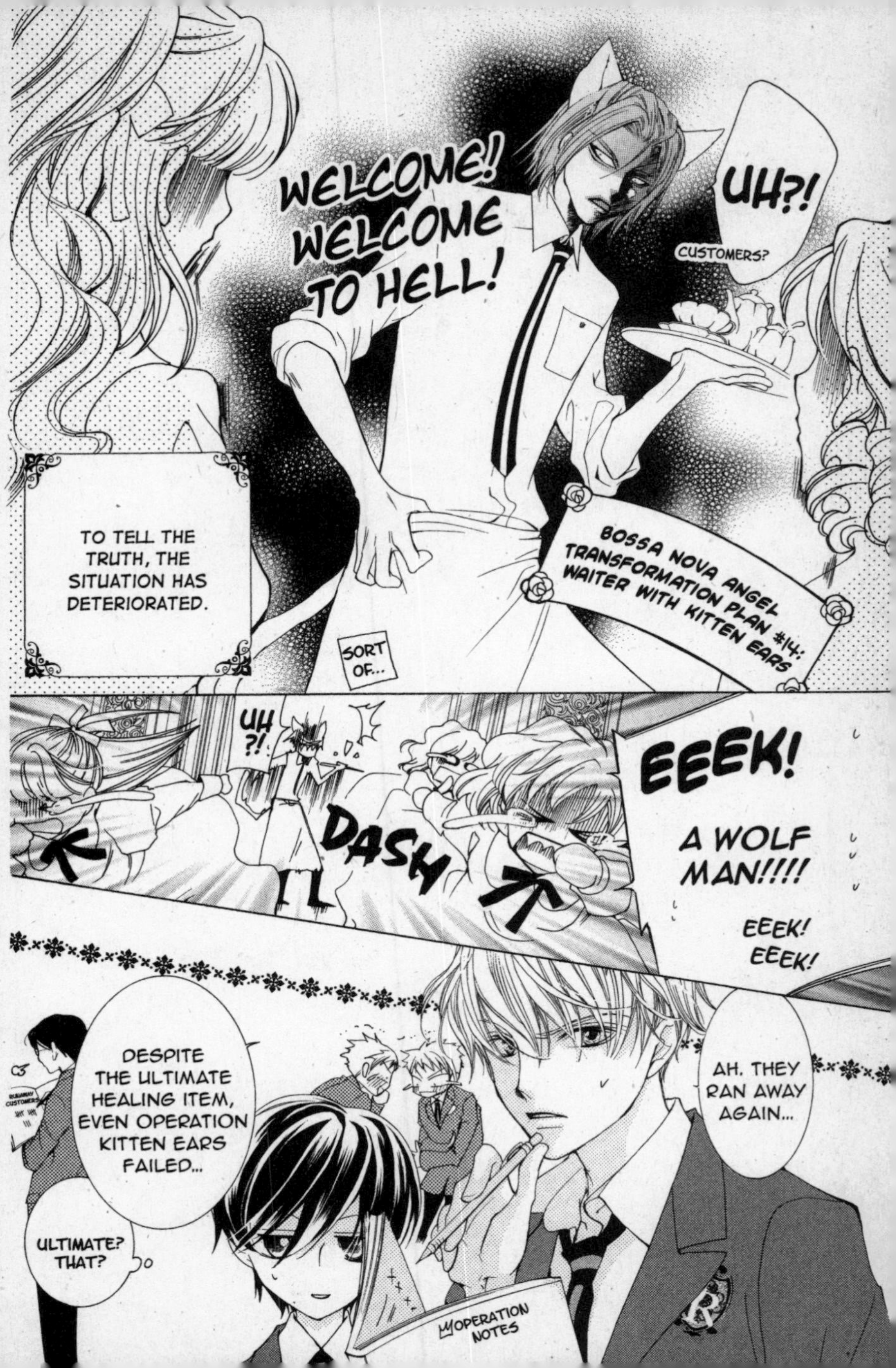
UH?!
CUSTOMERS?
WELCOME! WELCOME TO HELL!
BOSSA NOVA ANGEL TRANSFORMATION PLAN #14: WAITER WITH KITTEN EARS
SORT OF...
TO TELL THE TRUTH, THE SITUATION HAS DETERIORATED.
EEEK!
A WOLF MAN!!!!
EEEK! EEEK!
DASH
UH ?!
AH. THEY RAN AWAY AGAIN...
DESPITE THE ULTIMATE HEALING ITEM, EVEN OPERATION KITTEN EARS FAILED...
ULTIMATE? THAT?
OPERATION NOTES

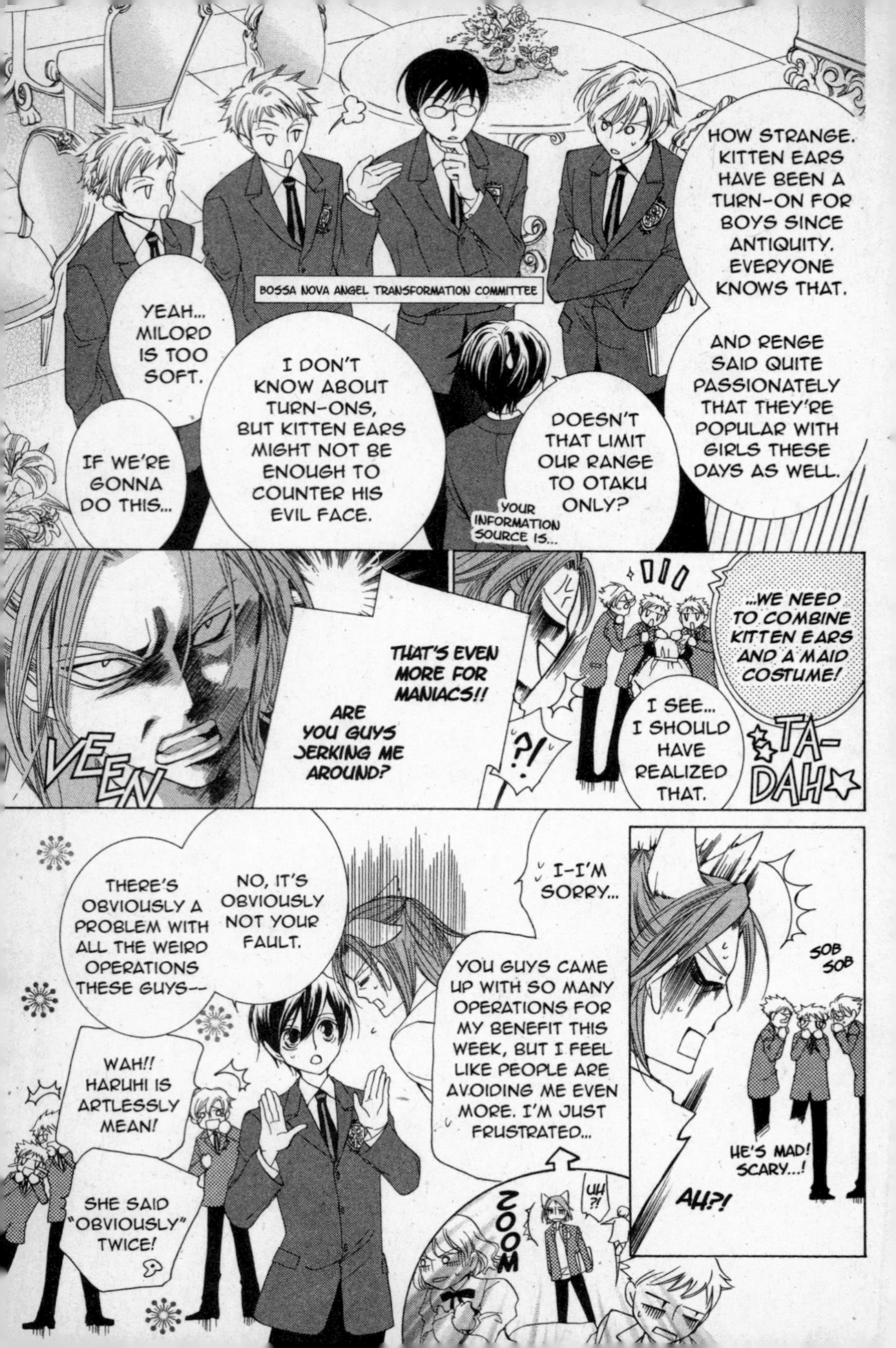
BOSSA NOVA ANGEL TRANSFORMATION COMMITTEE
HOW STRANGE. KITTEN EARS HAVE BEEN A TURN-ON FOR BOYS SINCE ANTIQUITY. EVERYONE KNOWS THAT.
AND RENGE SAID QUITE PASSIONATELY THAT THEY'RE POPULAR WITH GIRLS THESE DAYS AS WELL.
DOESN'T THAT LIMIT OUR RANGE TO OTAKU ONLY?
YOUR INFORMATION SOURCE IS...
I DON'T KNOW ABOUT TURN-ONS, BUT KITTEN EARS MIGHT NOT BE ENOUGH TO COUNTER HIS EVIL FACE.
YEAH... MILORD IS TOO SOFT.
IF WE'RE GONNA DO THIS...
...WE NEED TO COMBINE KITTEN EARS AND A MAID COSTUME!
TA-DAH
I SEE... I SHOULD HAVE REALIZED THAT.
?!
THAT'S EVEN MORE FOR MANIACS!!
ARE YOU GUYS JERKING ME AROUND?
VEEN
SOB SOB
HE'S MAD! SCARY...!
AH?!
I-I'M SORRY...
YOU GUYS CAME UP WITH SO MANY OPERATIONS FOR MY BENEFIT THIS WEEK, BUT I FEEL LIKE PEOPLE ARE AVOIDING ME EVEN MORE. I'M JUST FRUSTRATED...
UH ?!
ZOOM
NO, IT'S OBVIOUSLY NOT YOUR FAULT.
THERE'S OBVIOUSLY A PROBLEM WITH ALL THE WEIRD OPERATIONS THESE GUYS--
WAH!! HARUHI IS ARTLESSLY MEAN!
SHE SAID "OBVIOUSLY" TWICE!

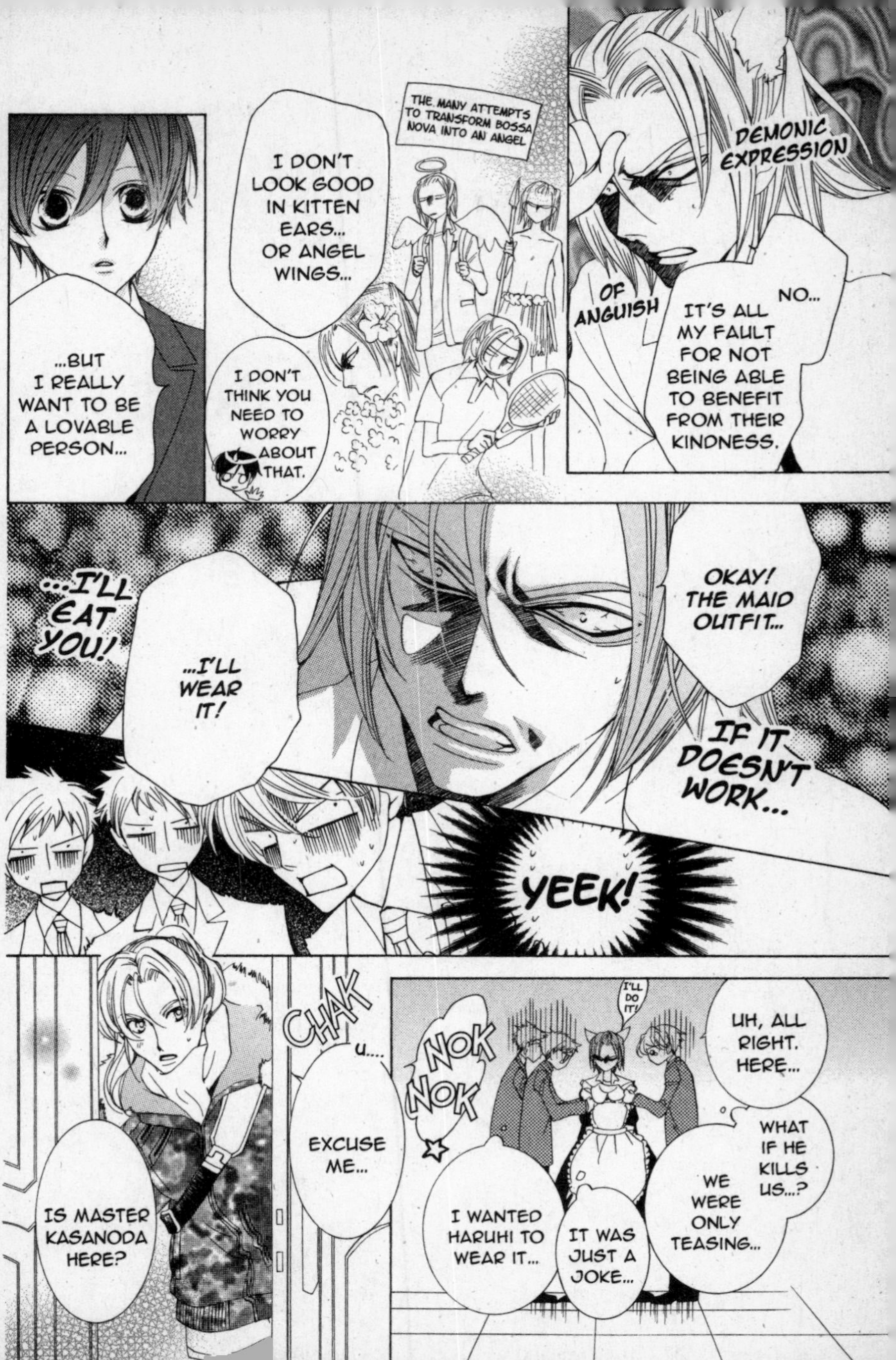

NO...
IT'S ALL MY FAULT FOR NOT BEING ABLE TO BENEFIT FROM THEIR KINDNESS.
DEMONIC EXPRESSION
OF ANGUISH
THE MANY ATTEMPTS TO TRANSFORM BOSSA NOVA INTO AN ANGEL
I DON'T LOOK GOOD IN KITTEN EARS... OR ANGEL WINGS...
I DON'T THINK YOU NEED TO WORRY ABOUT THAT.
...BUT I REALLY WANT TO BE A LOVABLE PERSON...
OKAY! THE MAID OUTFIT...
IF IT DOESN'T WORK...
...I'LL WEAR IT!
...I'LL EAT YOU!
YEEK!
UH, ALL RIGHT. HERE...
I'LL DO IT!
WHAT IF HE KILLS US...?
WE WERE ONLY TEASING...
IT WAS JUST A JOKE...
I WANTED HARUHI TO WEAR IT...
NOK NOK
CHAK
U...
EXCUSE ME...
IS MASTER KASANODA HERE?

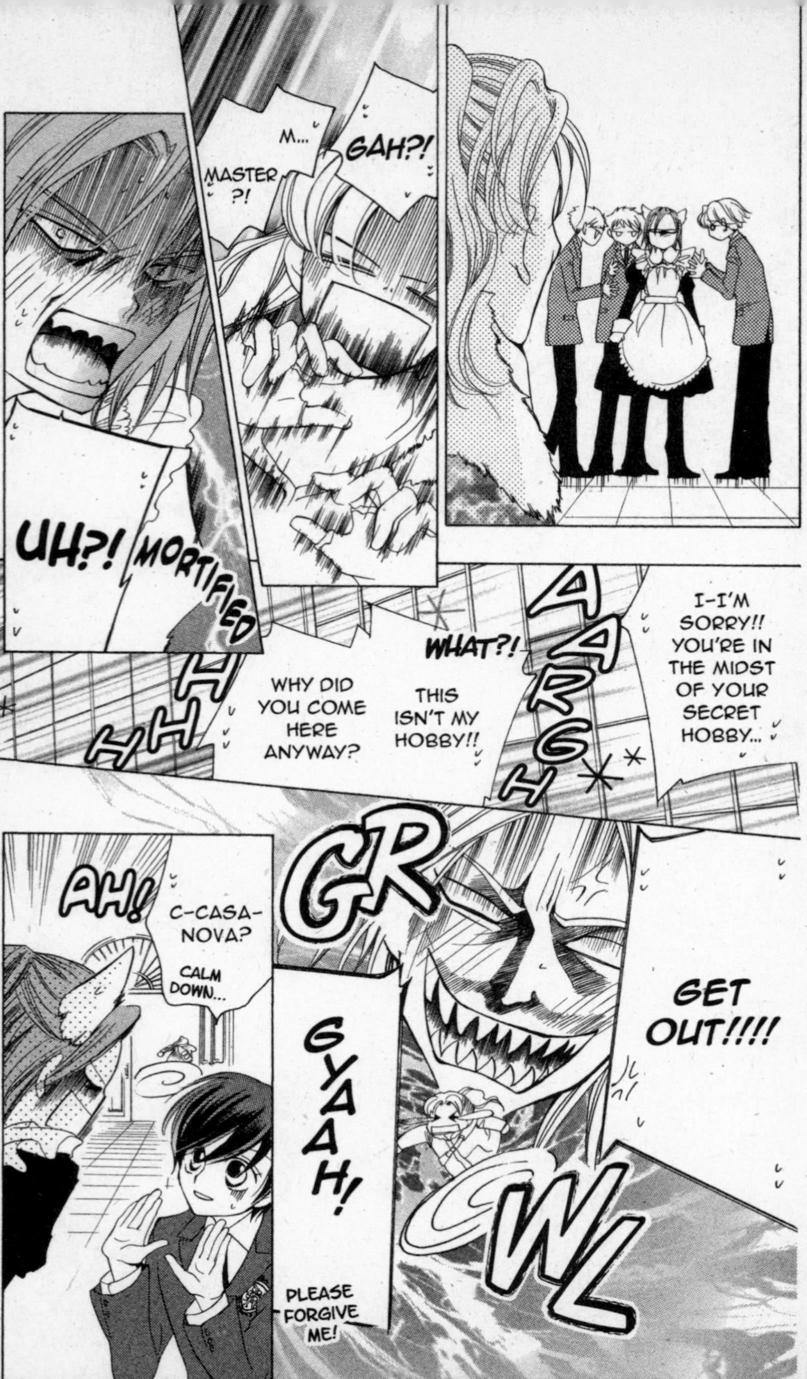
GAH?!
M... MASTER?!
UH?!
MORTIFIED
I-I'M SORRY!! YOU'RE IN THE MIDST OF YOUR SECRET HOBBY...
AARGH
WHAT?!
THIS ISN'T MY HOBBY!!
WHY DID YOU COME HERE ANYWAY?
HHHH
GR
GET OUT!!!!
GYAAH!
WL
PLEASE FORGIVE ME!
AH!
C-CASA-NOVA?
CALM DOWN...

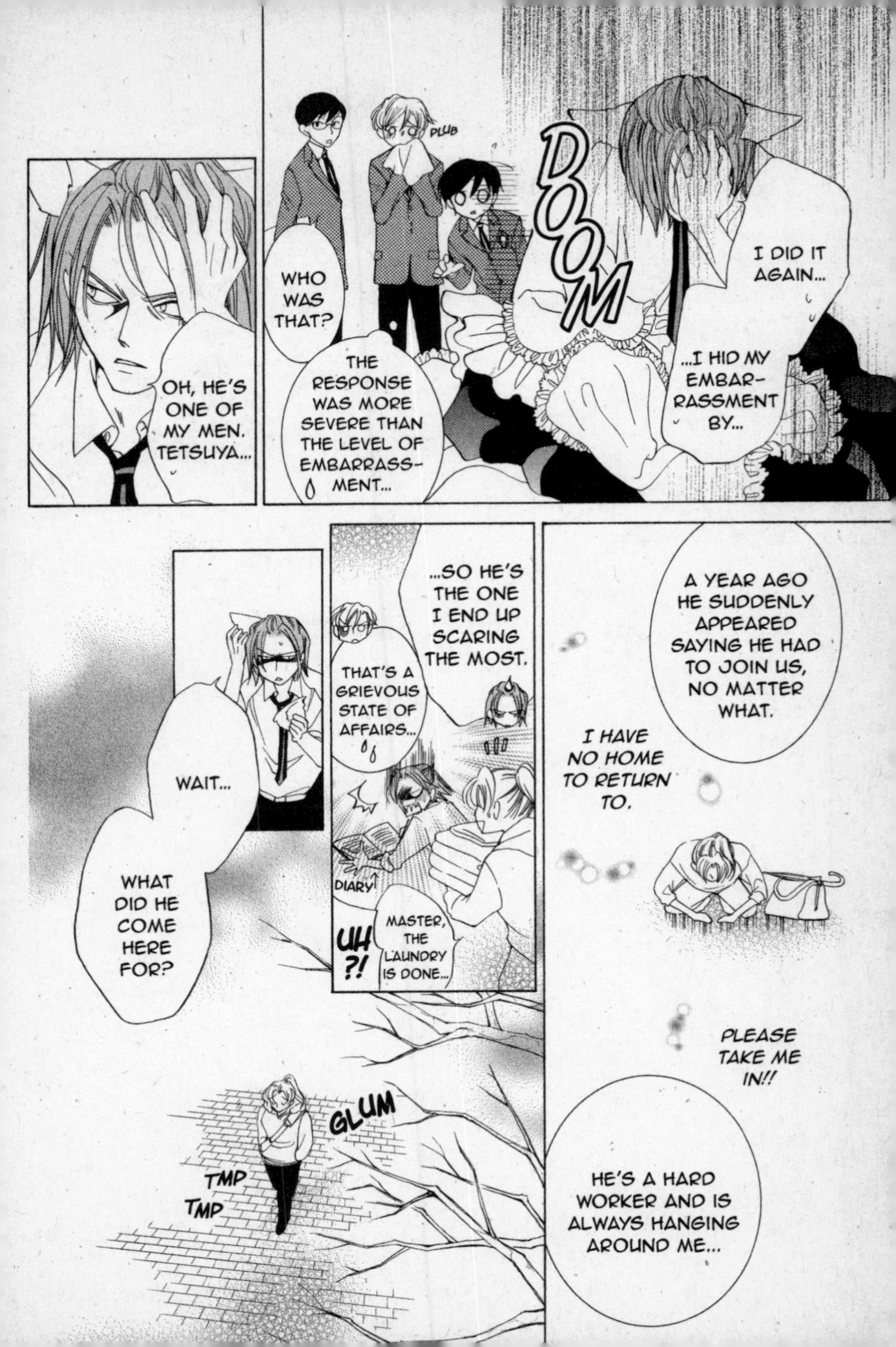
DOOM
I DID IT AGAIN...
...I HID MY EMBARRASSMENT BY...
PLUB
WHO WAS THAT?
THE RESPONSE WAS MORE SEVERE THAN THE LEVEL OF EMBARRASSMENT...
OH, HE'S ONE OF MY MEN. TETSUYA...
A YEAR AGO HE SUDDENLY APPEARED SAYING HE HAD TO JOIN US, NO MATTER WHAT.
I HAVE NO HOME TO RETURN TO.
PLEASE TAKE ME IN!!
HE'S A HARD WORKER AND IS ALWAYS HANGING AROUND ME...
...SO HE'S THE ONE I END UP SCARING THE MOST.
THAT'S A GRIEVOUS STATE OF AFFAIRS...
DIARY
UH?!
MASTER, THE LAUNDRY IS DONE...
WAIT...
WHAT DID HE COME HERE FOR?
GLUM
TMP
TMP

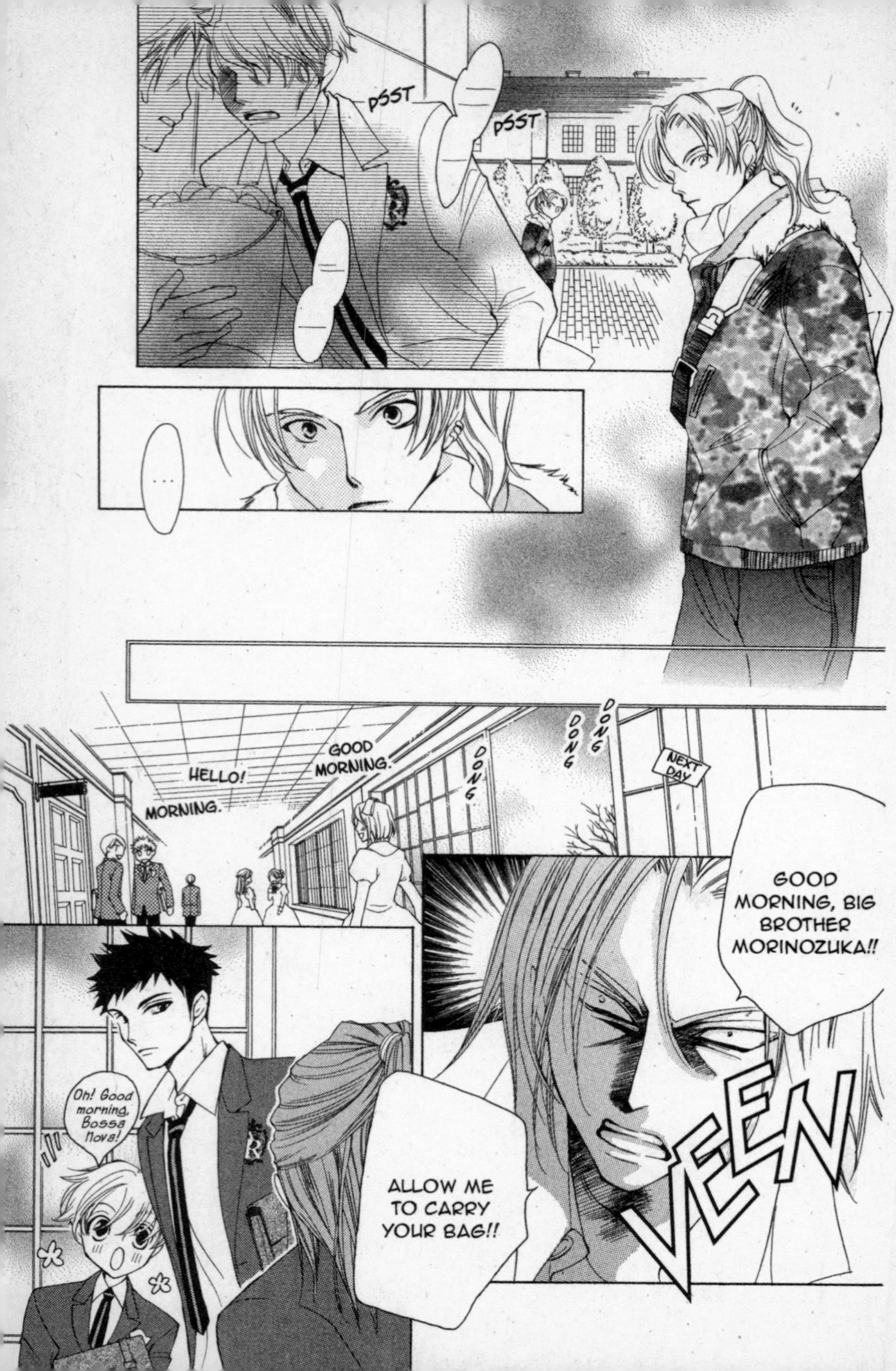
PSST
PSST
...
NEXT DAY
DONG DONG
DONG
GOOD MORNING.
HELLO!
MORNING.
GOOD MORNING, BIG BROTHER MORINOZUKA!!
VEEN
ALLOW ME TO CARRY YOUR BAG!!
Oh! Good morning, Bossa Nova!

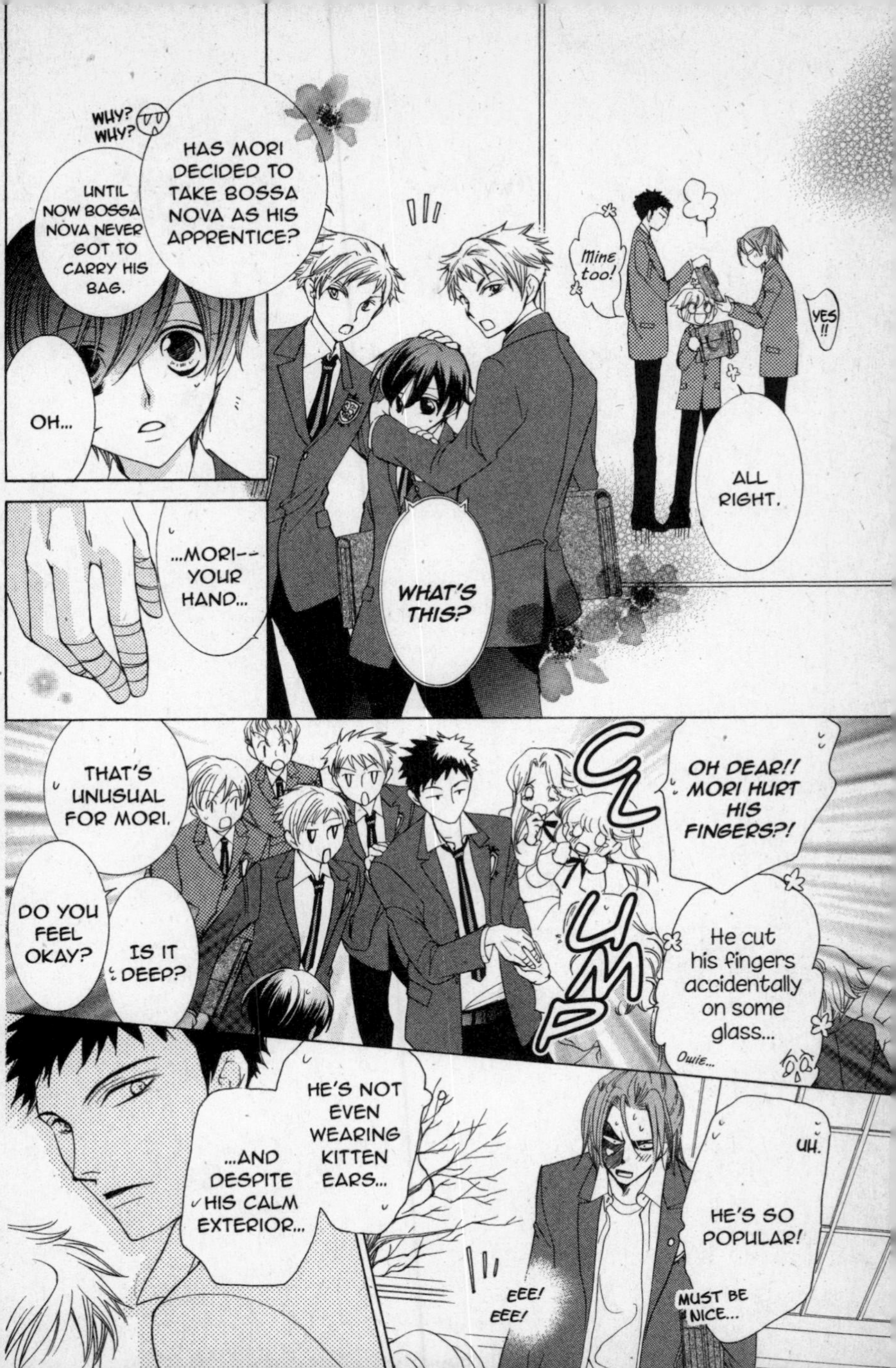
Mine too!
YES!!
ALL RIGHT.
HAS MORI DECIDED TO TAKE BOSSA NOVA AS HIS APPRENTICE?
WHY? WHY?
UNTIL NOW BOSSA NOVA NEVER GOT TO CARRY HIS BAG.
WHAT'S THIS?
OH...
...MORI-- YOUR HAND...
OH DEAR!! MORI HURT HIS FINGERS?!
He cut his fingers accidentally on some glass...
Owie...
CLUMP
THAT'S UNUSUAL FOR MORI.
IS IT DEEP?
DO YOU FEEL OKAY?
UH.
HE'S SO POPULAR!
MUST BE NICE...
EEE! EEE!
HE'S NOT EVEN WEARING KITTEN EARS...
...AND DESPITE HIS CALM EXTERIOR...

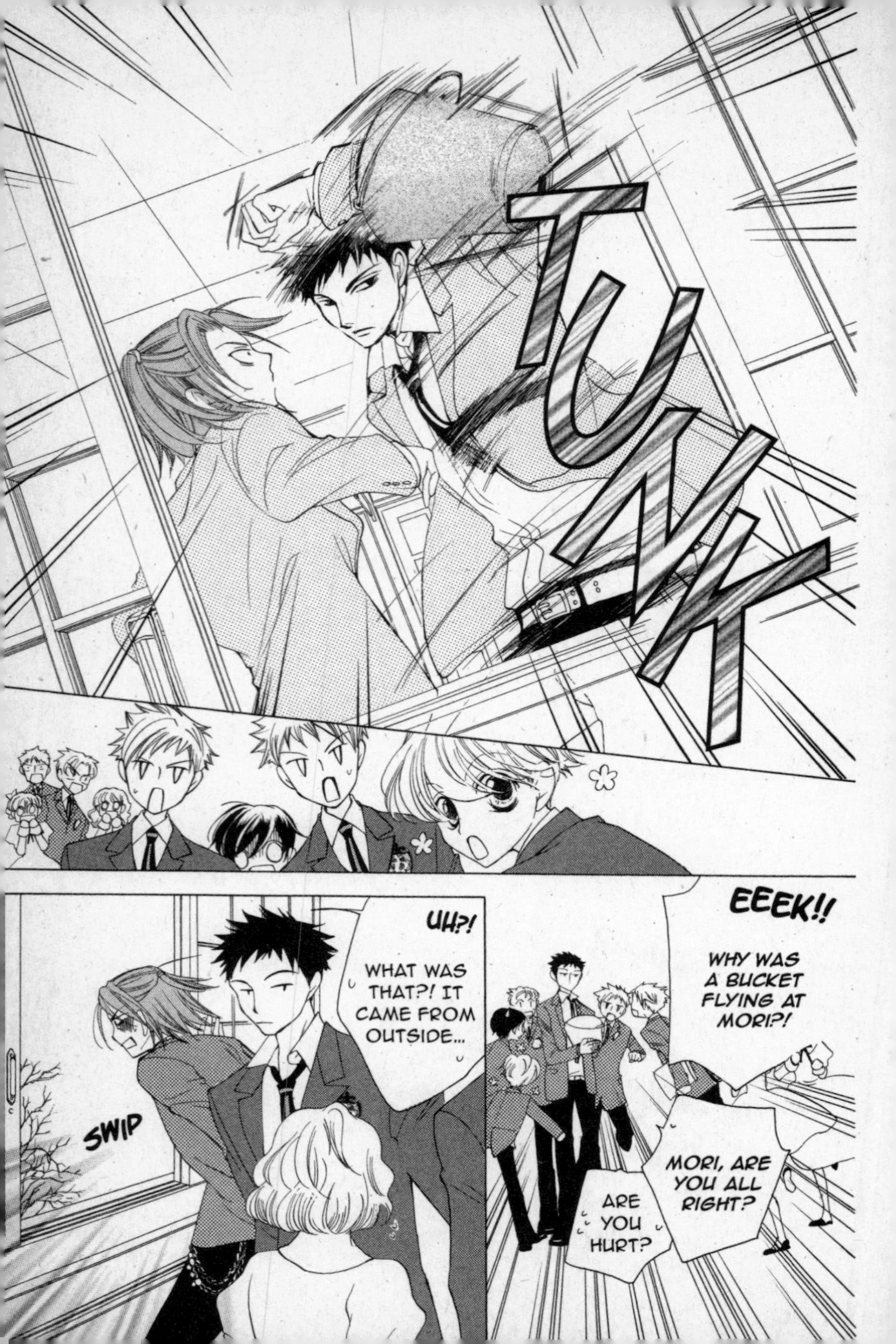
TUNK
EEEK!!
WHY WAS A BUCKET FLYING AT MORI?!
MORI, ARE YOU ALL RIGHT?
ARE YOU HURT?
UH?!
WHAT WAS THAT?! IT CAME FROM OUTSIDE...
SWIP

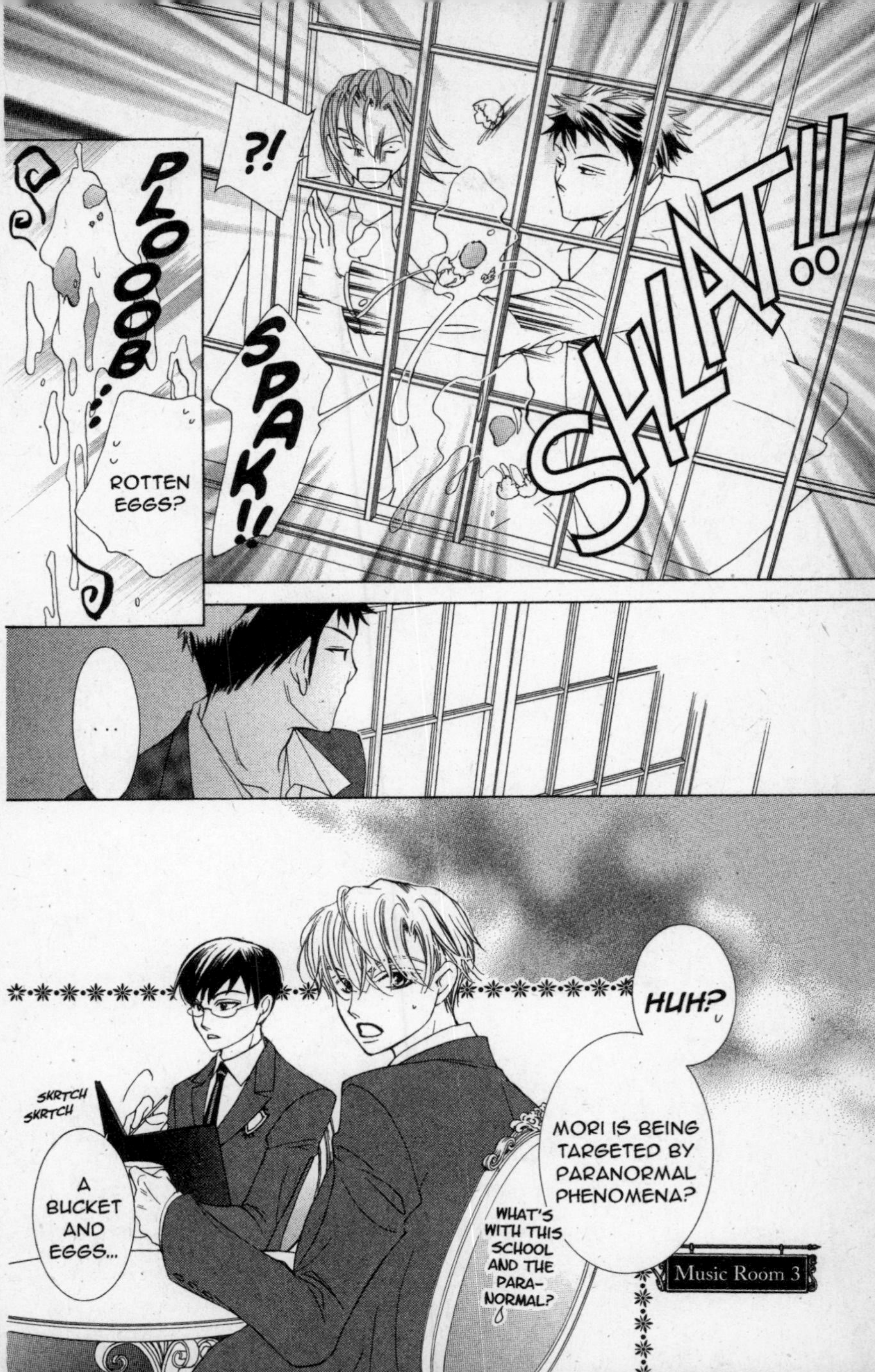
SHLAT!!
?!
SPAK!!
PLOOOOB...
ROTTEN EGGS?
...
Music Room 3
HUH?
MORI IS BEING TARGETED BY PARANORMAL PHENOMENA?
WHAT'S WITH THIS SCHOOL AND THE PARA-NORMAL?
SKRTCH SKRTCH
A BUCKET AND EGGS...

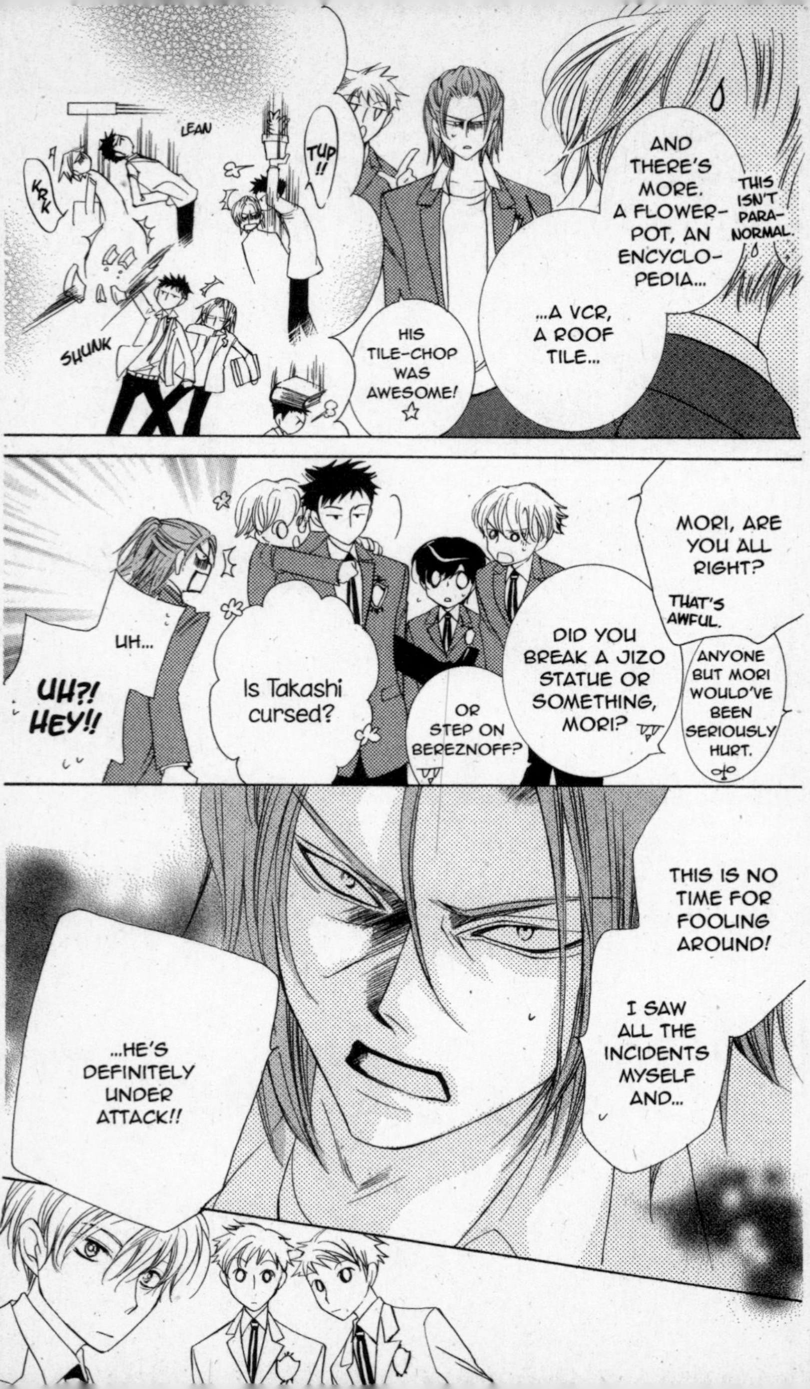
AND THERE'S MORE. A FLOWER-POT, AN ENCYCLO-PEDIA...
THIS ISN'T PARA-NORMAL.
...A VCR, A ROOF TILE...
HIS TILE-CHOP WAS AWESOME!
TUP!!
LEAN
KRK
SHUNK
MORI, ARE YOU ALL RIGHT?
THAT'S AWFUL.
ANYONE BUT MORI WOULD'VE BEEN SERIOUSLY HURT.
DID YOU BREAK A JIZO STATUE OR SOMETHING, MORI?
OR STEP ON BEREZNOFF?
Is Takashi cursed?
UH...
UH?! HEY!!
THIS IS NO TIME FOR FOOLING AROUND!
I SAW ALL THE INCIDENTS MYSELF AND...
...HE'S DEFINITELY UNDER ATTACK!!

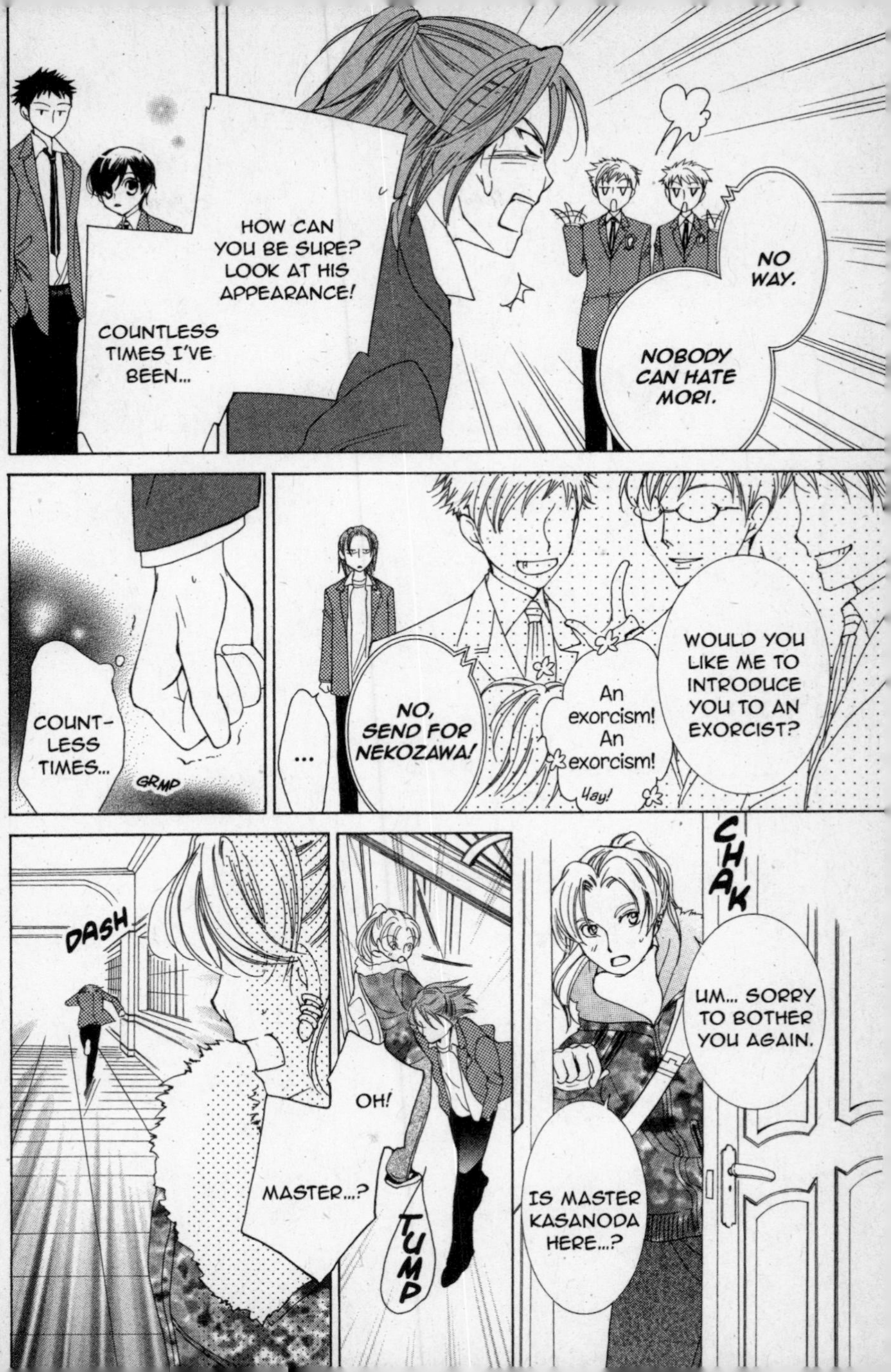
NO WAY.
NOBODY CAN HATE MORI.
HOW CAN YOU BE SURE? LOOK AT HIS APPEARANCE!
COUNTLESS TIMES I'VE BEEN...
WOULD YOU LIKE ME TO INTRODUCE YOU TO AN EXORCIST?
An exorcism! An exorcism!
Yay!
NO, SEND FOR NEKOZAWA!
...
COUNT-LESS TIMES...
GRMP
CHAK
UM... SORRY TO BOTHER YOU AGAIN.
IS MASTER KASANODA HERE...?
OH!
MASTER...?
TUMP
DASH

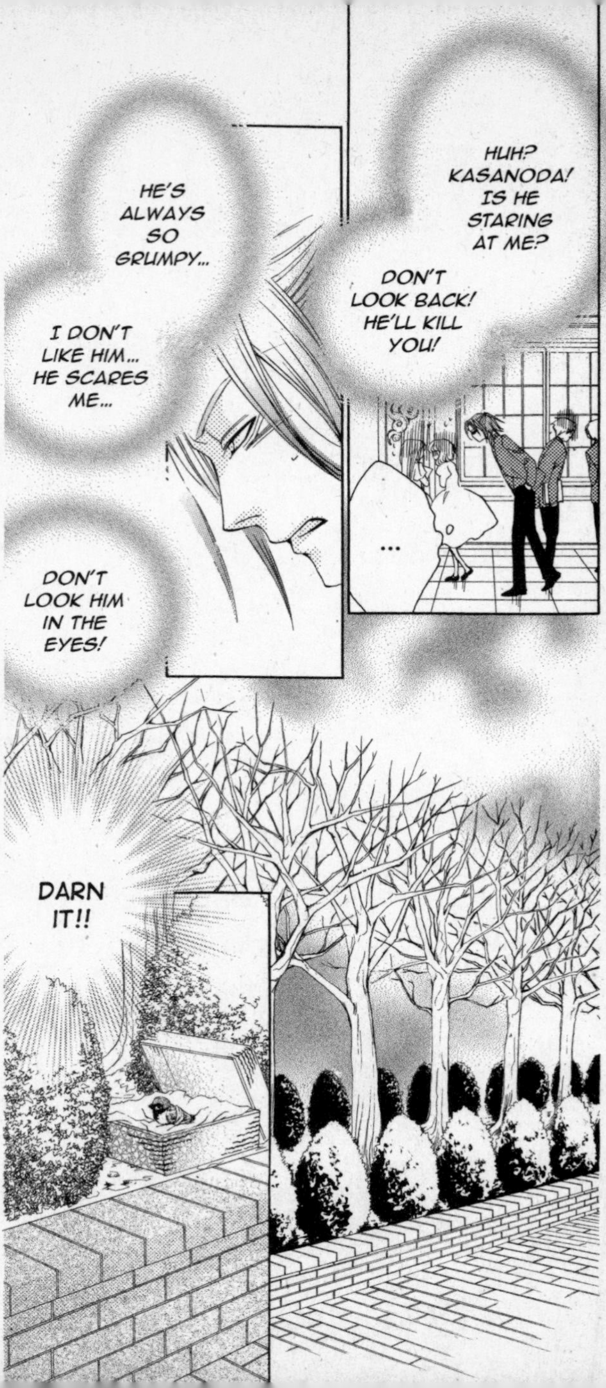
HUH? KASANODA! IS HE STARING AT ME?
DON'T LOOK BACK! HE'LL KILL YOU!
...
HE'S ALWAYS SO GRUMPY...
I DON'T LIKE HIM... HE SCARES ME...
DON'T LOOK HIM IN THE EYES!
DARN IT!!

✿HI! I HAVE IMPORTANT NEWS TODAY. *HOST CLUB* IS GOING TO BE A

TV ANIME!

IMPOSSIBLE...!!! W-WHAT SHOULD I DO?!!

SINCE I'M SUCH A WIMP, I'M A REAL BASKET CASE OVER THIS.

I THINK ABOUT HOW THERE MUST BE SO MANY^{x100} OTHER MANGA MUCH BETTER THAN THIS, SO WHY WAS *HOST CLUB* CHOSEN?

WHY WOULD A FAMOUS ANIMATION PRODUCTION COMPANY AND AN AMAZING DIRECTOR AND AMAZING CHARACTER DESIGNERS AND SCRIPT WRITERS AND ALL THESE PEOPLE WANT TO DEAL WITH *HOST CLUB*??!!

ARE YOU GUYS SURE ABOUT THIS?

ARE YOU REALLY SURE ABOUT THIS...?

AND SO ON...

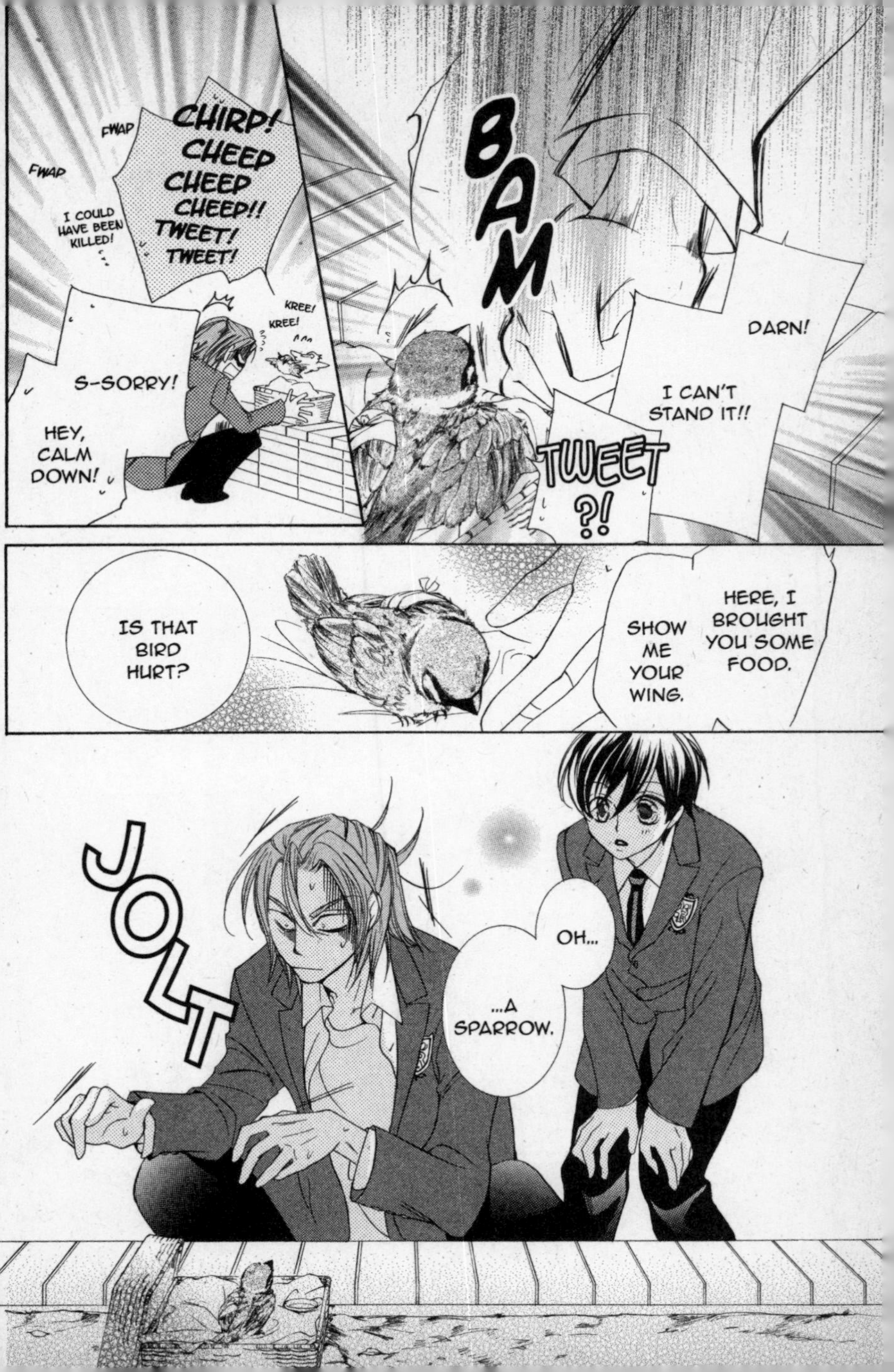
DARN!
I CAN'T STAND IT!!
BAM
TWEET ?!
CHIRP! CHEEP CHEEP CHEEP!! TWEET! TWEET!
FWAP
FWAP
I COULD HAVE BEEN KILLED!
KREE! KREE!
S-SORRY!
HEY, CALM DOWN!
HERE, I BROUGHT YOU SOME FOOD.
SHOW ME YOUR WING.
IS THAT BIRD HURT?
OH...
...A SPARROW.
JOLT

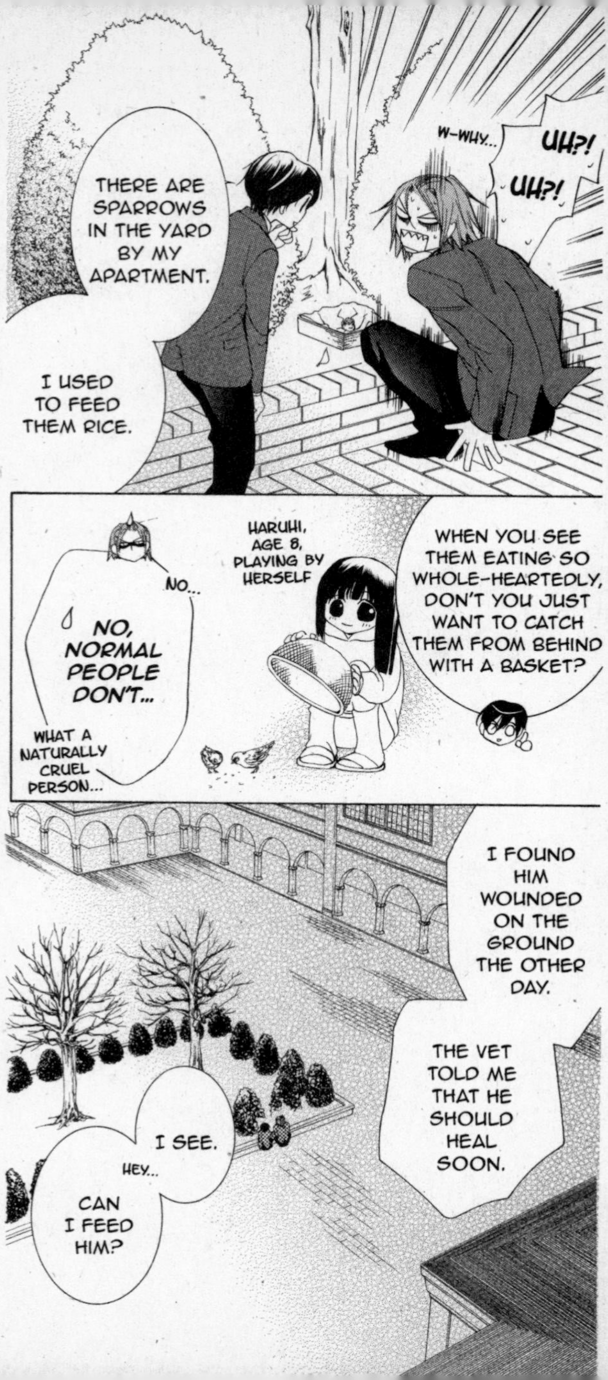
UH?!
UH?!
W-WHY...
THERE ARE SPARROWS IN THE YARD BY MY APARTMENT.
I USED TO FEED THEM RICE.
WHEN YOU SEE THEM EATING SO WHOLE-HEARTEDLY, DON'T YOU JUST WANT TO CATCH THEM FROM BEHIND WITH A BASKET?
HARUHI, AGE 8, PLAYING BY HERSELF
NO...
NO, NORMAL PEOPLE DON'T...
WHAT A NATURALLY CRUEL PERSON...
I FOUND HIM WOUNDED ON THE GROUND THE OTHER DAY.
THE VET TOLD ME THAT HE SHOULD HEAL SOON.
I SEE.
HEY...
CAN I FEED HIM?

THE ANIME IDEA CAME UP SOME TIME AGO, BUT THERE WAS A PERIOD WHEN NOT MUCH HAPPENED. QUITE FRANKLY, I THOUGHT NOTHING WOULD COME OF IT. BUT!! ONE DAY EVERYTHING STARTED ROLLING ALL AT ONCE. WOW!

EVERYONE!! ANIME IS AMAZING... ONCE THE DECISION TO DO IT IS MADE, IT TAKES OFF

LIKE CRAZY!!

WHILE I'M STRUGGLING OVER ROUGH DRAFTS FOR AN EPISODE OF THE MANGA, ALL THE ANIME SCENARIOS, CHARACTER DESIGNS, ART SETTINGS, VOICE ACTOR AUDITIONS, THEME SONG CANDIDATES, AND STORYBOARDS KEEP COMING AT ME!! IT'S REALLY SOMETHING! WHEN DOES EVERYONE SLEEP?

(I STILL DON'T QUITE GET HOW EACH PART OF THE PRODUCTION IS TAKEN OVER BY A DIFFERENT PERSON.)

AND PEOPLE IN THE ANIMATION INDUSTRY LOOK SO YOUNG!! THEY MAY LOOK LIKE THEY'RE THE SAME AGE OR YOUNGER THAN I AM, BUT THEY CAN BE MORE THAN 10 YEARS OLDER...

INCREDIBLE. I REALLY NEED TO LEARN THEIR SECRET.

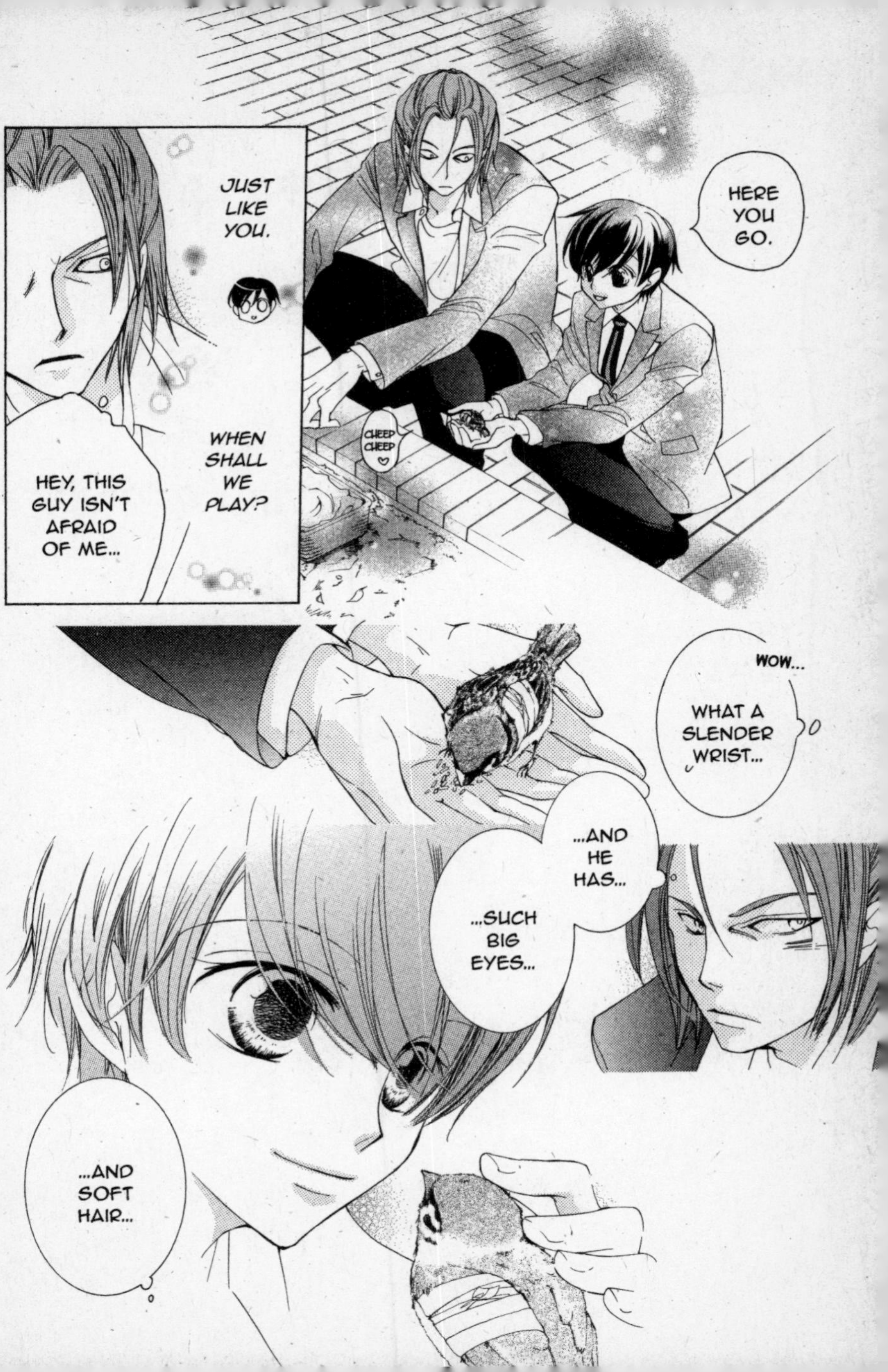
HERE YOU GO.
CHEEP CHEEP ♥
JUST LIKE YOU.
WHEN SHALL WE PLAY?
HEY, THIS GUY ISN'T AFRAID OF ME...
WOW...
WHAT A SLENDER WRIST...
...AND HE HAS...
...SUCH BIG EYES...
...AND SOFT HAIR...

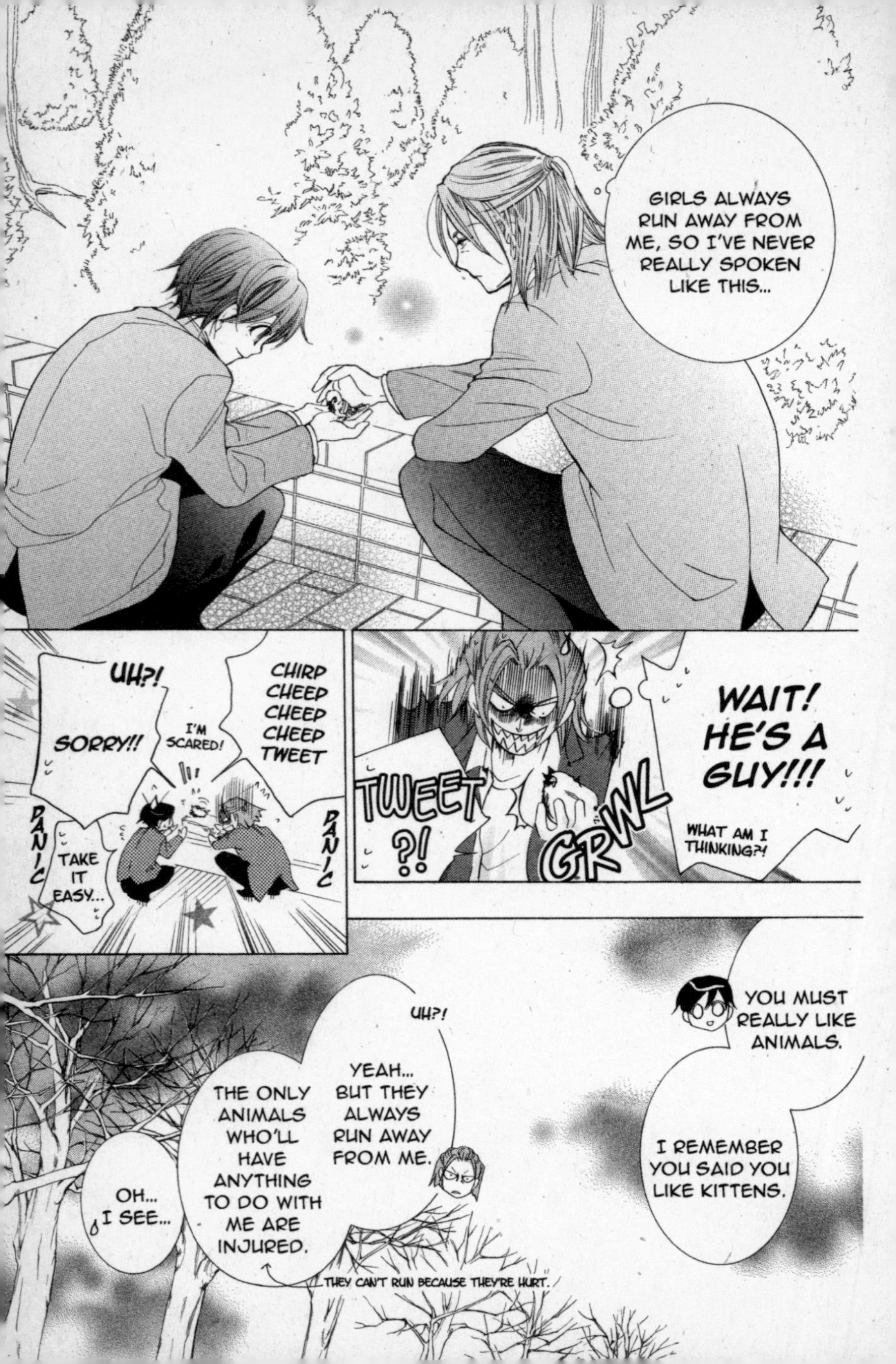
GIRLS ALWAYS RUN AWAY FROM ME, SO I'VE NEVER REALLY SPOKEN LIKE THIS...
WAIT! HE'S A GUY!!!
WHAT AM I THINKING?!
GRWL
TWEET ?!
CHIRP CHEEP CHEEP CHEEP TWEET
I'M SCARED!
UH?!
SORRY!!
PANIC
PANIC
TAKE IT EASY...
YOU MUST REALLY LIKE ANIMALS.
I REMEMBER YOU SAID YOU LIKE KITTENS.
UH?!
YEAH... BUT THEY ALWAYS RUN AWAY FROM ME.
THE ONLY ANIMALS WHO'LL HAVE ANYTHING TO DO WITH ME ARE INJURED.
THEY CAN'T RUN BECAUSE THEY'RE HURT.
OH... I SEE...

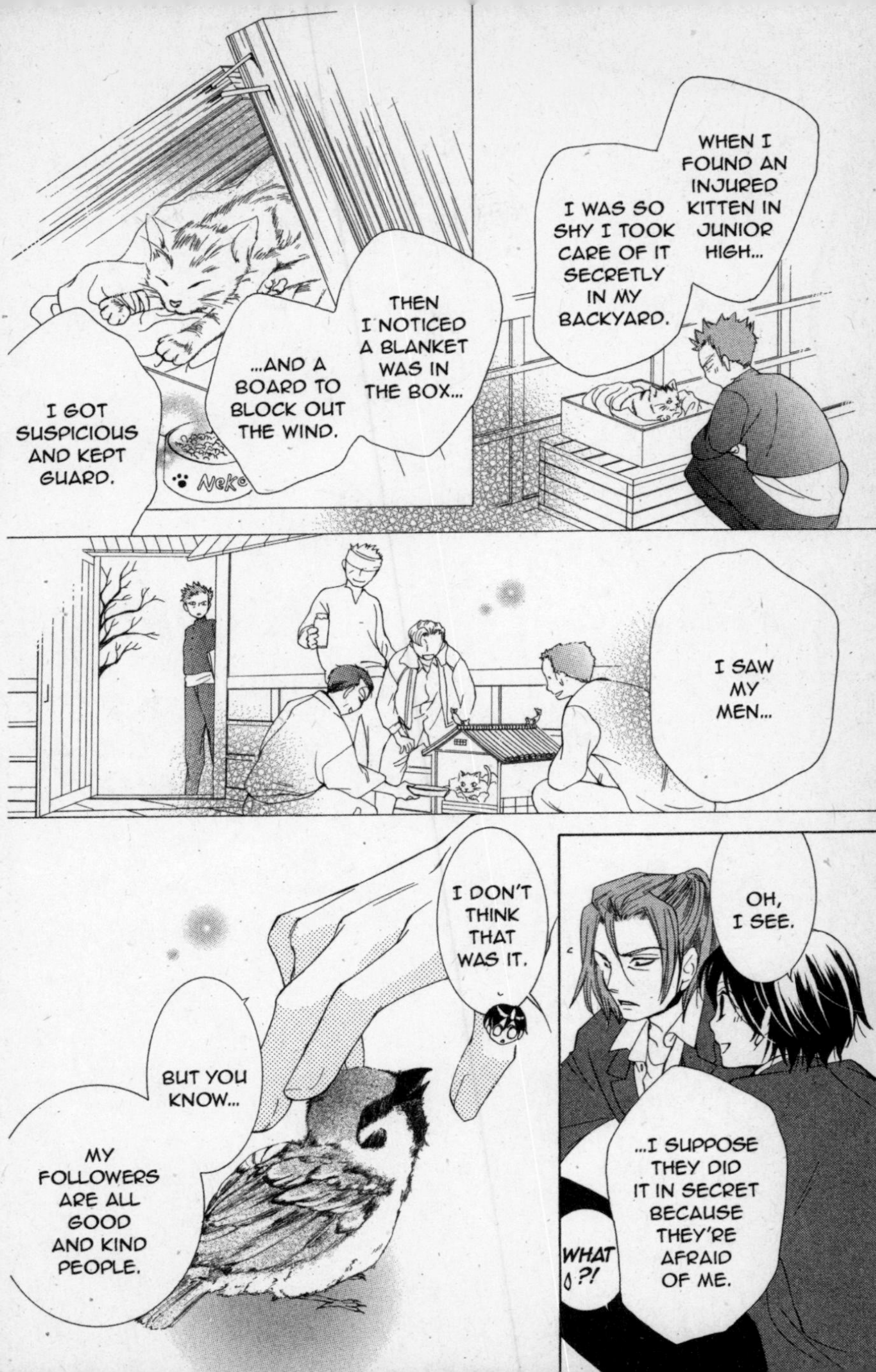
WHEN I FOUND AN INJURED KITTEN IN JUNIOR HIGH...
I WAS SO SHY I TOOK CARE OF IT SECRETLY IN MY BACKYARD.
THEN I NOTICED A BLANKET WAS IN THE BOX...
...AND A BOARD TO BLOCK OUT THE WIND.
I GOT SUSPICIOUS AND KEPT GUARD.
Neko
I SAW MY MEN...
OH, I SEE.
...I SUPPOSE THEY DID IT IN SECRET BECAUSE THEY'RE AFRAID OF ME.
WHAT?!
I DON'T THINK THAT WAS IT.
BUT YOU KNOW...
MY FOLLOWERS ARE ALL GOOD AND KIND PEOPLE.

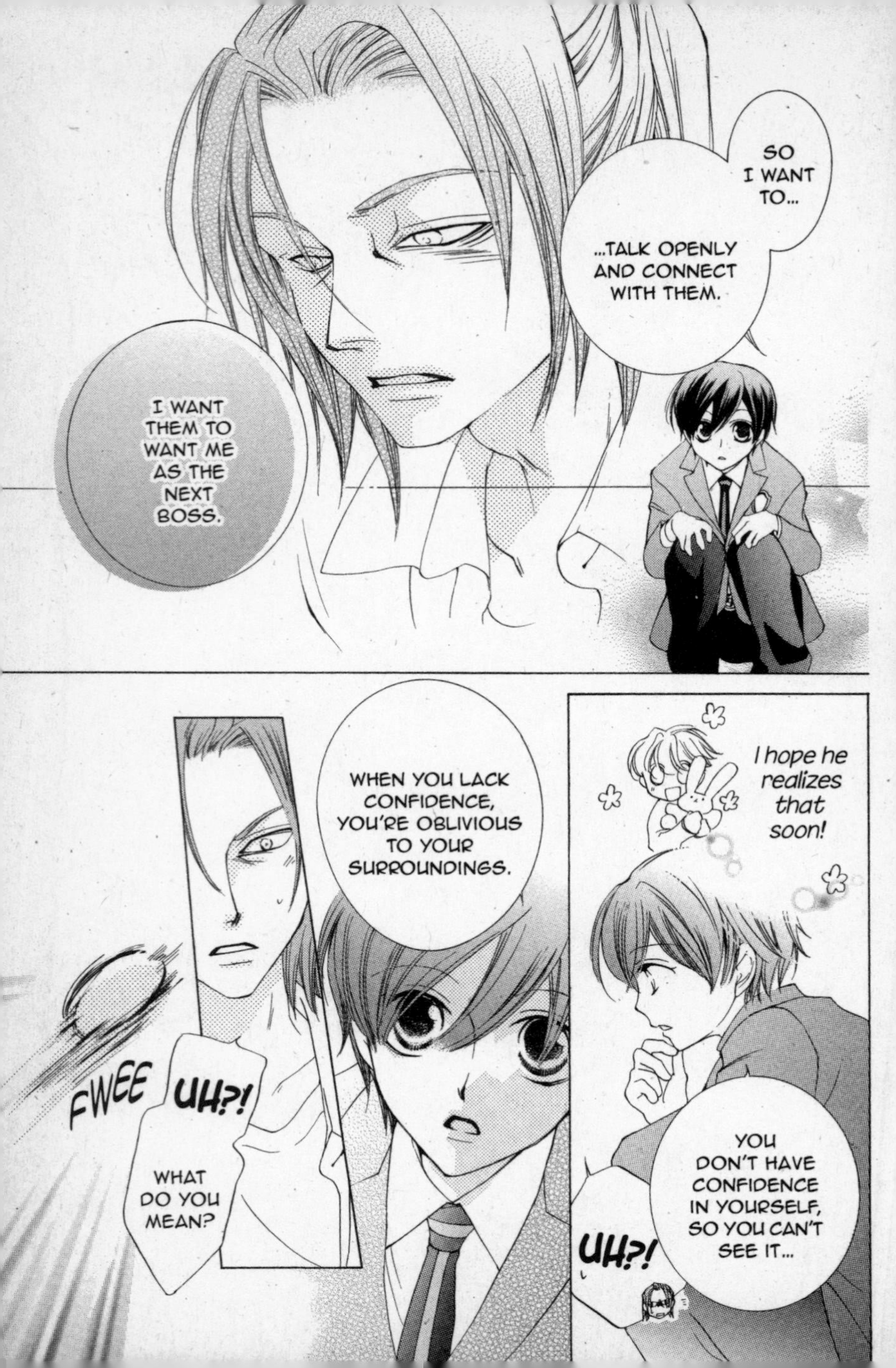
SO I WANT TO...
...TALK OPENLY AND CONNECT WITH THEM.
I WANT THEM TO WANT ME AS THE NEXT BOSS.
I hope he realizes that soon!
YOU DON'T HAVE CONFIDENCE IN YOURSELF, SO YOU CAN'T SEE IT...
UH?!
WHEN YOU LACK CONFIDENCE, YOU'RE OBLIVIOUS TO YOUR SURROUNDINGS.
UH?!
FWEE
WHAT DO YOU MEAN?

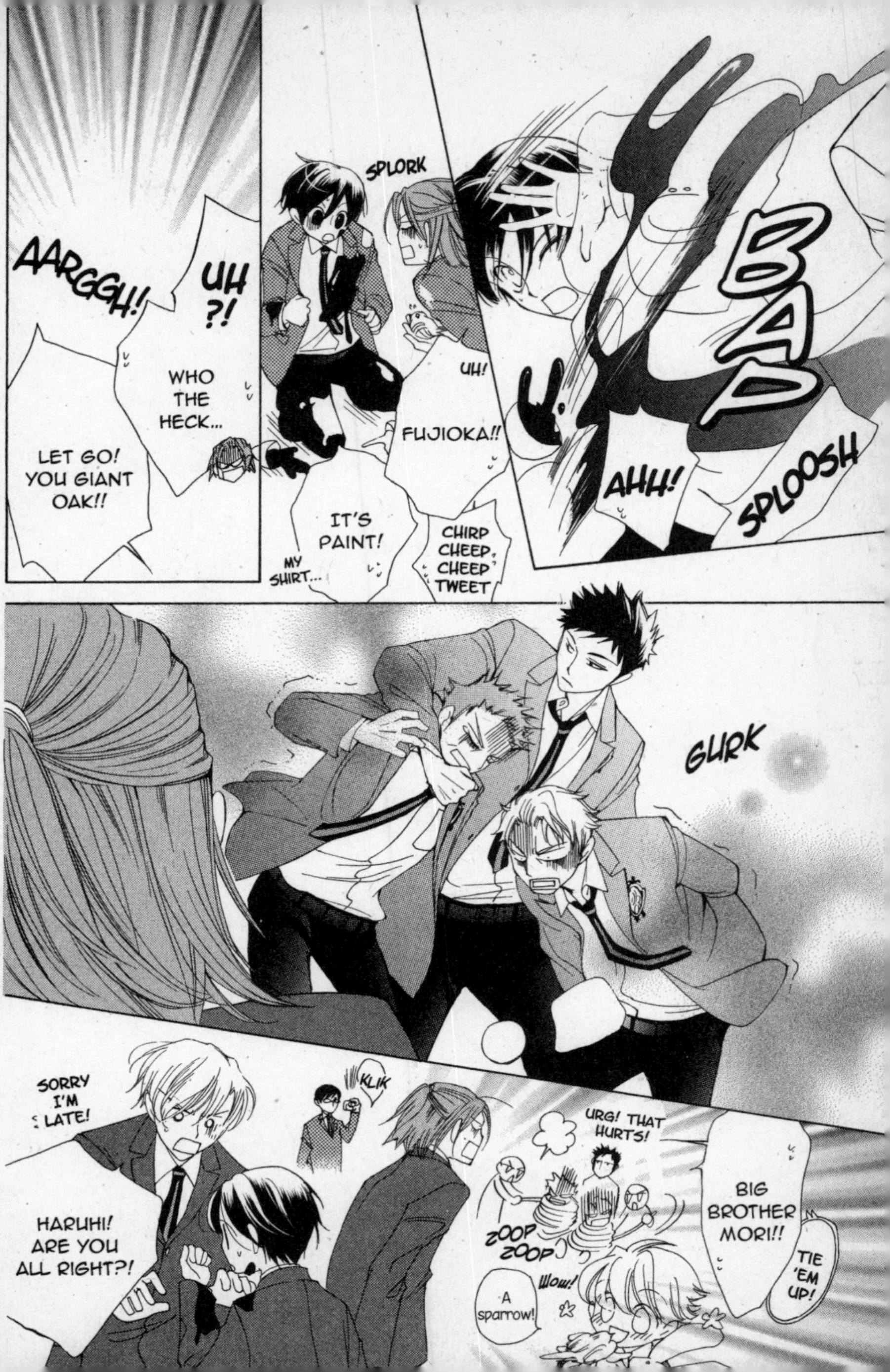

BAP
SPLOOSH
AHH!
SPLORK
UH!
FUJIOKA!!
CHIRP CHEEP, CHEEP TWEET
IT'S PAINT!
MY SHIRT...
UH ?!
AARGGH!
WHO THE HECK...
LET GO! YOU GIANT OAK!!
GURK
BIG BROTHER MORI!!
TIE 'EM UP!
URG! THAT HURTS!
ZOOP ZOOP
Wow!
A sparrow!
KLIK
SORRY I'M LATE!
HARUHI! ARE YOU ALL RIGHT?!

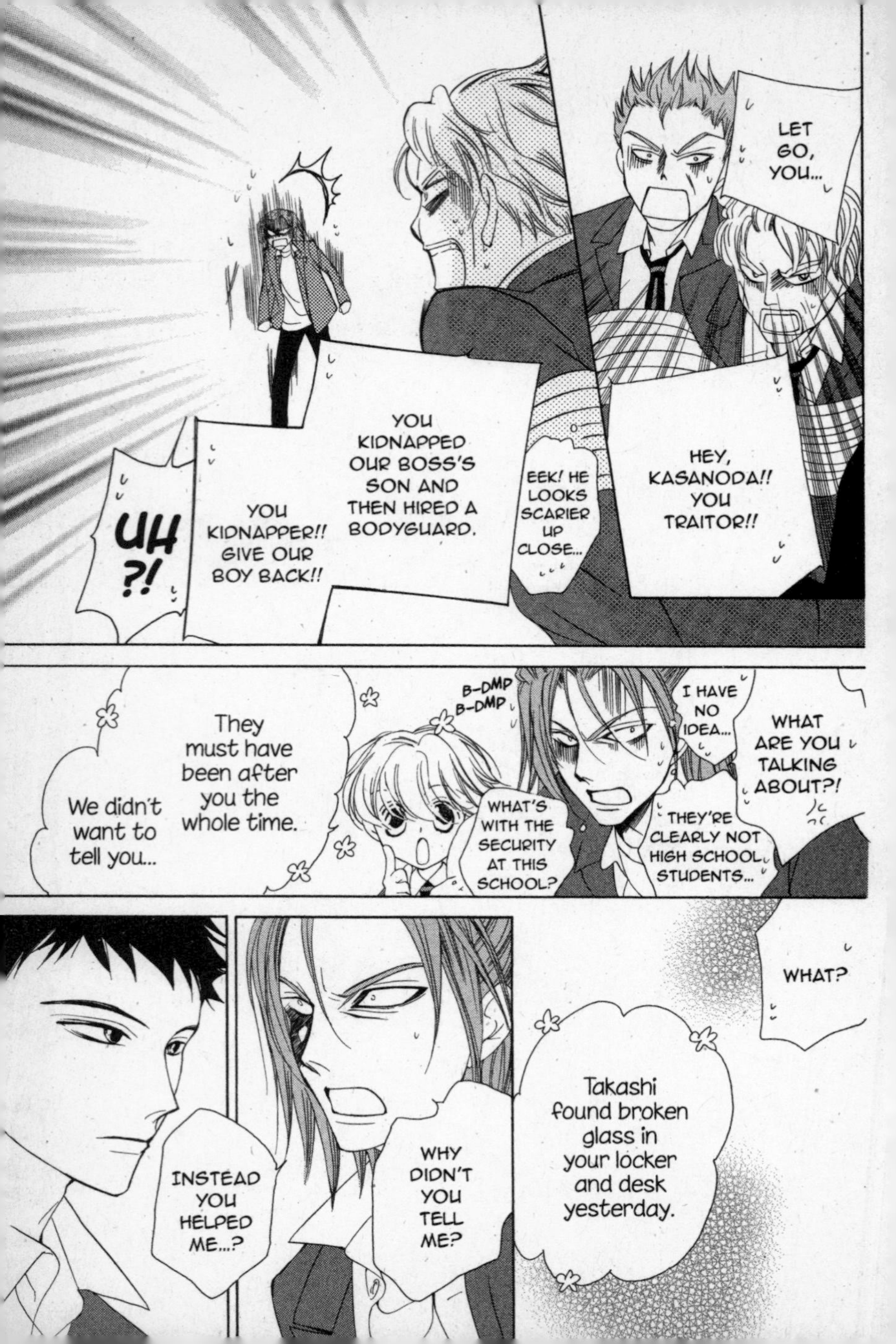
LET GO, YOU...
HEY, KASANODA!! YOU TRAITOR!!
EEK! HE LOOKS SCARIER UP CLOSE...
YOU KIDNAPPED OUR BOSS'S SON AND THEN HIRED A BODYGUARD.
YOU KIDNAPPER!! GIVE OUR BOY BACK!!
UH ?!
WHAT ARE YOU TALKING ABOUT?!
I HAVE NO IDEA...
THEY'RE CLEARLY NOT HIGH SCHOOL STUDENTS...
B-DMP B-DMP
WHAT'S WITH THE SECURITY AT THIS SCHOOL?
They must have been after you the whole time.
We didn't want to tell you...
WHAT?
Takashi found broken glass in your locker and desk yesterday.
WHY DIDN'T YOU TELL ME?
INSTEAD YOU HELPED ME...?

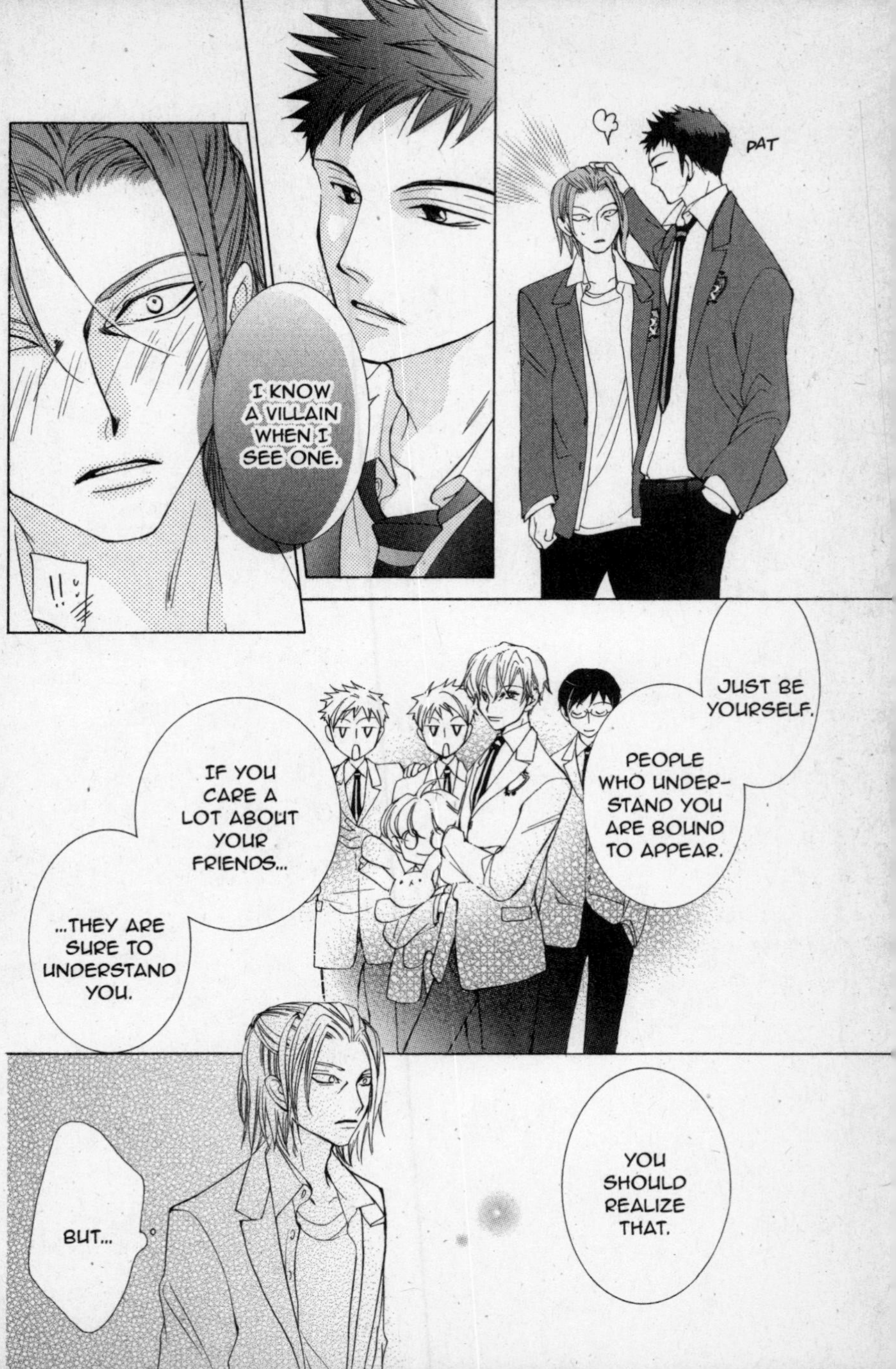
PAT
I KNOW A VILLAIN WHEN I SEE ONE.
!!
JUST BE YOURSELF.
PEOPLE WHO UNDER-STAND YOU ARE BOUND TO APPEAR.
IF YOU CARE A LOT ABOUT YOUR FRIENDS...
...THEY ARE SURE TO UNDERSTAND YOU.
YOU SHOULD REALIZE THAT.
BUT...

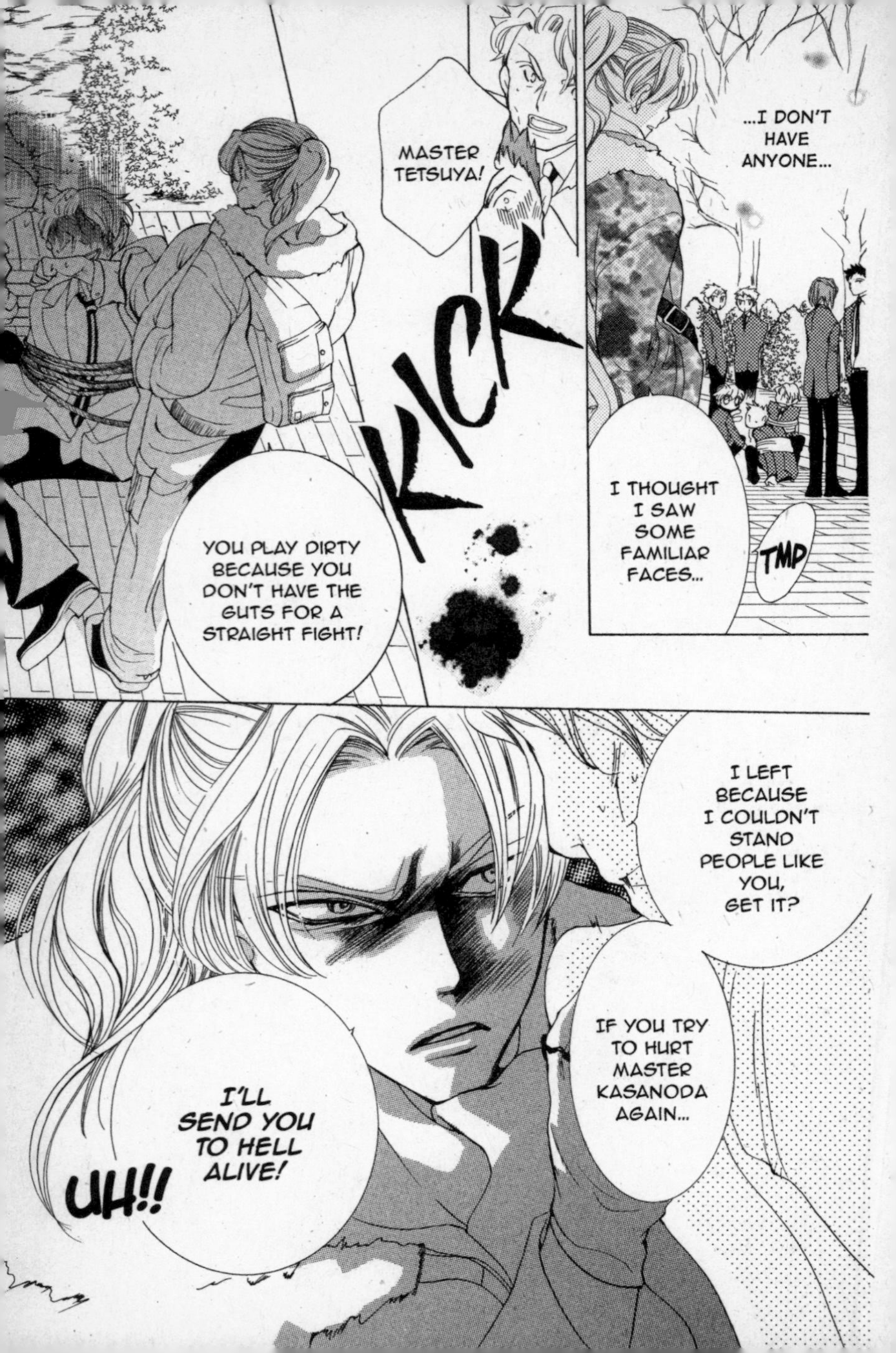
...I DON'T HAVE ANYONE...
I THOUGHT I SAW SOME FAMILIAR FACES...
TMP
MASTER TETSUYA!
KICK
YOU PLAY DIRTY BECAUSE YOU DON'T HAVE THE GUTS FOR A STRAIGHT FIGHT!
I LEFT BECAUSE I COULDN'T STAND PEOPLE LIKE YOU, GET IT?
IF YOU TRY TO HURT MASTER KASANODA AGAIN...
I'LL SEND YOU TO HELL ALIVE!
UH!!

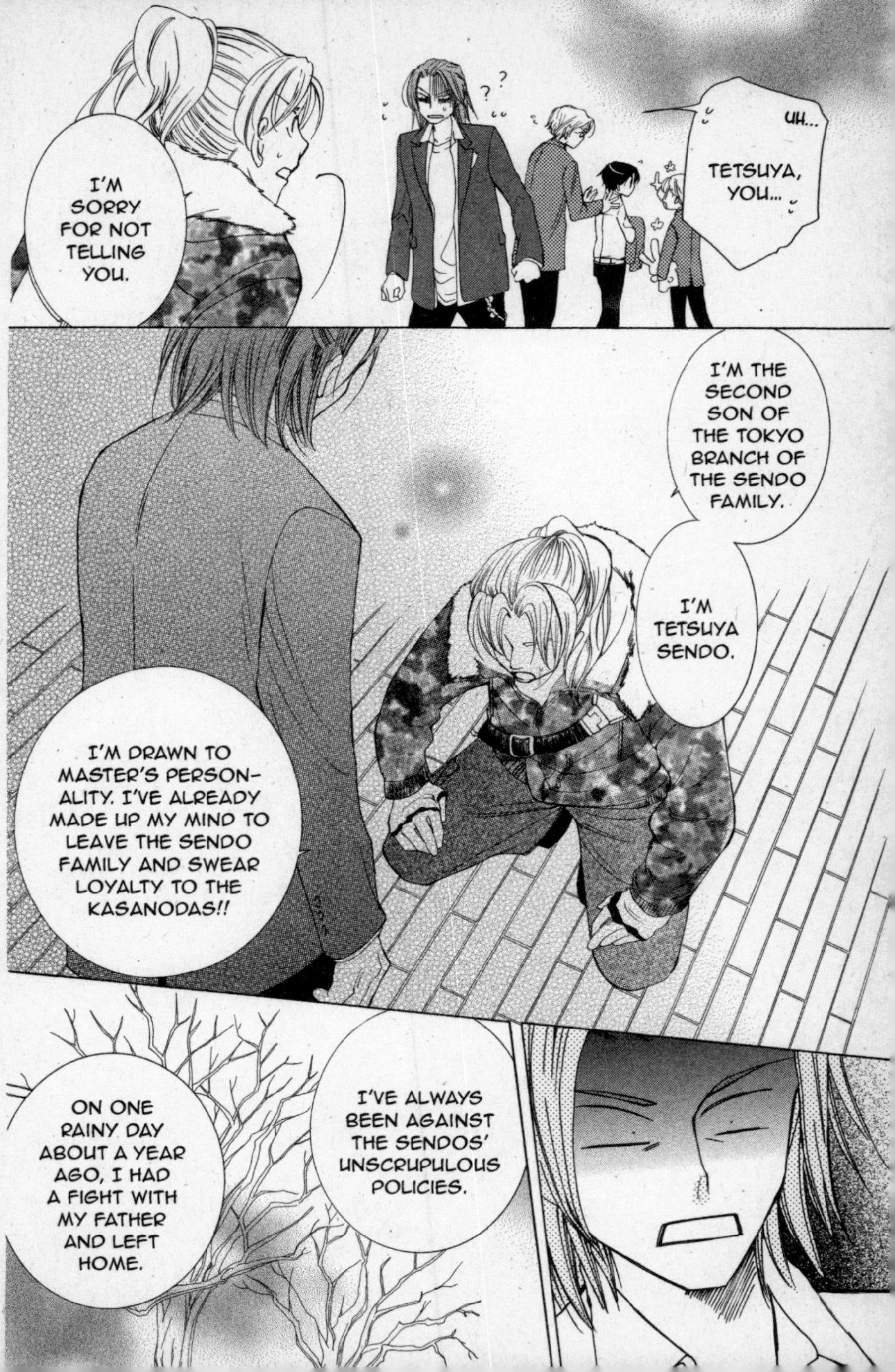
UH...
TETSUYA, YOU...
I'M SORRY FOR NOT TELLING YOU.
I'M THE SECOND SON OF THE TOKYO BRANCH OF THE SENDO FAMILY.
I'M TETSUYA SENDO.
I'M DRAWN TO MASTER'S PERSON-ALITY. I'VE ALREADY MADE UP MY MIND TO LEAVE THE SENDO FAMILY AND SWEAR LOYALTY TO THE KASANODAS!!
I'VE ALWAYS BEEN AGAINST THE SENDOS' UNSCRUPULOUS POLICIES.
ON ONE RAINY DAY ABOUT A YEAR AGO, I HAD A FIGHT WITH MY FATHER AND LEFT HOME.

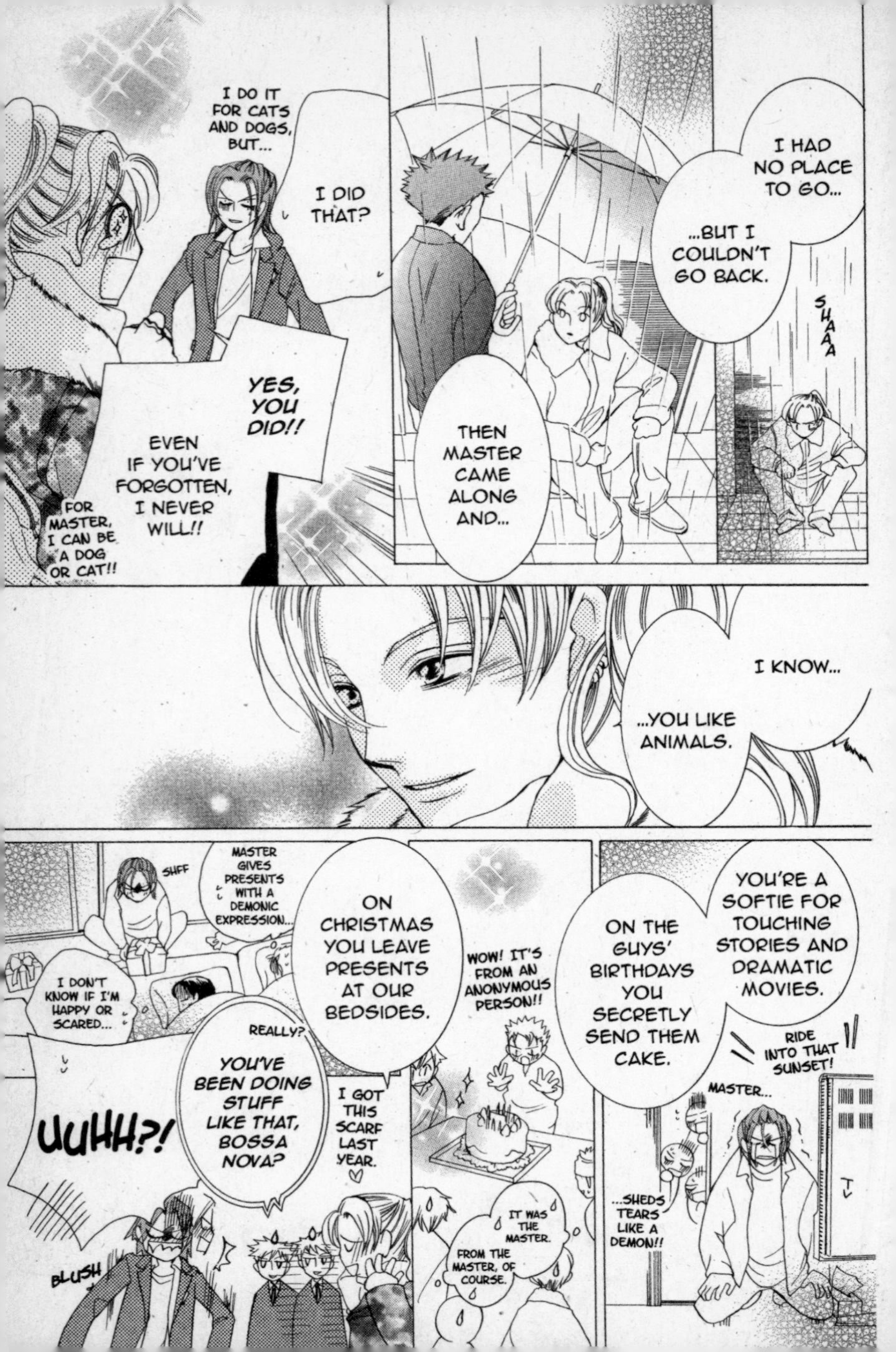
I HAD NO PLACE TO GO...
...BUT I COULDN'T GO BACK.
SHAAA
THEN MASTER CAME ALONG AND...
I DID THAT?
I DO IT FOR CATS AND DOGS, BUT...
YES, YOU DID!!
EVEN IF YOU'VE FORGOTTEN, I NEVER WILL!!
FOR MASTER, I CAN BE A DOG OR CAT!!
I KNOW...
...YOU LIKE ANIMALS.
YOU'RE A SOFTIE FOR TOUCHING STORIES AND DRAMATIC MOVIES.
RIDE INTO THAT SUNSET!
MASTER...
...SHEDS TEARS LIKE A DEMON!!
ON THE GUYS' BIRTHDAYS YOU SECRETLY SEND THEM CAKE.
WOW! IT'S FROM AN ANONYMOUS PERSON!!
IT WAS THE MASTER.
FROM THE MASTER, OF COURSE.
ON CHRISTMAS YOU LEAVE PRESENTS AT OUR BEDSIDES.
MASTER GIVES PRESENTS WITH A DEMONIC EXPRESSION...
SHUFF
I DON'T KNOW IF I'M HAPPY OR SCARED...
I GOT THIS SCARF LAST YEAR.
REALLY?
YOU'VE BEEN DOING STUFF LIKE THAT, BOSSA NOVA?
UUHH?!
BLUSH

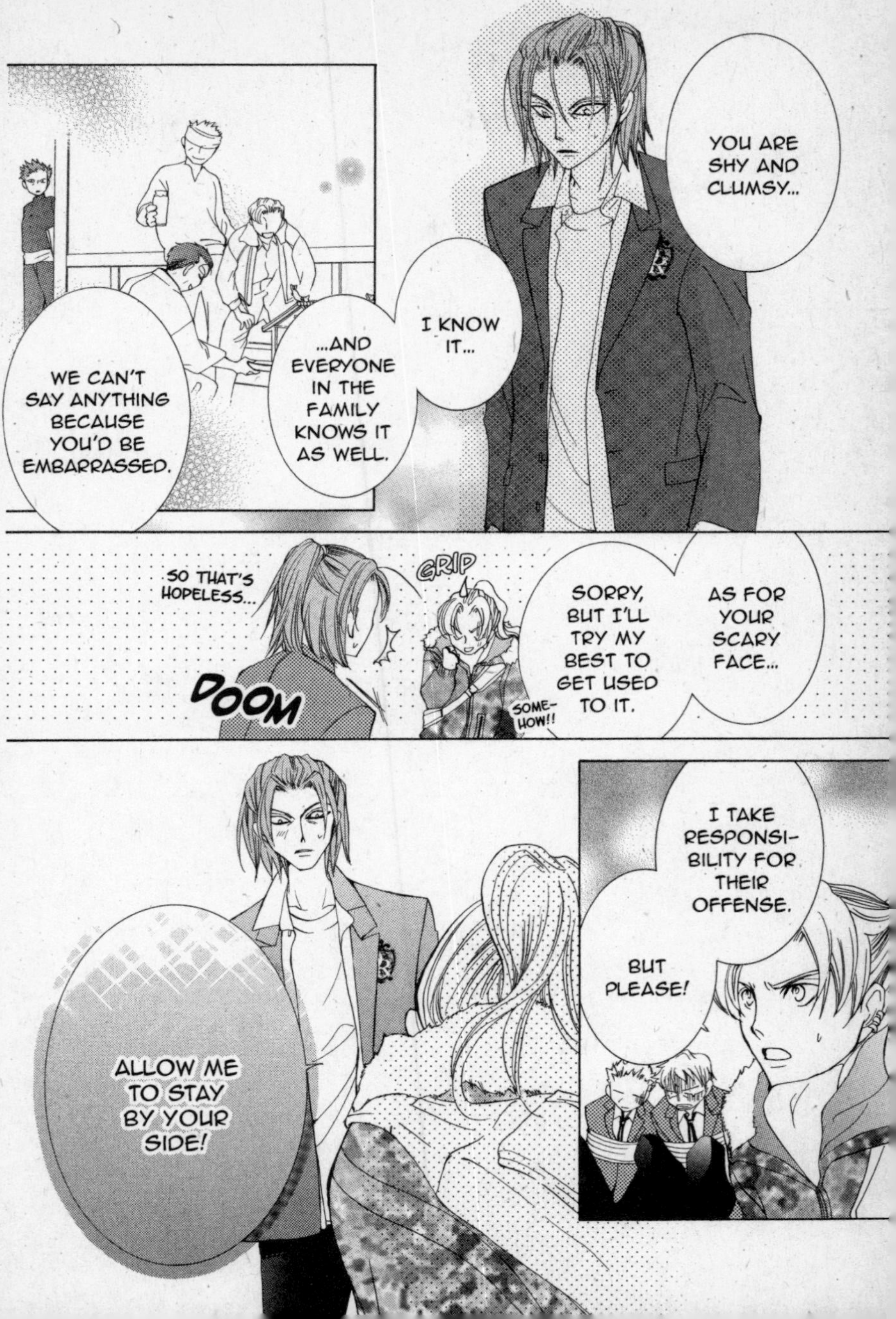
YOU ARE SHY AND CLUMSY...
I KNOW IT...
...AND EVERYONE IN THE FAMILY KNOWS IT AS WELL.
WE CAN'T SAY ANYTHING BECAUSE YOU'D BE EMBARRASSED.
AS FOR YOUR SCARY FACE...
SORRY, BUT I'LL TRY MY BEST TO GET USED TO IT.
SOME-HOW!!
GRIP
SO THAT'S HOPELESS...
DOOM
I TAKE RESPONSI-BILITY FOR THEIR OFFENSE.
BUT PLEASE!
ALLOW ME TO STAY BY YOUR SIDE!

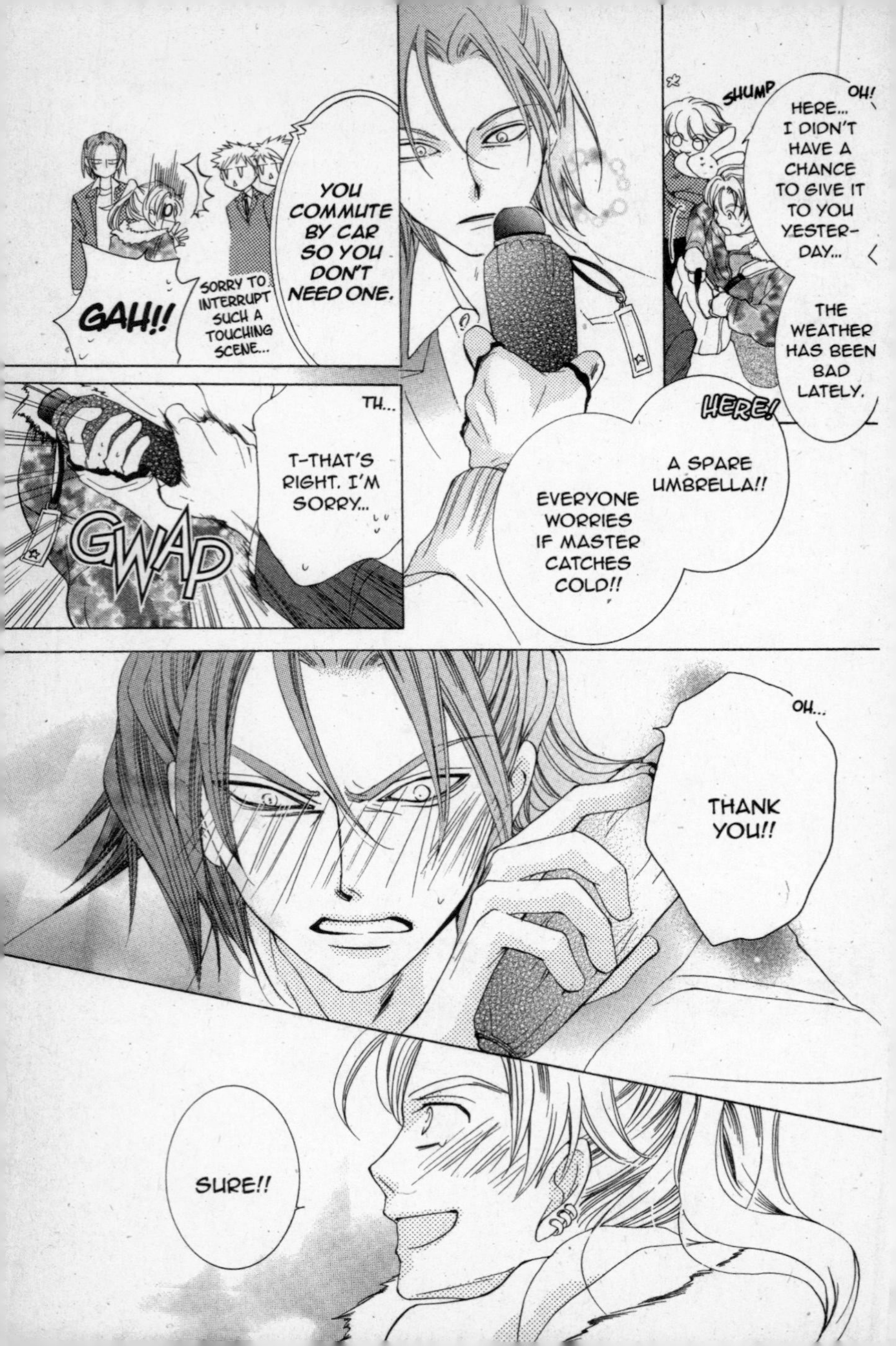
SHUMP
OH! HERE... I DIDN'T HAVE A CHANCE TO GIVE IT TO YOU YESTER-DAY...
THE WEATHER HAS BEEN BAD LATELY.
HERE!
A SPARE UMBRELLA!!
EVERYONE WORRIES IF MASTER CATCHES COLD!!
YOU COMMUTE BY CAR SO YOU DON'T NEED ONE.
SORRY TO INTERRUPT SUCH A TOUCHING SCENE...
GAH!!
TH...
T-THAT'S RIGHT. I'M SORRY...
GWAP
OH...
THANK YOU!!
SURE!!

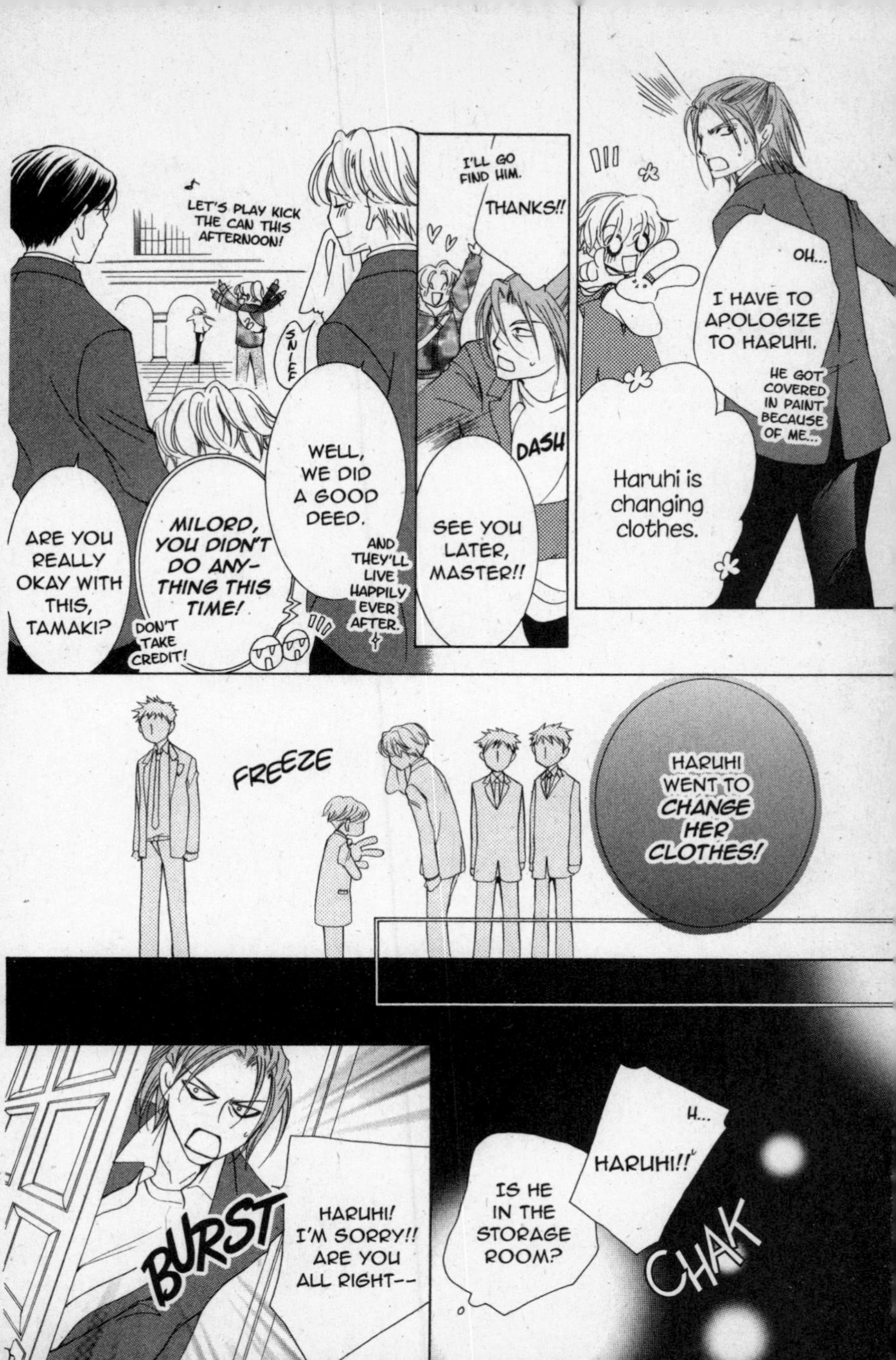
OH...
I HAVE TO APOLOGIZE TO HARUHI.
HE GOT COVERED IN PAINT BECAUSE OF ME...
Haruhi is changing clothes.
I'LL GO FIND HIM.
THANKS!!
DASH
SEE YOU LATER, MASTER!!
LET'S PLAY KICK THE CAN THIS AFTERNOON!
SNIFF
WELL, WE DID A GOOD DEED.
AND THEY'LL LIVE HAPPILY EVER AFTER.
MILORD, YOU DIDN'T DO ANY-THING THIS TIME!
DON'T TAKE CREDIT!
ARE YOU REALLY OKAY WITH THIS, TAMAKI?
HARUHI WENT TO CHANGE HER CLOTHES!
FREEZE
H...
HARUHI!!
CHAK
IS HE IN THE STORAGE ROOM?
HARUHI! I'M SORRY!! ARE YOU ALL RIGHT--
BURST

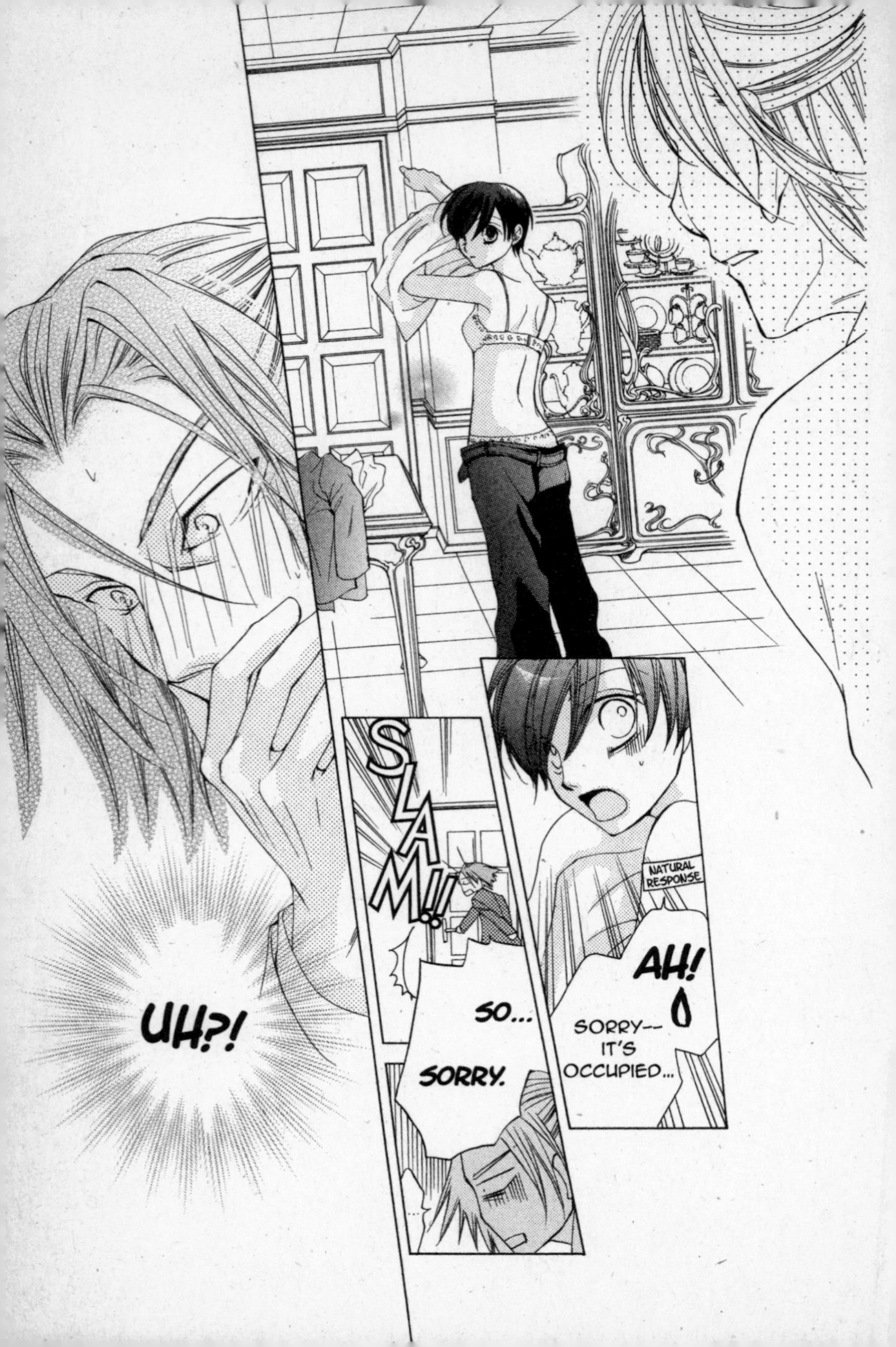
NATURAL RESPONSE
AH!
SORRY-- IT'S OCCUPIED...
SLAM!!
SO...
SORRY.
...
UH?!

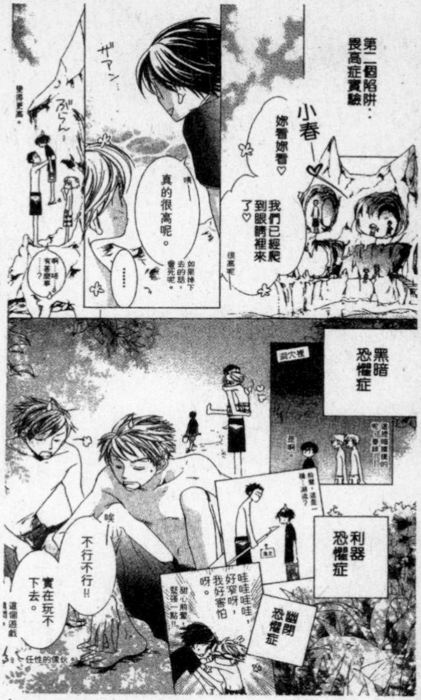
第二個陷阱：畏高症實驗
小春
妳看妳看♡
我們已經爬到眼睛裡來了♡
很高呢
如果掉下去的話，會死呢。
咦— 真的很高呢。
……
ザァン…
ぶらん…
黑暗恐懼症
洞穴裡
咳
不行不行!!
實在玩不下去。
利器恐懼症
哇哇哇哇，好窄呀，我好害怕呀。
幽閉恐懼症
任性的傢伙

↑"SENPAI" IS WRITTEN "前輩."
I SEE...

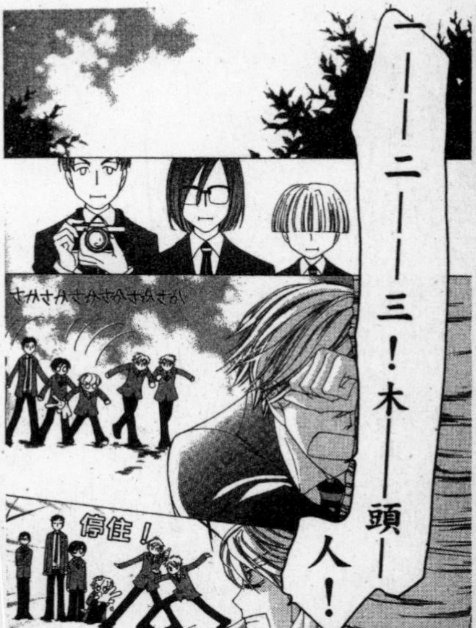
一——二——三！木——頭——人！
停住！

✿HONG KONG VERSION✿ ↓→
HARUHI IS WRITTEN "春緋"
BUT "HARU-CHAN" IS WRITTEN "小春".
THE WAY HUNNY IS WRITTEN, "甜心",
IS CUTE TOO.

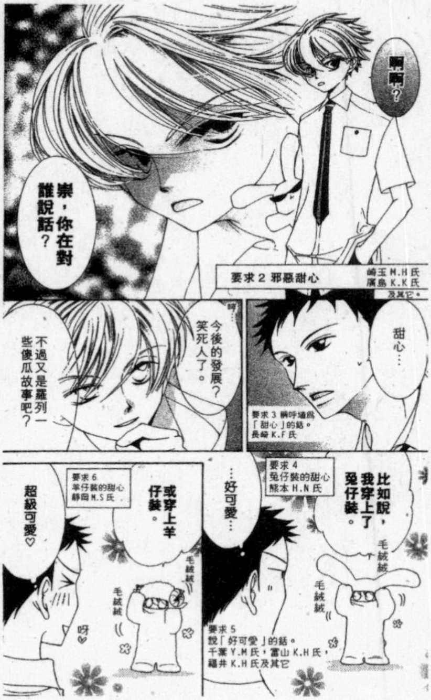
啊—啊？
崇，你在對誰說話？
要求2 邪惡甜心
崎玉 M.H氏
廣島 K.K氏
及其它
今後的發展？笑死人了。
不過又是羅列一些傻瓜故事吧？
甜心…
要求3 稱呼埴爲「甜心」的話。長崎 K.F氏
比如說，我穿上了兔仔裝。
要求4 兔仔裝的甜心 熊本 H.N氏
…好可愛…
或穿上羊仔裝。
要求6 羊仔裝的甜心 靜岡 M.S氏
超級可愛♡
毛絨絨
呀♡
要求5 說「好可愛」的話。千葉 Y.M氏，富山 K.H氏，福井 K.H氏及其它

✿TAIWAN VERSION✿ →↓
THE "DOWN FELL DARUMA" HAS
BEEN CHANGED INTO A TAIWANESE
VERSION OF THE GAME?
VERY INTERESTING.

THIS LOOKS
REALLY PAINFUL...

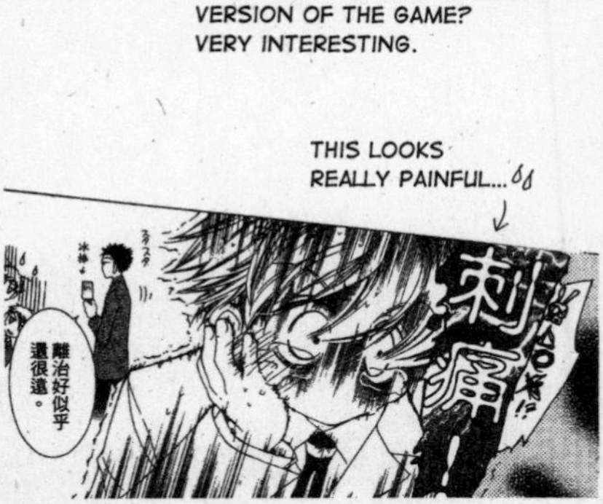
刺痛!!
離治好似乎還很遠。

Episode 36

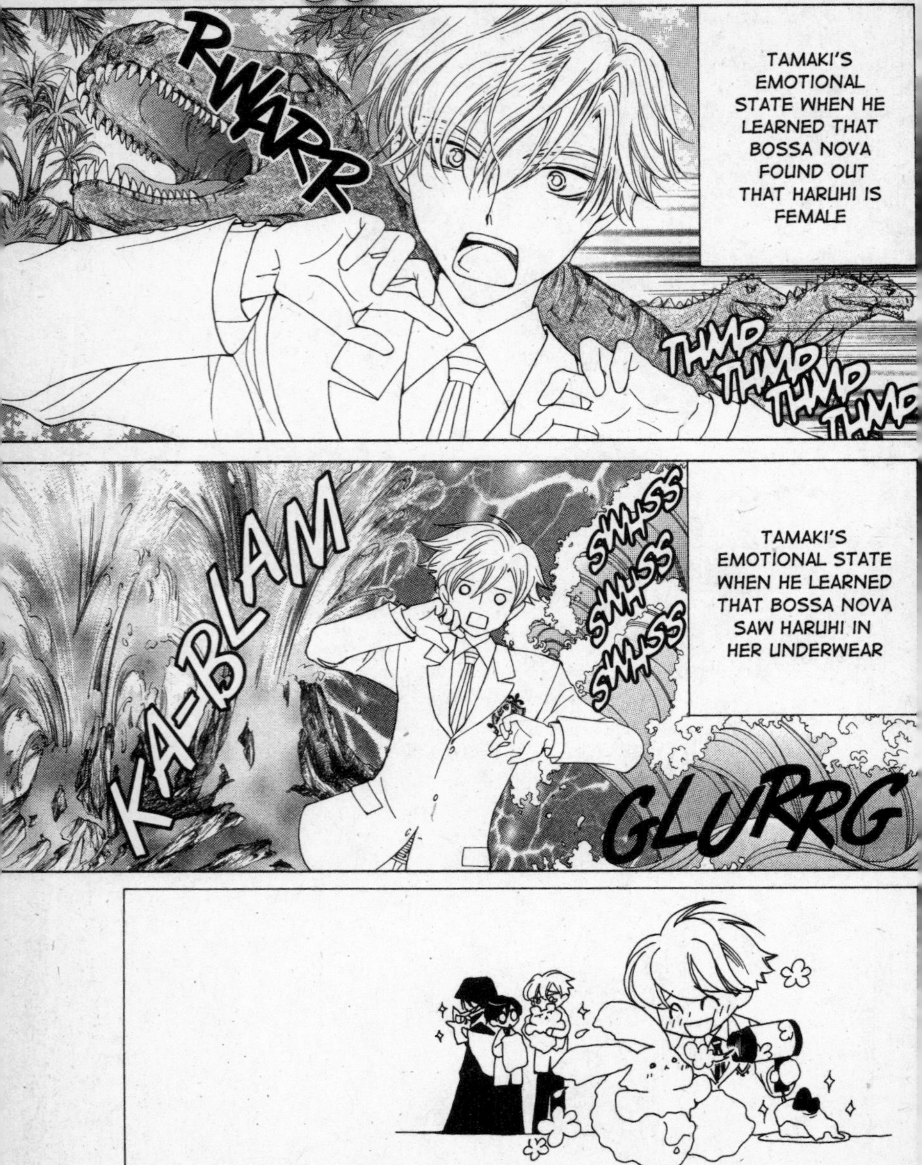
TAMAKI'S EMOTIONAL STATE WHEN HE LEARNED THAT BOSSA NOVA FOUND OUT THAT HARUHI IS FEMALE
RWARR
THUMP THUMP THUMP THUMP
TAMAKI'S EMOTIONAL STATE WHEN HE LEARNED THAT BOSSA NOVA SAW HARUHI IN HER UNDERWEAR
SWUSS SWUSS SWUSS
KA-BLAM
GLURRG

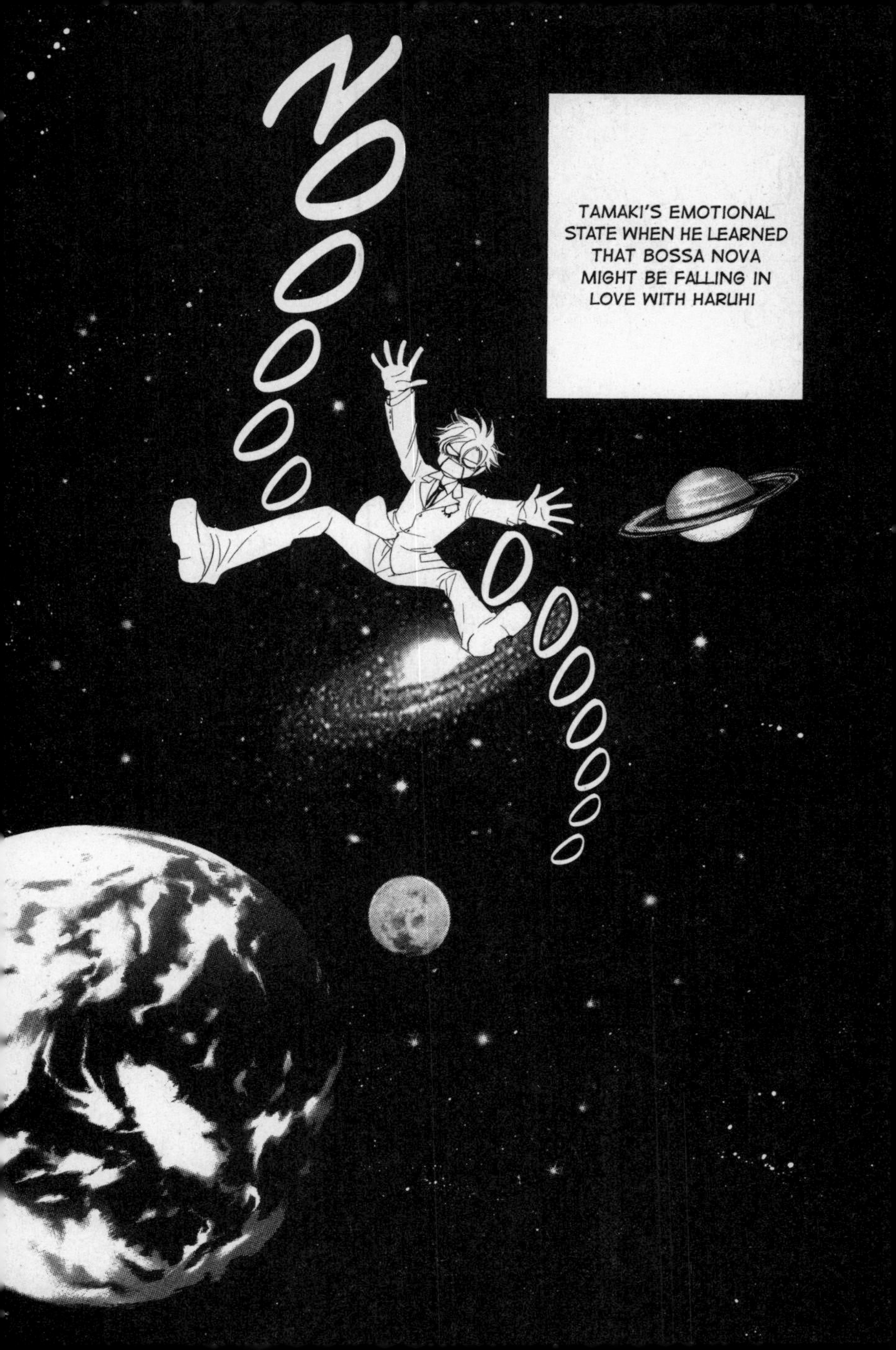
TAMAKI'S EMOTIONAL STATE WHEN HE LEARNED THAT BOSSA NOVA MIGHT BE FALLING IN LOVE WITH HARUHI
NOOOOOOOOOOOOOOOOO

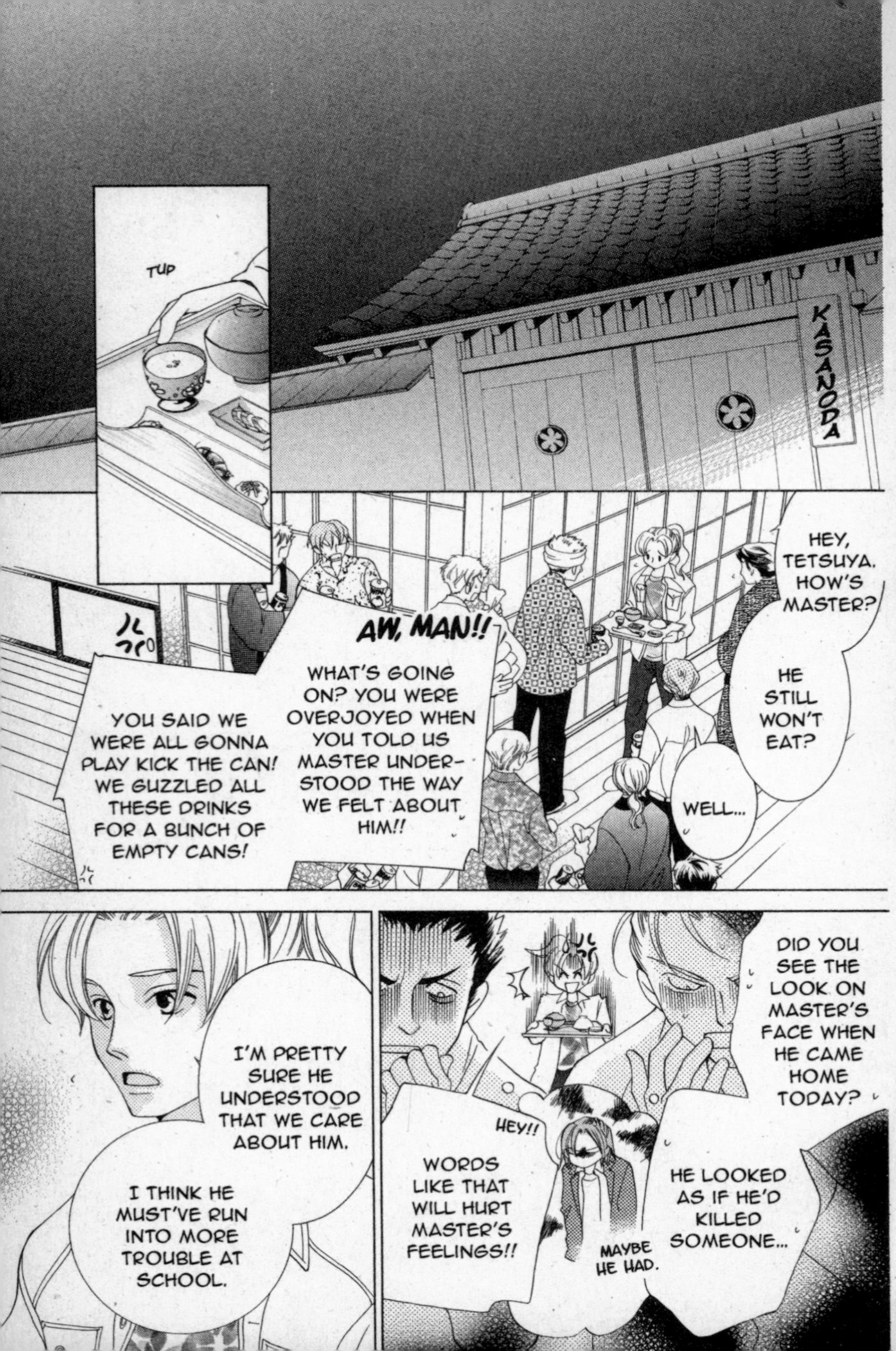
KASANODA
TUP
HEY, TETSUYA. HOW'S MASTER?
HE STILL WON'T EAT?
WELL...
AW, MAN!!
WHAT'S GOING ON? YOU WERE OVERJOYED WHEN YOU TOLD US MASTER UNDER-STOOD THE WAY WE FELT ABOUT HIM!!
YOU SAID WE WERE ALL GONNA PLAY KICK THE CAN! WE GUZZLED ALL THESE DRINKS FOR A BUNCH OF EMPTY CANS!
DID YOU SEE THE LOOK ON MASTER'S FACE WHEN HE CAME HOME TODAY?
HE LOOKED AS IF HE'D KILLED SOMEONE...
MAYBE HE HAD.
HEY!!
WORDS LIKE THAT WILL HURT MASTER'S FEELINGS!!
I'M PRETTY SURE HE UNDERSTOOD THAT WE CARE ABOUT HIM.
I THINK HE MUST'VE RUN INTO MORE TROUBLE AT SCHOOL.

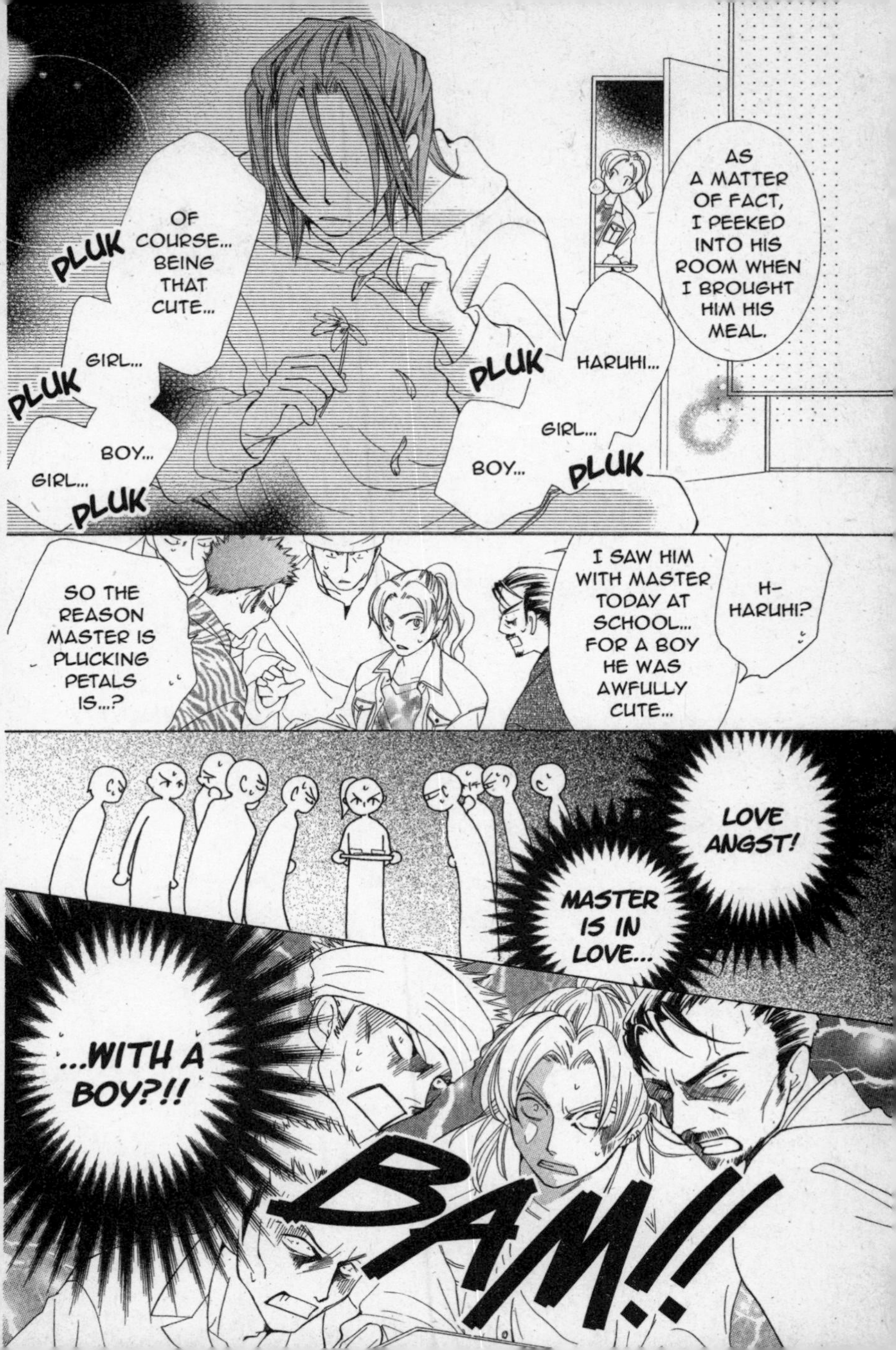
AS A MATTER OF FACT, I PEEKED INTO HIS ROOM WHEN I BROUGHT HIM HIS MEAL.
PLUK
HARUHI...
GIRL...
BOY...
PLUK
OF COURSE... BEING THAT CUTE...
PLUK
GIRL...
PLUK
BOY...
GIRL...
PLUK
H-HARUHI?
I SAW HIM WITH MASTER TODAY AT SCHOOL... FOR A BOY HE WAS AWFULLY CUTE...
SO THE REASON MASTER IS PLUCKING PETALS IS...?
LOVE ANGST!
MASTER IS IN LOVE...
...WITH A BOY?!!
BAM!!

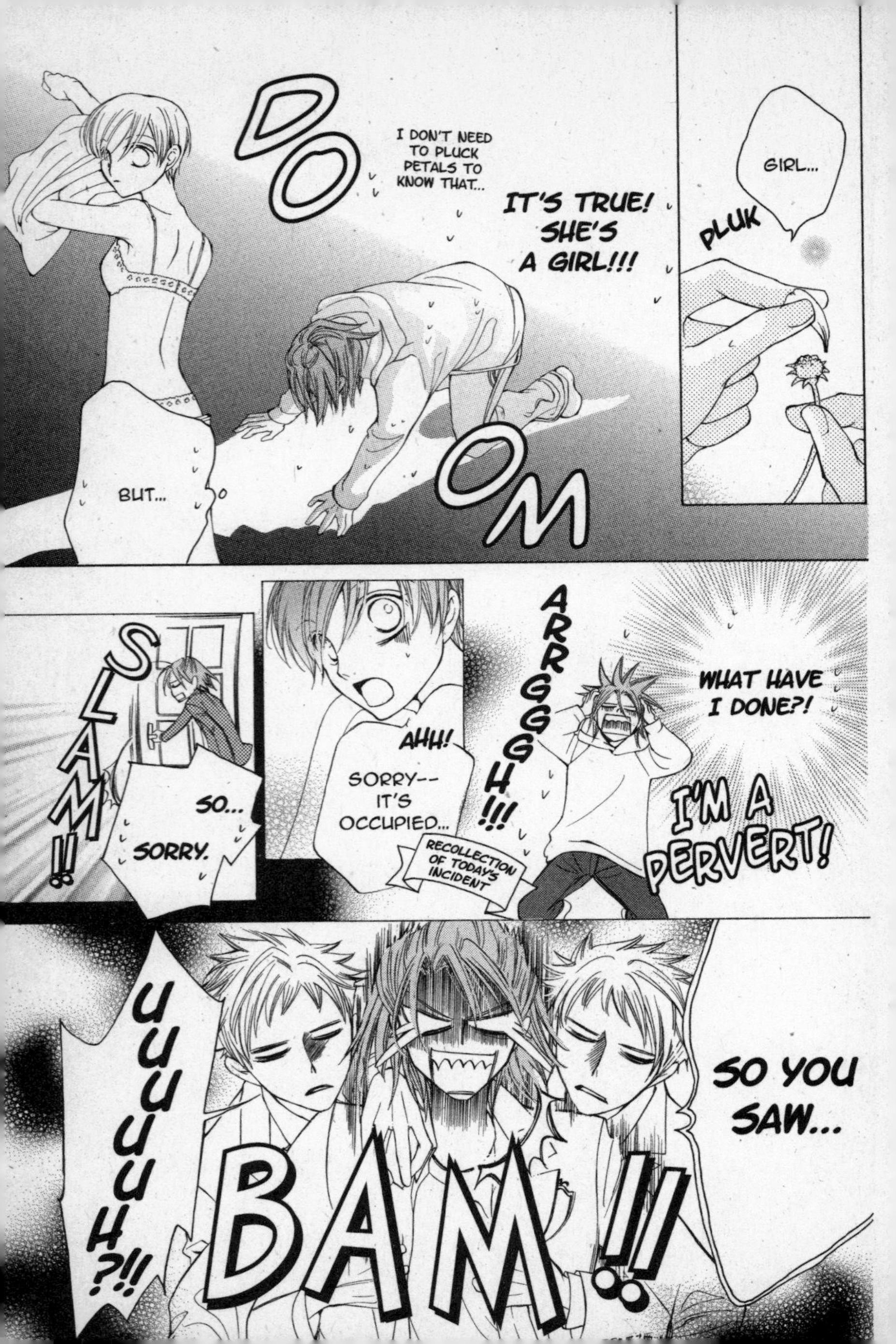
GIRL...
PLUK
IT'S TRUE! SHE'S A GIRL!!!
I DON'T NEED TO PLUCK PETALS TO KNOW THAT...
DOOM
BUT...
WHAT HAVE I DONE?!
I'M A PERVERT!
ARRGGGH!!!
RECOLLECTION OF TODAY'S INCIDENT
AHH!
SORRY-- IT'S OCCUPIED...
SLAM!!
SO...
SORRY.
SO YOU SAW...
BAM!!
UUUUUH?!!

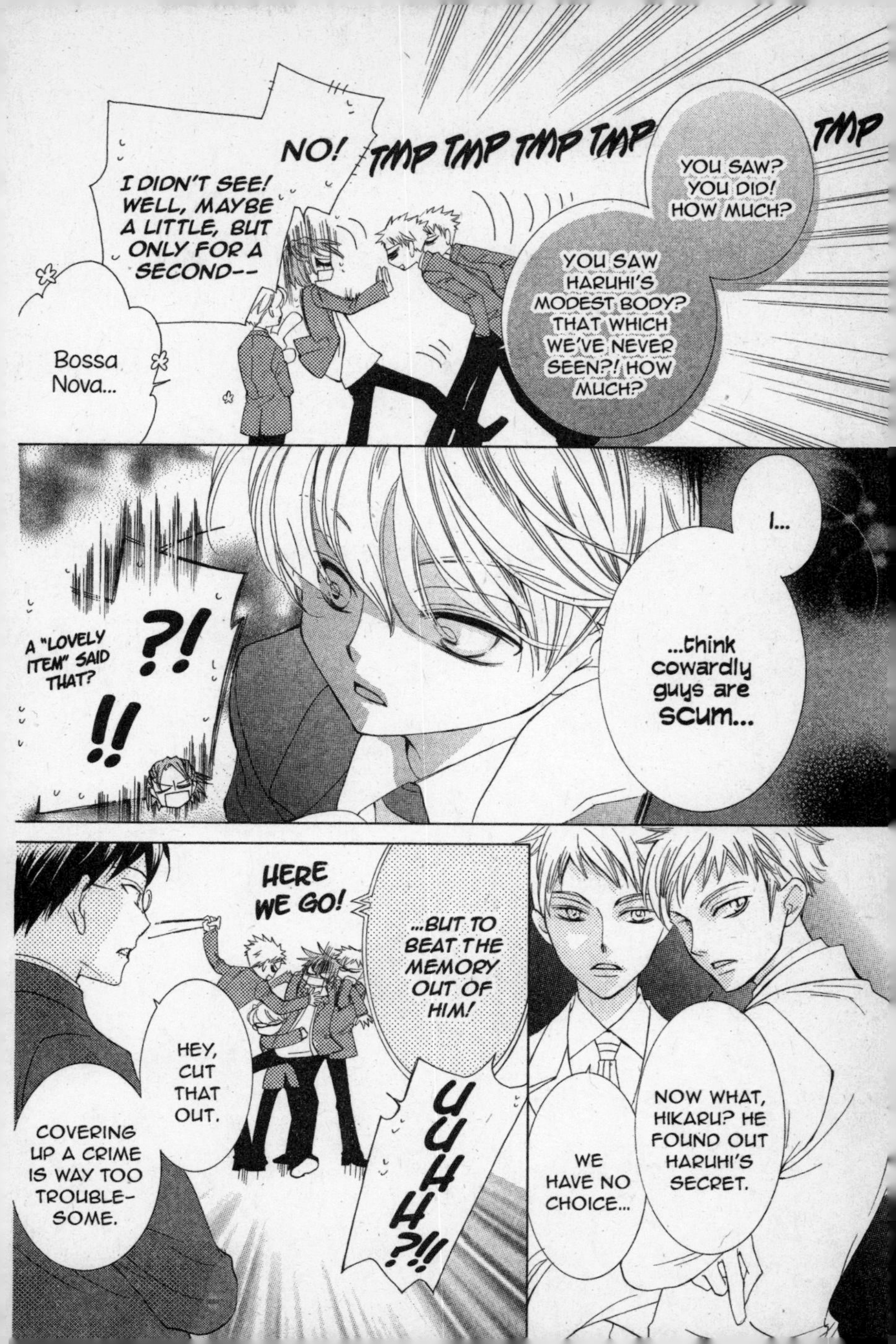
TMP
TMP TMP TMP TMP
YOU SAW? YOU DID! HOW MUCH?
YOU SAW HARUHI'S MODEST BODY? THAT WHICH WE'VE NEVER SEEN?! HOW MUCH?
NO!
I DIDN'T SEE! WELL, MAYBE A LITTLE, BUT ONLY FOR A SECOND--
Bossa Nova...
I...
...think cowardly guys are scum...
?!
A "LOVELY ITEM" SAID THAT?
!!
NOW WHAT, HIKARU? HE FOUND OUT HARUHI'S SECRET.
WE HAVE NO CHOICE...
...BUT TO BEAT THE MEMORY OUT OF HIM!
HERE WE GO!
UUHH?!!
HEY, CUT THAT OUT.
COVERING UP A CRIME IS WAY TOO TROUBLE-SOME.

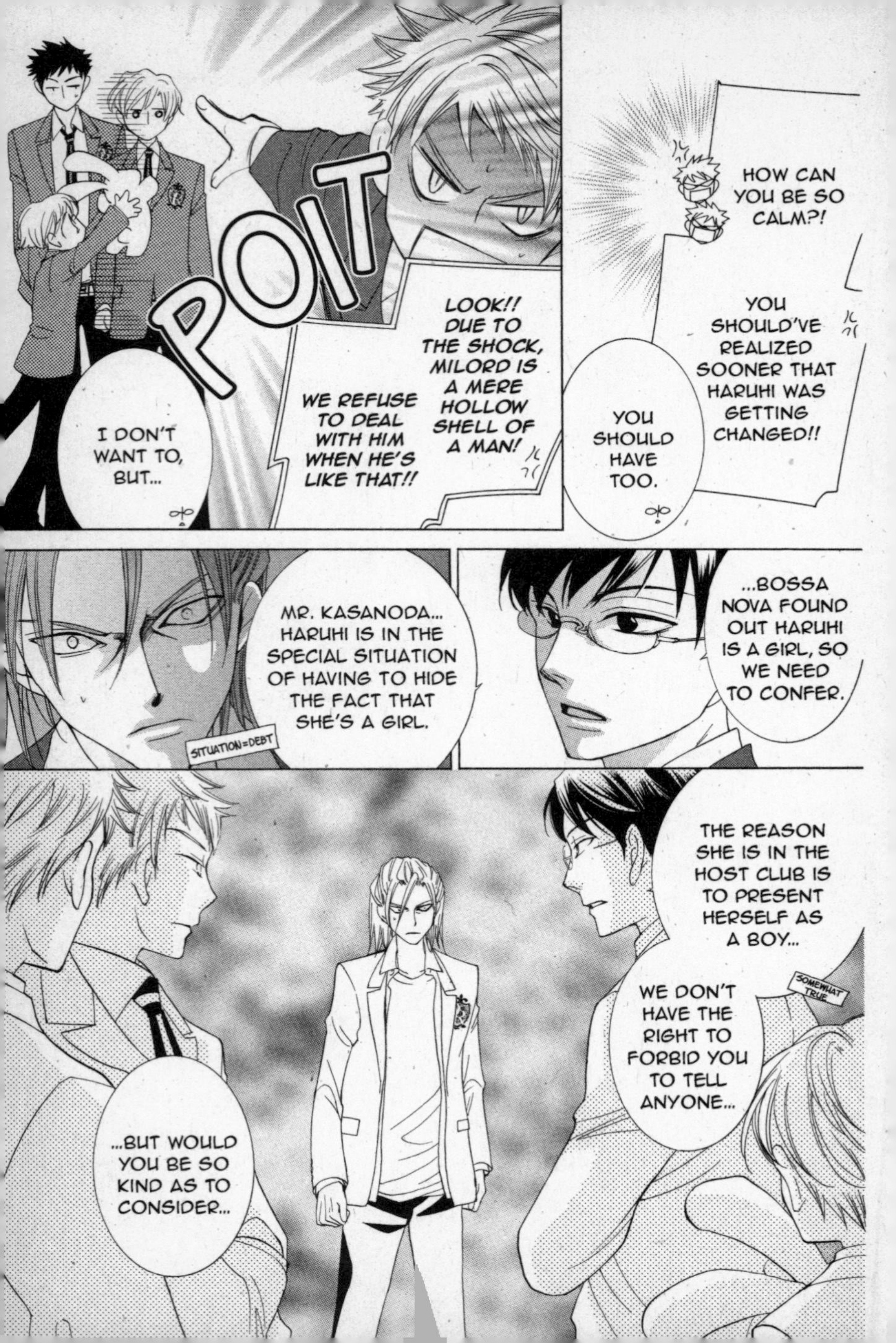
HOW CAN YOU BE SO CALM?!
YOU SHOULD'VE REALIZED SOONER THAT HARUHI WAS GETTING CHANGED!!
YOU SHOULD HAVE TOO.
LOOK!! DUE TO THE SHOCK, MILORD IS A MERE HOLLOW SHELL OF A MAN!
WE REFUSE TO DEAL WITH HIM WHEN HE'S LIKE THAT!!
POIT
I DON'T WANT TO, BUT...
...BOSSA NOVA FOUND OUT HARUHI IS A GIRL, SO WE NEED TO CONFER.
MR. KASANODA... HARUHI IS IN THE SPECIAL SITUATION OF HAVING TO HIDE THE FACT THAT SHE'S A GIRL.
SITUATION=DEBT
THE REASON SHE IS IN THE HOST CLUB IS TO PRESENT HERSELF AS A BOY...
SOMEWHAT TRUE
WE DON'T HAVE THE RIGHT TO FORBID YOU TO TELL ANYONE...
...BUT WOULD YOU BE SO KIND AS TO CONSIDER...

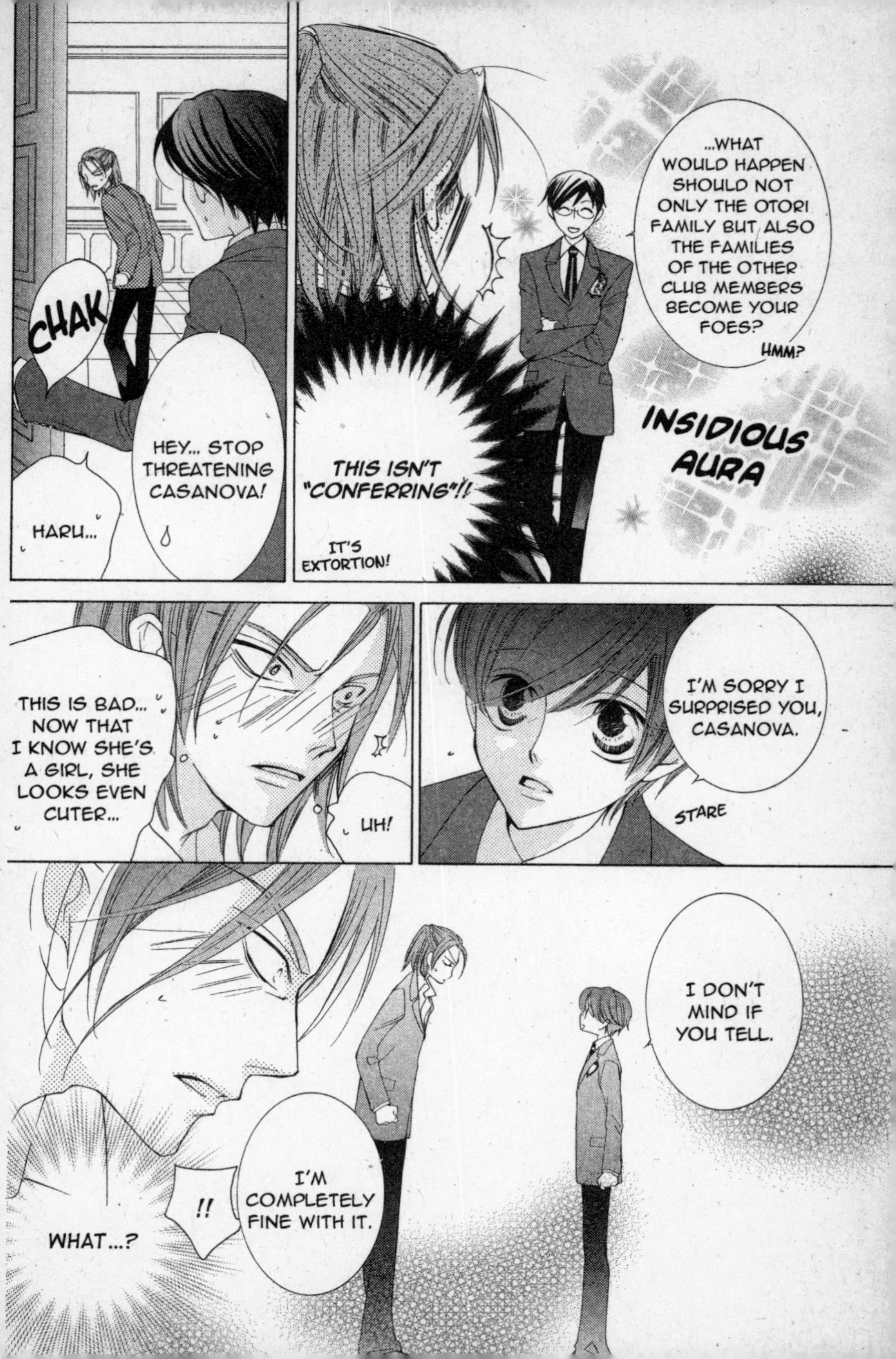
...WHAT WOULD HAPPEN SHOULD NOT ONLY THE OTORI FAMILY BUT ALSO THE FAMILIES OF THE OTHER CLUB MEMBERS BECOME YOUR FOES?
HMM?
INSIDIOUS AURA
THIS ISN'T "CONFERRING"!!
IT'S EXTORTION!
CHAK
HEY... STOP THREATENING CASANOVA!
HARU...
I'M SORRY I SURPRISED YOU, CASANOVA.
STARE
THIS IS BAD... NOW THAT I KNOW SHE'S A GIRL, SHE LOOKS EVEN CUTER...
UH!
I DON'T MIND IF YOU TELL.
I'M COMPLETELY FINE WITH IT.
!!
WHAT...?

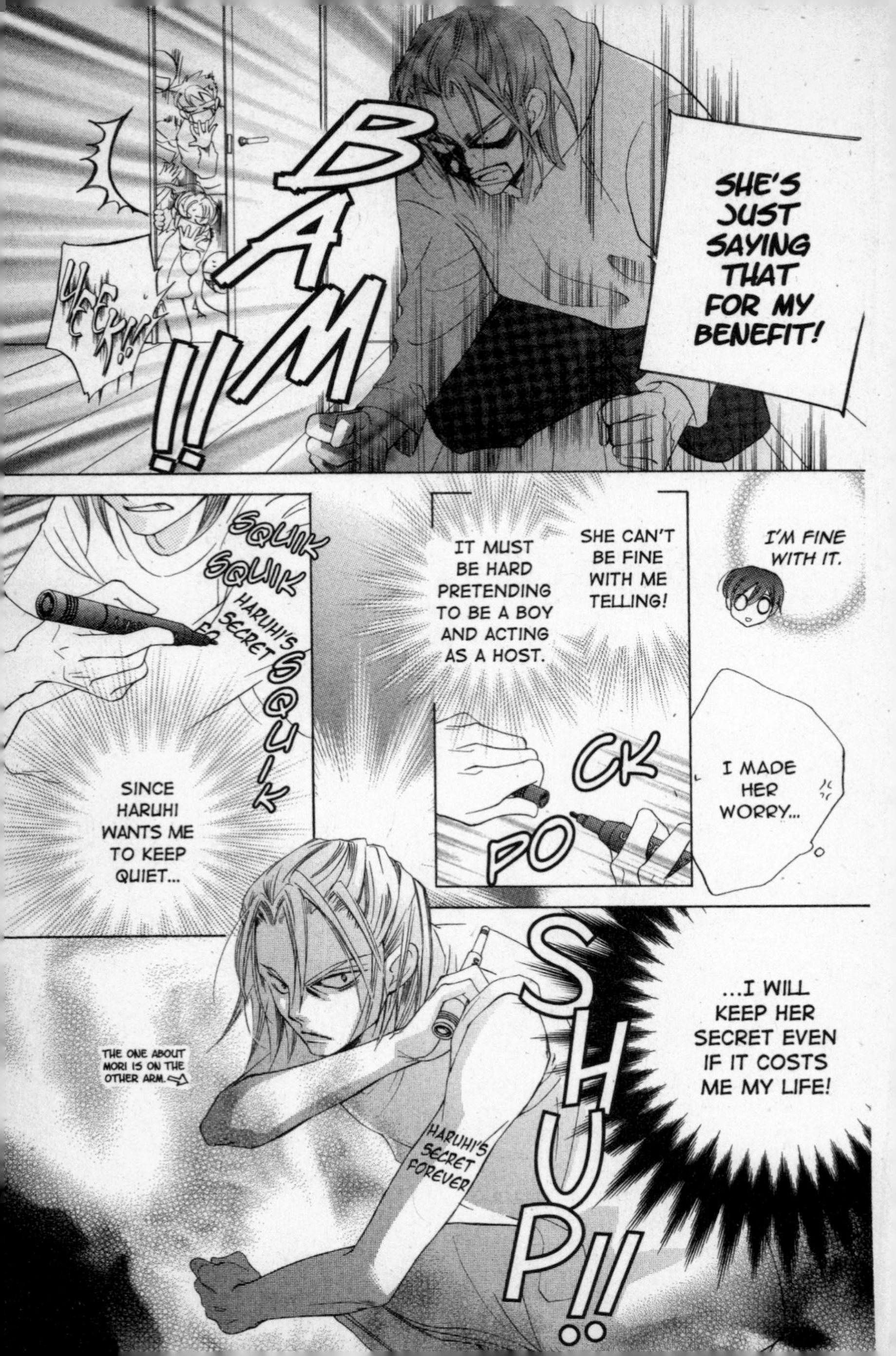

SHE'S JUST SAYING THAT FOR MY BENEFIT!
BAM!!
YEEK!!
I'M FINE WITH IT.
I MADE HER WORRY...
SHE CAN'T BE FINE WITH ME TELLING!
IT MUST BE HARD PRETENDING TO BE A BOY AND ACTING AS A HOST.
POCK
SQUIK SQUIK
HARUHI'S SECRET FO
SQUIK
SINCE HARUHI WANTS ME TO KEEP QUIET...
...I WILL KEEP HER SECRET EVEN IF IT COSTS ME MY LIFE!
SHUP!!
HARUHI'S SECRET FOREVER
THE ONE ABOUT MORI IS ON THE OTHER ARM.

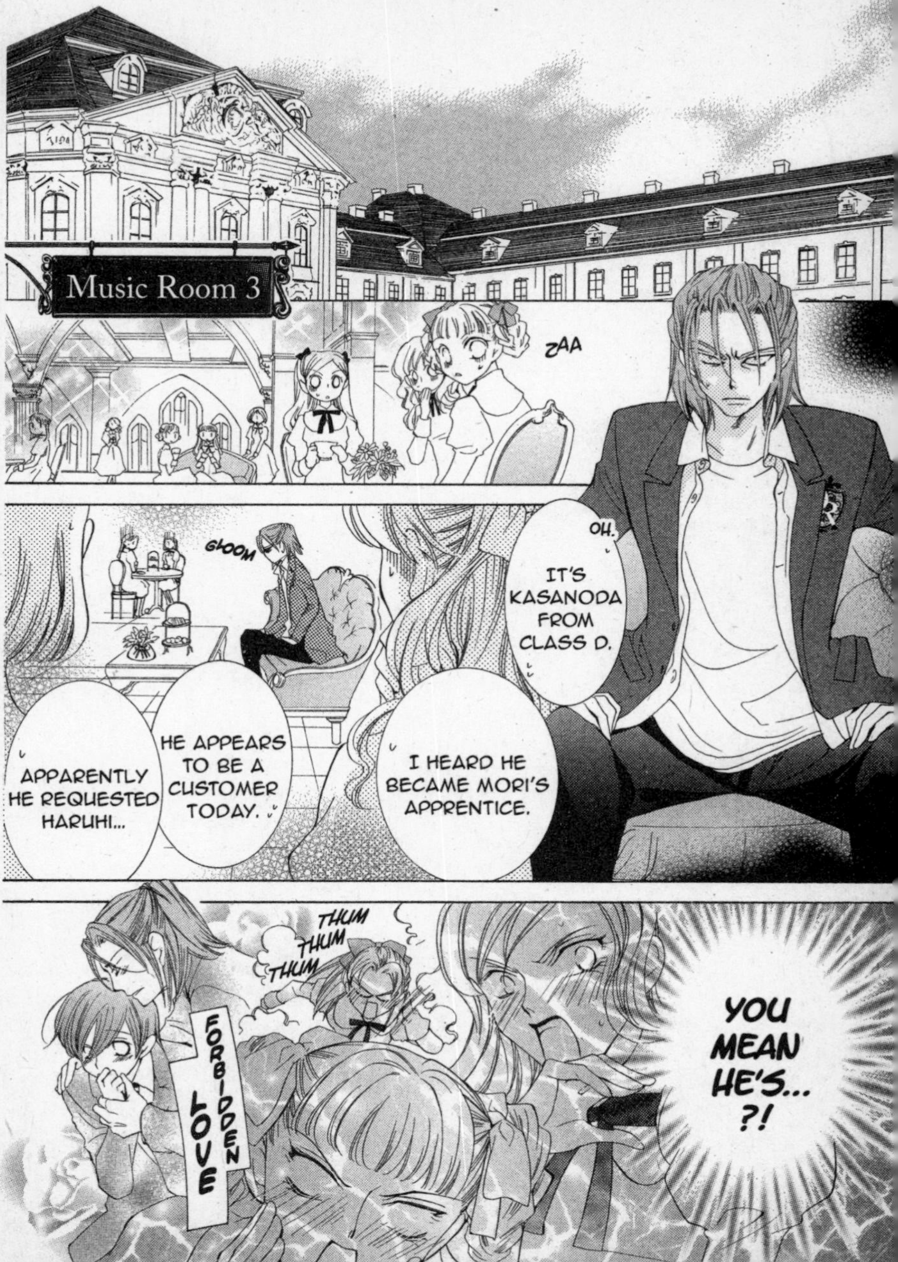
Music Room 3
ZAA
OH.
IT'S KASANODA FROM CLASS D.
I HEARD HE BECAME MORI'S APPRENTICE.
HE APPEARS TO BE A CUSTOMER TODAY.
APPARENTLY HE REQUESTED HARUHI...
GLOOM
YOU MEAN HE'S... ?!
THUM THUM THUM
FORBIDDEN LOVE

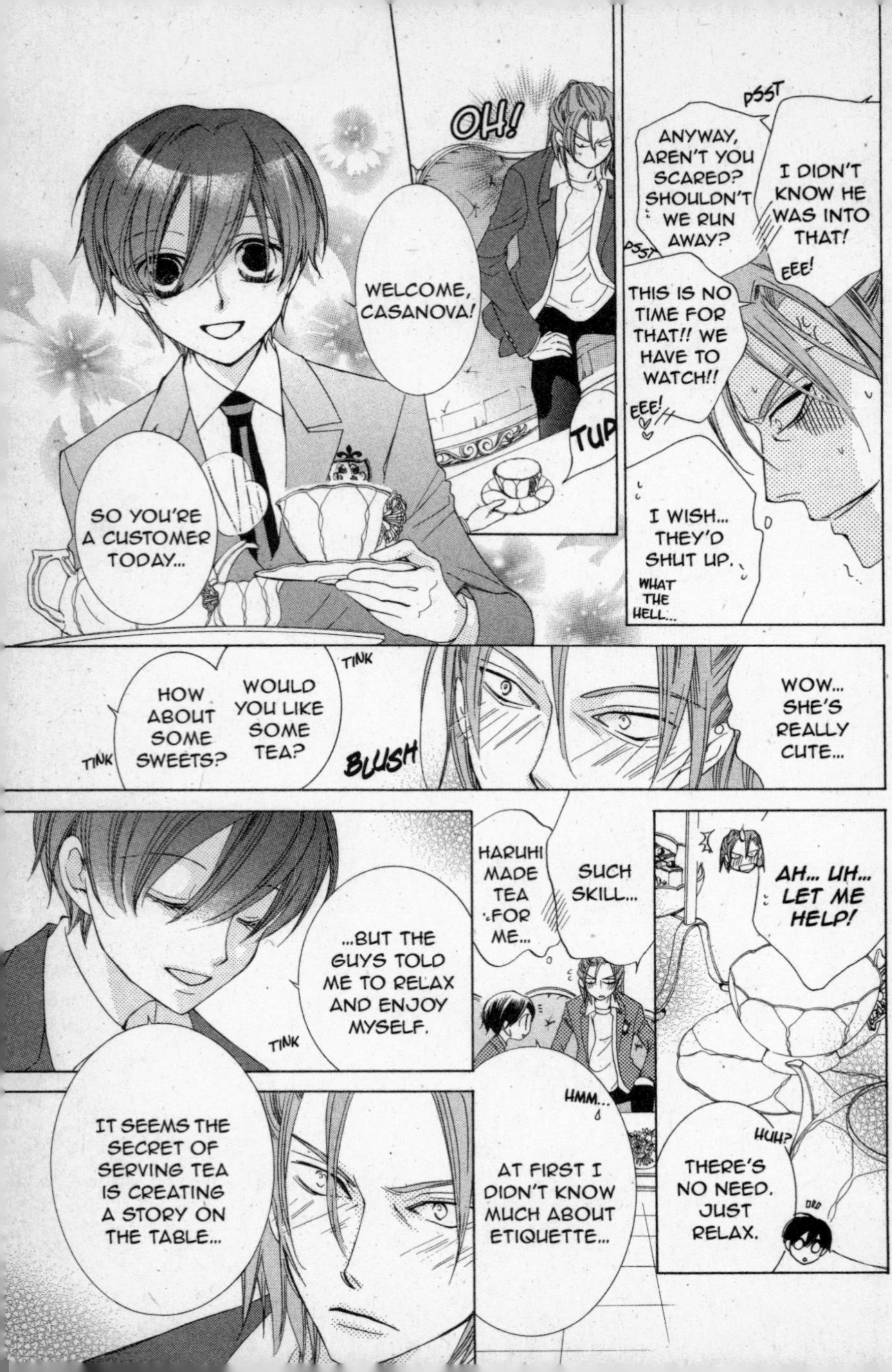
PSST
I DIDN'T KNOW HE WAS INTO THAT!
ANYWAY, AREN'T YOU SCARED? SHOULDN'T WE RUN AWAY?
PSST
EEE!
THIS IS NO TIME FOR THAT!! WE HAVE TO WATCH!!
EEE!
I WISH... THEY'D SHUT UP.
WHAT THE HELL...
OH!
WELCOME, CASANOVA!
TUP
SO YOU'RE A CUSTOMER TODAY...
WOW... SHE'S REALLY CUTE...
BLUSH
TINK
WOULD YOU LIKE SOME TEA?
HOW ABOUT SOME SWEETS?
TINK
AH... UH... LET ME HELP!
HUH?
THERE'S NO NEED. JUST RELAX.
SUCH SKILL...
HARUHI MADE TEA FOR ME...
HMM...
AT FIRST I DIDN'T KNOW MUCH ABOUT ETIQUETTE...
...BUT THE GUYS TOLD ME TO RELAX AND ENJOY MYSELF.
TINK
IT SEEMS THE SECRET OF SERVING TEA IS CREATING A STORY ON THE TABLE...

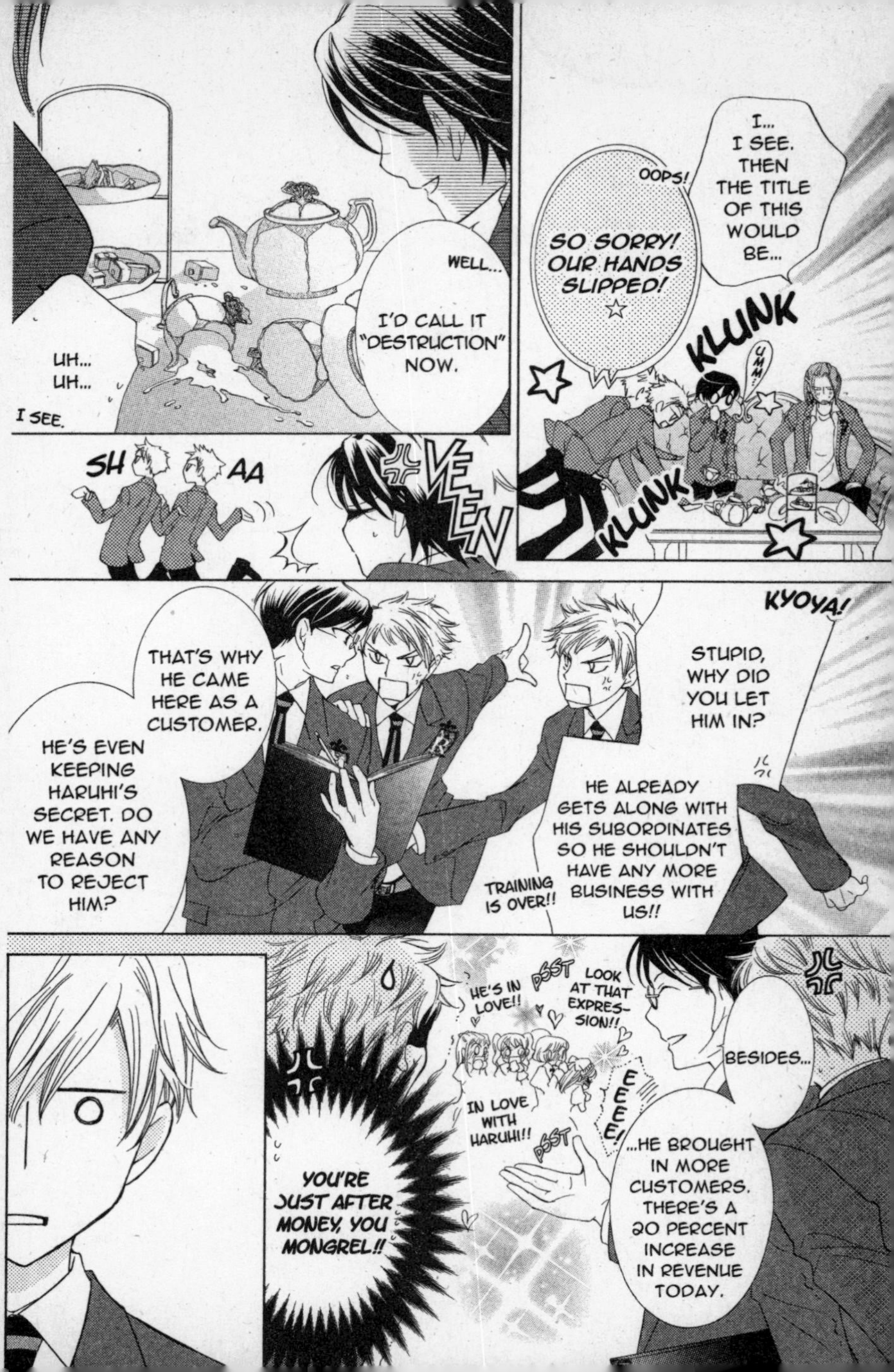
I...
I SEE. THEN THE TITLE OF THIS WOULD BE...
OOPS!
SO SORRY! OUR HANDS SLIPPED! ☆
KLUNK
UMM...
KLUNK
WELL...
I'D CALL IT "DESTRUCTION" NOW.
UH... UH...
I SEE.
SH
AA
VEEEN
KYOYA!
STUPID, WHY DID YOU LET HIM IN?
HE ALREADY GETS ALONG WITH HIS SUBORDINATES SO HE SHOULDN'T HAVE ANY MORE BUSINESS WITH US!!
TRAINING IS OVER!!
THAT'S WHY HE CAME HERE AS A CUSTOMER.
HE'S EVEN KEEPING HARUHI'S SECRET. DO WE HAVE ANY REASON TO REJECT HIM?
BESIDES...
...HE BROUGHT IN MORE CUSTOMERS. THERE'S A 20 PERCENT INCREASE IN REVENUE TODAY.
LOOK AT THAT EXPRES-SION!!
PSST
HE'S IN LOVE!!
EEEE!
IN LOVE WITH HARUHI!!
PSST
YOU'RE JUST AFTER MONEY, YOU MONGREL!!

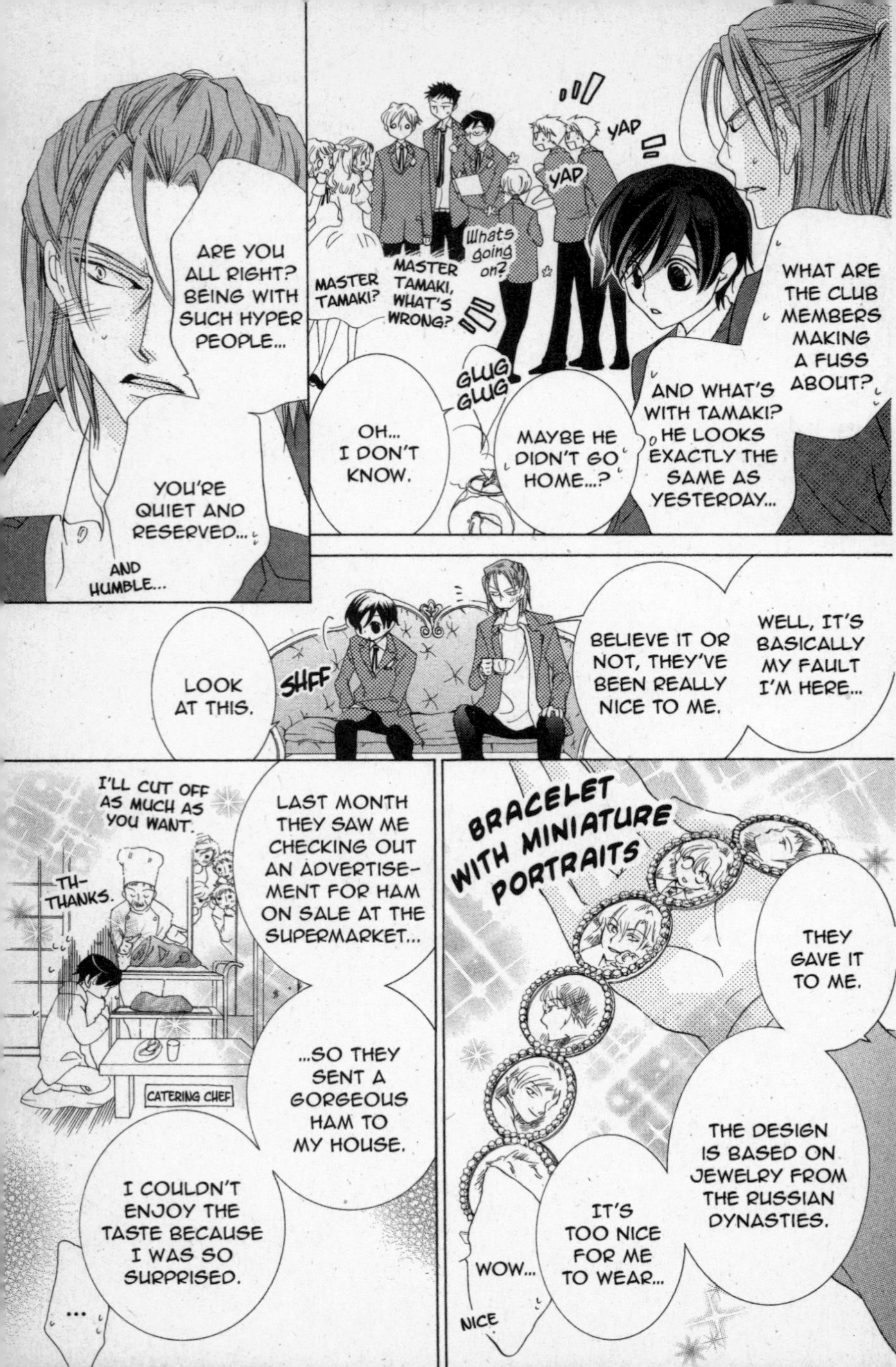
WHAT ARE THE CLUB MEMBERS MAKING A FUSS ABOUT?
AND WHAT'S WITH TAMAKI? HE LOOKS EXACTLY THE SAME AS YESTERDAY...
YAP
YAP
MAYBE HE DIDN'T GO HOME...?
Whats going on?
MASTER TAMAKI, WHAT'S WRONG?
MASTER TAMAKI?
GLUG GLUG
OH... I DON'T KNOW.
ARE YOU ALL RIGHT? BEING WITH SUCH HYPER PEOPLE...
YOU'RE QUIET AND RESERVED...
AND HUMBLE...
WELL, IT'S BASICALLY MY FAULT I'M HERE...
BELIEVE IT OR NOT, THEY'VE BEEN REALLY NICE TO ME.
SHFF
LOOK AT THIS.
BRACELET WITH MINIATURE PORTRAITS
THEY GAVE IT TO ME.
THE DESIGN IS BASED ON JEWELRY FROM THE RUSSIAN DYNASTIES.
IT'S TOO NICE FOR ME TO WEAR...
WOW...
NICE
LAST MONTH THEY SAW ME CHECKING OUT AN ADVERTISE-MENT FOR HAM ON SALE AT THE SUPERMARKET...
I'LL CUT OFF AS MUCH AS YOU WANT.
TH-THANKS.
...SO THEY SENT A GORGEOUS HAM TO MY HOUSE.
CATERING CHEF
I COULDN'T ENJOY THE TASTE BECAUSE I WAS SO SURPRISED.
...

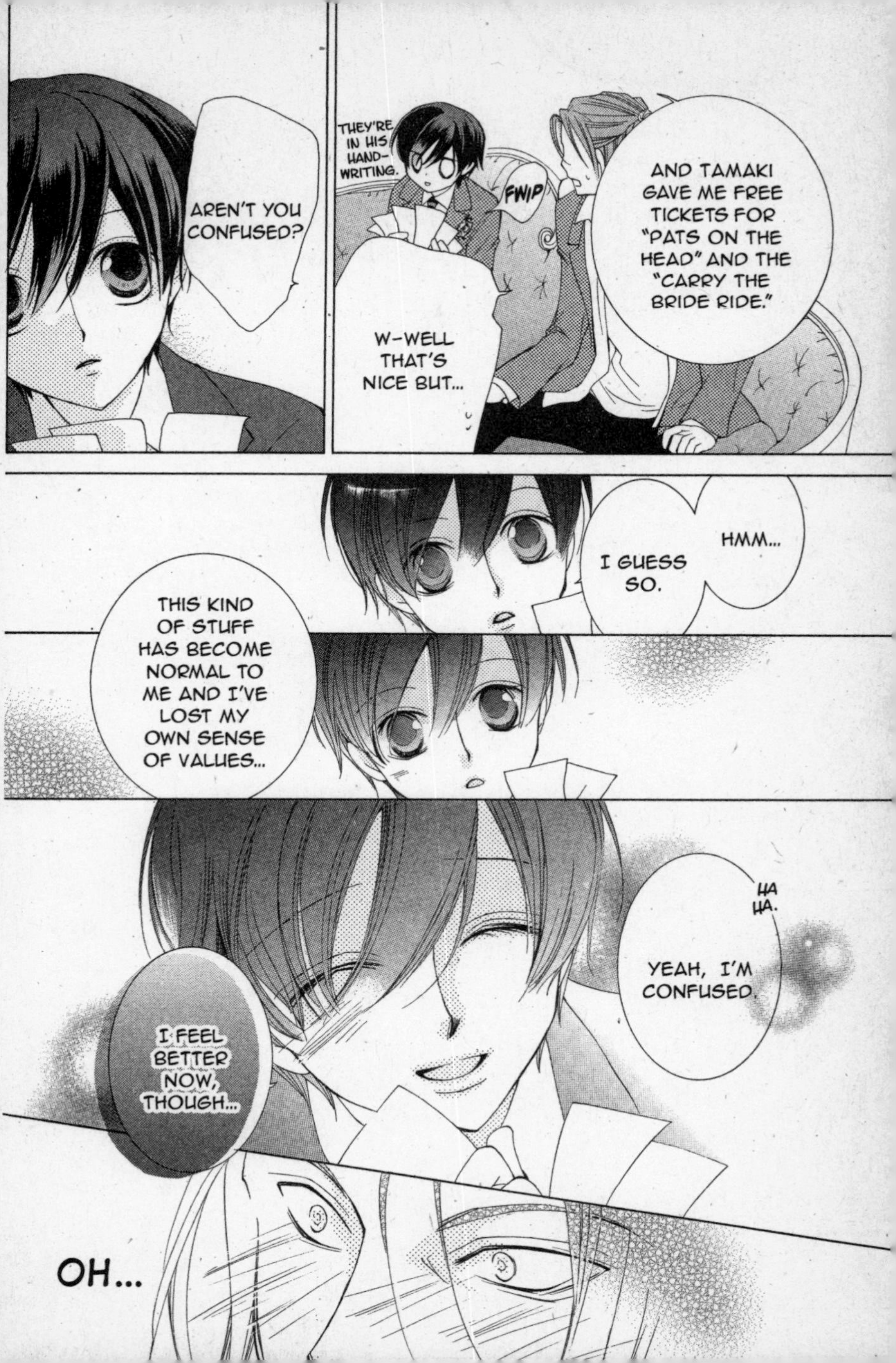

AND TAMAKI GAVE ME FREE TICKETS FOR "PATS ON THE HEAD" AND THE "CARRY THE BRIDE RIDE."
FWIP
THEY'RE IN HIS HAND-WRITING.
W-WELL THAT'S NICE BUT...
AREN'T YOU CONFUSED?
HMM...
I GUESS SO.
THIS KIND OF STUFF HAS BECOME NORMAL TO ME AND I'VE LOST MY OWN SENSE OF VALUES...
HA HA.
YEAH, I'M CONFUSED.
I FEEL BETTER NOW, THOUGH...
OH...

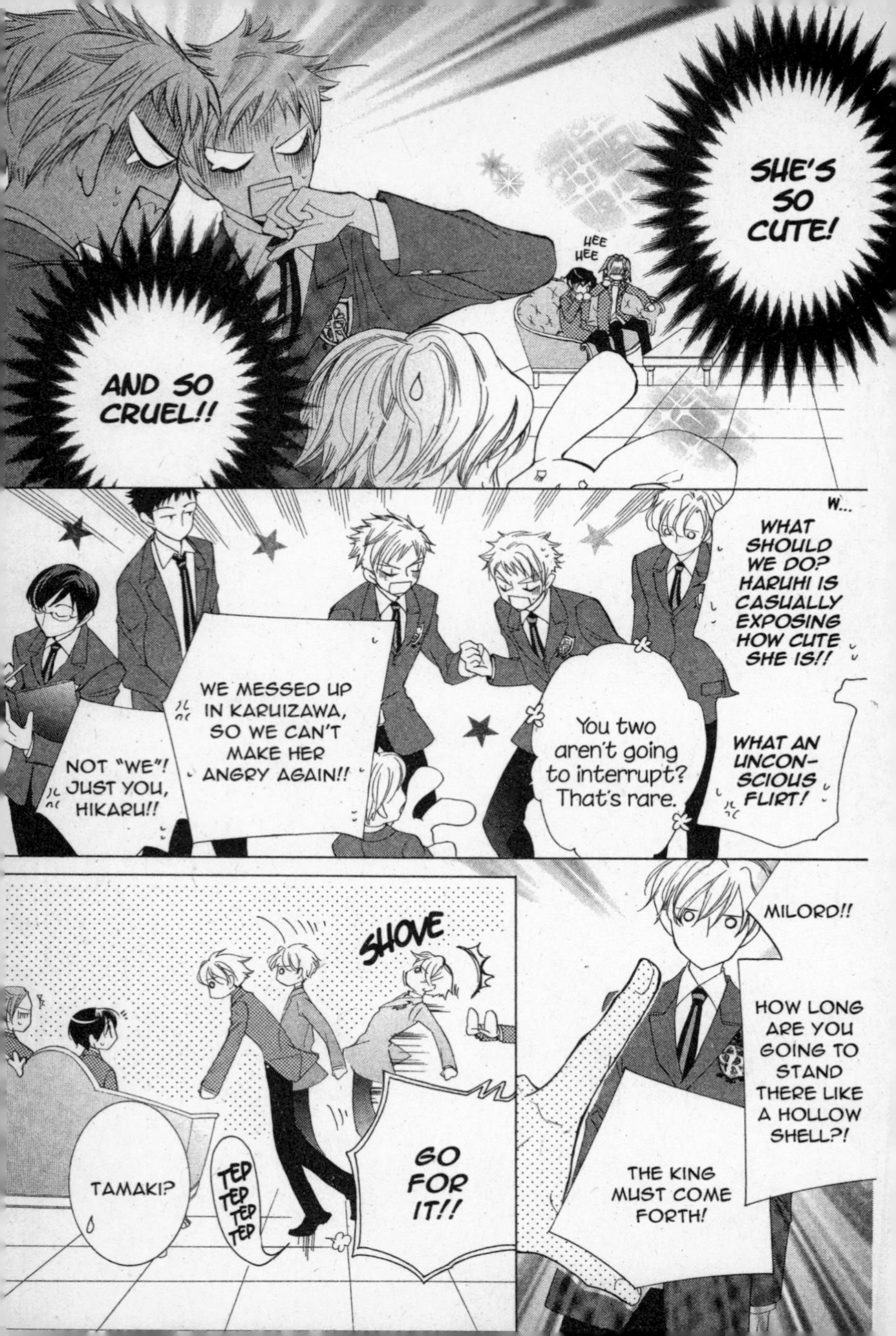
SHE'S SO CUTE!
HEE HEE
AND SO CRUEL!!
W... WHAT SHOULD WE DO? HARUHI IS CASUALLY EXPOSING HOW CUTE SHE IS!!
WHAT AN UNCON-SCIOUS FLIRT!
You two aren't going to interrupt? That's rare.
WE MESSED UP IN KARUIZAWA, SO WE CAN'T MAKE HER ANGRY AGAIN!!
NOT "WE"! JUST YOU, HIKARU!!
MILORD!!
HOW LONG ARE YOU GOING TO STAND THERE LIKE A HOLLOW SHELL?!
THE KING MUST COME FORTH!
SHOVE
GO FOR IT!!
TEP TEP TEP TEP
TAMAKI?

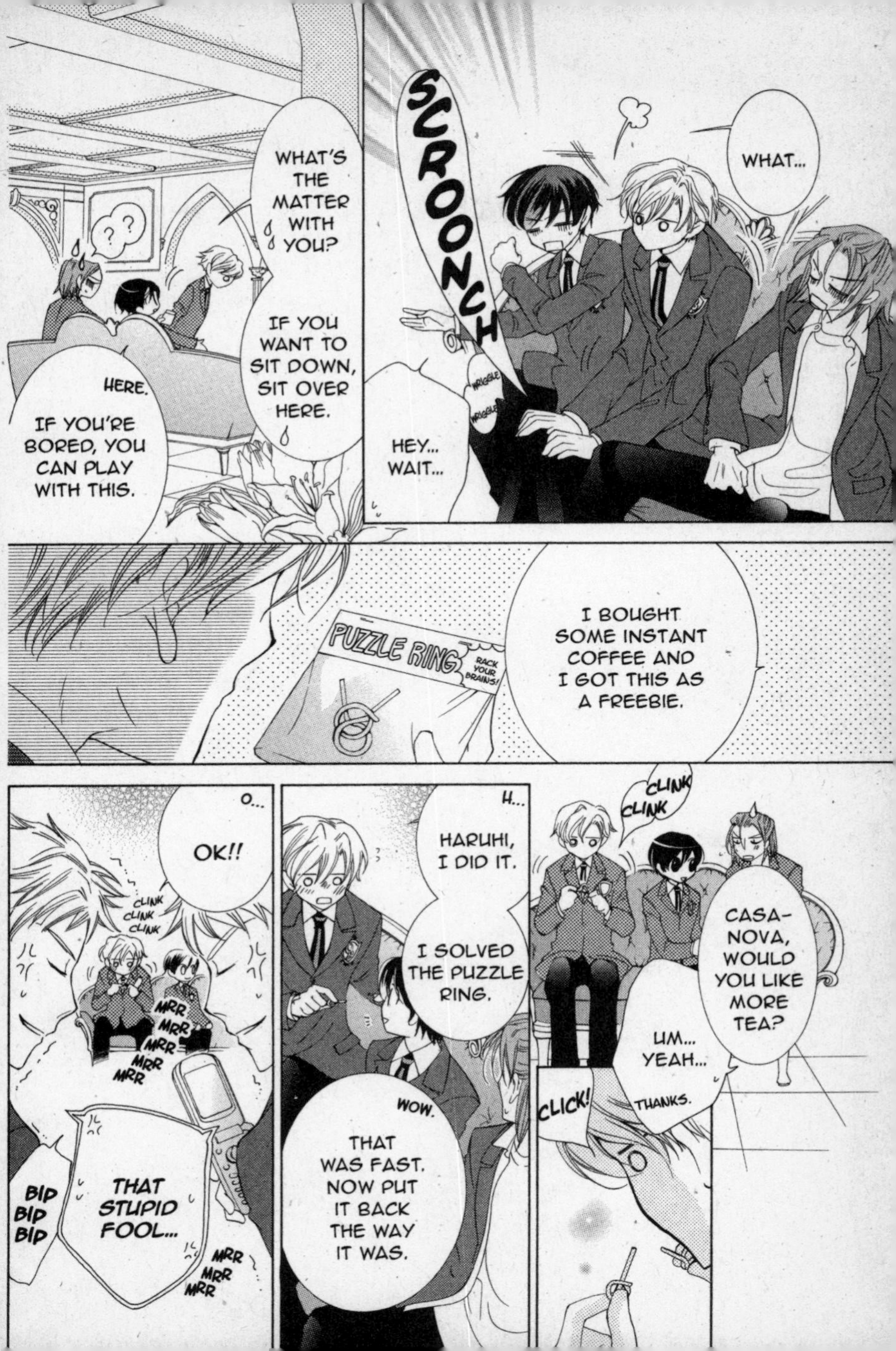
WHAT...
SCROONCH
WRIGGLE WRIGGLE
HEY... WAIT...
WHAT'S THE MATTER WITH YOU?
IF YOU WANT TO SIT DOWN, SIT OVER HERE.
??
HERE.
IF YOU'RE BORED, YOU CAN PLAY WITH THIS.
I BOUGHT SOME INSTANT COFFEE AND I GOT THIS AS A FREEBIE.
PUZZLE RING
RACK YOUR BRAINS!
CLINK CLINK
CASA-NOVA, WOULD YOU LIKE MORE TEA?
UM... YEAH...
THANKS.
CLICK!
H...
HARUHI, I DID IT.
I SOLVED THE PUZZLE RING.
WOW.
THAT WAS FAST. NOW PUT IT BACK THE WAY IT WAS.
O...
OK!!
CLINK CLINK CLINK
MRR MRR MRR MRR MRR
BIP BIP BIP
THAT STUPID FOOL...
MRR MRR MRR

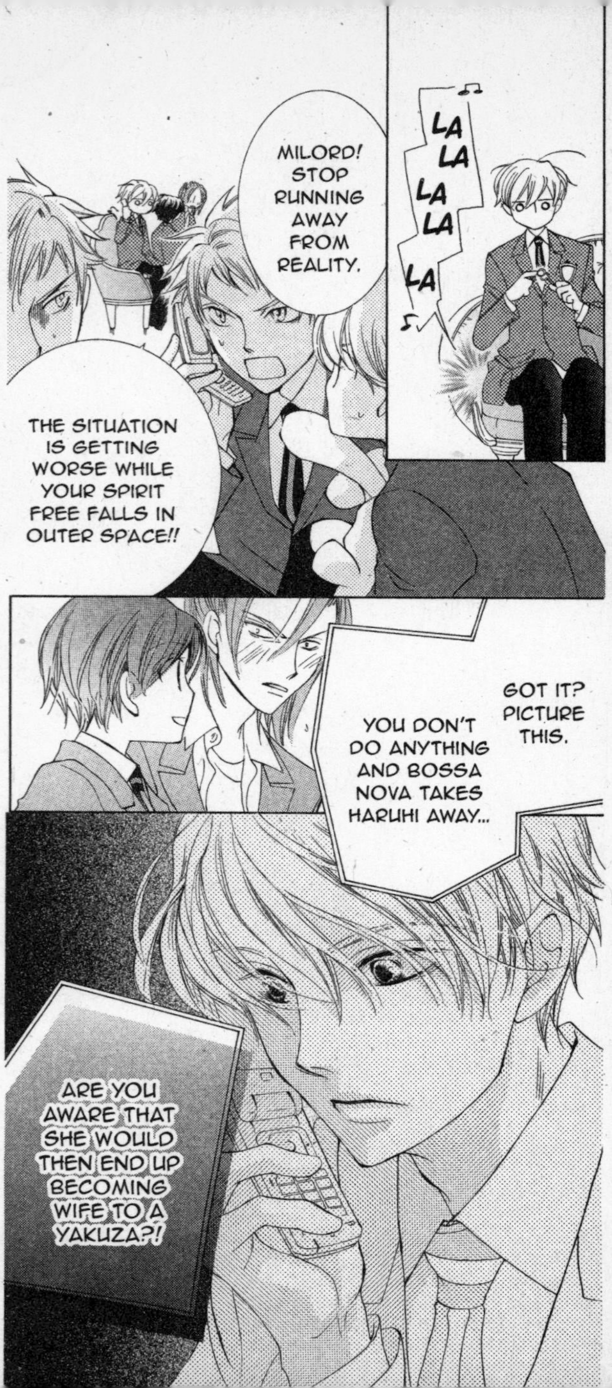
LA LA LA LA LA
MILORD! STOP RUNNING AWAY FROM REALITY.
THE SITUATION IS GETTING WORSE WHILE YOUR SPIRIT FREE FALLS IN OUTER SPACE!!
GOT IT? PICTURE THIS.
YOU DON'T DO ANYTHING AND BOSSA NOVA TAKES HARUHI AWAY...
ARE YOU AWARE THAT SHE WOULD THEN END UP BECOMING WIFE TO A YAKUZA?!

✿ ANYWAY, THIS IS NO TIME TO BE AGITATED, SO I'LL CONTINUE DOING MY BEST TO ILLUSTRATE *HOST CLUB* IN MY OWN FASHION. THE CHARACTER DESIGNS ARE REALLY, REALLY GREAT AND THE BACKGROUND ART REALLY IMPRESSED ME AND MY ASSISTANTS. THE SCRIPTS ARE AMUSING, AND THE STORYBOARDS ARE JUST AMAZING. THE THEME SONGS ARE VERY NICE TOO!! BOTH THE OPENING AND THE CLOSING SONGS!!!!

I'D REALLY LIKE TO THANK ALL YOU READERS FOR SUPPORTING ME. I MUST HAVE USED UP MY ENTIRE LIFE'S WORTH OF GOOD FORTUNE!!

EVERYONE, PLEASE WATCH THE ANIME. ♡ I'LL BE ON THE EDGE OF MY SEAT, BUT I'LL HIDE IN THE BATHROOM DURING THE ENDING (I DREW THAT...) PLEASE ENJOY IT, EVERYONE!!!

BANANA

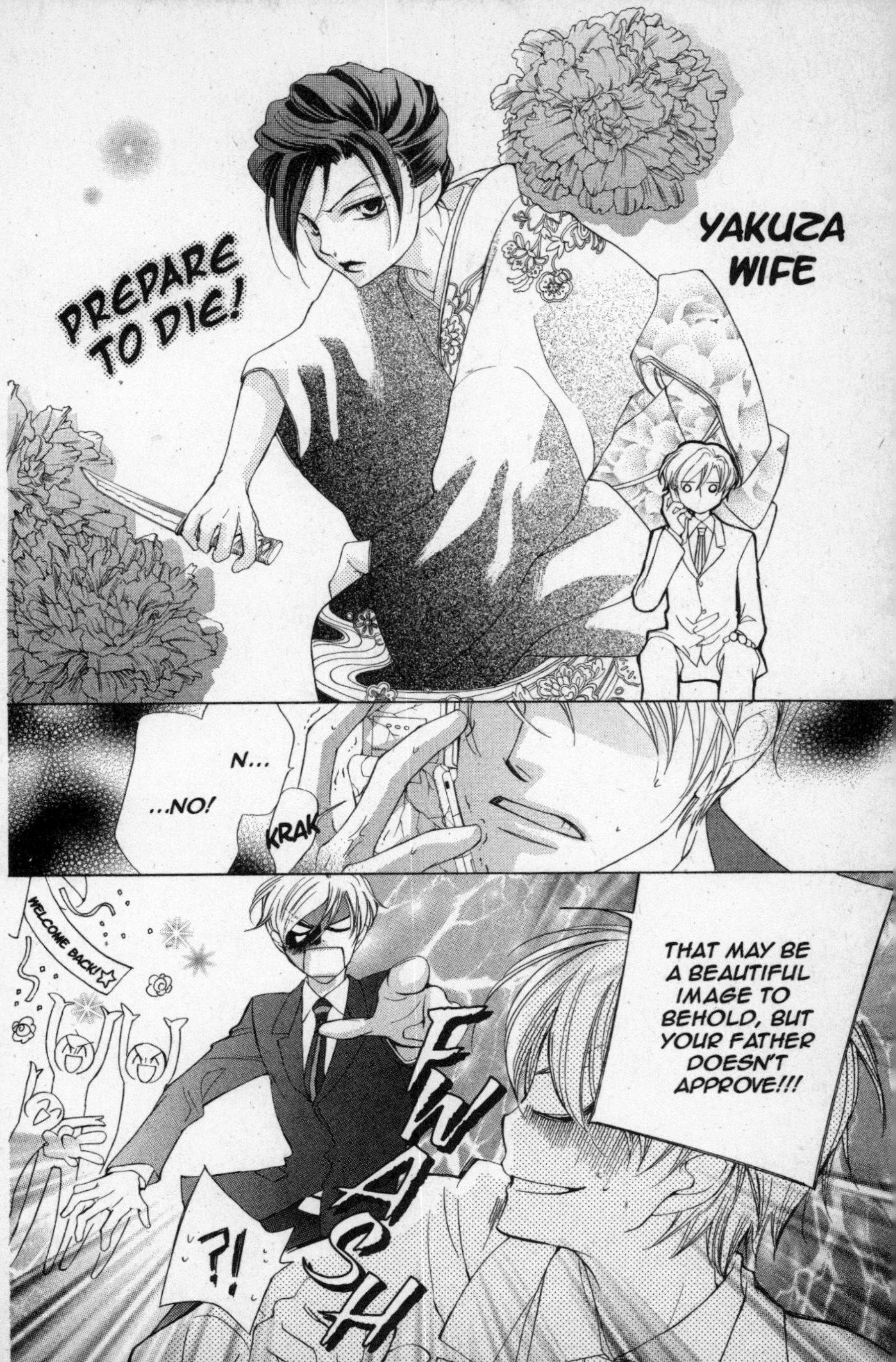
YAKUZA WIFE
PREPARE TO DIE!
N...
...NO!
KRAK
THAT MAY BE A BEAUTIFUL IMAGE TO BEHOLD, BUT YOUR FATHER DOESN'T APPROVE!!!
FWASH
?!
WELCOME BACK!☆

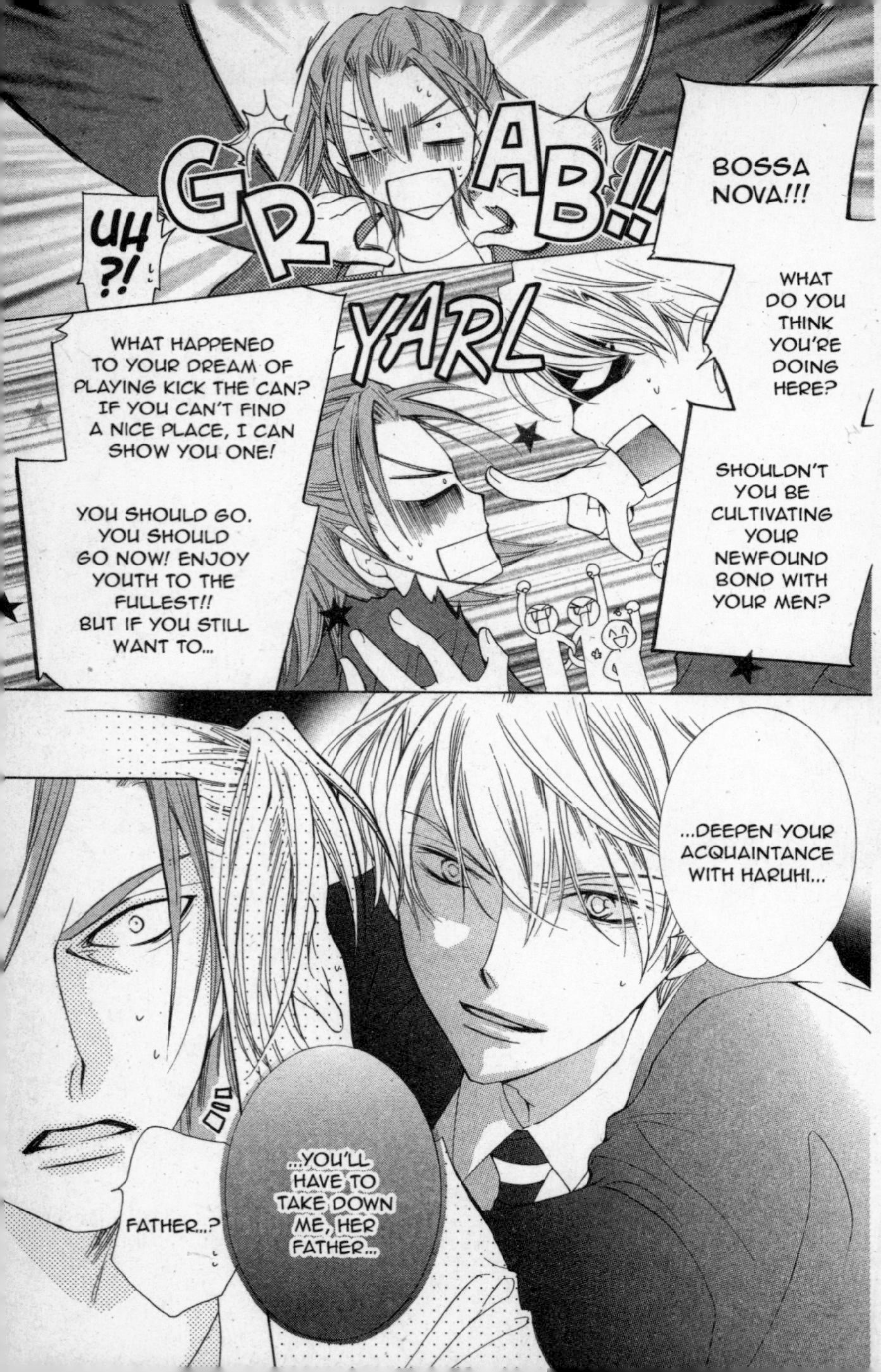
BOSSA NOVA!!!
GRAB!!
UH?!
WHAT DO YOU THINK YOU'RE DOING HERE?
SHOULDN'T YOU BE CULTIVATING YOUR NEWFOUND BOND WITH YOUR MEN?
YARL
WHAT HAPPENED TO YOUR DREAM OF PLAYING KICK THE CAN? IF YOU CAN'T FIND A NICE PLACE, I CAN SHOW YOU ONE!
YOU SHOULD GO. YOU SHOULD GO NOW! ENJOY YOUTH TO THE FULLEST!! BUT IF YOU STILL WANT TO...
...DEEPEN YOUR ACQUAINTANCE WITH HARUHI...
...YOU'LL HAVE TO TAKE DOWN ME, HER FATHER...
FATHER...?

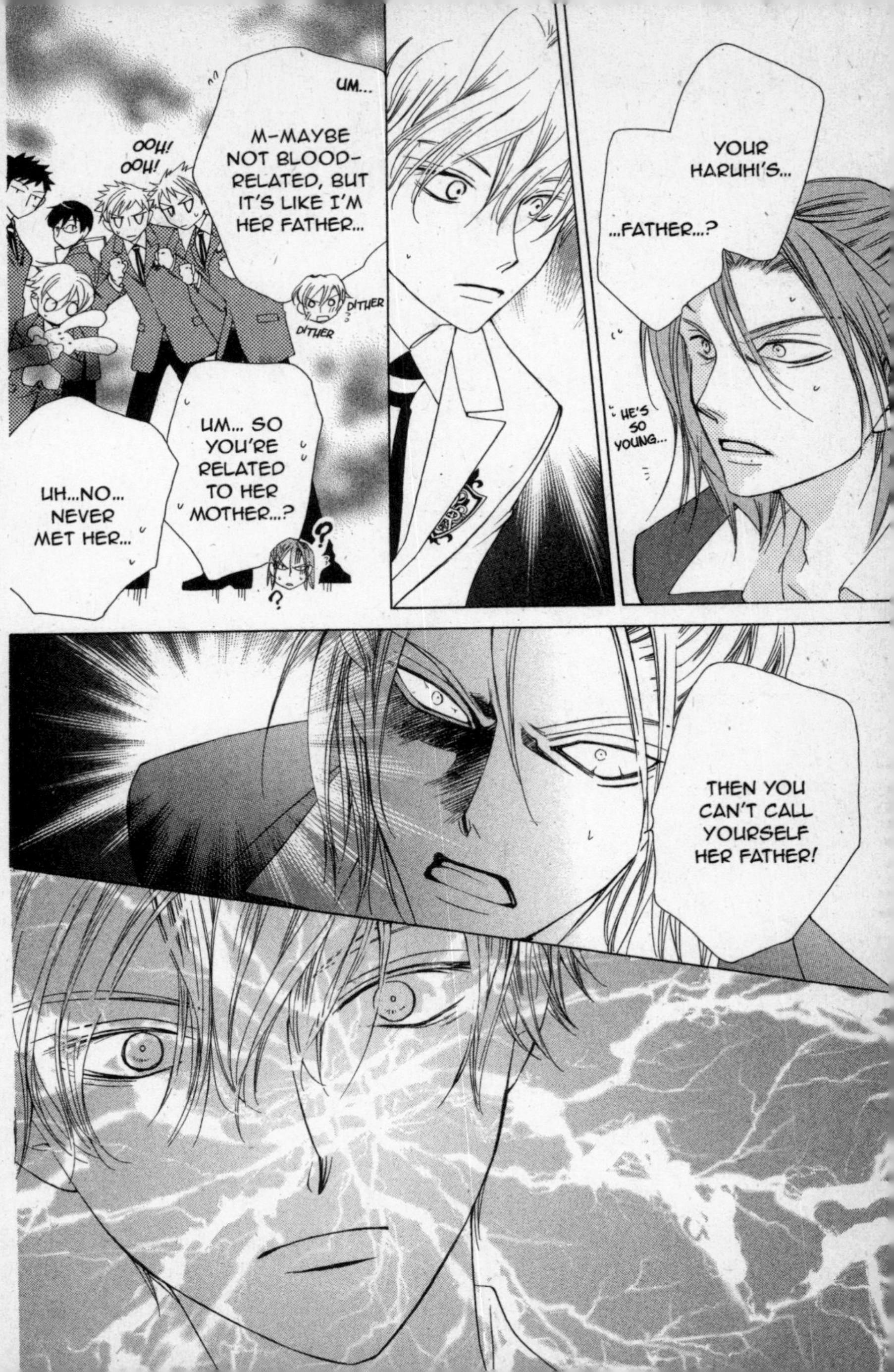
YOUR HARUHI'S...
...FATHER...?
HE'S SO YOUNG...
UM...
M-MAYBE NOT BLOOD-RELATED, BUT IT'S LIKE I'M HER FATHER...
OOH! OOH!
DITHER
DITHER
UM... SO YOU'RE RELATED TO HER MOTHER...?
UH...NO... NEVER MET HER...
THEN YOU CAN'T CALL YOURSELF HER FATHER!

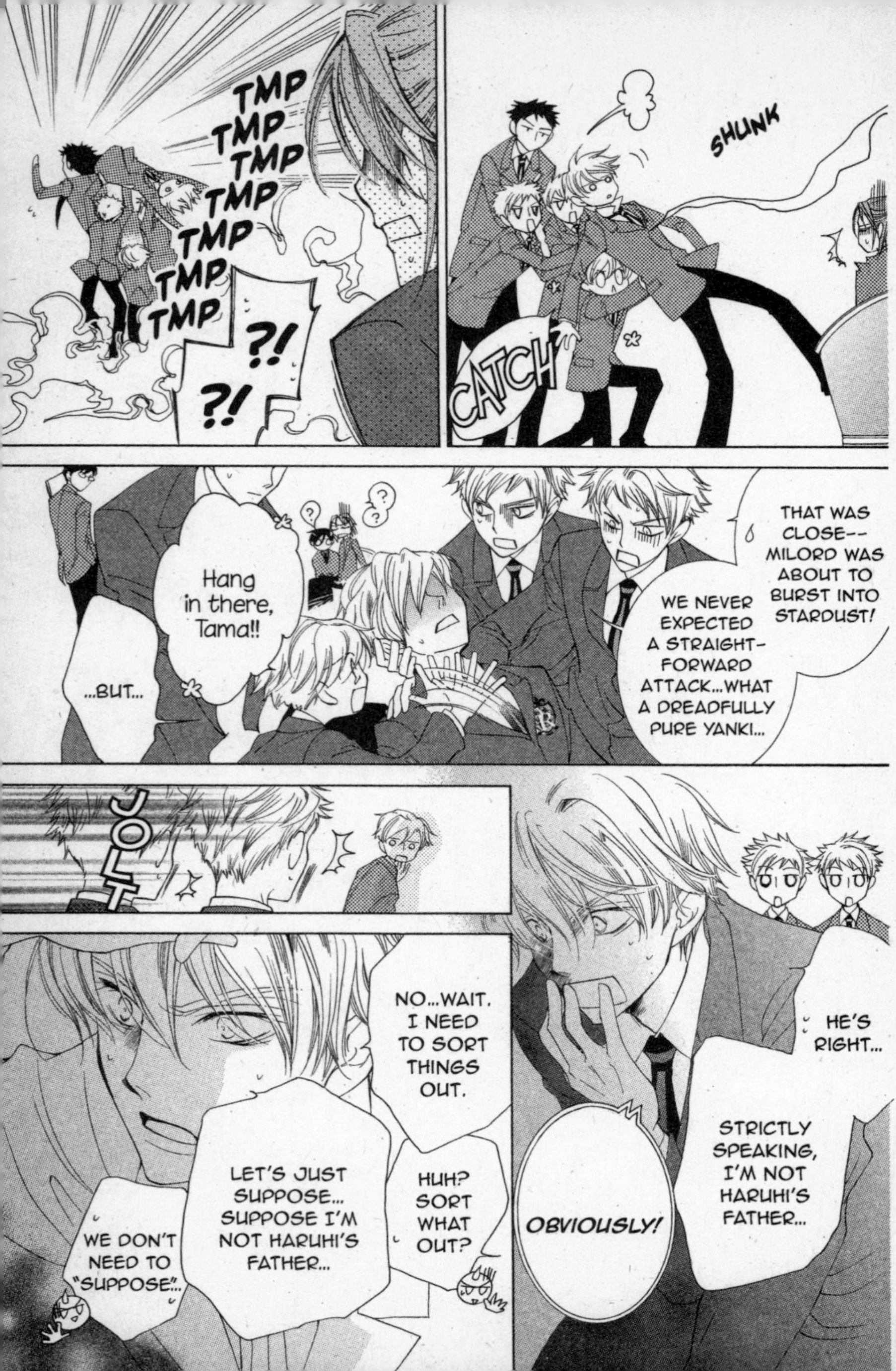
SHUNK
CATCH
TMP TMP TMP TMP TMP TMP TMP
?!
?!
THAT WAS CLOSE-- MILORD WAS ABOUT TO BURST INTO STARDUST!
WE NEVER EXPECTED A STRAIGHT-FORWARD ATTACK...WHAT A DREADFULLY PURE YANKI...
Hang in there, Tama!!
...BUT...
HE'S RIGHT...
STRICTLY SPEAKING, I'M NOT HARUHI'S FATHER...
OBVIOUSLY!
JOLT
NO...WAIT. I NEED TO SORT THINGS OUT.
HUH? SORT WHAT OUT?
LET'S JUST SUPPOSE... SUPPOSE I'M NOT HARUHI'S FATHER...
WE DON'T NEED TO "SUPPOSE"...

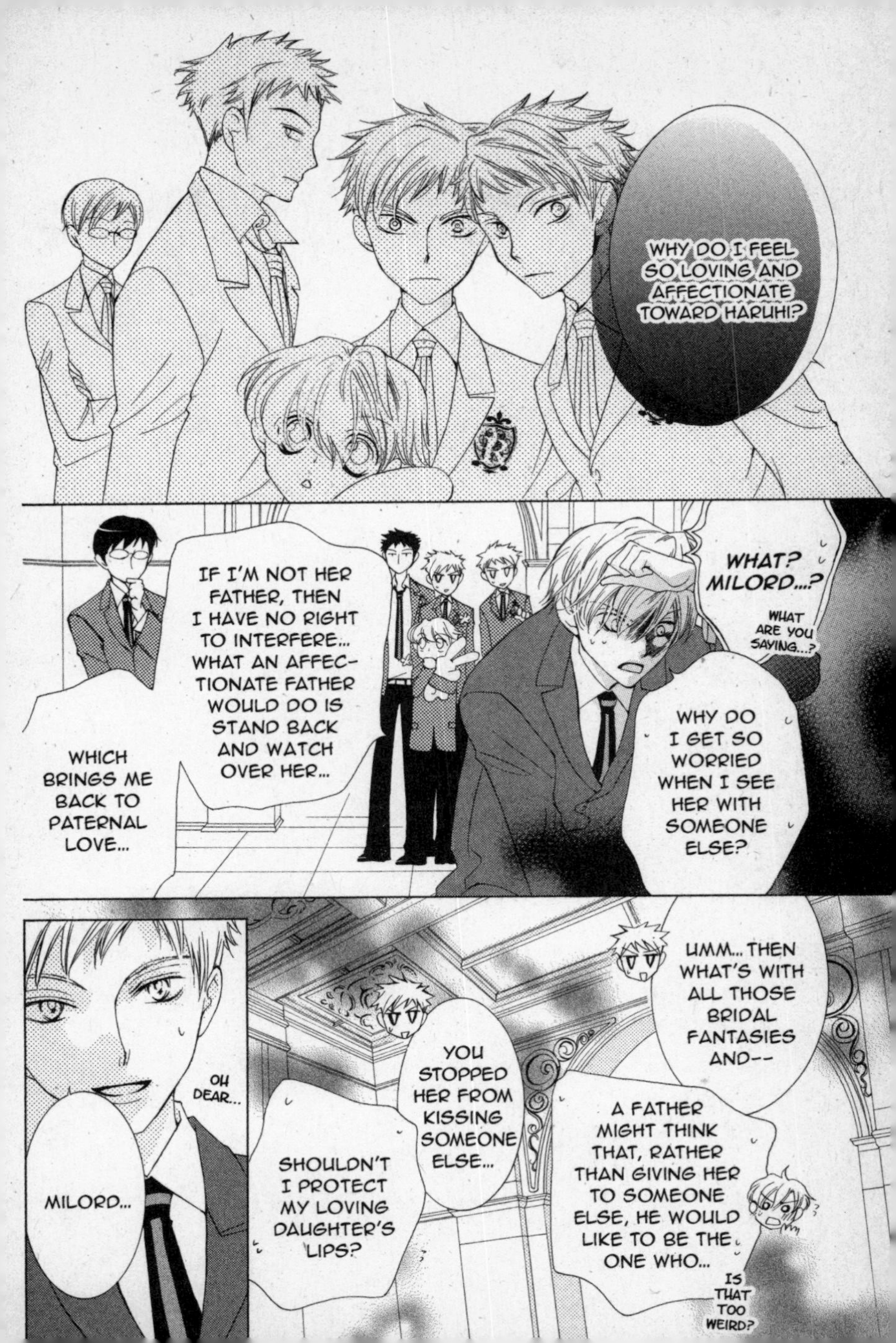
WHY DO I FEEL SO LOVING AND AFFECTIONATE TOWARD HARUHI?
WHAT? MILORD...?
WHAT ARE YOU SAYING...?
WHY DO I GET SO WORRIED WHEN I SEE HER WITH SOMEONE ELSE?
IF I'M NOT HER FATHER, THEN I HAVE NO RIGHT TO INTERFERE... WHAT AN AFFECTIONATE FATHER WOULD DO IS STAND BACK AND WATCH OVER HER...
WHICH BRINGS ME BACK TO PATERNAL LOVE...
UMM... THEN WHAT'S WITH ALL THOSE BRIDAL FANTASIES AND--
YOU STOPPED HER FROM KISSING SOMEONE ELSE...
A FATHER MIGHT THINK THAT, RATHER THAN GIVING HER TO SOMEONE ELSE, HE WOULD LIKE TO BE THE ONE WHO...
IS THAT TOO WEIRD?
SHOULDN'T I PROTECT MY LOVING DAUGHTER'S LIPS?
OH DEAR...
MILORD...

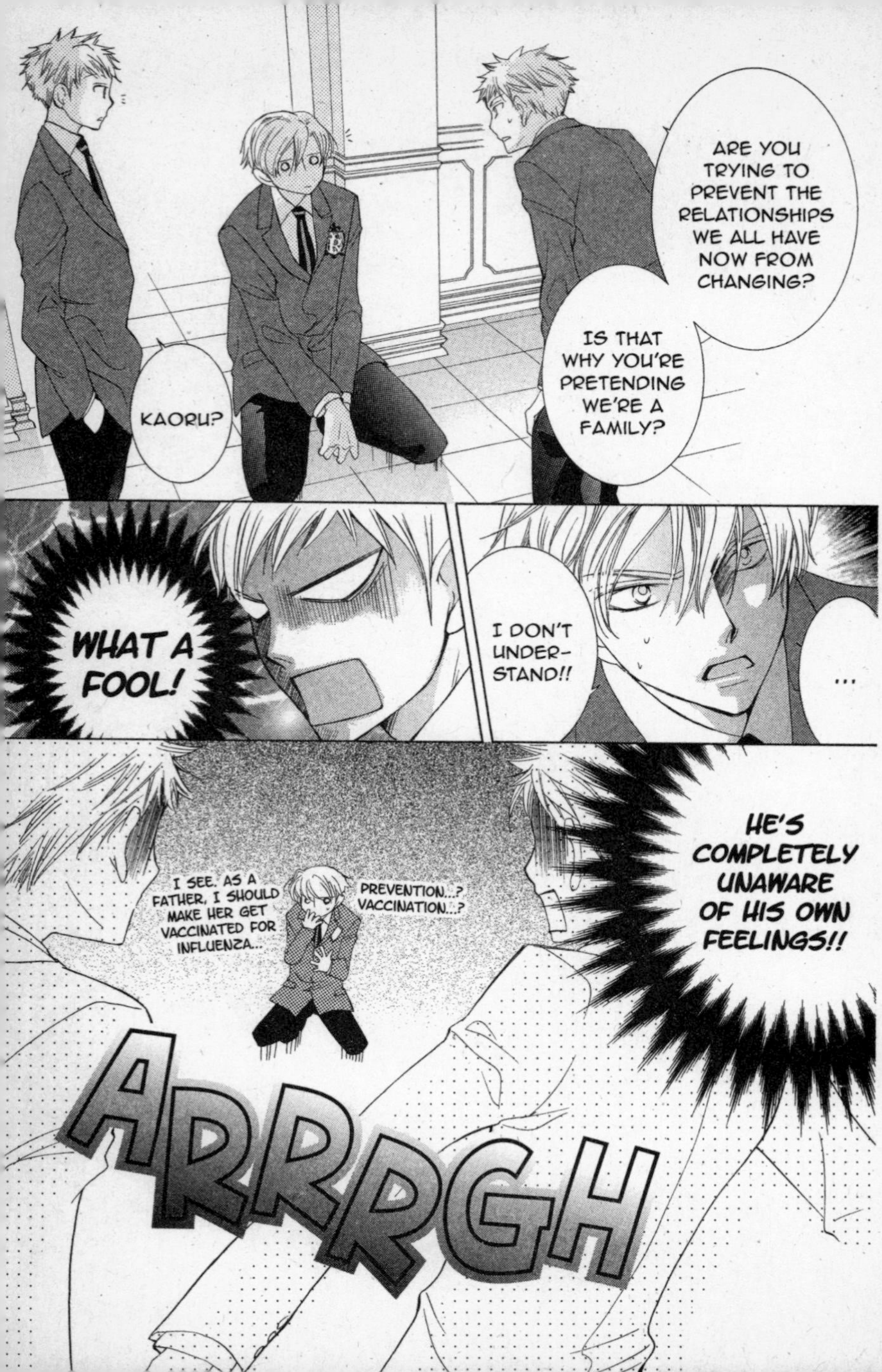
ARE YOU TRYING TO PREVENT THE RELATIONSHIPS WE ALL HAVE NOW FROM CHANGING?
IS THAT WHY YOU'RE PRETENDING WE'RE A FAMILY?
KAORU?
...
I DON'T UNDER-STAND!!
WHAT A FOOL!
HE'S COMPLETELY UNAWARE OF HIS OWN FEELINGS!!
PREVENTION...? VACCINATION...?
I SEE. AS A FATHER, I SHOULD MAKE HER GET VACCINATED FOR INFLUENZA...
ARRRGH

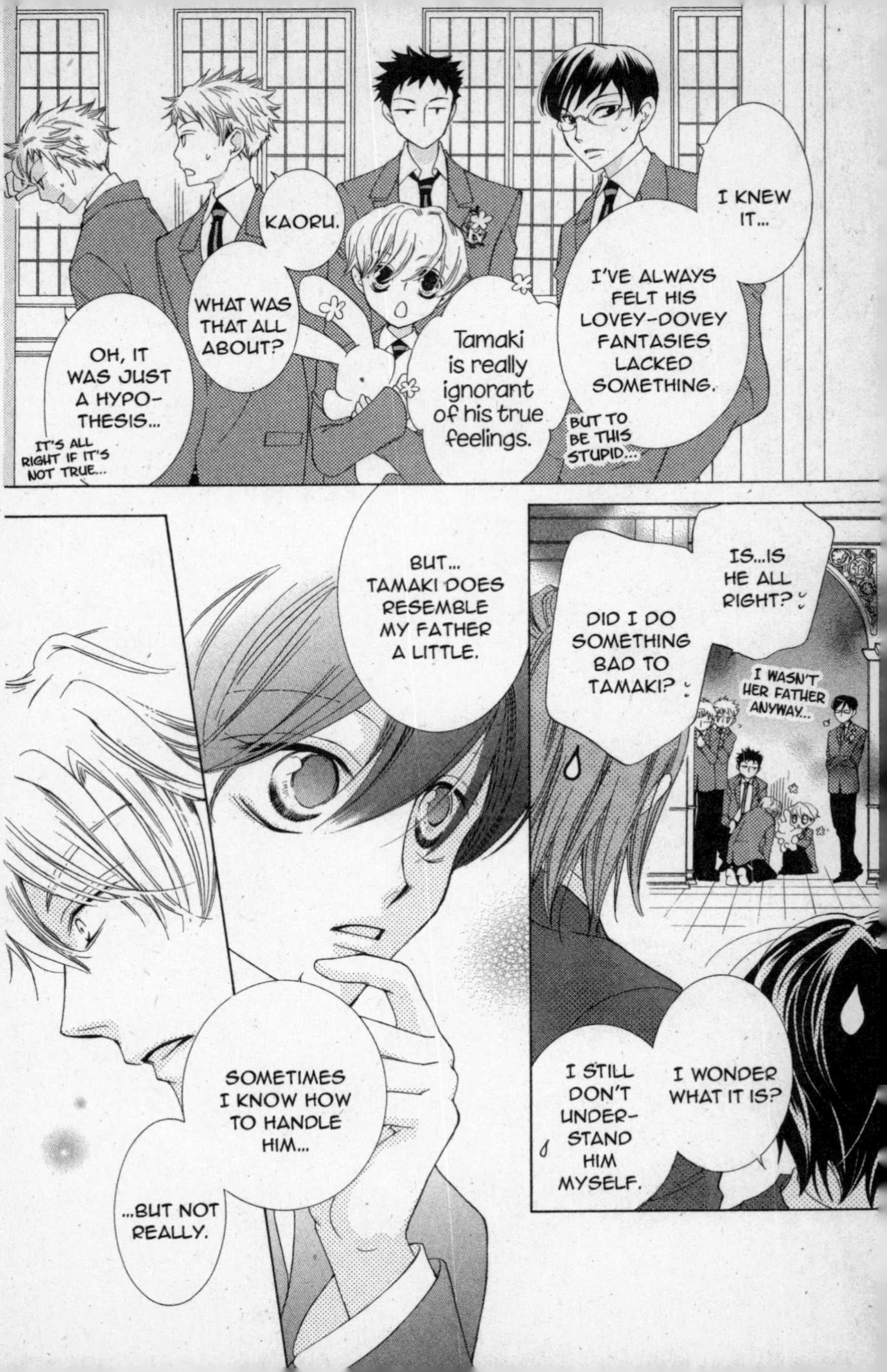
I KNEW IT...
I'VE ALWAYS FELT HIS LOVEY-DOVEY FANTASIES LACKED SOMETHING.
BUT TO BE THIS STUPID...
Tamaki is really ignorant of his true feelings.
KAORU.
WHAT WAS THAT ALL ABOUT?
OH, IT WAS JUST A HYPO-THESIS...
IT'S ALL RIGHT IF IT'S NOT TRUE...
IS...IS HE ALL RIGHT?
DID I DO SOMETHING BAD TO TAMAKI?
I WASN'T HER FATHER ANYWAY...
I WONDER WHAT IT IS?
I STILL DON'T UNDER-STAND HIM MYSELF.
BUT... TAMAKI DOES RESEMBLE MY FATHER A LITTLE.
SOMETIMES I KNOW HOW TO HANDLE HIM...
...BUT NOT REALLY.

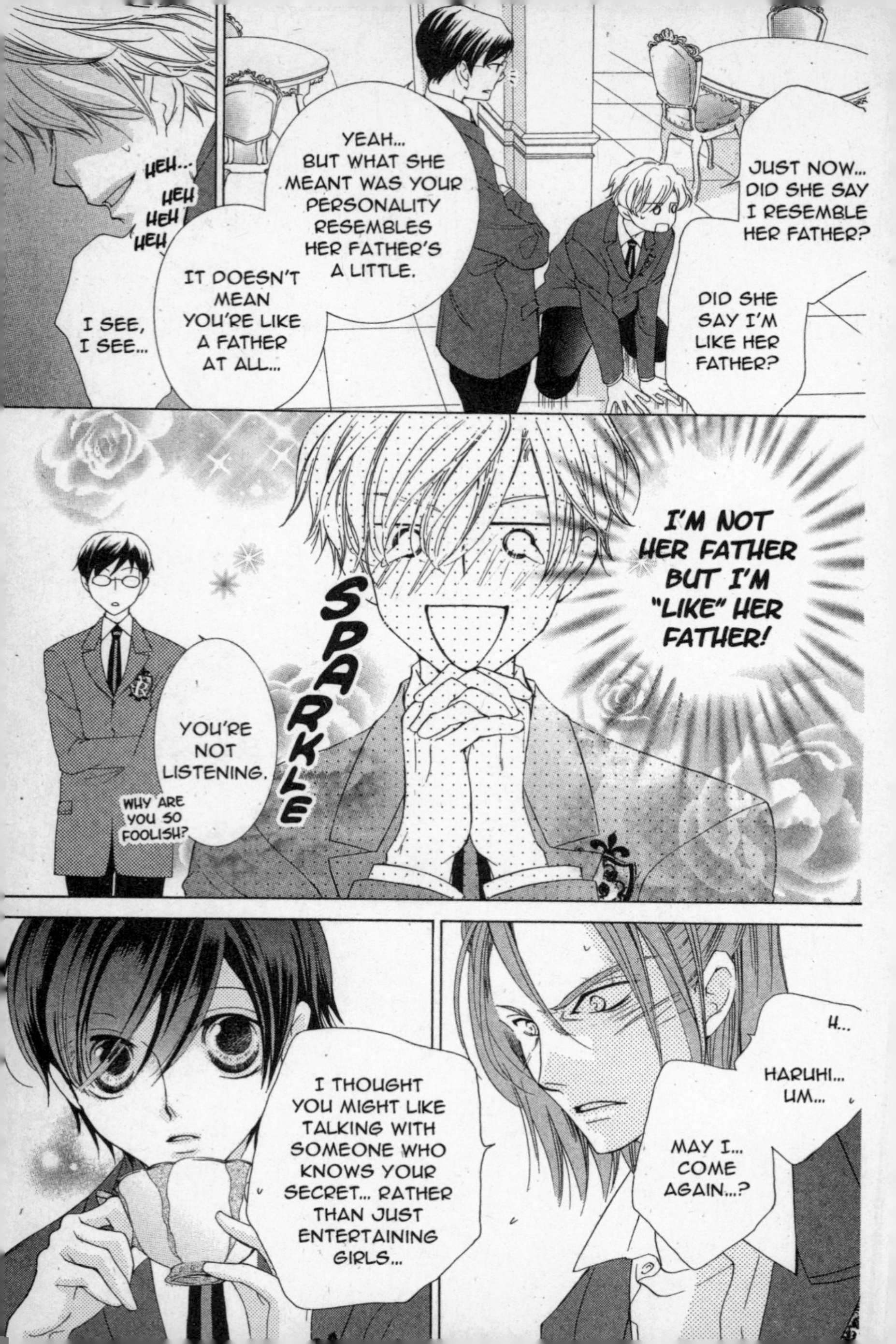
JUST NOW... DID SHE SAY I RESEMBLE HER FATHER?
DID SHE SAY I'M LIKE HER FATHER?
YEAH... BUT WHAT SHE MEANT WAS YOUR PERSONALITY RESEMBLES HER FATHER'S A LITTLE.
IT DOESN'T MEAN YOU'RE LIKE A FATHER AT ALL...
HEH... HEH HEH HEH
I SEE, I SEE...
I'M NOT HER FATHER BUT I'M "LIKE" HER FATHER!
SPARKLE
YOU'RE NOT LISTENING.
WHY ARE YOU SO FOOLISH?
H...
HARUHI... UM...
MAY I... COME AGAIN...?
I THOUGHT YOU MIGHT LIKE TALKING WITH SOMEONE WHO KNOWS YOUR SECRET... RATHER THAN JUST ENTERTAINING GIRLS...

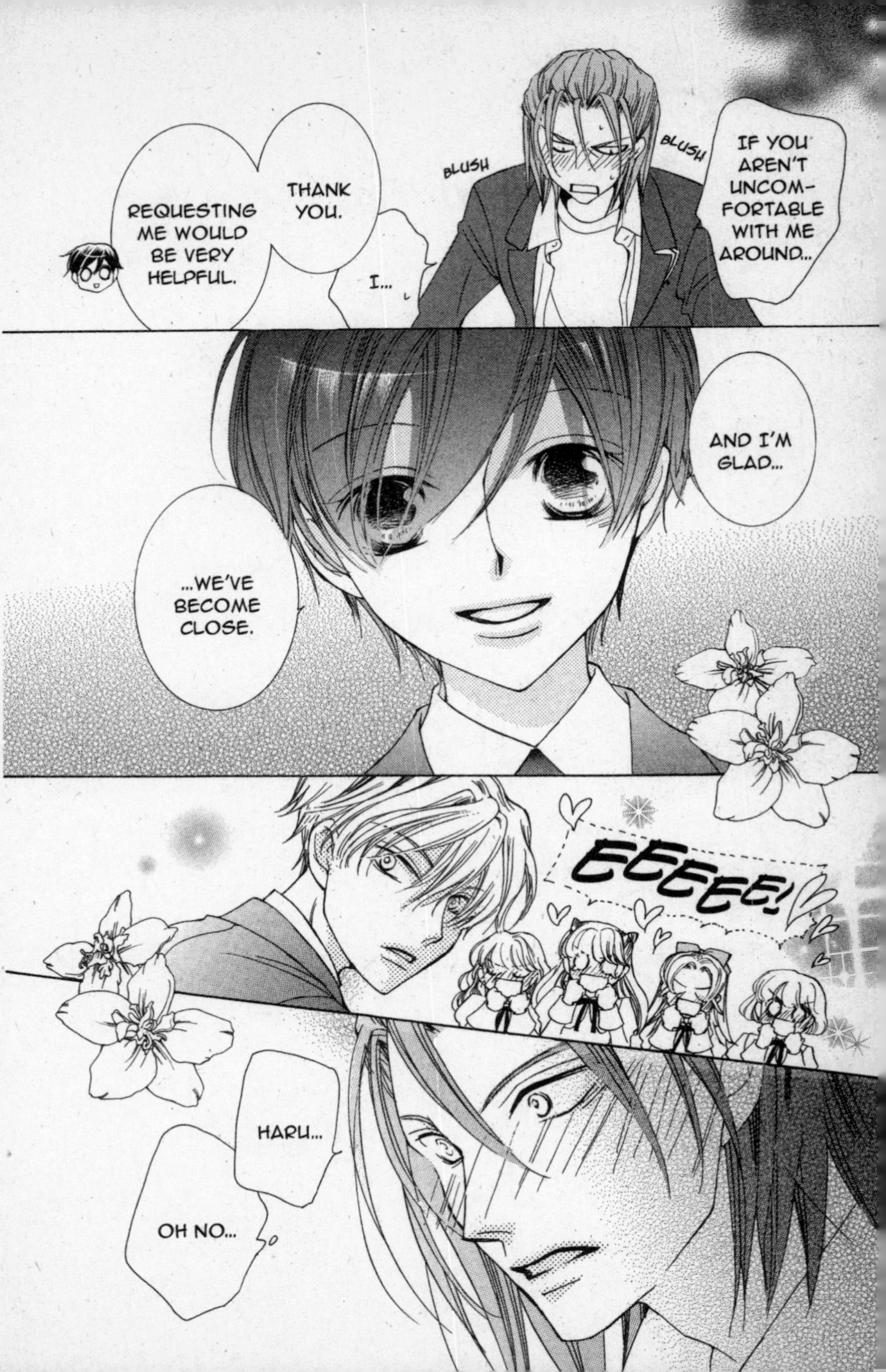
IF YOU AREN'T UNCOM-FORTABLE WITH ME AROUND...
BLUSH
BLUSH
I...
THANK YOU.
REQUESTING ME WOULD BE VERY HELPFUL.
AND I'M GLAD...
...WE'VE BECOME CLOSE.
EEEEEE!
HARU...
OH NO...

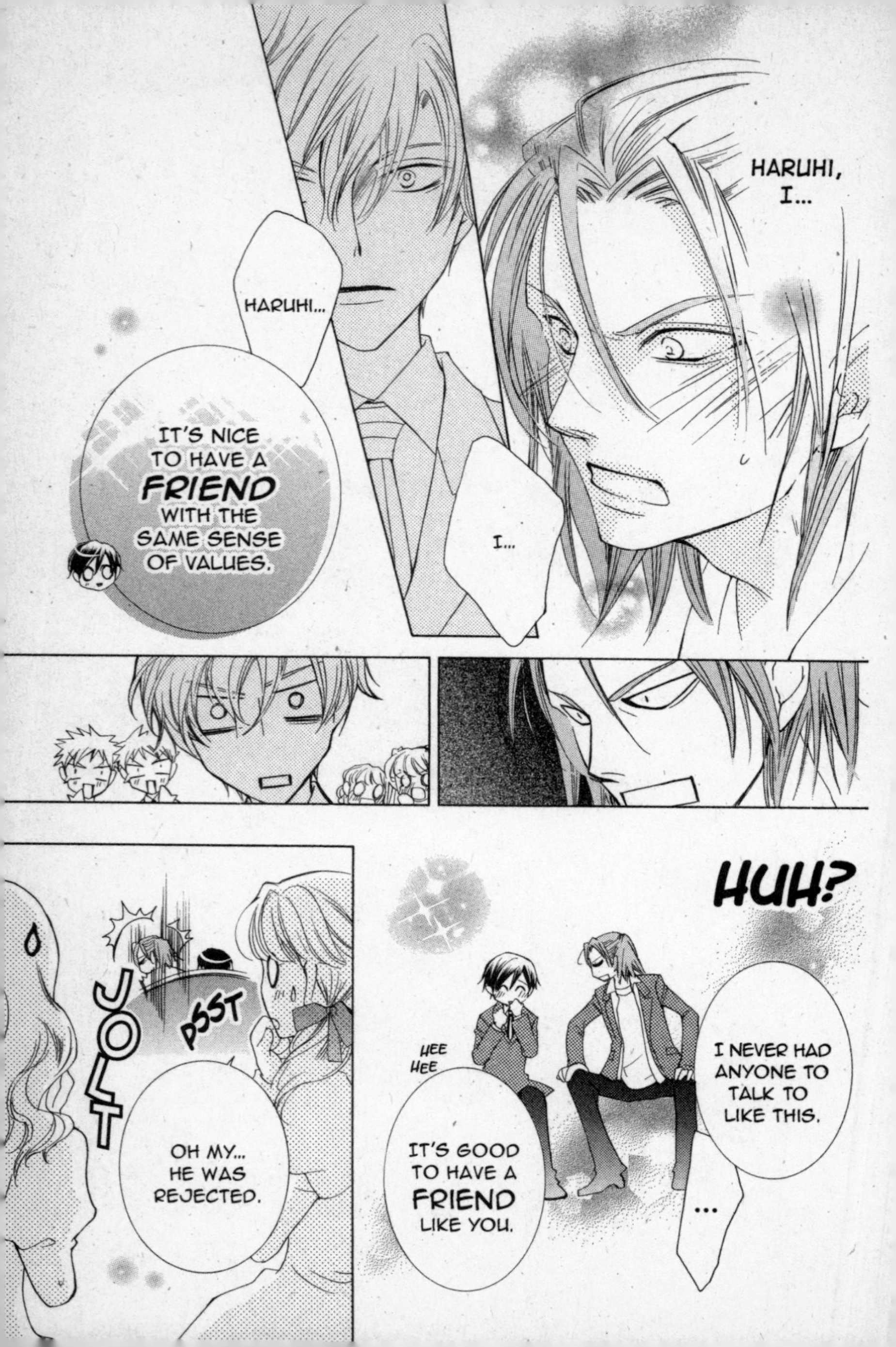
HARUHI, I...
I...
HARUHI...
IT'S NICE TO HAVE A FRIEND WITH THE SAME SENSE OF VALUES.
HUH?
I NEVER HAD ANYONE TO TALK TO LIKE THIS.
...
HEE HEE
IT'S GOOD TO HAVE A FRIEND LIKE YOU.
JOLT
PSST
OH MY... HE WAS REJECTED.

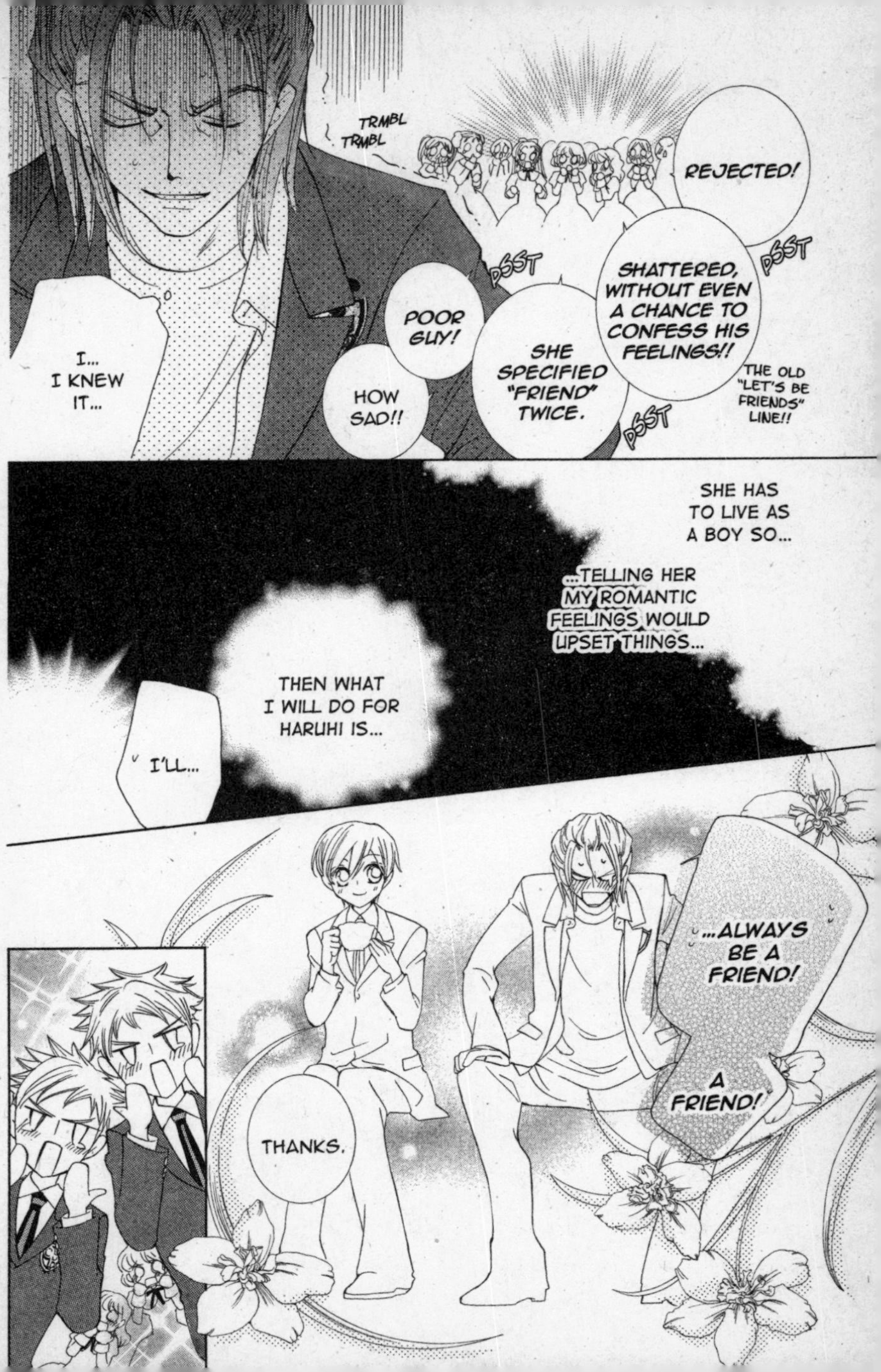
REJECTED!
SHATTERED, WITHOUT EVEN A CHANCE TO CONFESS HIS FEELINGS!!
PSST
PSST
THE OLD "LET'S BE FRIENDS" LINE!!
PSST
SHE SPECIFIED "FRIEND" TWICE.
POOR GUY!
HOW SAD!!
TRMBL TRMBL
I... I KNEW IT...
SHE HAS TO LIVE AS A BOY SO...
...TELLING HER MY ROMANTIC FEELINGS WOULD UPSET THINGS...
THEN WHAT I WILL DO FOR HARUHI IS...
I'LL...
...ALWAYS BE A FRIEND!
A FRIEND!
THANKS.

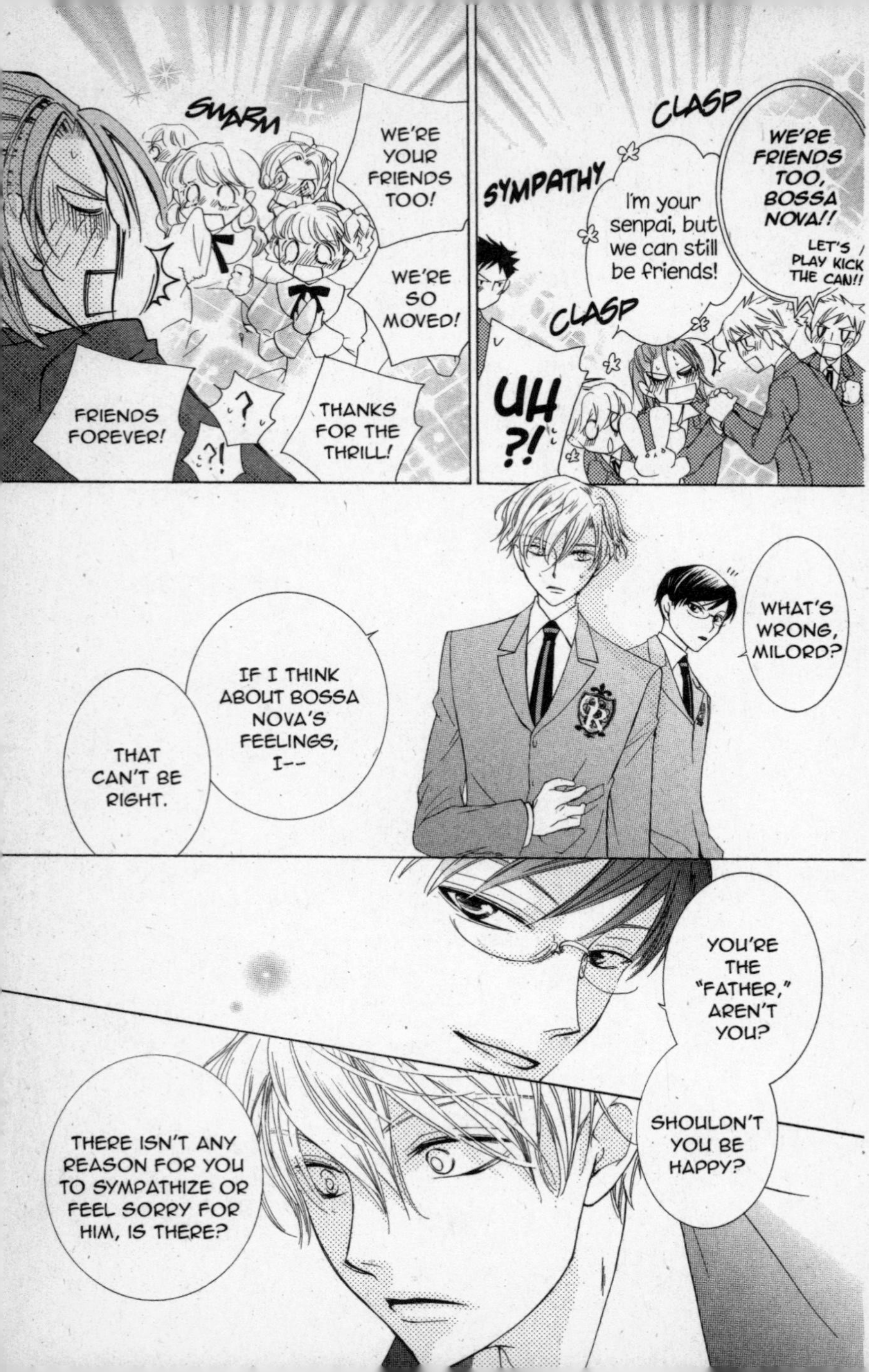
WE'RE FRIENDS TOO, BOSSA NOVA!!
LET'S PLAY KICK THE CAN!!
CLASP
I'm your senpai, but we can still be friends!
SYMPATHY
CLASP
UH ?!
SWARM
WE'RE YOUR FRIENDS TOO!
WE'RE SO MOVED!
THANKS FOR THE THRILL!
?
FRIENDS FOREVER!
?!
WHAT'S WRONG, MILORD?
IF I THINK ABOUT BOSSA NOVA'S FEELINGS, I--
THAT CAN'T BE RIGHT.
YOU'RE THE "FATHER," AREN'T YOU?
SHOULDN'T YOU BE HAPPY?
THERE ISN'T ANY REASON FOR YOU TO SYMPATHIZE OR FEEL SORRY FOR HIM, IS THERE?

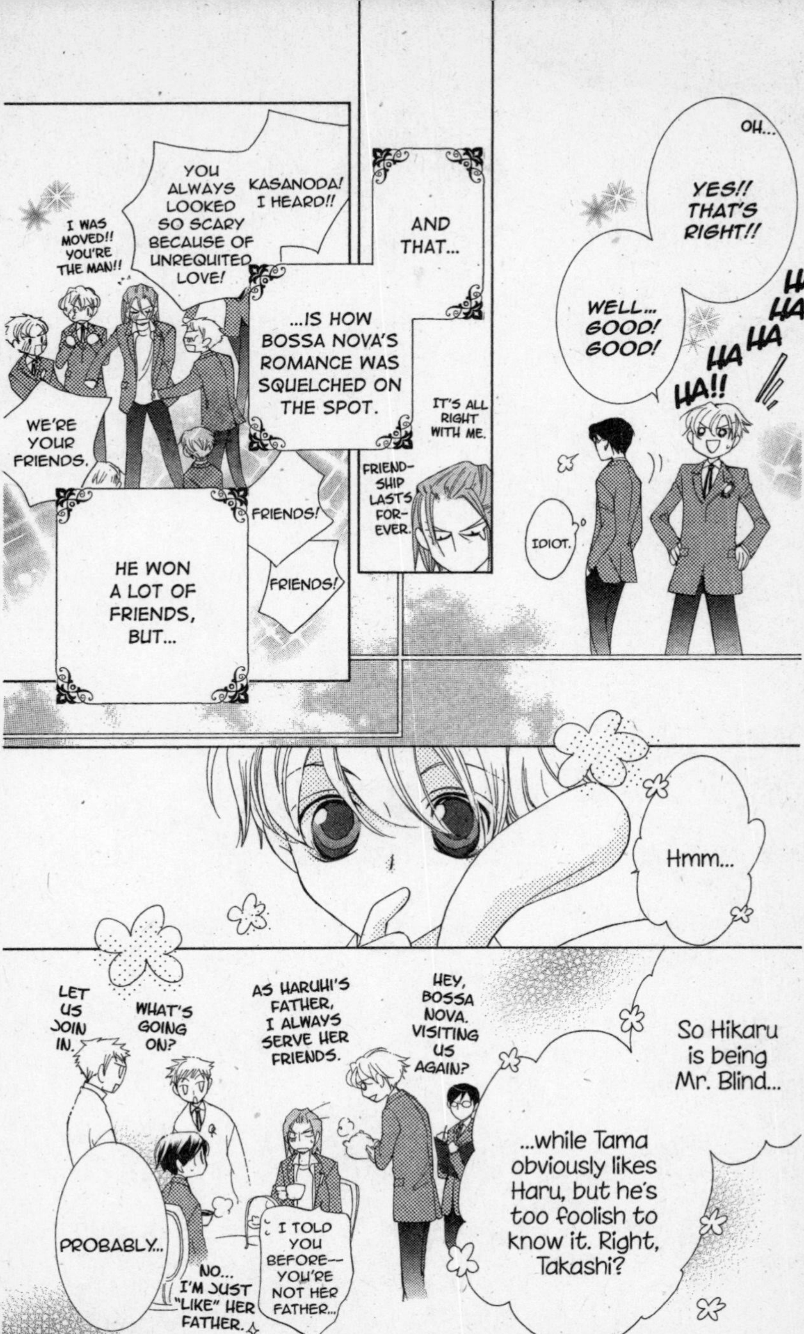
OH...
YES!! THAT'S RIGHT!!
WELL... GOOD! GOOD!
HA HA HA HA HA!!
IDIOT.
AND THAT...
...IS HOW BOSSA NOVA'S ROMANCE WAS SQUELCHED ON THE SPOT.
IT'S ALL RIGHT WITH ME.
FRIENDSHIP LASTS FOREVER.
KASANODA! I HEARD!!
YOU ALWAYS LOOKED SO SCARY BECAUSE OF UNREQUITED LOVE!
I WAS MOVED!! YOU'RE THE MAN!!
WE'RE YOUR FRIENDS.
FRIENDS!
FRIENDS!
HE WON A LOT OF FRIENDS, BUT...
Hmm...
So Hikaru is being Mr. Blind...
...while Tama obviously likes Haru, but he's too foolish to know it. Right, Takashi?
HEY, BOSSA NOVA. VISITING US AGAIN?
AS HARUHI'S FATHER, I ALWAYS SERVE HER FRIENDS.
I TOLD YOU BEFORE-- YOU'RE NOT HER FATHER...
NO... I'M JUST "LIKE" HER FATHER.
WHAT'S GOING ON?
LET US JOIN IN.
PROBABLY...

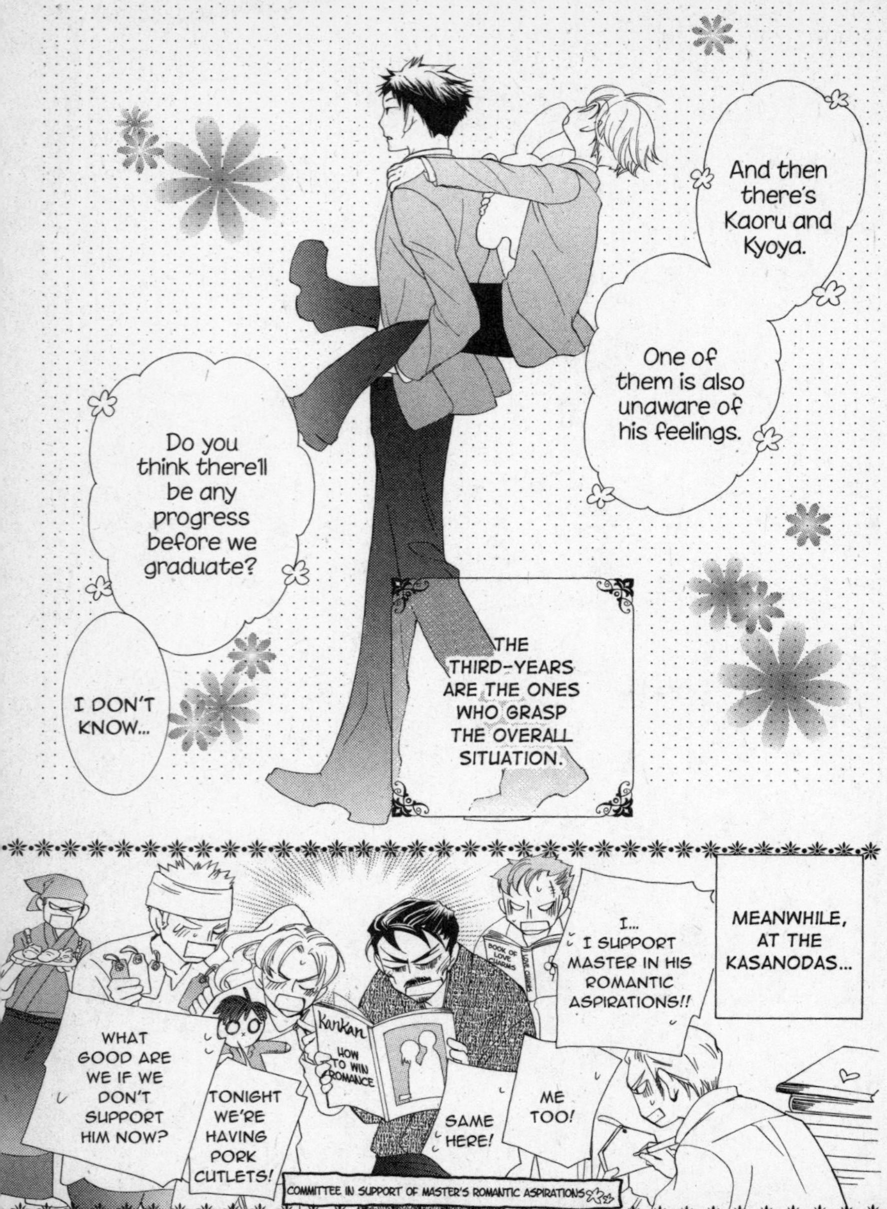
And then there's Kaoru and Kyoya.
One of them is also unaware of his feelings.
Do you think there'll be any progress before we graduate?
THE THIRD-YEARS ARE THE ONES WHO GRASP THE OVERALL SITUATION.
I DON'T KNOW...
MEANWHILE, AT THE KASANODAS...
I... I SUPPORT MASTER IN HIS ROMANTIC ASPIRATIONS!!
BOOK OF LOVE CHARMS
ME TOO!
KanKan
HOW TO WIN ROMANCE
SAME HERE!
TONIGHT WE'RE HAVING PORK CUTLETS!
WHAT GOOD ARE WE IF WE DON'T SUPPORT HIM NOW?
COMMITTEE IN SUPPORT OF MASTER'S ROMANTIC ASPIRATIONS

OURAN HIGH SCHOOL HOST CLUB, VOL. 8/THE END

✿AMERICAN VERSION✿
"Ouran High School Host Club"
IT LOOKS REALLY POP. CUTE!!
IT LOOKS LIKE A RESPECTABLE MANGA
(IN MY IMAGINATION)!!

SOMETIMES THE EFFECTS ARE A LITTLE OVERPOWERING... POOR TAMAKI... (LAUGH)

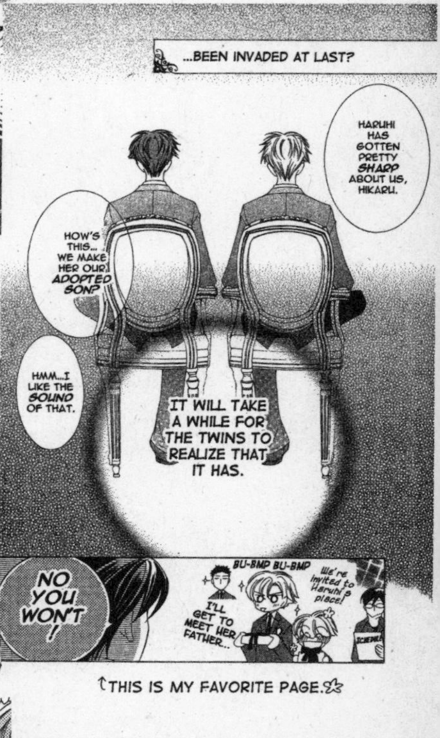
...BEEN INVADED AT LAST?
HARUHI HAS GOTTEN PRETTY SHARP ABOUT US, HIKARU.
HOW'S THIS... WE MAKE HER OUR ADOPTED SON?
HMM...I LIKE THE SOUND OF THAT.
IT WILL TAKE A WHILE FOR THE TWINS TO REALIZE THAT IT HAS.
We're invited to Haruhi's place!
BU-BMP BU-BMP
I'LL GET TO MEET HER FATHER...
NO YOU WON'T!

↑THIS IS MY FAVORITE PAGE.✿

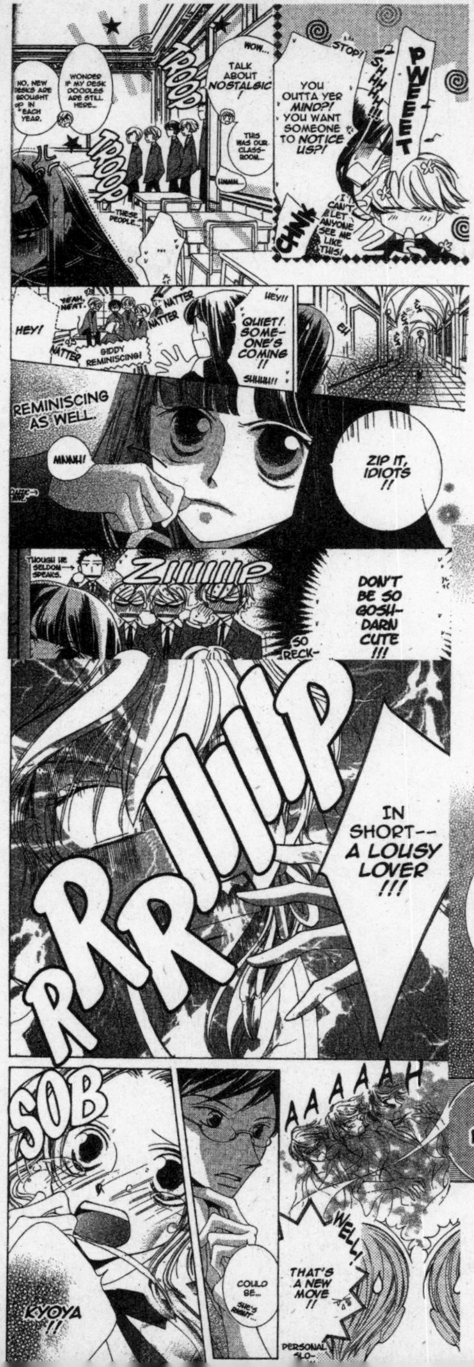
PWEEEET
STOP!
SHHHH!!!
YOU OUTTA YER MIND?! YOU WANT SOMEONE TO NOTICE US?!
I CAN'T LET ANYONE SEE ME LIKE THIS!
CHINK
WOW... TALK ABOUT NOSTALGIC!
THIS WAS OUR CLASSROOM...
HMMM...
TROOP
TROOP
WONDER IF MY DESK DOODLES ARE STILL HERE...
NO, NEW DESKS ARE BROUGHT UP IN EACH YEAR.
THESE PEOPLE...
...
HEY!!
QUIET! SOMEONE'S COMING!!
SHHHH!!
NATTER
NATTER
YEAH, NEAT.
NATTER
GIDDY REMINISCING!
HEY!
ZIP IT, IDIOTS!!
REMINISCING AS WELL.
MMMH!
DON'T BE SO GOSH-DARN CUTE!!!
SO RECK-
ZIIIIIIP
THOUGH HE SELDOM SPEAKS.
IN SHORT-- A LOUSY LOVER!!!
RRRIIIIIP
AAAAAAH
WELL!
THAT'S A NEW MOVE!!
PERSONAL SLO-
COULD BE... SHE'S RIGHT...
SOB
KYOYA!!

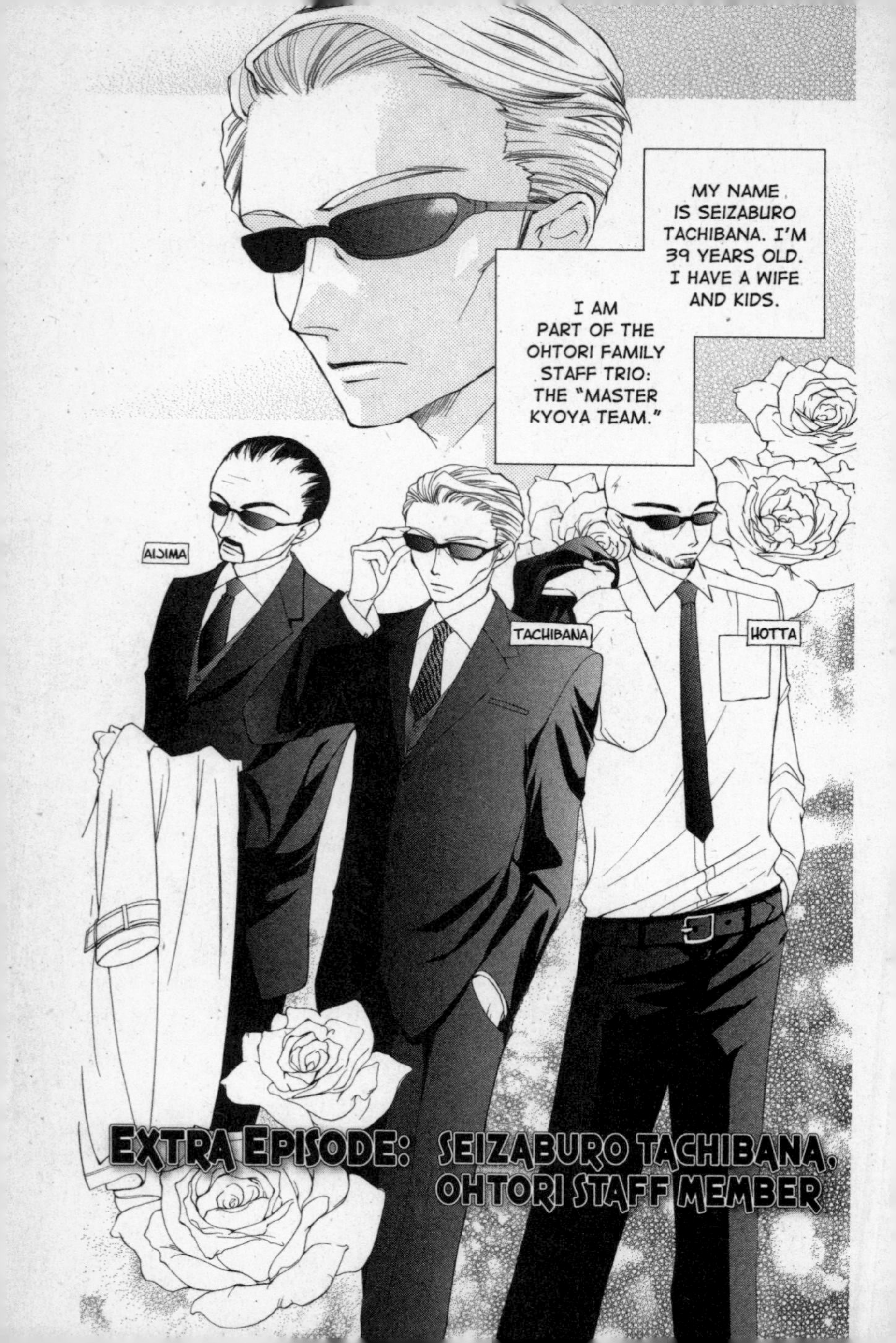
MY NAME IS SEIZABURO TACHIBANA. I'M 39 YEARS OLD. I HAVE A WIFE AND KIDS.
I AM PART OF THE OHTORI FAMILY STAFF TRIO: THE "MASTER KYOYA TEAM."
HOTTA
TACHIBANA
AIJIMA
EXTRA EPISODE: SEIZABURO TACHIBANA, OHTORI STAFF MEMBER

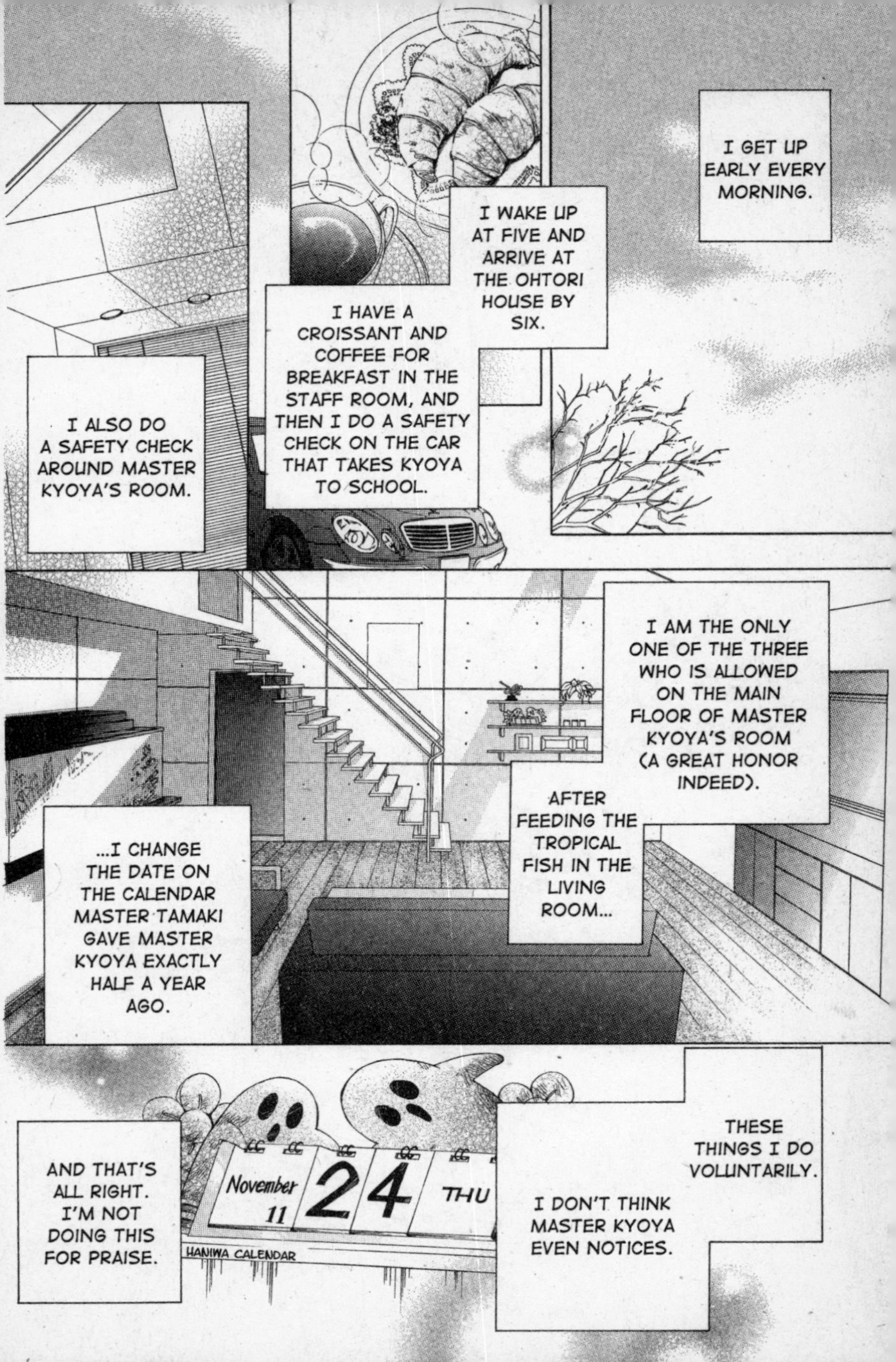
I GET UP EARLY EVERY MORNING.
I WAKE UP AT FIVE AND ARRIVE AT THE OHTORI HOUSE BY SIX.
I HAVE A CROISSANT AND COFFEE FOR BREAKFAST IN THE STAFF ROOM, AND THEN I DO A SAFETY CHECK ON THE CAR THAT TAKES KYOYA TO SCHOOL.
I ALSO DO A SAFETY CHECK AROUND MASTER KYOYA'S ROOM.
I AM THE ONLY ONE OF THE THREE WHO IS ALLOWED ON THE MAIN FLOOR OF MASTER KYOYA'S ROOM (A GREAT HONOR INDEED).
AFTER FEEDING THE TROPICAL FISH IN THE LIVING ROOM...
...I CHANGE THE DATE ON THE CALENDAR MASTER TAMAKI GAVE MASTER KYOYA EXACTLY HALF A YEAR AGO.
THESE THINGS I DO VOLUNTARILY.
I DON'T THINK MASTER KYOYA EVEN NOTICES.
November
11
24
THU
HANIWA CALENDAR
AND THAT'S ALL RIGHT. I'M NOT DOING THIS FOR PRAISE.

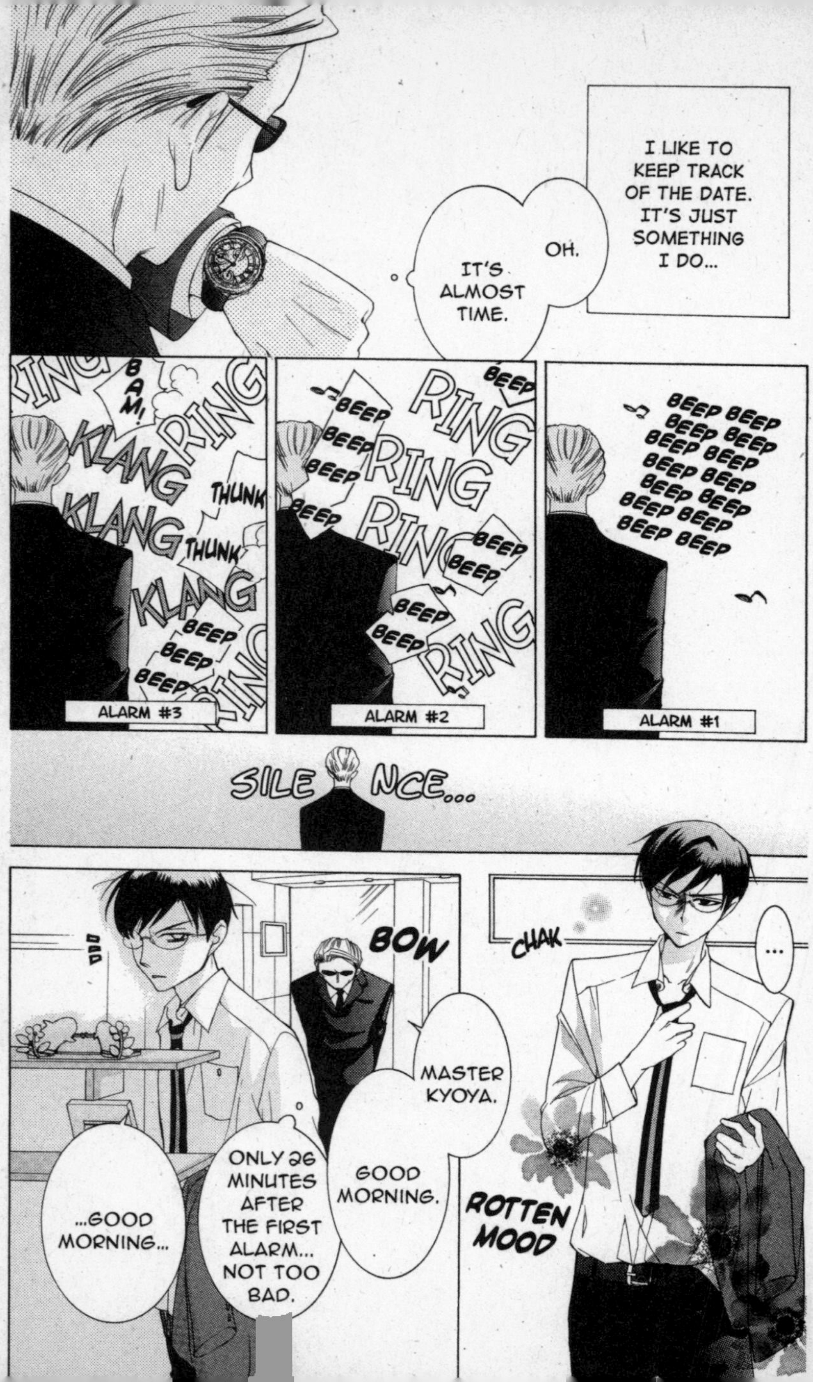
I LIKE TO KEEP TRACK OF THE DATE. IT'S JUST SOMETHING I DO...
OH.
IT'S ALMOST TIME.
BEEP BEEP BEEP BEEP BEEP BEEP BEEP BEEP BEEP BEEP BEEP BEEP BEEP BEEP
ALARM #1
RING RING RING RING
BEEP BEEP BEEP BEEP BEEP BEEP BEEP BEEP BEEP
ALARM #2
RING BAM! KLANG KLANG THUNK THUNK KLANG RING
BEEP BEEP BEEP
ALARM #3
SILENCE...
...
CHAK
ROTTEN MOOD
BOW
MASTER KYOYA.
GOOD MORNING.
ONLY 26 MINUTES AFTER THE FIRST ALARM... NOT TOO BAD.
...GOOD MORNING...

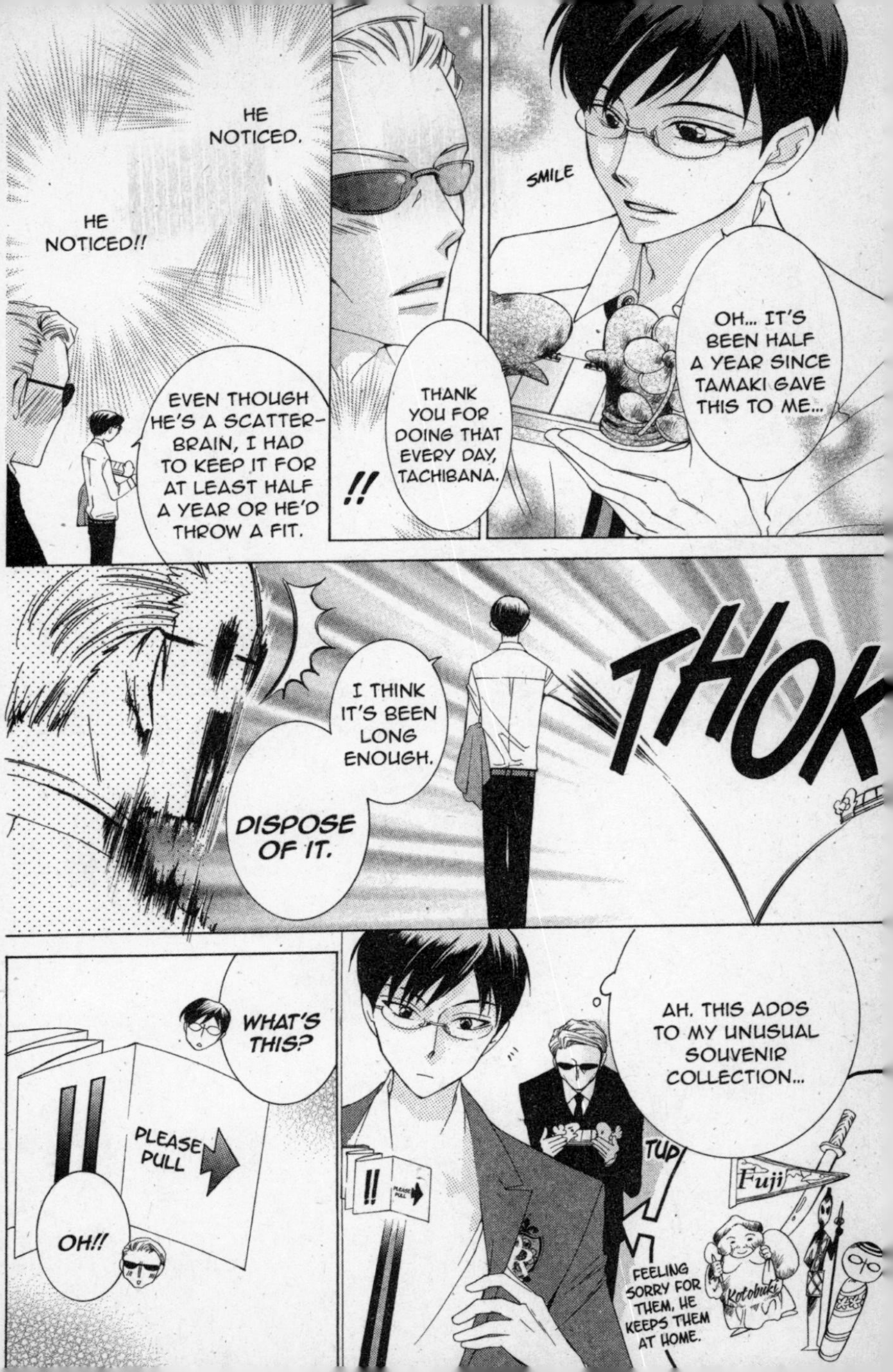
SMILE
OH... IT'S BEEN HALF A YEAR SINCE TAMAKI GAVE THIS TO ME...
THANK YOU FOR DOING THAT EVERY DAY, TACHIBANA.
!!
HE NOTICED.
HE NOTICED!!
EVEN THOUGH HE'S A SCATTER-BRAIN, I HAD TO KEEP IT FOR AT LEAST HALF A YEAR OR HE'D THROW A FIT.
THOK
I THINK IT'S BEEN LONG ENOUGH.
DISPOSE OF IT.
AH. THIS ADDS TO MY UNUSUAL SOUVENIR COLLECTION...
TUP
Fuji
Kotobuki
FEELING SORRY FOR THEM, HE KEEPS THEM AT HOME.
!!
PLEASE PULL
WHAT'S THIS?
!!
PLEASE PULL
OH!!

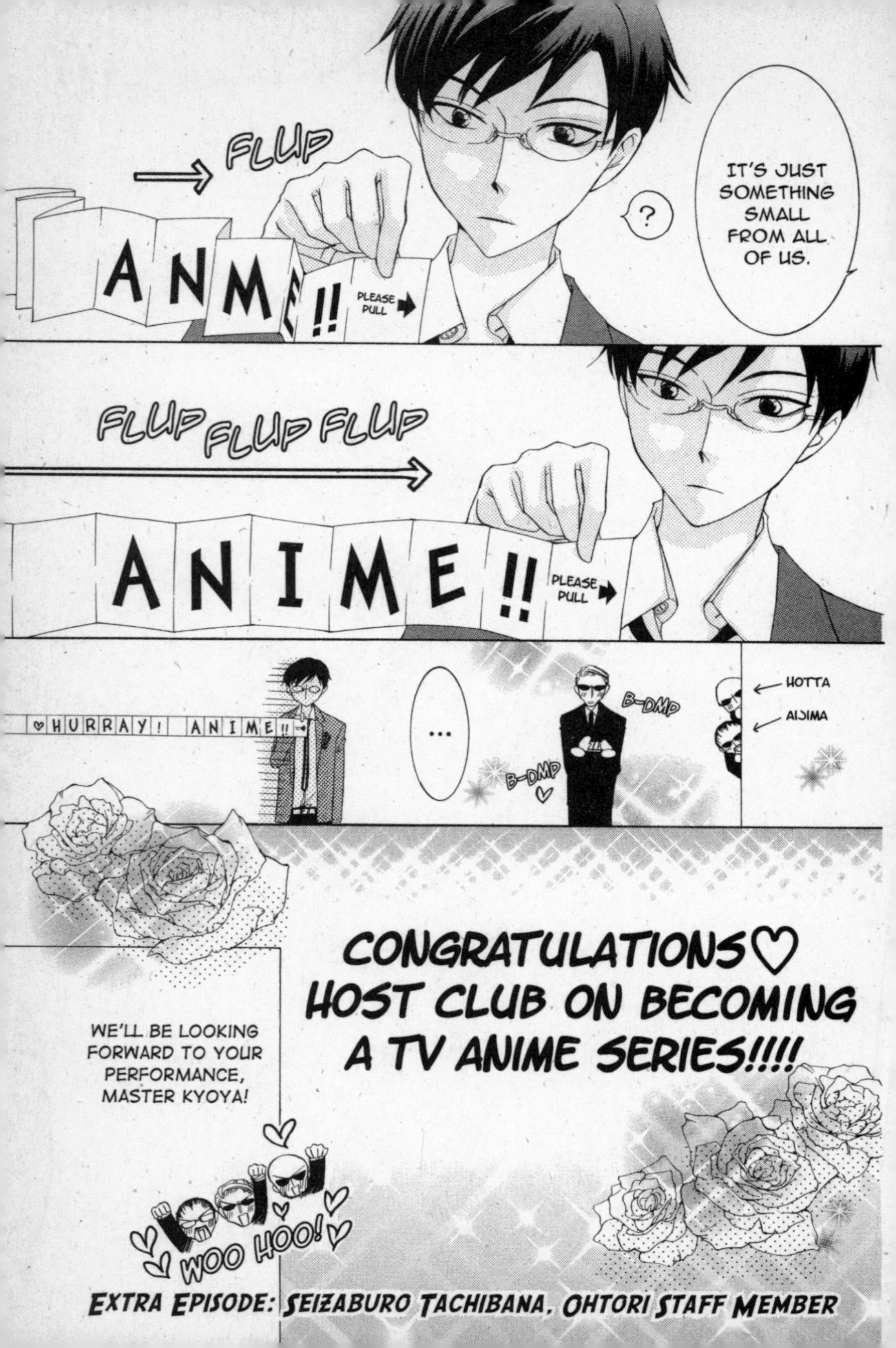
IT'S JUST SOMETHING SMALL FROM ALL OF US.
?
FLUP
ANME!!
PLEASE PULL
FLUP FLUP FLUP
ANIME!!
PLEASE PULL
HOTTA
AIJIMA
B-DMP
B-DMP
...
HURRAY! ANIME!!
CONGRATULATIONS♡ HOST CLUB ON BECOMING A TV ANIME SERIES!!!!
WE'LL BE LOOKING FORWARD TO YOUR PERFORMANCE, MASTER KYOYA!
WOO HOO!
EXTRA EPISODE: SEIZABURO TACHIBANA, OHTORI STAFF MEMBER

MU
HA
HA
HA
HA
♥
♥

THE NEKOZAWA
SIBLINGS SINCE WE
LAST SAW THEM

EGOISTIC CLUB

HELLO EVERYONE!!
THIS IS BISCOFF III.

SOMEONE SENT ME
A LETTER WHICH SAID:
"YOU'RE ALWAYS DRESSED
IN SUCH RAGGED OUTFITS.
PLEASE WEAR SOMETHING
THAT ISN'T RAGGED."
I DECIDED TO TAKE THIS
SIMPLE AND JUST
OPINION AND DRESS UP.

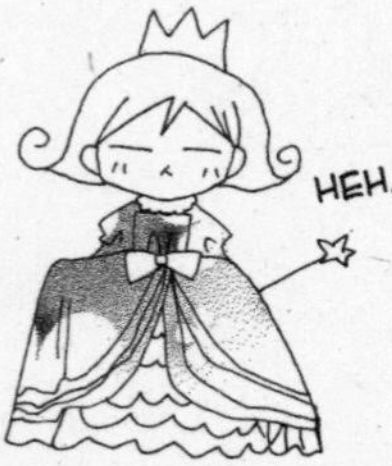
HEH.

※ BUT I REALIZED THAT JUST WEARING NORMAL CLOTHES WAS AN IMPROVEMENT, SO I DIDN'T REALLY HAVE TO "DRESS UP."

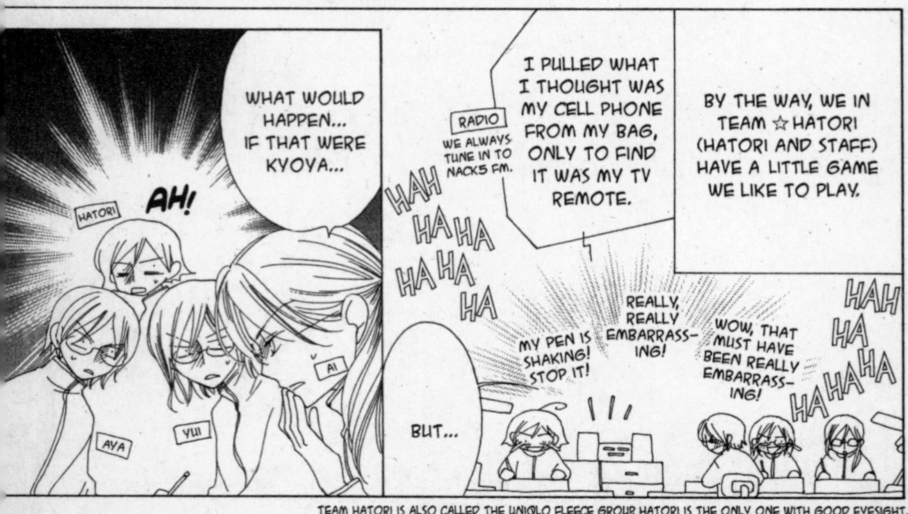
BY THE WAY, WE IN TEAM ☆ HATORI (HATORI AND STAFF) HAVE A LITTLE GAME WE LIKE TO PLAY.
I PULLED WHAT I THOUGHT WAS MY CELL PHONE FROM MY BAG, ONLY TO FIND IT WAS MY TV REMOTE.
RADIO
WE ALWAYS TUNE IN TO NACK5 FM.
HAH HA HA HAHAHA
WOW, THAT MUST HAVE BEEN REALLY EMBARRASS-ING!
HAH HA HA HA HA
REALLY, REALLY EMBARRASS-ING!
MY PEN IS SHAKING! STOP IT!
HAH HA HA HA HA HA
BUT...
WHAT WOULD HAPPEN... IF THAT WERE KYOYA...
AH!
HATORI
AI
YUI
AYA

TEAM HATORI IS ALSO CALLED THE UNIQLO FLEECE GROUP. HATORI IS THE ONLY ONE WITH GOOD EYESIGHT.

AND

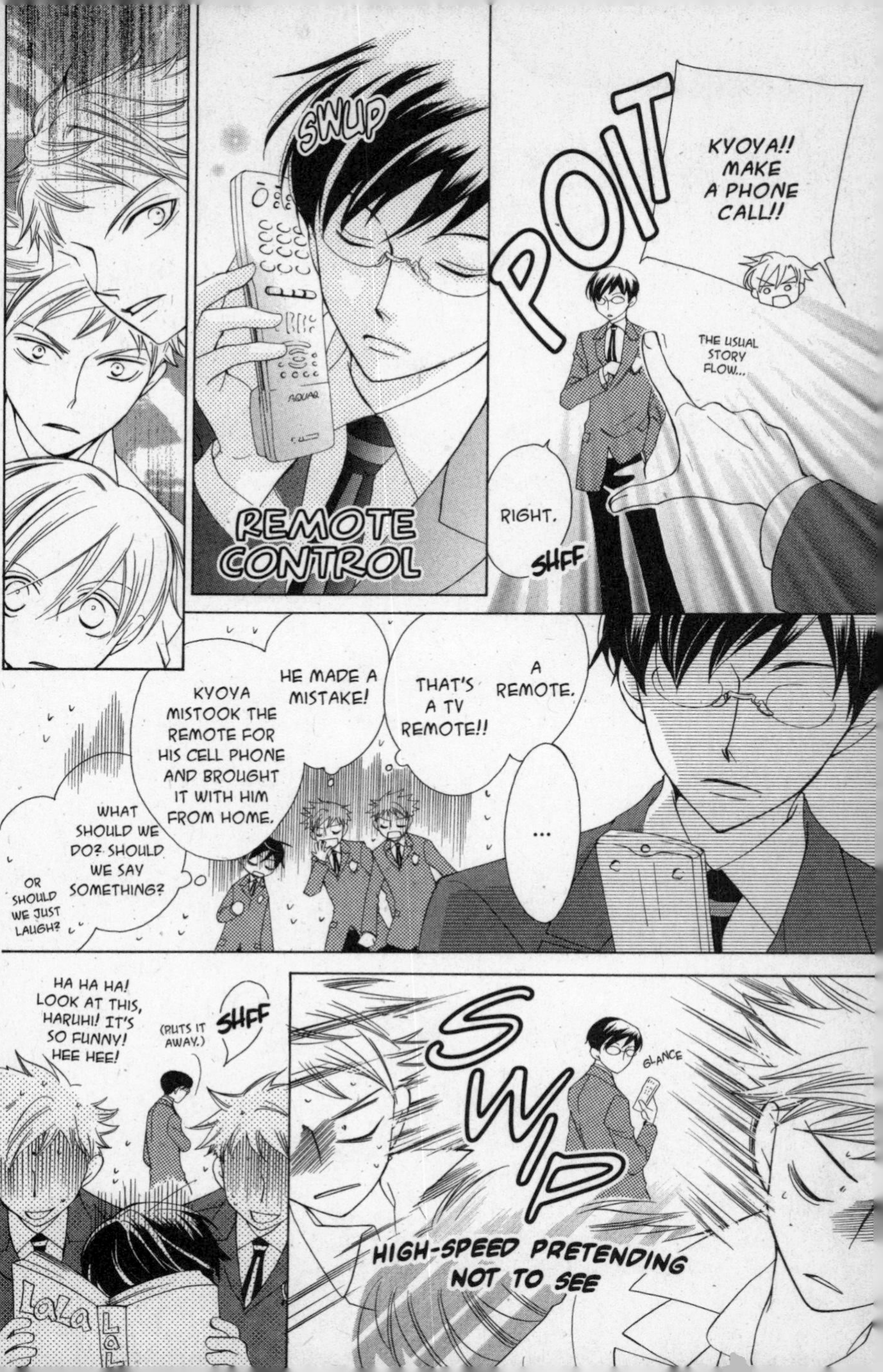
KYOYA!! MAKE A PHONE CALL!!
POIT
THE USUAL STORY FLOW...
RIGHT.
SHFF
SWUP
REMOTE CONTROL
A REMOTE.
...
THAT'S A TV REMOTE!!
HE MADE A MISTAKE!
KYOYA MISTOOK THE REMOTE FOR HIS CELL PHONE AND BROUGHT IT WITH HIM FROM HOME.
WHAT SHOULD WE DO? SHOULD WE SAY SOMETHING?
OR SHOULD WE JUST LAUGH?
SWIP
GLANCE
HIGH-SPEED PRETENDING NOT TO SEE
SHFF
(PUTS IT AWAY.)
HA HA HA! LOOK AT THIS, HARUHI! IT'S SO FUNNY! HEE HEE!
LaLa

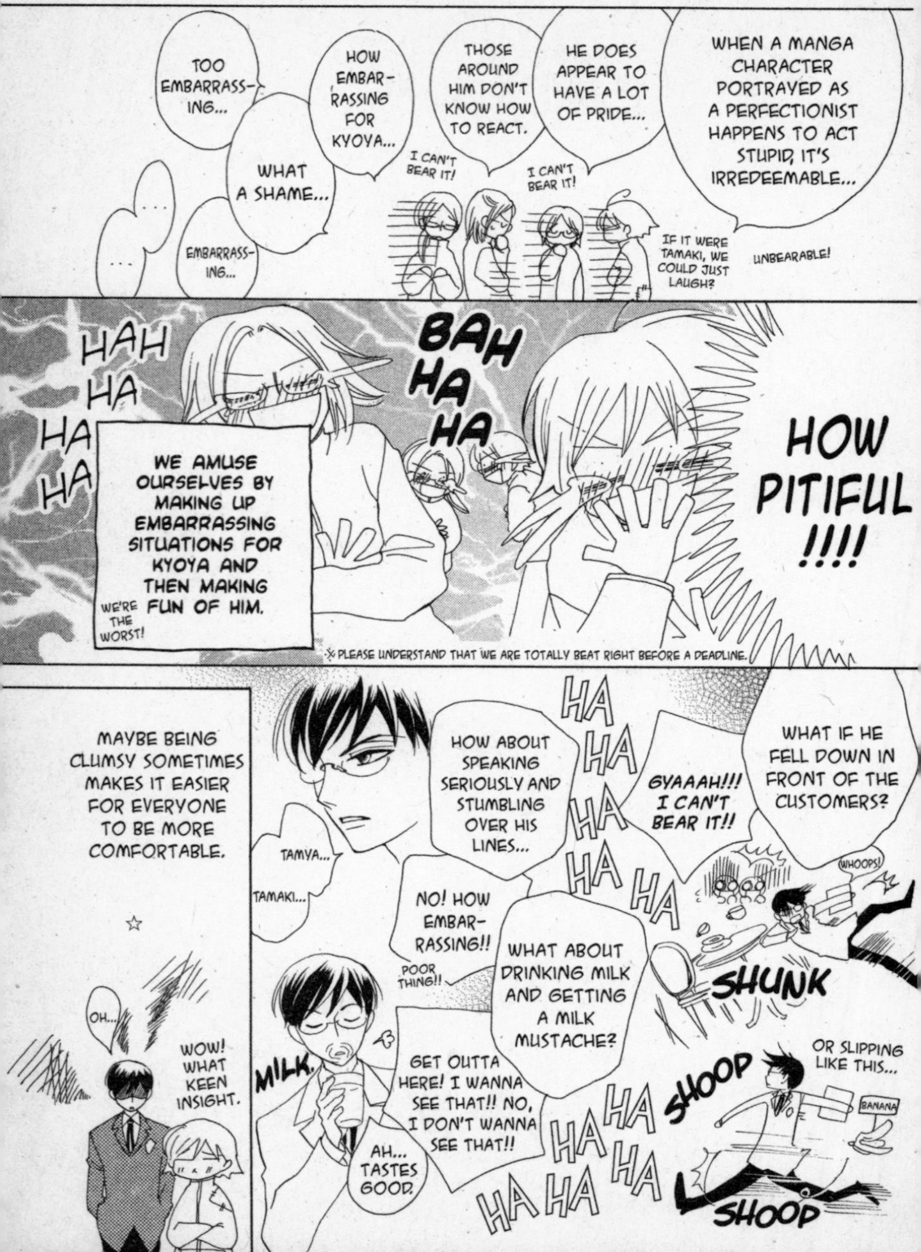
WHEN A MANGA CHARACTER PORTRAYED AS A PERFECTIONIST HAPPENS TO ACT STUPID, IT'S IRREDEEMABLE...
UNBEARABLE!
IF IT WERE TAMAKI, WE COULD JUST LAUGH?
HE DOES APPEAR TO HAVE A LOT OF PRIDE...
I CAN'T BEAR IT!
THOSE AROUND HIM DON'T KNOW HOW TO REACT.
I CAN'T BEAR IT!
HOW EMBAR-RASSING FOR KYOYA...
TOO EMBARRASS-ING...
WHAT A SHAME...
EMBARRASS-ING...
...
...
HOW PITIFUL!!!!
BAH HA HA
HAH HA HA HA
WE AMUSE OURSELVES BY MAKING UP EMBARRASSING SITUATIONS FOR KYOYA AND THEN MAKING FUN OF HIM.
WE'RE THE WORST!
※ PLEASE UNDERSTAND THAT WE ARE TOTALLY BEAT RIGHT BEFORE A DEADLINE.
WHAT IF HE FELL DOWN IN FRONT OF THE CUSTOMERS?
GYAAAH!!! I CAN'T BEAR IT!!
WHOOPS!
SHUNK
HA HA HA HA HA HA
HOW ABOUT SPEAKING SERIOUSLY AND STUMBLING OVER HIS LINES...
TAMYA...
TAMAKI...
NO! HOW EMBAR-RASSING!!
POOR THING!!
WHAT ABOUT DRINKING MILK AND GETTING A MILK MUSTACHE?
OR SLIPPING LIKE THIS...
BANANA
SHOOP
SHOOP
HA HA HA HA HA HA HA HA
GET OUTTA HERE! I WANNA SEE THAT!! NO, I DON'T WANNA SEE THAT!!
MILK.
AH... TASTES GOOD.
MAYBE BEING CLUMSY SOMETIMES MAKES IT EASIER FOR EVERYONE TO BE MORE COMFORTABLE.
☆
OH...
WOW! WHAT KEEN INSIGHT.

PLEASE SEND US YOUR OPINIONS♡♡
AND REMARKS.
YOUR LETTERS REALLY DO KEEP ME GOING!!

〒BISCO HATORI
C/O OURAN HIGH SCHOOL HOST CLUB EDITOR
P.O. BOX 77064
SAN FRANCISCO, CA 94107☆

✿ Special Thanks ✿

TO MR. YAMASHITA, EVERYONE IN THE EDITORIAL DEPARTMENT, AND EVERYONE WHO CONTRIBUTED TO THIS MANGA. AND THANKS TO ALL THE STAFF: YUI NATSUKI, AYA AOMURA, RIKU, YUTORI HIZAKURA, AND NATSUMI SATO.

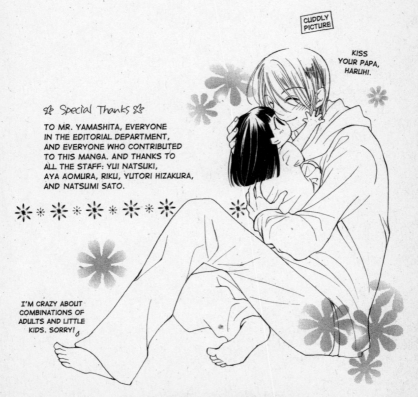

CUDDLY PICTURE
KISS YOUR PAPA, HARUHI.
I'M CRAZY ABOUT COMBINATIONS OF ADULTS AND LITTLE KIDS. SORRY!

EGOISTIC CLUB / THE END

EDITOR'S NOTES

EPISODE 32

Page 19: *Konnyaku*, or "devil's tongue," is a root similar to a yam that is made into a gelatinous substance. It is used in cooking as a thickening agent.

EPISODE 33

Page 53: Tamaki wants to see the *daibutsu*, or large statue of Buddha, located in Nara. Goryokaku fort, located in Hakodate, Hokkaido, was built during the Tokugawa Shogunate. *Shisa* are decorative statues that adorn rooftops and entranceways in Okinawa to ward off evil spirits.

Page 58: *Binboudai kazoku monogatari*, or "The Large Poor Family Story," is a TV documentary show about impoverished families who have many children.

Page 66: *Hannya* is a mask used in Noh theater to represent a woman who has been turned into a demon through jealousy and vengefulness.

EPISODE 34

Page 77: *Bushido* means "way of the warrior." It refers to a code of conduct adopted officially by the Shinsengumi during the Late Tokugawa Shogunate (1853-1867).

Page 77: "I could eat three bowls of rice!" Renge is saying that imagining Hijikata gives her enough *okazu* (literally a side dish to accompany rice) for a full meal. Here *okazu* refers to something that is a turn-on.

Page 81: A *yanki* is a delinquent.

EPISODE 35

Page 134: *Daruma-san ga koronda*, or "Down Fell Daruma," is a game similar to Red Light/Green Light.

EXTRA EPISODE

Page 168: *Haniwa* are clay figurines that were placed in Japanese burial mounds during the Kofun period (300-552 A.D.).

Author Bio

Bisco Hatori made her manga
debut with *Isshun kan no
Romance* (A Moment of
Romance) in *LaLa DX*
magazine. The comedy *Ouran
High School Host Club* is her
breakout hit. When she's stuck
thinking up characters' names,
she gets inspired by loud,
upbeat music (her radio is set
to NACK5 FM). She enjoys
reading all kinds of manga, but
she's especially fond of the sci-fi
drama *Please Save My Earth*
and *Slam Dunk*, a basketball
classic.

OURAN HIGH SCHOOL HOST CLUB
Vol. 8

The Shojo Beat Manga Edition

STORY AND ART BY BISCO HATORI

Translation/RyoRca, Honyaku Center Inc.
English Adaptation/John Werry, Honyaku Center Inc.
Touch-up Art & Lettering/George Caltsoudas
Graphic Design/Izumi Evers
Editor/Nancy Thistlethwaite

Managing Editor/Megan Bates
Editorial Director/Elizabeth Kawasaki
VP & Editor in Chief/Yumi Hoashi
Sr. Director of Acquisitions/Rika Inouye
Sr. VP of Marketing/Liza Coppola
Exec. VP of Sales & Marketing/John Easum
Publisher/Hyoe Narita

Printed in Canada

Published by VIZ Media, LLC
P.O. Box 77010
San Francisco, CA 94107

Shojo Beat Manga Edition
10 9 8 7 6 5 4 3 2 1
First printing, January 2007

store.viz.com